The Antifederalists

CRITICS OF THE CONSTITUTION

1781–1788

The Antifederalists

CRITICS OF THE CONSTITUTION

1781–1788

JACKSON TURNER MAIN

Foreword by Edward Countryman

Published for the
Omohundro Institute of Early American History and Culture
Williamsburg, Virginia
by the
University of North Carolina Press
Chapel Hill and London

*The Omohundro Institute of Early American History
and Culture is sponsored jointly by the College of William
and Mary and the Colonial Williamsburg Foundation.
On November 15, 1996, the Institute adopted its present
name in honor of a bequest from Malvern H. Omohundro, Jr.*

The paper in this book meets the guidelines for permanence
and durability of the Committee on Production Guidelines
for Book Longevity of the Council on Library Resources.

The Library of Congress has cataloged the
original edition of this book as follows:

Main, Jackson Turner
The antifederalists : critics of the Constitution, 1781–1788 /
by Jackson Turner Main
p. cm.
Includes bibliographical references and index
1. Constitutional history—United States. 2. United States—
History—Confederation, 1783–1789
JK 116 .M2
342.73'029   61017904

ISBN 0-8078-5544-8

08 07 06 05 04   5 4 3 2 1

To my Mother and Father

CONTENTS

Jackson Turner Main: A Historical Life, 1917–2003 ix
Foreword: *The Antifederalists*, Four Decades On,
by Edward Countryman xiii
Preface xxi
Introduction xxiii

Chapter I. Social and Political Background 1
Chapter II. Society and Politics in the South 21
Chapter III. Society and Politics in the North 41
Chapter IV. Antifederalists vs. Nationalists: The Impost 72
Chapter V. Antifederalists vs. Nationalists:
Commutation, Commerce, and the Convention 103
Chapter VI. Antifederal Objections to the Constitution,
Part I 119
Chapter VII. Antifederal Objections to the Constitution,
Part II 143
Chapter VIII. The Antifederal Solution 168
Chapter IX. Ratification: November to May 187
Chapter X. Ratification: The Final Defeat 221
Chapter XI. Conclusion 249

Appendix A. Separate Confederacies 283
Appendix B. The Antifederal Majority in Virginia 285
Appendix C. Authorship of Anonymous Articles 287
Appendix D. Chronology of Ratification 288
Appendix E. Occupational Tables 289
Appendix F. Socio-Economic Divisions in Maryland 291

Historiographical and Bibliographical Essay 293
Index 299

Jackson Turner Main

A HISTORICAL LIFE, 1917–2003

AFTER his death on October 19, 2003, Jackson Turner Main made one last journey back to the historical roots of his family and his career in Madison, Wisconsin. This place nourished Main's progressive vision of the American past. His grandfather Frederick Jackson Turner had grown up nearby and attended the University of Wisconsin, where he subsequently researched, wrote, and taught, shaping the understanding of American history with his theory of frontier democracy. Born on August 6, 1917, Jackson Turner Main was the son of John Smith Main and Dorothy Turner Main. After a stint at Harvard, the young Main went home to Madison, where he earned his B.A., M.A., and following the interruption of World War II, his Ph.D. from the university. After serving with the U.S. Army Signal Corps, he completed his graduate work in 1949. The New Deal and postwar reformist perspectives permeated Wisconsin's history department, whose faculty included the Socialist William Hesseltine and the progressives Merle Curti and Merrill Jensen. Under Jensen's supervision, Main wrote his dissertation on the Antifederalists. In these opponents to the Constitution, Main located a radical democratic tradition in the nation's origins.

Years later, reflecting on his career as a historian, Main recalled:

In Jensen's seminar I had chosen to tackle Beard's *Economic Interpretation* with the notion that Beard erred, but discovered that the secondary literature supported him, at least in general if not in detail. The view that the Constitution reflected its time and the ideas of an economic and social upper class fitted with the general thrust of scholarship and teaching at Wisconsin, and, to judge from the literature, elsewhere. The implication followed that the Antifederalists represented, in some degree, the ordinary folk, and that they might have been correct. My dissertation therefore sided with the Antifederalists and concentrated on the faults that they perceived in the new plan. It stressed economic and social influences on politics but with little attention to cultural or ideological forces except for the ideas of the Antifederalists themselves, and it failed to offer the Federalists equal time. The latter flaw occurs in most books on political groups, as does the concentration on party cores that limits such studies to a small minority of politicians, oversimplifying the actual diversity of opinion. Further research never removed these faults, which at the time did not seem deficiencies, and they survived in the subsequent book.[1]

The Antifederalists: Critics of the Constitution, 1781–1788, was published in 1961 by the University of North Carolina Press for the Institute of Early American History and Culture and was the winner of the Jamestown Manuscript Prize. Main went on to publish five more books on Revolutionary America: He brought out a second with the Institute and North Carolina in 1973, *Political Parties before the Constitution*, which won the Fraunces Tavern Museum Book Award, and also authored *The Social Structure of Revolutionary America* (Princeton, 1965), *The Upper House in Revolutionary America, 1763–1788* (Madison, 1967), *The Sovereign States, 1775–1783* (New York, 1973), and *Society and Economy in Colonial Connecticut* (Princeton, 1985). In addition, he published a number of influential articles, including "The One Hundred" in the *William and Mary Quarterly* (1954).

In the midst of an indefatigable research schedule, logging many thousands of miles to depositories before the days of microfilm and the Internet, he pursued a teaching career in early American history. After a time as an instructor at Wisconsin, his first job was at Washington and Jefferson College, where he taught between 1948 and 1950. For a decade, from 1953 to 1965, he was at San Jose State College (now University), where he met Gloria Lund, whom he married in 1956, forming one of those partnerships, personal and professional, in which envisioning one without the other is difficult. Moving

1. "Main-Traveled Roads," *William and Mary Quarterly*, 3d ser., XLI (1984), 446.

east in the mid-1960s, Main became director of the Institute for Colonial Studies at the State University of New York at Stony Brook in
1966. He was professor there until he became emeritus in 1983. He
and Gloria then moved to the University of Colorado at Boulder,
where she became a professor of early American history, and he offered courses as well.

Jackson Turner Main had a long association with the Institute of
Early American History and Culture. Besides publishing two of his
books with the Institute and contributing regularly to the *William
and Mary Quarterly*, he served twice on the Institute Council, in
1966–1969 and 1974–1977, and belonged to the Associates. At
SUNY–Stony Brook in 1968 he cosponsored with the Institute a national conference on the new social history that featured the emerging school of New England town studies. In 1982–1983, he graced
the Institute's halls while serving as the Visiting James Pinckney Harrison Professor of History at the College of William and Mary. At historical conventions, he regularly dropped by the Institute's book
booth to check the new publications and greet the staff with his wry
humor and friendly manner. The last time he swung by was in 2003,
obviously frail but still his affable self. With the reissuing of *The Antifederalists* under the Institute and University of North Carolina
Press's joint imprint, the association lives on.

Fredrika J. Teute
Editor of Publications, Omohundro Institute
of Early American History and Culture

Foreword

THE ANTIFEDERALISTS, FOUR DECADES ON

A S I BEGAN preparing this foreword, a chapter of the Sons of the American Revolution asked me to address their monthly meeting. They wanted about twenty minutes on the Confederation period. My little talk for them one Saturday morning rested firmly on what Jackson Turner Main achieved in this book. So does a great deal of major scholarship.

When Jack Main published *The Antifederalists*—his first book—in 1961, his subjects did not enjoy a good reputation. At best they were "Men of Little Faith," as political scientist Cecelia Kenyon called them in 1955.[1] Cold War American culture (or at least its dominant strain) was in a mood to stress our cohesion and our achievements as a people, and the Constitution's opponents did not fit that mood. They belonged instead to the "states' rights" tradition. In the context of mid-twentieth-century black American protest, that phrase—states' rights—could only evoke the defense of what was indefensible: slavery and Jim Crow. But during the ratification debates of 1787 and 1788, those problems had not been the issue. As a good historian must do, Main asked his readers to understand his subjects rather than judge them or claim them as forebears.

Jackson Turner Main was the grandson of Frederick Jackson Turner. Though he spent time at Harvard as an undergraduate, he chose to be a doctoral student at Wisconsin, working with Merrill Jensen. By his midwestern origins, his blood descent, and his intellectual forming, he belonged within the progressive tradition in American historiography. As of the date of this book's publication,

1. Cecelia M. Kenyon, "Men of Little Faith: The Anti-Federalists on the Nature of Representative Government," *William and Mary Quarterly*, 3d ser., XII (1955), 3–43.

that tradition seemed in disarray. That was partly because of the larger cultural climate of "consensus" within a supposedly monolithic "American mind" or "liberal tradition," but the seeming disarray also emerged from hard monographic research and close criticism of what the progressives had written.

By 1961 Robert E. Brown had advanced his thesis that the American Revolution was a matter of defending "middle-class democracy" and was beginning his frontal assault on the reputations of progressive historians Charles A. Beard and Carl Lotus Becker.[2] Forrest McDonald had taken on Beard's argument that the Constitution's framers stood to make a financial killing by using the new government's tax power to restore value to worthless securities. Examining all available records, he showed that the Constitution's opponents held the same kind of paper. Whatever separated the two sides, the prospect of simple financial gain for some did not explain it.[3] Clinton Rossiter had taken important early steps along the path leading to what we now call "the linguistic turn" in American Revolution studies.[4] Nor, for historians in the 1950s, were the Constitution's opponents the true bearers of the heritage of 1776. To Richard B. Morris, "the Federalists, not the Antifederalists, were the real radicals of their day."[5] Edmund S. Morgan wrote a powerful synthesis of Revolution scholarship whose descriptive nouns are all-embracing: colonists, revolutionaries, Americans. More precise terms did not seem necessary.[6] The time seemed long past for regarding the Confederation years as the "critical period of American history."[7] The Antifed-

2. Robert E. Brown, *Middle-Class Democracy and the Revolution in Massachusetts, 1691–1780* (Ithaca, N.Y., 1955); Brown, *Charles Beard and the Constitution: A Critical Analysis of "An Economic Interpretation of the Constitution"* (Princeton, N.J., 1956); Brown, *Carl Becker on History and the American Revolution* (East Lansing, Mich., 1970). See also Robert E. Brown and B. Katherine Brown, *Virginia, 1705–1786: Democracy or Aristocracy?* (East Lansing, Mich., 1964).

3. Forrest McDonald, *We the People: The Economic Origins of the Constitution* (Chicago, 1958).

4. Clinton Rossiter, *Seedtime of the Republic: The Origins of the American Tradition of Political Liberty* (New York, 1953).

5. Richard B. Morris, "The Confederation Period and the American Historian," *WMQ*, 3d ser., XIII (1956), 139–156, quote at 156.

6. Edmund S. Morgan, *The Birth of the Republic* (Chicago, 1956).

7. John Fiske, *The Critical Period of American History, 1783–1789* (Boston, 1888).

eralists seemed like a negligible, transient group. To the consensus-minded historian of one intensely fought state ratification campaign, antifederalism simply disappeared after its cause was lost.[8]

Such historiography was formidable. For a first-book author to write in opposition to it required courage. Jackson Turner Main was not a noisy man. But he was not a historian to follow fashion, and he always displayed indomitable courage. The book that he produced and that is reissued here speaks for itself. He showed in these pages that the Antifederalists had serious points to make, and that they deserve even now to be heard. Without being reductionist or determinist about their motives, he demonstrated that they had good reasons in their own lives for making those points. During the debate on the Constitution, they found themselves both out-argued and out-maneuvered. They ended up among history's losers. But they spoke for a majority of the people eligible to vote. In a fair plebiscite under the rules of their time, they would have won. As E. P. Thompson was doing for the English working class, Main was rescuing his subjects from "the enormous condescension of posterity."[9] They do not belong in history's dustbin.

In the four decades since this book was published, scholarship has vindicated Main's position. Main uncovered a very real and very important debate about the meaning of the American Revolution and about the direction of the American future. His opening sentence set his theme (as, of course, an opening sentence should do): "The United States consisted in the 1780's of a number of sections and subsections, each with a distinctive social structure, economy, and set of political objectives." There was no point in talking about "Americans" or "revolutionaries" in blanket, undifferentiated terms. The people who inhabit this book had shared a moment of great decision when, for their many separate reasons, they had chosen the path of independence. They had shared the struggle to achieve what Congress had declared. But they were not yet a single "people." For most of them identity was local and specific. So were the sources of well-being in their lives.

8. Linda Grant De Pauw, *The Eleventh Pillar: New York State and the Federal Constitution* (Ithaca, N.Y., 1966).

9. E. P. Thompson, *The Making of the English Working Class* (New York, 1963), 12.

Yet, will they, nil they, Main's people were living through a very large change. They faced problems that transcended their separate polities and their separate identities. Main constructed this book in terms of states and regions, but he showed that an emerging national economy vexed all his people, wherever they were. In this sense, as in many others, their "Nationalist" opponents did have the advantage. The trans-state issues over which the two emerging groups contended prior to 1787 were the congressional impost, the commutation of the salaries of Continental army officers, and the regulation of commerce between the states. Emergent Antifederalists were coalescing around each of these questions across sectional and state lines. But they did not realize it. Their opponents held positions in common, too, and much more than the people who would be Antifederalists, they understood that point. They had the great advantages of knowing one another, of understanding that they shared a perspective and a set of interests and goals, and, ultimately, of deciding the questions that were going to be put for debate. They were setting the agenda, and in any debate on any subject that is the greatest advantage of all. In an oft-quoted sentence Thompson once wrote that "class happens when some men, as a result of common experiences . . . feel and articulate the identity of their interests as between themselves, and as against other men whose interests are different from . . . theirs."[10] In this sense the people whom the Antifederalists opposed were not just "Nationalists," as Main insisted they should be called rather than "Federalists," but a national class.[11]

Not until well into the final stage of debate, when ratification of the Constitution was all but assured, did its opponents realize their own need to organize and cooperate across the lines that had kept them separate. For the most part these were men who spent their Revolution at the state level. Their best leaders were the likes of Governor George Clinton of New York, who must figure large in any account of the Constitution's critics. In the second half of the 1780s Clinton and his state could look back on a revolution that seemed both supremely trying and supremely successful.

10. Ibid., 9.

11. Gary J. Kornblith and John M. Murrin, "The Making and Unmaking of an American Ruling Class," in Alfred F. Young, ed., *Beyond the American Revolution: Explorations in the History of American Radicalism* (DeKalb, Ill., 1993), 27–79.

Few states had suffered as much as New York during the war years. Yet by 1786, on the eve of the writing of the federal Constitution and the struggle over its ratification, matters were very different. The state was economically prosperous and politically stable. There seemed little reason for major change. Most New Yorkers probably agreed. After their votes for the state's ratifying convention, when the delegates gathered in Poughkeepsie, forty-six were pledged to oppose the Constitution and only nineteen to support it. Governor George Clinton presided. He also led the Antifederalist forces.

Clinton's own path in the Revolution had led him from the moderate prominence of a seat in the old provincial assembly to unquestioned dominance in his own state. Unopposed in 1786, he won his fourth successive three-year term as governor. Future Federalist (or Nationalist) John Jay, who was the author of New York's constitution, had looked forward in the 1777 gubernatorial election to calling one of Clinton's opponents, Philip Schuyler, by the governor's title of "your excellency." Schuyler, another future Federalist and father-in-law of Alexander Hamilton, had fully expected to "command them all." He thought after Clinton's first victory that the new governor had neither the "family" nor "the connections" to qualify for "so distinguished a predominance." Jay and Schuyler's friend, the loyalist lawyer William Smith, Jr., who had taught Clinton, disparaged him now as "George the Governor."[12]

Clinton did not begin his state-level career as an outright partisan. He sought in good faith to work with the likes of Schuyler and Jay and later with Hamilton. But Clinton proved to be a consummate politician. By 1786 he had a loyal following among both electors and legislators. He was master of his state, and he wielded patronage to shore up his position. He was not, however, a national figure, and he had very little national experience. New York was what counted to him, just as Virginia counted most to Patrick Henry and Richard Henry Lee and Massachusetts did to Samuel Adams. Together with the state legislators, county judges, and militia officers who rallied to them, these were men who had made their own Revolution and whom the Revolution had for the most part made. But they had done it at the

12. Edward Countryman, *A People in Revolution: The American Revolution and Political Society in New York, 1760–1790* (Baltimore, 1981), 196, 198, 286.

state level. Such men, their followers in lower offices and at the state ratifying conventions, and the voters who chose them are the Anti-federalists whom Jackson Turner Main describes in this book. What he achieved here has influenced many historians since 1961.

The best evidence of Main's influence is the book that still dominates study of the Confederation period, Gordon S. Wood's *Creation of the American Republic, 1776–1787*,[13] published eight years after *The Antifederalists*. Wood worked from printed literary sources, and his method was very different from Main's. Yet he found strong evidence of the same deep divisions of social experience, historical interpretation, and future vision that Main found between the Antifederalists and their ultimately victorious opponents. One might read Wood as validating the Federalists' side and Main his own subjects' position, but their interpretations of the underlying issues match. Like Wood's *Creation of the American Republic*, Roger H. Brown's *Redeeming the Republic* was not written from an Antifederalist point of view. But it used sources and methods akin to Main's own to present strong evidence that a debate about fundamental issues of taxation took place in the states during the 1780s, with very real interests at stake. In an argument that Main could have made, Brown showed how the separate state debates about taxation fed into the great national discussion of 1787–1788.[14]

Main went on to expand the argument of *The Antifederalists* in three separate books about what transpired in the states between the Declaration of Independence and the ratification of the Constitution.[15] While Wood was finishing his book, I was a beginning graduate student, encountering and resisting Main's ideas. I planned originally to write my study of revolutionary New York in opposition to his views, but my own immersion in the sources led me to do otherwise.[16] (Actually, I shudder to look back at the marginalia I scrawled in my

13. Gordon S. Wood, *The Creation of the American Republic, 1776–1787* (Chapel Hill, N.C., 1969).

14. Roger H. Brown, *Redeeming the Republic: Federalists, Taxation, and the Origins of the Constitution* (Baltimore, 1993).

15. Jackson Turner Main, *The Upper House in Revolutionary America, 1776–1788* (Madison, Wisc., 1967); *The Sovereign States, 1775–1783* (New York, 1973); and *Political Parties before the Constitution* (Chapel Hill, N.C., 1973).

16. Countryman, *A People in Revolution.*

copy of *The Antifederalists*. And I have it on good authority that I was muttering its author's name in my sleep.) People who worked on other states are in debt to him in the same way.[17] None of them found simple "middle-class democracy." Instead they discovered and told stories of transforming conflict.

Like Roger Brown and like Main himself, most state-level historians were more interested in bringing out patterns of political and social experience than in the close study of the texts and ideas of the ratification debate. But in 1981 those texts and ideas received their due with the posthumous publication of the University of Chicago political scientist Herbert Storing's multivolume compilation, *The Complete Anti-Federalist* (finished by his associate Murray Dry).[18] Their collection is not actually "complete," but Storing and Dry compiled massive evidence that Main's subjects deserved to be taken seriously as political thinkers. The seven volumes and Storing's separately published introduction, *What the Anti-Federalists Were For: The Political Thought of the Opponents of the Constitution*, added Antifederalist voices, as well as their votes and organization, to the great national discussion that was underway. Acknowledging their debt to Main, Storing and Dry demonstrated that "those who opposed the Constitution must be seen as playing an indispensable . . . part in the founding process. They contributed to the dialogue of the American founding. . . . The political life of the community continues to be a dialogue, in which the Anti-Federalist concerns and principles still play an important part."[19] This is why their view must count in any discussion of the "original intent" of the founding generation.[20]

Finally, consider this book's next-generation successor, *The Other*

---

17. As examples, see Stephen E. Patterson, *Political Parties in Revolutionary Massachusetts* (Madison, Wisc., 1973); Ronald Hoffman and Peter J. Albert, eds., *Sovereign States in an Age of Uncertainty* (Charlottesville, Va., 1981); Norman K. Risjord, *Chesapeake Politics, 1781–1800* (New York, 1978); Ronald Hoffman, *A Spirit of Dissension: Economics, Politics, and the Revolution in Maryland* (Baltimore, 1973); and Jerome J. Nadelhaft, *The Disorders of War: The Revolution in South Carolina* (Orono, Maine, 1981).

18. Herbert J. Storing, ed., *The Complete Anti-Federalist*, 7 vols. (Chicago, 1981).

19. Herbert J. Storing, *What the Anti-Federalists Were For: The Political Thought of the Opponents of the Constitution* (Chicago, 1981), 3.

20. Jack N. Rakove, *Original Meanings: Politics and Ideas in the Making of the Constitution* (New York, 1996).

Founders by historian Saul Cornell.[21] Publishing through the Omohundro Institute imprint, like Main and Wood, Cornell does not set
out to "replace" Main's work, let alone to "disprove" it. On the contrary, he takes Main's insights as fully established and turns to the
question of the language the Antifederalists used. Like Main, he un-
derstands that blanket, all-encompassing terms will not do. This even
applies to the term "Antifederalist." Main distinguished them by state
and region, and elsewhere he showed an enduring interest in the economic and social distinctions that separated Americans within specific places.[22] Cornell shows that "elite" and "popular" Antifederalists
had very different approaches to the problem that ratifying the Constitution presented. He takes the ratification debates onto new
ground in two ways. One is by demonstrating that the debate involved not just the actual issues of 1787–1788, but also the appropriate place and rights of dissenters in the American public sphere. The
other is by making clear that even though actual opposition to the
Constitution died, the substantive issues the Antifederalists raised
continued to be vital for decades.

Cornell does not simply argue that Antifederalists were plebeian,
and therefore "democratic." Many were not plebeian, just as many of
the Constitution's supporters were not members of the elite. The real
Antifederalist contribution to evolving American democracy was that
by dissenting from the Constitution they kept open the public sphere
of debate that the Revolution had made possible. The Antifederalists
and what they stood for did not disappear at all.

This book began that large discussion. It still bears reading, which
is why the Omohundro Institute of Early American History and Culture and the University of North Carolina Press are bringing it out in
a new paperback edition. As I was writing this foreword, I learned of
Jack Main's death. He lived a long and good life and wrote many good
books, beginning with this one. Its republication signifies that his
quiet but determined voice should, and will, continue to be heard.

                                                    Edward Countryman

21. Saul Cornell, *The Other Founders: Anti-Federalism and the Dissenting Tradition in America, 1788–1828* (Chapel Hill, N.C., 1999).

22. Jackson Turner Main, *The Social Structure of Revolutionary America* (Princeton, N.J., 1965).

PREFACE

IT is curious that after all that has been written on the subject there is still no adequate history of the Constitution, of its making and ratification. Merrill Jensen's *The New Nation* furnishes much of the background, but stops short of the Constitutional Convention, and other general histories of the period either are out-of-date or never were much good. Moreover the lack of monographs is so serious that a satisfactory book can hardly be written at present. There are few good histories of state politics, fewer of economic developments, and fewer still of social and cultural matters. We have some reliable studies of the ideas of prominent individuals, but no general investigation of Federalist political thought has been made, nor has there hitherto been one of the opposition.

The present volume is therefore intended only to fill a gap, not to furnish a complete account of post-Revolutionary politics. In order to identify the Antifederalists and to discover what they thought, it was necessary to examine in the various states the political controversies that culminated in the conflict over ratification. In doing so, certain conclusions were reached and are stated; however they must be regarded as tentative only, and the broader implications of this book must await further research.

The author's principal obligation is acknowledged in the dedication. Secondly, I am indebted to my teachers, especially those at the University of Wisconsin, and most of all to Merrill Jensen, who first criticized this study as a term paper, then as a dissertation, and finally through several drafts. Every historian is glad to state that his book could not have been written without the facilities provided by great libraries and historical societies. I was especially aided at the following: American Antiquarian Society,

Boston Public Library, Charleston Library Company, Connecticut Historical Society, Connecticut State Library, Historical Society of Pennsylvania, Library of Congress, Massachusetts Historical Society, Massachusetts State Archives, New Hampshire Historical Society, New York Historical Society, New York Public Library, New York State Library, Philadelphia Library Company, Rhode Island Historical Society, South Carolina Historical Society, United States Archives, Alderman Library of the University of Virginia, Virginia Historical Society, Virginia State Library, and the Wisconsin Historical Society.

INTRODUCTION

T HEY are called the Antifederalists, but it should be made clear at once that they were not antifederal at all. In reality they were determined to preserve the Confederation, and the name, far from being their own choice, was imposed upon them by their opponents, the so-called "Federalists." The attachment to them of a word which denotes the reverse of their true beliefs, and which moreover implies that they were mere obstructionists, without any positive plan to offer, was part of the penalty of defeat. The victors took what name they chose, and fastened on the losers one which condemned them. Since the victory was a lasting one, the name and the stigma have endured.

It was a nice piece of misdirection by the Federalists. Originally the word "federal" meant anyone who supported the Confederation. Several years before the Constitution was promulgated, the men who wanted a strong national government, who might more properly be called "nationalists," began to appropriate the term "federal" for themselves. To them, the man of "federal principles" approved of "federal measures," which meant those that increased the weight and authority or extended the influence of the Confederation Congress. The word "antifederal" by contrast implied hostility to Congress. According to this definition, the antifederal man was opposed to any effort to strengthen the government and was therefore unpatriotic. Eventually the term became a general word of opprobrium applied by the Nationalists to anyone who opposed their designs. So we find David Humphreys referring to "Antifederalists & Advocates for Mobs & Conventions." [1]

1. To George Washington, Nov. 16, 1786, Washington Papers, CCXXXVI, No. 133, Lib. Cong. For the use of the word during this early period see also James Madison to James Monroe, Aug. 7, 1785, Gaillard Hunt, ed., *The*

Naturally the unpleasant connotation of the name thus attached to the Antifederalists was injurious to their cause—as the Federalists surely foresaw.[2] It suggested that they were against a federal government, which was diametrically opposite to the truth, and the negative form implied that an "anti" was nothing but an obstructor. The Antifederalists indignantly rejected the name, insisting that the proponents of the Constitution really deserved the appellation, and they tried to recover for themselves the more accurate designation of "Federalists." For example, in *The American Herald* (Boston) of December 10, 1787, appeared the following: " A FEDERALIST is a Friend to a Federal Government—An ANTI-FEDERALIST is an Enemy to a Confederation.—Therefore, the FRIENDS to the New Plan of CONSOLIDATION, are Anti-Federal, and its Opposers are firm Federal Patriots."

When the Antifederalists selected pseudonyms for their published tracts they made the same point. Richard Henry Lee chose "A Federal Farmer" as his pen name, and no fewer than eight other writers used the word as part of a nom de plume.[3] Numer-

---

Writings of James Madison, 9 vols. (New York, 1900-1910), II, 158; Robert A. East, "The Massachusetts Conservatives in the Critical Period," in Richard B. Morris, ed., *The Era of the American Revolution* (New York, 1939), 373; *Massachusetts Centinel* (Boston), Dec. 20, 1786; *Daily Advertiser* (N. Y.), May 11, 1786, Jan. 31, 1787; *New Haven Gazette,* Feb. 8, 1787; *New-Hampshire Spy* (Portsmouth), Apr. 20, 1787; David Humphreys to Thomas Jefferson, June 5, 1786, in Julian P. Boyd, ed., *The Papers of Thomas Jefferson,* 13 vols. (in progress, Princeton, 1950 to date), IX, 609.

2. The French minister Joseph Fauchet wrote some years later, "The primitive divisions of opinion as to the political form of the State, and as to the limits of the sovereignty of the whole over each State individually sovereign had created the federalists and the anti-federalists. From a whimsical contrast between the name and the real opinion of the parties, a contrast hitherto little understood in Europe, the former aimed and still aim, with all their power to annihilate federalism, whilst the latter have always wished to preserve it. This contrast was created by the *consolidators* or the Constitutionalists who being first in giving the denominations (a matter so important in a revolution!) took for themselves that which was the most popular, altho' in reality it contradicted their Ideas, and gave to their rivals one which would draw on them the attention of the people, notwithstanding they really wished to preserve a System whose prejudices should cherish at least the memory and the name." To the French Commissioner to Foreign Relations, Oct. 31, 1794, Edmund Randolph Papers, Lib. Cong.

3. *Norfolk and Portsmouth Journal,* Mar. 5, 1788; *Pennsylvania Packet, and Daily Advertiser* (Phila.), Oct. 23, 1787; *Boston Gazette, and the Country Journal,* Nov. 26, 1787; *Pennsylvania Herald, and General Adver-*

ous writers and speakers insisted that the Federalists did not believe in Federalism but that the Antifederalists did, while "A Countryman" remarked that the use of the term "was the way some great men had to deceive the common people, and prevent their knowing what they were about." [4] When John Lamb and others organized a committee in New York to oppose the Constitution, they called it the "Federal Republican Committee." [5] Indeed a principal objection to the Constitution was that it set up a national, not a federal, government. But they lost, and Antifederalists they remain.

Antifederalism was not a single, simple, unified philosophy of

---

tiser (Phila.), Oct. 27, 1787; *Mass. Centinel* (Boston), Dec. 29, 1787 to Feb. 2, 1788; *United States Chronicle: Political, Commercial, and Historical* (Providence), Mar. 27, 1788; *Freeman's Journal: or, North-American Intelligencer* (Phila.), Mar. 26, 1788.

4. *New York Journal*, Dec. 13, 1787. See also John Smilie, in John Bach McMaster and Frederick D. Stone, *Pennsylvania and the Federal Constitution, 1787-1788* (Lancaster, 1888), 768; "Algernon Sidney," in *Independent Gazetteer; or, Chronicle of Freedom* (Phila.), Feb. 13, 1788; *ibid.*, Jan. 16, 1788; "John Wilkes," in *ibid.*, Jan. 26, 1788; William Irvine in Irvine Papers, IX, Hist. Soc. Pa.; Thomas Tredwell in Jonathan Elliot, ed., *The Debates in the Several State Conventions, on the Adoption of the Federal Constitution, as Recommended by the General Convention at Philadelphia, in 1787 . . .*, 5 vols. (Washington, 1854), II, 405; Melancton Smith in *ibid.*, 224; Luther Martin in Max Farrand, ed., *The Records of the Federal Convention of 1787*, 3 vols. (New Haven, 1911), III, 195; Joshua Atherton to John Lamb, Feb. 23, 1789, John Lamb Papers, Box 5, N. Y. Hist. Soc.; Nathan Dane to Samuel Adams, May 10, 1788, Samuel Adams Papers, N. Y. Pub. Lib.; Mercy Warren to Mrs. Macauley, May 1788, in Charles Warren, "Elbridge Gerry, James Warren, Mercy Warren and the Ratification of the Federal Constitution in Massachusetts," Mass. Hist. Soc., *Proceedings*, 64 (1930-1931), 158; *Freeman's Journal* (Phila.), Jan. 16, 1788; *Providence Gazette; and Country Journal*, Mar. 15, 1788; *New York Journal*, Feb. 11, 1788; Elbridge Gerry in [Annals of Congress] *Debates and Proceedings in the Congress of the United States, 1789-1824*, 42 vols. (Washington, 1834-55), I, 731; Samuel Chase to John Lamb, June 13, 1788, in Isaac Q. Leake, *Memoir of the Life and Times of General John Lamb* (Albany, 1850), 311; Richard Henry Lee to Patrick Henry, Sept. 14, 1789, in James Curtis Ballagh, ed., *The Letters of Richard Henry Lee*, 2 vols. (New York, 1911-1914), II, 502. *The Government of Nature Delineated, . . .* (Carlisle, 1788) has an excellent discussion of the point.

5. John Lamb Papers, N. Y. Hist. Soc. However in Albany, when the Federalists organized first under the name "Federal," their opponents were forced to adopt "Antifederal," one of the very few cases in which they used the name. See broadsides in the New York Historical Society, such as that dated Mar. 15, 1788, and the *Albany Gazette*, Mar. 27, 1788.

government. It was rather a combination, a mixture of two somewhat different points of view adhered to by two different groups
of men. It was, first, the doctrine of those who preferred a weak
central government. This concept attracted many well-to-do
thinkers, most frequently from the agricultural interest, and these
men provided the Antifederalists with their ablest and best-
educated leaders. The origins of this body of thought lay far back
in colonial and English political history, and it became especially
relevant during the last years before independence and the period
of constitution-making, when fundamental principles of government had to be defined and applied. From the broadest point of
view, the issue was whether authority or liberty should be emphasized. Once the authority of the British government had been
overthrown, many were satisfied with the degree of liberty thus
achieved and were willing to retain or reconstruct a strong central
government at home; but others continued the struggle for local
self-rule and individual freedom from restraint. In an equally general way, the former view was defended by those who desired a
political system which would protect property and maintain order
in society, while the latter was held by those who feared oppression: the former wished to exert power, the latter feared the
effects of it.

The second ingredient of Antifederalism was provided by the
smaller property holders, in particular by the small farmers. All of
the socio-economic groups had their peculiar, often conflicting
interests, which they attempted to further by political action.
Because the small property holders were a majority in Revolutionary times, they wanted a government dominated by the many
rather than the few, and they therefore favored democratic ideas.
Thus the Antifederalists included two major elements: those who
emphasized the desirability of a weak central government, and
those who encouraged democratic control. The democrats at this
time accepted the doctrine of weak government, but the advocates of weak government did not always believe in democracy.

Strictly speaking, Antifederalism came into existence only when
the Constitution was made public and lasted until opposition to
its adoption ceased. But it is clear that the origins of Antifederal
ideas must be sought long before 1787, deep in the colonial past.

In order to explain why the Constitution aroused such intense hostility and where that hostility came from, it will be necessary first to describe the social structure of the new nation; second, to point out some of the most important political ideas which the Antifederalists adopted. Two chapters will be devoted to an analysis of the political conditions in the states. The final step before treating the Constitution itself will be to describe the earlier attempts to revise the Articles of Confederation, in which both sides rehearsed their arguments in preparation for the decisive conflict.

Chapter I

SOCIAL AND POLITICAL BACKGROUND

THE United States consisted in the 1780's of a number of sections and subsections, each with a distinctive social structure, economy, and set of political objectives. From Maine to Georgia, by way of Vermont, the Wyoming Valley, the Alleghany district, and the Wateree, stretched the frontier. Except where great land-holders with their tenants and slaves pursued the retreating supply of topsoil, frontier society did not include extremes of wealth and poverty. There was an embryonic class structure but it was potential only; property was, in comparison with other sections, equally distributed, and from the bottom to the top was but a short step. The men of the frontier wanted to keep it that way: thus the first Kentucky convention, meeting in the winter of 1784-85, declared: "That to grant any Person a larger quantity of Land than he designs Bona Fide to seat himself or his Family on, is a greevance, Because it is subversive of the fundamental Principles of a free republican Government to allow any individual, or Company or Body of Men to possess such large tracts of Country in their own right as may at a future Day give them undue influence." [1] Along the whole arc of the frontier, expansion was the essential need—expansion of geographical area, of available capital, of facilities for transportation, and of political organization.

What frontier society became, once the frontier had passed on, depended upon a number of circumstances, of which two were particularly important during the 1780's: soil and transportation

1. Quoted in Thomas Perkins Abernethy, *Western Lands and the American Revolution* (New York, 1937), 305.

1

facilities. If the soil was fertile and easily worked, a surplus could be produced; if this surplus could be marketed, farming on a commercial basis was possible. But if the soil was not fertile, or if transportation facilities were poor, it was more difficult to raise produce for market and the farmer was limited to a near-subsistence level. One or the other of these inhibiting factors was present over wide areas. In most of New England, for example, the soil precluded raising a surplus; in most of North Carolina, lack of transportation facilities rendered a surplus of little value. In the great stretches of uplands, between the river valleys, there existed a society of subsistence or subsistence-plus farmers—a frontier in arrested development. Here, as on the frontier itself, no wealthy class existed because there was little chance to accumulate wealth; property was widely distributed, and although it was easy to acquire land, upward social mobility was limited by the ceiling which rivers and soil imposed.

Those who achieved riches usually lived on the valley lands, not the uplands. Here farming was profitable, and the subsistence farmer could become a wealthy planter. He could, that is, so long as the region was undergoing development; for after a period during which wealth was accumulated rapidly, large estates were formed, and then the newcomer was confronted with expensive land, which he could perhaps rent but hardly buy. In contrast with the social structure of the frontier and uplands, the society of the valley was characterized by greater class distinctions. The emergence of an aristocracy of wealth was balanced by the growth of a far larger lower class, and between these groups the small property holders were proportionately less numerous. Although agricultural, the interest of such a region was also commercial, for its prosperity depended upon selling the surplus overseas or in a nearby city. The city developed still another type of class structure, but this society is not of such importance to us because Antifederalism was rural rather than urban.

In referring to a class structure of society during the Revolutionary era one might be accused of interpreting the past with words of the present. The existence of classes, however, was clearly recognized in the eighteenth century. Usually three were distinguished. These were, as Patrick Henry expressed it, the well-born, the middle, and the lower "ranks." [2] There is, and was, no clear dividing line between the first two. The term "well born" implied a hereditary aristocracy, and it is true that by the 1780's such a thing did exist in America, but its basis was pecuniary; property, not birth, was the major factor in determining class structure. Phrases such as "the rich," "men of wealth and ability," "men of Sense and Property" describe the upper class as the Revolutionary generation saw it. John Jay defined this class as "the better kind of people, by which I mean the people who are orderly and industrious, who are content with their situation and not uneasy in their circumstances." [3] Such men were frequently termed "gentlemen," a word which usually implied superior wealth as well as superior status and behavior, as the phrase "gentlemen of property" suggests.[4] Indeed, wealth was essential in order to acquire the attributes of a gentleman: to dress fashionably, become educated, patronize arts, purchase luxuries, and conduct oneself in society as gentlemen were supposed to do.

The distinction between gentlemen and other sorts of men existed everywhere in some degree. John Adams pretended that it was a phenomenon known only outside New England. In 1775 he wrote to Joseph Hawley from Philadelphia: "Gentlemen in other colonies have large plantations of slaves, and the common people among them are very ignorant and very poor. These gentlemen are [more] . . . habituated to higher notions of themselves, and the distinction between them and the common people, than we are." [5] But Hawley could have set him right, for a decade earlier he had pleaded that a writ was defective because it desig-

2. Elliot, ed., *Debates*, III, 140; Richard Henry Lee in Paul Leicester Ford, ed., *Pamphlets on the Constitution of the United States* (Brooklyn, N.Y., 1888), 295.
3. To George Washington, June 27, 1786, in Henry P. Johnston, ed., *The Correspondence and Public Papers of John Jay*, 4 vols. (New York, 1890-1893), III, 205; Melancton Smith in Elliot, ed., *Debates*, II, 248; "Sydney," in Paul Leicester Ford, ed., *Essays on the Constitution of the United States* (Brooklyn, N.Y., 1892), 307.
4. For example, John Lloyd, quoted in Ulrich B. Phillips, "The South Carolina Federalists, I," *American Historical Review*, 14 (1908-1909), 537; Robert Livingston, quoted in E. Wilder Spaulding, *New York in the Critical Period, 1783-1789* (New York, 1932), 146-47.
5. Nov. 25, 1775 in Edmund Cody Burnett, ed., *Letters of Members of the Continental Congress*, 8 vols. (Washington, 1921-1936), I, 260.

nated the defendant as a yeoman when he was really a gentle-man! [6] It is undoubtedly true, however, that the upper class was larger and more conspicuous in the South than in most parts of the North.

There were obviously great variations among the well-to-do. They were persons of different degrees of wealth and, above all, of varying interests. Greater and lesser planters, debtors and creditors, merchants in towns and in cities, speculators and land-lords, lawyers and shipowners, "River Gods" and "manor lords"— each had particular economic and political aspirations. They did not always agree with one another, yet they did share similar attitudes toward property and politics. In 1787, gentlemen of property provided the Antifederalists with many of their ablest leaders, but the great majority gave the Federalists vigorous support.

In contrast with the better sort, the rest of the people were sometimes simply lumped together and identified as "common" or "lower." [7] As a rule, however, a distinction was made between those who had property and those who had not. The former were referred to as the "middle" or "middling" classes (or sorts, or ranks), and the latter were designated as "lower," or "inferior." [8] The number of men who belonged to this latter group varied from only 25 or 30 per cent of the total in rural New England to well over half in some Southern counties.[9] Their political influence was as slight as their prestige.

6. Ernest F. Brown, *Joseph Hawley, Colonial Radical* (New York, 1931), 55.

7. Samuel Osgood to John Adams, Dec. 7, 1783, Burnett, ed., *Letters*, VII, 378; Peter Tappen to George Clinton, Sept. 29, 1787, Clinton Papers, Bancroft Transcripts, N.Y. Pub. Lib.; *Maryland Journal and Baltimore Advertiser*, May 16, 1788; Louis B. Wright and Marion Tinling, eds., *Quebec to Caroline in 1785-1786. Being the Travel Diary and Observations of Robert Hunter, Jr., a Young Merchant of London* (San Marino, Calif., 1943), 119.

8. James M. Hughes to General Gates, Nov. 20, 1787, Emmett Coll., No. H, N.Y. Pub. Lib.; Edmund Pendleton in Elliot, ed., *Debates*, III, 295; William Findley in McMaster and Stone, *Pennsylvania and the Constitution*, 778; Aedanus Burke, quoted in Charles Gregg Singer, *South Carolina in the Confederation* (Philadelphia, 1941), 32.

9. This material on social structure is drawn from a wide variety of sources. Especially worth noting are the tax records for North Carolina,

Most significant was the middle class, from which the Antifederalists drew their greatest strength. The majority of white Americans, and by far the largest number of voters, were farmers who owned their land and who lived at a subsistence-plus level.[10] It is difficult to generalize about their economic status, but two major groups can be distinguished. First, many lived on the good soil of the river valleys, in well-established communities, where transportation facilities made marketing easy. Such farmers were fairly well-to-do. They might contract debts in order to improve their holdings or, like the rich, to purchase luxuries, but they were generally solvent. Their prosperity depended upon commerce, and they were interested in stability. Hence they were often allied politically with the mercantile interest and the conservative elements of society in defense of a favorable status quo. On the other hand many farmers were poor. In North Carolina a few surviving tax records reveal that the median amount of cash in hand held by landowners was £17— this at a time when large quantities of paper money had been is-

available on microfilm as listed in William S. Jenkins and Lillian A. Hamrick, eds., *Guide to the Microfilm Collection of Early State Records* (Washington, 1950), 73-74; discussion and sources cited in Jackson Turner Main, "The Distribution of Property in Post-Revolutionary Virginia," *Mississippi Valley Historical Review*, 41 (1954-55), 241-58, and "The One Hundred," *William and Mary Quarterly*, 3rd Ser., 11 (1954), 354-84; Francis G. and Phyllis May Morris, "Economic Conditions in North Carolina about 1780," *North Carolina Historical Review*, 16 (1939), 107-33, 296-327; Charles A. Barker, *The Background of the Revolution in Maryland* (New Haven, 1940), Appendix I; Chilton Williamson, "The Connecticut Property Test and the East Guilford Voter: 1800," Conn. Hist. Soc., *Bulletin*, 19 (1954), 101-4; Stella Sutherland, *Population Distribution in Colonial America* (New York, 1936); United States Bureau of the Census, *A Century of Population Growth from the first census of the United States to the twelfth, 1790-1900* (Washington, 1909); Evarts B. Greene and Virginia D. Harrington, *American Population before the Federal Census of 1790* (New York, 1932).

10.   What percentage of the men could vote is a moot point. In the South, where it was usually necessary to own land, about half were disenfranchised, but in New England probably between 60 and 90 per cent had the suffrage. At present not enough research has been done. See A. E. McKinley, *The Suffrage Franchise in the Thirteen English Colonies in America* (Philadelphia, 1905); Charles S. Sydnor, *Gentlemen Freeholders: Political Practices in Washington's Virginia* (Chapel Hill, 1952); Robert E. Brown, *Middle-Class Democracy and the Revolution in Massachusetts, 1691-1780* (Ithaca, 1955); Richard P. McCormick, *Experiment in Independence: New Jersey in the Critical Period, 1783-1789* (New Brunswick, 1950); Williamson, "Connecticut Property Test," Conn. Hist. Soc., *Bulletin*, 19 (1954).

sued.[11] One of the best farms in Rhode Island made a profit of only £31½ cash in 1785 while another made just over £5½.[12] The income of farmers in Worcester County, Massachusetts, during the depression year 1786 was about £9 per poll.[13] The great variation in farm value is suggested by the fact that the legislature of Connecticut estimated that the annual income from land ranged from 7¢ to $1.67 per acre.[14] Many farmers must have been living near the margin, with little cash income, so that they were obliged to obtain necessities by barter or credit. They had little left over for taxes and were especially vulnerable if there was a depression or a scarcity of money.

It appears that a large proportion of the farmers, especially of this second type, were in debt. To acquire a farm often demanded a fairly large capital investment. Even 100 acres would cost not far from £50 to £100 in the South, and much more than that in the North, unless one sought out poor, discarded, or isolated land and thereby sentenced oneself to permanent penury. The purchase of essential farm animals, equipment, and supplies would raise the cost still higher. Since wages were not high enough to enable laborers to save such a sum easily, the number of landless men and of tenant farmers was increasing, while those who owned land often had to borrow in order to pay for it.[15] Suits for debt were everywhere numerous, as were complaints concerning debts. The situation was most serious during the period of money shortage that followed the Revolution. During the 1780's there were riots among debtors in Massachusetts, New Hampshire, Connec-

11. Tax lists cited in *n.* 9, above.

12. Douglas S. Robertson, ed., *An Englishman in America in 1785 being the Diary of Joseph Hadfield* (Toronto, 1933), 219; Wright and Tinling, eds., *Quebec to Caroline,* 127-28.

13. John G. Metcalf, *Annals of the Town of Mendon, from 1659 to 1880* (Providence, 1880), 432.

14. Williamson, "Connecticut Property Test," Conn. Hist. Soc., *Bulletin,* 19 (1954), 103.

15. The extent of rural indebtedness is suggested by a recent article which indicates that Virginians of the Piedmont owed a good deal of money to Scotch merchants. See Jacob M. Price, "The Rise of Glasgow in the Chesapeake Tobacco Trade, 1707-1775," *Wm. and Mary Qtly.,* 3rd Ser., 11 (1954), 179-99. That land was hard to obtain, as a freehold, in the longer settled parts of New York, is made clear by the article of E. Marie Becker, "The 801 Westchester County Freeholders of 1763," N. Y. Hist. Soc., *Quarterly,* 35 (1951), 283-321.

ticut, Rhode Island, New Jersey, Maryland, Virginia, and South Carolina; paper money laws were passed or strongly supported in every state.

Debts were a factor which motivated farmers to take an interest in politics; they were also vitally concerned about tax policy and the payment of the state debts. Seeking to transfer their tax burdens to different shoulders, farmers and other small property holders opposed poll taxes and heavy taxes on cultivated land. They tried to reduce government expenses and official salaries in order to keep taxes low. To ease the burden of discharging public debts, they variously tried to delay payment, to depreciate the value of public securities, to levy taxes payable in securities, or to pay the interest in paper money or in certificates created for the purpose. When taxes were levied, they preferred payment in kind, and in depression years they tried to postpone payment of the whole or part of the tax. Unwilling to grant Congress as much money as it asked, they adopted various expedients to lower the amount to be paid, and tried to avoid any form of payment which would require state taxes to be collected in hard money. It would not be fair to say that they refused to support their governments, but a considerable gap sometimes separated what the governments thought was needed and what the farmers were willing to give. The isolation of many farmers, their lack of formal education, and the limited horizons of their experience, also made them unwilling to surrender local advantages for the more general good.

An attractive solution to the farmers' financial problems was paper money. It could be issued to pay the expenses of government, discharge public debts, and reduce the hardship of paying taxes. Private debts could also be more easily paid. As a debtor, the farmer also hoped that the judicial process might be made more favorable to him. He demanded the more convenient location of courts, lower court costs and lawyer fees, laws obliging creditors to accept property at a "fair" value, the abolition of imprisonment for debt, and laws delaying the recovery of debts. Such measures as these occasionally attracted the support of larger property holders, especially during the years 1784-86 when the complex of debts involved both rich and poor; but the principal support came from the small farmers.

Everywhere the small farmers, like all other economic and social groups, tried to increase their political power in order to achieve their objectives. In doing so, they could draw upon their experience as colonials and revolutionists, and they could also select out of the great body of the world's political literature those doctrines which were most useful. These doctrines, though their origins were doubtless unknown to the rank and file of Americans, were their common property, and had been made familiar first during the pre-Revolutionary years, when they were incorporated into sermons, pamphlets, and newspaper articles, and then extended into the first period of constitution-making after independence.

Different aspects of this experience and different parts of this literature appealed to different groups. Future Federalists as well as future Antifederalists accepted the great body of English political thought incorporated into the Whig tradition, which emphasized individual liberty and the ultimate authority of the people. The Antifederalists, however, advanced much further toward democratic political ideas, so that the background of their thought is to be found in what might be called the left wing of Whiggism. Two works in particular are relevant to their ideas. *Cato's Letters*, the joint product of Thomas Gordon and John Trenchard, was written during 1720-23 and had passed through a number of English editions by the time of the Revolution.[16] Although it was never published in America, it was widely read in the colonies and became "a favorite textbook of the patriots." [17] The writers who adopted "Cato" as their nom de plumes were probably thinking as often of the British authors as of the Roman original. The other major source of Antifederal thought was James Burgh's *Political Disquisitions*.

16. [Thomas Gordon and John Trenchard], *Cato's Letters: or, Essays on Liberty, Civil, and Religious, and other important Subjects*, 4 vols., 5th ed. (London, 1748).

17. Arthur M. Schlesinger, *Prelude to Independence* (New York, 1958), 96, 137. Among those who consulted "Cato" were Joseph Hawley, Benjamin Franklin, Josiah Quincy, Jr., John Adams, and Thomas Jefferson. Brown, *Hawley*, 93; Sidney Kobre, *The Development of the Colonial Newspaper* (Pittsburgh, 1944), 32; Caroline Robbins, "Algernon Sidney's *Discourses Concerning Government*: Textbook of Revolution," *Wm. and Mary Qtly.*, 3rd Ser., 4 (1947), 269-70; H. Trevor Colbourn, "Thomas Jefferson's Use of the Past," *ibid.*, 15 (1958), 65.

An American edition, published in 1775, was "encouraged" by some seventy-five prominent Americans.[18]

The basic concept stressed in both of these works was the evil effect of power. "The love of power is natural," wrote Burgh, "it is insatiable; it is whetted, not cloyed, by possession."[19] Gordon and Trenchard observed that "Power renders men wanton, insolent to others, and fond of themselves.... All history affords but few Instances of Men trusted with great Power without abusing it, when with Security they could." The people must retain power in their own hands, grant it but sparingly, and then only under the strictest supervision. [20] "The people can never be too jealous of their liberties," warned Burgh. "Power is of an elastic nature, ever extending itself and encroaching on the liberties of the subjects."[21] "Cato" also believed that "Political Jealousy, ... in the People, is a necessary and laudable Passion." Therefore the people must select their rulers with care, and these must be "narrowly watched, and checked with Restraints stronger than their Temptation to break them."[22]

This mistrust of power was characteristic of American political thought during this period. Long before the doctrine was applied to the Constitution, it was frequently expressed by men who became Antifederalists. For example, Samuel Adams asserted that "there is a Degree of Watchfulness over all Men possessed of Power or Influence upon which the Liberties of Mankind much depend. It is necessary to guard against the Infirmities of the best as well as the Wickedness of the worst of Men." Therefore, "Jealousy is the best Security of publick Liberty."[23] So also Hugh

18. James Burgh, *Political Disquisitions; or, an Enquiry into public Errors, Defects, and Abuses. Illustrated by, and established upon Facts and Remarks, extracted from a Variety of Authors, Ancient and Modern*, 3 vols. (Philadelphia, 1775). Caroline Robbins has discussed the English Whig background of political thought in *The Eighteenth-Century Commonwealthman* (Cambridge, Mass., 1959).

19. Burgh, *Disquisitions*, I, 106.

20. *Ibid.*, II, 36, 230.

21. *Ibid.*, III, 311.

22. *Ibid.*, I, 260, III, 82. See also on power, [Gordon and Trenchard], *Cato's Letters*, I, 184, 225, II, 233, III, 80-81, IV, 82; Burgh, *Disquisitions*, I, 112 (where he refers to Harrington).

23. To Elbridge Gerry, Apr. 23, 1784, in Harry Alonzo Cushing, ed., *The Writings of Samuel Adams*, 4 vols. (New York, 1904-1908), IV, 302; to John Winthrop, Dec. 21, 1778, Burnett, ed., *Letters*, III, 545.

Hughes, a New York City Antifederalist, warned, "From the Conduct of our Church and the Senate, we see how *absolutely requisite* it is, to continually guard against Power; for, when once Bodies of Men, in authority, get Possession of, or become invested with, Property or Prerogative, whether it be by Intrigue, Mistake, or Chance, they scarcely ever relinquish their Claim, even if founded in Iniquity itself." [24]

The power to govern must therefore be retained by the people, who alone can be trusted to know their own will, and who, as "Cato" believed, "generally, if not always, judge well." Since all men are equal, there is no reason to grant power to the "Great Men," who indeed are most apt to be oppressors.[25] "Democritus" warned the Massachusetts voters that even if the well-educated and well-to-do had good intentions, they had been taught to look upon their inferiors as their property, so that they would have "very little compassion." Only those could be trusted who earned their living by "honest industry" and who were men "in middling circumstances." [26]

Still another condition was necessary to ensure that the government would express the popular will. Such a government, wrote "Cato," required a relatively equal division of property. Since "Dominion follows Property, . . . An Equality of Estate will give an Equality of Power; and an Equality of Power is a Commonwealth, or Democracy," whereas "Very great Riches in private Men . . . destroy, amongst the Commons, that Balance of Property and Power, which is necessary to a Democracy." If property is thus equally divided, "there is no hindering a popular Form of Government, unless sudden Violence takes away all Liberty, and, to preserve itself, alters the Distribution of Property again." [27]

Years before, James Harrington had written that where an equality of estates existed there must be equality of power.[28] This

24. To Charles Tillinghast, Mar. 7, 1787, John Lamb Papers, N.Y. Hist. Soc. See also, for example, "Cassius," in the *Hudson Weekly Gazette* (N.Y.), Dec. 14, 1786.

25. [Gordon and Trenchard], *Cato's Letters*, I, 156, 177-79, II, 85, 88.

26. Quoted in Ralph Volney Harlow, *Samuel Adams* (New York, 1923), 281.

27. [Gordon and Trenchard], *Cato's Letters*, I, 113, III, 161, 207. See also III, 151. The authors note the necessity of a law prohibiting entail.

28. James Harrington, *The Commonwealth of Oceana*, ed. Henry Morley

doctrine contained radical implications which few followed to the logical conclusion, yet the relationship between power and property was observed in America, and among the Antifederalists there were at least some who attacked any trend toward the inequality of wealth as being dangerous to democracy. They recognized, as Thomson Mason wrote in 1783, that "power is the constant, the necessary attendant on property." [29] Connecticut, as Captain Welton observed, had a government that was "popular or democratical," which God had given as the best system, and "for this purpose an equal distribution of property was necessary." [30] It followed that where property was widely distributed, a democratic or popular government was most agreeable. Joseph Reed in Pennsylvania and Joseph Warren in Massachusetts were two who noted that a democracy would be congenial to Americans only so long as an excessive concentration of wealth was avoided.[31]

In order to guard against the tyranny of power and preserve popular rule, the men entrusted with power had to be kept responsive to public opinion. If they were allowed to act independently, history proved that the results were evil, and the former colonials did not have to look far into the past to perceive this truth. The Revolutionary generation needed only to recall events out of their own experiences: the behavior of the royal governors or of officials appointed by them; the failure of councilors and even of elective officers to heed the people's will. The corruption of power, the oppression of strong government, had been vital, immediate dangers to those who waged the Revolution because of them. How could responsibility be maintained?

(London, 1887), 64. See also Robbins, *Commonwealthman*, 38-39, 190-92, 207-8, 353.

29. To the Freeholders of Stafford County, June 10, 1783, in Kate Mason Rowland, *The Life of George Mason*, 2 vols. (New York, 1892), II, 53. Thomson Mason was the father of Stevens Thomson Mason and the brother of George Mason.

30. *Middlesex Gazette* (Middletown, Conn.), June 18, 1787. Welton, who was speaking in the House of Representatives, came from Woodbridge, a town which opposed the Constitution. He was an advocate of paper money.

31. Reed to Anthony Wayne, June 13, 1781, in John F. Roche, *Joseph Reed: a Moderate in the American Revolution* (New York, 1957), 187; Warren to Edmund Dana, Mar. 19, 1766, Richard Frothingham, *Life and Times of Joseph Warren* (Boston, 1865), 20-21. On the relation between

Frequent and regular elections were certainly essential. In England and in many colonies, elections had been held only at long intervals and might be delayed by the executive, so that when an important new issue arose, the vote of the legislators did not always reflect a changing public opinion. It was therefore recognized that to preserve popular rule, elections must be held every year. "Where annual elections end, slavery begins," Burgh declared, and the Pennsylvania democrat William Findley agreed: "Annual Elections are an annual Recognition of the Sovereignty of the People." [32] In addition, there was the danger that an official might remain in office so long that he ceased to sympathize with the people. Rotation in office, according to "Cato," was "essentially necessary to a free Government: It is indeed the Thing itself; and constitutes, animates, and informs it, as much as the Soul institutes the Man. It is a Thing sacred and inviolable, where-ever Liberty is thought sacred." [33] This principle was forcibly expressed by the Pennsylvania constitution of 1776, which required a rota-

---

power and property and democracy, see also "A Spartan," *New York Packet and American Advertiser,* Feb. 16, 1786; petition of Albemarle County, Nov. 3, 1787, *Wm. and Mary Qtly.,* 2nd Ser., 2 (1922), 213-16; Samuel Adams to Elbridge Gerry, Sept. 9, 1783, in Cushing, ed., *Writings of Adams,* IV, 287; John Francis Mercer in Worthington Chauncey Ford, ed., *Journals of the Continental Congress, 1774-1789,* 34 vols. (Washington, 1904-1937), XXV, 916; James Otis, *The Rights of the British Colonies Asserted and Proved* (Boston, 1764), 8; Philadelphia convention of 1776 and Mecklenburg instructions of 1776 quoted in Elisha P. Douglass, *Rebels and Democrats* (Chapel Hill, 1955), 226, 127; *Hampshire Herald: Or, Weekly Advertiser* (Springfield), May 7, 1785; *Cumberland Gazette* (Falmouth, Maine), June 8, 1786; "Brutus," in the *Boston Gazette,* Apr. 2, 1787. At an earlier date Governor Tryon of New York had seen the same point and advocated large grants as a means of preventing democracy. Virginia D. Harrington, *New York Merchants on the Eve of the Revolution* (New York, 1935), 142. The success of his policy caused a New Yorker later to regret the separation of Vermont, for had that not occurred he saw that the "Democratic Spirit" would have been strengthened against the aristocracy which, he recognized, had resulted from an unequal distribution of property. Chilton Williamson, *Vermont in Quandary: 1763-1825* (Montpelier, 1949), 67. For an extremely interesting discussion of the economic basis of politics, see "The Free Republican" in the *Boston Magazine,* Aug. 1784, 420-23.

32. Burgh, *Disquisitions,* I, 83, 87; McMaster and Stone, *Pennsylvania and the Constitution,* 776.

33. [Gordon and Trenchard], *Cato's Letters,* II, 240; see also Burgh, *Disquisitions,* I, 175-76.

tion in office in order that "the danger of establishing an inconvenient aristocracy will be effectually prevented."[34]

The Antifederalists, like most Americans, believed that if the government were truly to represent the people, the principal power should rest in the popular branch. There was, however, some disagreement as to whether this branch of government should be all-powerful or restrained by a coequal upper house and executive. "Cato" had favored a political system of three parts: the magistracy, to prevent confusion; the people, to prevent oppression; and the senate, consisting of men distinguished for their fortunes and abilities. Such an arrangement was made familiar by many other writers, including Locke. On the other hand, Burgh argued that there ought to be no checks whatever on the people's representatives by king or lords.[35] Certainly the trend in America had consistently been toward the elevation of the lower house at the expense of the upper house and the governor. The citizens of Ashfield, Massachusetts, represent the extreme: they wished no governor except God, as they said, and under him a states general. They envisaged the state legislature as a unicameral body, annually elected; any acts pertaining to the towns were to be approved by the towns. Even the judiciary was to be under popular control, for each town was to choose its own judges.[36] Antifederal thought did not always insist on the complete elimination of the senate, as in this instance, but it did require a readjustment of power in favor of the more democratic lower house. A reduction in the executive authority was almost universally demanded after 1776 because of a reaction against the royal governors.

Many Antifederalists also wished to reduce the high property qualifications for holding office. Arguing against any special requirement for the election of the governor, the town of Petersham, Massachusetts (soon to be a Shaysite center and then Antifed-

34. Francis Newton Thorpe, comp., *The Federal and State Constitutions, Colonial Charters, and other Organic Laws of the States, Territories, and Colonies Now or Heretofore Forming the United States of America*, 7 vols. (Washington, 1909), V, 3087.

35. [Gordon and Trenchard], *Cato's Letters*, III, 12-14; Burgh, *Disquisitions*, I, 116.

36. Resolutions of Oct. 4, 1776, in Harlow, *Adams*, 282-83. See also, for example, the *Cumberland Gazette* (Falmouth), May 11, 1786.

eral), resolved, "Riches and Dignity neither make the head wiser nor the heart better. The overgrown Rich we consider the most dangerous to the Liberties of a free State." [37] Orange County in the North Carolina uplands, various little New Hampshire towns, and other spokesmen of democracy demanded that the suffrage be extended. [38] The inhabitants of Westminster, Massachusetts (presently to be Antifederal), accepted this point of view when in 1778 they resolved,

The oftener power Returns into the hands of the people the Better, and when for the good of the whole the power is Delligated it ought to be done by the whole . . . Where can the power be lodged so Safe as in the Hands of the people and who can Delligate it So Well as they, or who has the boldness without Blushing to Say that the people are not Suitable to putt in their own officers—if so why do we wast our blood and Treasure to obtain that which when obtained we are not fitt to Enjoy, or if but a Selected few only are fitt to appoint our Rulers, why were we uneasie under George? [39]

Oppression could be avoided if a government was made popular, and also if it was denied powers which might be abused. It was hardly necessary to warn Englishmen concerning the powers of "the sword." Burgh and "Cato" agreed that no nation which had a standing army could preserve its liberty; "a free parliament and a standing army are absolutely incompatible." [40] So also in America, Samuel Adams warned that "the Sins of America may be

37.   Quoted in Douglass, *Rebels and Democrats*, 207. For other objections to property qualifications for the governor in Massachusetts, see Samuel Eliot Morison, "The Struggle over the Adoption of the Constitution of Massachusetts, 1780," Mass. Hist. Soc., *Proceedings*, 50 (1916-1917), 385. Most of the towns mentioned were Antifederal.

38.   Instructions to Thomas Burke, in Elisha P. Douglass, "Thomas Burke, Disillusioned Democrat," *N. C. Hist. Rev.*, 26 (1949), 160; Richard Francis Upton, *Revolutionary New Hampshire* (Hanover, 1936), 184, 190; Peter Force, ed., *American Archives . . . a Documentary History of . . . the North American Colonies*, 4th Ser., 6 vols. (Washington, 1837-53), V, 1119; discussion and references given in Merrill Jensen, "Democracy and the American Revolution," *Huntington Library Quarterly*, 20 (1957), 328-38.

39.   Quoted in Lee N. Newcomer, *The Embattled Farmers; a Massachusetts Countryside in the American Revolution* (New York, 1953), 98.

40.   Burgh, *Disquisitions*, II, 348, 355; [Gordon and Trenchard], *Cato's Letters*, I, 115, III, 234-57.

punished by a standing Army," and Richard Henry Lee agreed with James Monroe that it led to "the destruction of liberty." [41] The suspicion of a standing army and the Antifederal determination to keep in local hands the control over the military had important consequences during and after the Revolution. Equally important in its effects was the conviction that the power to tax must be retained by the people. The long struggle with the governors and the decade of controversy with king and parliament re-emphasized and intensified a doctrine shared by all Englishmen. This distrust of centralization existed, indeed, long before the Revolutionary period. One of the principal causes of the rejection of the famous Albany Plan in 1754 was that the Grand Council would have the right to raise troops and levy taxes as well as other critical powers. [42]

When the Articles of Confederation were being considered, fears of excessive concentration of authority were often expressed. The town of West Springfield, Massachusetts, reminded its representatives of the "weakness of human nature and the growing thirst for power," and continued: "It is *freedom*, Gentlemen, it is *freedom*, & not a choice of the *forms of servitude* for which we contend, and we rely on your fidelity, that you will not consent to the present *plan* of Union, til after the most calm & dispassionate examination you are fully convinced it is well calculated to secure so great & desirable an object." The powers granted to Congress, the town feared, were too great, and "the sovereignty and independence of particular states nearly annihilated.... We entertain no jealousy of the present Congress but who knows but in some future corrupt times there may be a Congress which will form a design upon the liberties of the People & will it be difficult

41. Adams to James Warren, Oct. 20, 1788, Burnett, ed., *Letters*, III, 458; Lee to Monroe, Jan. 5, 1784, Ballagh, ed., *Lee*, II, 287; see also William Gordon to Washington, Aug. 13, 1783, Washington Papers, CCXXIV, No. 26, Lib. Cong.; instructions of Leicester, Mass., July 13, 1775, Massachusetts towns, Force Transcripts, V, Lib. Cong.

42. For examples of opposition to the Albany Plan, see Albert B. Hart, ed., *Commonwealth History of Massachusetts, Colony, Province and State*, 5 vols. (New York, 1927-1930), II, 461; Report of Committee of the General Assembly, "The Fitch Papers," Conn. Hist. Soc., *Collections*, 17 (1918), 34-36.

to execute such a design when they have the absolute command of the navy, the army & the purse?"[43]

It was in accordance with such principles that under the Articles most powers were reserved to the states and that Article II guaranteed the sovereignty and independence of the states.[44] It was also in accord with this political tradition that there was no independent executive—executive functions were performed by Congress through committees or, later, by departments responsible to Congress. Similarly, there was no judiciary except Congress itself, and that body appointed all officers. It might be supposed that the absence of a check and balance system, the lack of any division of power, might result in an excessive centralization of authority. But there were two important limitations which prevented the delegates to Congress from violating their trust. First, they could not act independently. It is true that they were chosen by the legislatures rather than by the people—a fact which drew scattered criticisms[45]—but the elections were annual, the delegates could serve only for three years out of six, and they could be recalled at any time. Members of Congress recognized their responsibility and continually reported to the state governments, giving information and seeking advice.[46] A second check

43. Feb. 16, 1778, Massachusetts towns, Force Transcripts, II, Lib. Cong. West Springfield, a farming community in the heart of Shaysite country, was typical of such towns; on every issue in Massachusetts politics it was to be found following, so to speak, the Antifederalist party line.

44. Illustrations of this doctrine are: Instructions of the Assembly of Rhode Island to the delegates to Congress, May 1776, John Russell Bartlett, ed., *Records of the Colony of Rhode Island and Providence Plantations, in New England*, 10 vols. (Providence, 1856-65), VII, 526; George Mason to Edmund Randolph, Oct. 19, 1782, Rowland, *Mason*, II, 28-29; William Bradford, Jr., to Joseph Reed, July 12, 1781, Reed Papers, N.Y. Hist. Soc. William Plumer remarked that in New Hampshire the constitution makers' task was arduous, "for the prejudices which the revolution had engendered against the arbitrary government of Great Britain, made the people jealous of giving to their own officers so much power as was necessary to establish an efficient government." Upton, *Revolutionary New Hampshire*, 184.

45. See extracts from the town records of Stafford, Salisbury, Stratford, Waterbury, and Windham, Conn. State Lib.

46. Almost all of this correspondence was with the governor. Since the democrats emphasized the superior authority of the legislature, their correspondence ought to have been with it, whenever that was feasible, instead of with the executive. Among the few delegates who did direct some of their letters to the popular branch, nearly all were Antifederalists, including

was that the critical powers were withheld. For matters of the highest importance the agreement of the states was essential, and this was especially true of financial affairs, since Congress possessed no revenue of its own but could only request money from the independent states. The Articles grew out of a political tradition widely accepted in Revolutionary America, and it was from the same tradition that Antifederalism grew.

Eleven of the original thirteen states, and Vermont, too, altered the structure of their governments during the Revolutionary era; only Rhode Island and Connecticut retained the inherited form. The political ideas of the Revolution were incorporated into all twelve of the new constitutions, but they were most prominent in those drafted by conventions in which, as one critic complained, "everyone who had the least pretensions to be a gentleman is borne down *per ignobile vulgus.*" [47] In Pennsylvania, North Carolina, Georgia, and Vermont, property qualifications for the suffrage were reduced or abolished: in Georgia any man could vote who had property worth £10 and paid taxes; in Pennsylvania and North Carolina all taxpayers could vote; and in Vermont there were no qualifications at all. In other states the usual requirement was fifty acres of land or an estate worth about £50 —a provision which reflects the widely-held opinion that only property owners were sufficiently responsible to be entrusted with the management of public affairs; yet the more democratic view was gaining ground. It was expressed not only in the liberal franchise granted by a few states, but in protests against other restrictions.[48] Each of the four states just mentioned and two others specified that voting should be by ballot rather than viva voce.

Thomas Burke, Timothy Bloodworth, Elbridge Gerry, and John Francis Mercer. See Burnett, ed., *Letters, passim.*

47. Samuel Johnson, quoted in Allan Nevins, *The American States During and After the Revolution, 1775-1789* (New York, 1924), 141.

48. See resolutions of Lenox, Mass., quoted in Robert J. Taylor, *Western Massachusetts in the Revolution* (Providence, 1954), 89; also the statement of Douglas, Mass., in Morison, "Constitution of Massachusetts," Mass. Hist. Soc., *Proceedings,* 50 (1916-1917), 390, and citations in Douglass, *Rebels and Democrats,* especially 15, 116-17, 179. Democratic views concerning the ability of the people to judge aright were also expressed by "Democraticus," in Force, ed., *American Archives,* 4th Ser., VI, 731; and Joseph Hawley to Elbridge Gerry, Oct. 13, 1776, in Brown, *Hawley,* 170.

Vermont and Pennsylvania virtually eliminated property qualifications for serving in the lower house by making any voter eligible. Everywhere except in South Carolina the lower house was chosen annually. Although most of the states stressed frequent elections, they usually left it to the voters to rotate officeholders; in Pennsylvania, however, representatives were limited to four years in seven.

The provisions in regard to an upper house are especially revealing. Georgia, Pennsylvania, and Vermont refused to provide for a senate, so the more democratic lower house was supreme.[49] The other constitutions provided for an upper house equal in power to the lower. That the senates were intended to represent the larger property holders is evident from the special qualifications for membership, which were almost everywhere higher than for the other branch. Yet the doctrine that legislators must be watched was recognized: senate terms were either annual or rotational (except in the case of Maryland). The prevalent fear of strong authority in government is also to be seen in the provisions regarding the executive branch. The power of the governor was strikingly limited; only one state—Massachusetts—allowed him a veto.[50] Usually he was merely a creature of the legislature, chosen by a joint ballot of the houses; his term was seldom more than a single year, and half of the states limited his re-eligibility.

Striking also was the change in regard to other officials. Prior to the Revolution most of them were responsible to the governor, holding office at his pleasure. Now, in many cases, the governor lost the power of appointment, and the officials served during good behavior rather than at the pleasure of the governor. In many states—notably in Georgia, Pennsylvania, Vermont, New Jersey, and Delaware—local officials were made more responsible to local constituencies; their terms were shorter and re-eligibility was limited. The constitution of Pennsylvania obliged judges to

49. The exception was North Carolina, where property qualifications for senators were unusually low.

50. For examples of objections to the governor's veto, see Samuel Holten to Samuel Adams, Jan. 4, 1780, Adams Papers, XIV, Lib. Cong.; George Bryan to Samuel Adams, Jan. 5, 1780, *ibid.* Suspicion of the executive authority was frequently expressed, as in Thomas McKean to Samuel Adams, July 8, 1781, Burnett, ed., *Letters*, VI, 139.

seek reappointment every seven years and provided that justices of the peace be chosen by the freemen for the same term, while all other local officials were elected annually.[51]

The liberties of the people were protected in other ways. Three of the four most democratic constitutions and four of the other eight contained bills of rights, which among other provisions warned against standing armies and asserted the subordination of the military to the civil authority. All four of the more democratic constitutions, and two of the other eight, favored tax-supported education; three of the four, and only these, abolished imprisonment for debt; entail was regulated by all four, and by these only.

The ideas expressed by Burgh and "Cato" thus found acceptance in the new constitutions, especially those of Vermont, Pennsylvania, North Carolina, and Georgia, which expressed clearly the doctrine that power should be concentrated in that branch which was most responsive to public opinion. Here, and above all among future Antifederalists, was to be seen a willingness to widen the franchise, to limit terms of office, to reject checks by a senate or the governor—in general, to extend popular control. The attitude of this group was well expressed by a minority address of the Pennsylvania Council of Censors, defending the state's constitution against attempts to change it. Those who wanted reform were dissatisfied with the existing Constitution, the report declared, because "it retains too much power in the hand of the people, who do not know how to use it, so well as gentlemen of fortune, . . . and it gives no advantage to the rich over the poor." "To remedy these inconveniences," the gentlemen wanted a senate "to accomodate the *better sort of people*" and obstruct the wishes of "honest farmers"; they hoped in addition to give the governor a veto. The judiciary, warned the future Antifederalists, would then also come under the control of the "better sort," and popular rights would be endangered; and "that you may finally despair of ever having it in your power without bloodshed to counteract an ambitious tyrant at the head of your government, it is farther

51. For an argument in favor of popular control over local officials see Force, ed., *American Archives*, 4th Ser., V, 451-52. The author insists that the people are better able to judge than their representatives, and are not so liable to be corrupted: "No business that can be done by the people themselves should ever be trusted to their Delegates."

proposed to give him absolute power to appoint and commission every officer in the state."[52] Perhaps Reverend William Gordon best summarized the Antifederal position when he remarked, "The rich will have enough advantages against the poor without political advantages."[53]

52. *Pennsylvania Journal, and Weekly Advertiser* (Phila.), Jan. 31, 1784.
53. Quoted in Douglass, *Rebels and Democrats,* 153.

Chapter II

SOCIETY AND POLITICS
IN THE SOUTH

A S THE YEAR 1781 drew to a close, the people were increasingly able to turn their attention away from the war and consider who was to rule the country in peace. Each state witnessed a struggle between various sections and classes for political power, and the outcome had significant economic and social consequences. Fortunately, it is not necessary to describe all of the local issues and local contests, but only those aspects of state politics which are vital to an understanding of Antifederalism. The South will be discussed first, and attention will be particularly focused on those states in which the significant features appear most sharply: South Carolina and Virginia.

The sectional division of South Carolina was a fundamental element in the state's history.[1] In Revolutionary times there were two major sections: east and west. The former, which was the commercial part of the state, lay entirely within the Tidewater and extended perhaps forty or fifty miles inland. The metropolis of this region, Charleston, was the economic, social, and political center of the state and its capital until 1789.[2] Within the city society was divided along class lines. On one side were the wealthy merchants, lawyers, and planters, closely connected by marriage and economic interest. Labeled by their opponents as a "Nabob Phalanx,"[3] they had dominated the city before the Revo-

1. William A. Schaper, "Sectionalism and Representation in South Carolina," Am. Hist. Assn., *Annual Report*, 1900 (Washington, 1901), 237-463.
2. A new site was chosen in 1786 but the move was delayed, so that the ratifying convention met in Charleston—a fact of some importance.
3. *Gazette of the State of South-Carolina* (Charleston), Aug. 19, 1784.

21

lution and had never lost control. The other side, led by Alexander Gillon, consisted of the less well-to-do, who were characterized by their opponents as "Drunken Tavern-keepers, Montebank Doctors, Pettifogging Attornies, and necessitous Speculators" and "a mob."[4] The Gillon supporters were handicapped by a three shilling poll tax which, they complained, prevented many from voting. They concentrated their fire on tories and British aliens, who supported and were in turn defended by the aristocracy. Although the aristocracy was hard pressed for a short time during the Revolution, it quickly resumed its usual dominance, and the city cast an almost solid vote in the legislature. On matters of state politics the Gillon group was often allied with the back-country, but this was not true of national affairs.[5]

Charleston usually furnished political leadership to the eastern parishes of the state. These parishes (the "Low Country") contained 108,000 persons in 1790, but of these about 78,000 were slaves, who outnumbered the whites in most of the parishes by four to one.[6] Only some six thousand adult white males occupied this region of large plantations, in which there were, on the average, twenty Negroes available for each white man, and in two parishes, over sixty. In contrast, the rest of the state contained nearly five times as many whites but far fewer slaves. The great planters of the coast were economically and socially a part of Charleston, and although the city and the rural low country parishes were sometimes opposed, on most issues they united against the west.

4. *South-Carolina Gazette and General Advertiser* (Charleston), Nov. 20, 1784.

5. The conflict and alignment can be followed in the newspapers. See especially the *South Carolina Weekly Gazette* (Charleston), May 22, 1784; *Charleston Evening Gazette*, Feb. 16, 1786; *Gazette of State of S.-C.*, (Charleston), Aug. 12, 19, Sept. 9, 1784; *S. C. Gazette and General Advertiser* (Charleston), Sept. 14, 16, Nov. 20, 1784; *South Carolina Gazette, and Public Advertiser* (Charleston), Sept. 29, 1784, July 12, Sept. 1, 3, 1785; *Charleston Morning Post, and Daily Advertiser*, Feb. 5, 7, 8, 1787. See also Arthur Bryan to George Bryan, Apr. 9, 1788, George Bryan Papers, Box A24, Hist. Soc. Pa. There is a good discussion in Phillips, "South Carolina Federalists," *Am. Hist. Rev.*, 14 (1908-1909), 533-37.

6. This is true with the exceptions of St. Phillips and St. Michael (Charleston), Prince Frederick's, Prince George, St. George (Dorchester) and Beaufort District. Greene and Harrington, *American Population*, 177-79.

In spite of its much greater population, the west had far less political strength than the eastern lowland because it was under-represented in the legislature. During the transition to independence the planters had retained control of the new state and had adopted a constitution which assured their continued dominance. Just how one assesses the sectional imbalance in representation depends upon how "west" and "east" are defined. If the alignment as indicated by actual votes is taken as the guide, the eastern section had 143 seats in the lower house (at full strength) whereas the western had only 93; according to population in 1790 the east should have had only 50 and the west, 186. Obviously the west could not achieve its aims unaided, but support was sometimes forthcoming from a group of parishes which lay along the dividing line between the two sections.[7] These parishes were transitional both in geographical location and in socio-economic character-istics, and with their 43 votes they held the balance of power.

Inequality of representation was not the only cause of the west's political difficulties. The state constitution discriminated not only against that stronghold of self-sufficient farmers but also against small property-holders in general. Limitations on the franchise were not unusually large,[8] and any voter could serve in the House of Representatives, which, aside from the inequitable distribution of seats, was therefore a popular body. Nor could the governor check the will of the majority, for although he had to be rich (£10,000 clear of debt) in order to qualify for his office, he did not have a veto over legislation. The Senate, however, did have a veto, and since that body consisted principally of easterners and entirely of men owning a settled estate or freehold worth £2,000 clear of debt, or £7,000 in the case of non-residents, no measure favorable to western or to middle-class interests could be passed unless it was also backed by some of the wealthy planters.

No basic political or economic reform, no real shift of political power, could occur unless changes were made in the constitution.

7. St. Peter's, Prince William, St. Bartholomew, St. George's (Dor-chester), St. John's (Berkeley), St. Stephen's, Prince George's, and Prince Frederick. Their Federalism in 1788 proved decisive in the ratification of the Constitution in the state.

8. Any adult male who owned 50 acres or a town lot or who paid a tax equal to that on 50 acres could vote. Thorpe, comp., *Constitutions*, VI, 3252.

Demands for its revision were heard continually. The west was especially anxious to abolish the Senate and redistribute seats in the House.[9] In 1785 the House approved a convention but the Senate rejected it.[10] Two years later the House again approved a convention, but the Senate shared the fears of an opponent who warned that "the general mass of the people were so much bent for a democratical government, that he feared a convention at this time would do more harm than good," and the proposal was again defeated.[11] Still another attempt was made the following year with the same result. On this occasion the nature of the division in the lower house is indicated by two roll-call votes. When a report calling for revision was brought in, a motion to postpone consideration was favored by the eastern members; but the west, supported by the border area, defeated the delaying action. A second vote approved the report by a narrow margin, supplied mainly by the west.[12] The alignment on this bill corresponds to the vote on a bill, which was considered about the same time, to establish the governor's salary at £1,000 per year.[13] The amount seemed excessive to the western delegates, and they rejected it by a very large majority. To the easternmost representatives it seemed reasonable, and they approved it by an equally large margin. In this instance the border divided, and the bill lost.

Many issues grew out of the financial problems of the state and of individuals. Wartime losses had been extensive, and after the war the planters hastened to repair their plantations and purchase slaves, borrowing very heavily. Even though exports increased rapidly, imports also rose sharply; from 1783 on the state had a large unfavorable balance of trade and a corresponding increase of private debts. To some extent these new debts were justified,

9. David Ramsay to Benjamin Rush, Aug. 16, 1784, Rush Papers, Phila. Lib. Co.; *Charleston Morning Post*, Mar. 16, 1787.

10. *Columbian Herald, or Patriotic Courier of North-America* (Charleston), Mar. 28, 1785. The Constitution could be altered by majority vote of both branches after a 90 day interval, or by a convention.

11. *Charleston Evening Gazette*, Feb. 21, 1786.

12. *State Gazette of South-Carolina* (Charleston), Mar. 19, 1787. On the first vote the division was, extreme east 37-16 for postponement, west 56-7 against, border area 21-8 against.

13. *Ibid.*, Feb. 8, 1787.

since they represented capital outlays, but the planters greatly overextended themselves, counting on good crops and high prices. Too much of the buying was for luxuries: "If we are undone," wrote "Senex" sourly, "we are the most splendidly ruined of any nation in the universe."[14] The excessive imports drew specie out of the state, creating a shortage which was further aggravated by the necessity of levying heavy taxes to discharge an enormous public debt incurred during the Revolution. It became exceedingly difficult to pay taxes and private debts.[15] Debtors suffered severely, and their situation was made worse by crop failures.[16] A series of prosecutions resulted in heavy losses for debtors who were forced to sell their property at a fraction of its true value. Mounting protest led to violence. In some parts of the state legal affairs were forcibly halted, and the government was confronted almost with a revolt.[17] Not only small farmers but wealthy planters were involved. The merchant John Lloyd, president of the Senate, was unable to collect debts owed to him by men of "Rank, dignity and wealth";[18] and Henry Laurens asserted that he had been unable to collect so much as a farthing of the money due him, even though most of it was "owing by People of the first Characters in the State beginning with the Supreme Magistrate's Excellency."[19] One is not surprised to find his Excellency appealing to the legislature in October 1785 for laws to remedy a situation

14. *S. C. Gazette, and Public Advertiser* (Charleston), May, 21, 1785.

15. For imports and exports, see the *Columbian Herald* (Charleston), Mar. 7, Oct. 5, 1785, Jan. 30, 1786, Jan. 3, 1788; *Charleston Morning Post,* Feb. 28, 1787; *Pa. Herald* (Phila.), Dec. 20, 1786. For the general situation at this time, see John Lloyd to Francis Simmons, Jan. 30, 1785, Charleston Lib. Soc.; David Ramsay to Benjamin Rush, Jan. 31, 1785, Rush Papers, Phila. Lib. Co.; David Ramsay, *The History of South-Carolina, from its First Settlement in 1670, to the Year 1808,* 2 vols. (Charleston, 1809), II, 428; Phillips, "South Carolina Federalists," *Am. Hist. Rev.,* 14 (1908-1909), 537-40.

16. *Columbian Herald* (Charleston), May 8, 1786.

17. *Charleston Evening Gazette,* Sept. 30, 1785; address of Burke in *ibid.,* Feb. 21, 1786; *Pa. Herald* (Phila.), Oct. 5, 1785; Ford, ed., *Journals of Congress,* XXXI, 787-88.

18. To his nephew, Apr. 15, 1786, Charleston Lib. Soc.

19. To Daniel Roberdeau (of Alexandria, Virginia), Apr. 20, 1786, Laurens Papers, Letter Book No. 13, S. C. Hist. Soc.; also Singer, *South Carolina,* 20, 117.

which had led to "your courts being insulted, your laws set at defiance, and civil process confined to a small part of this state."[20]

Not only were both rich and poor in economic distress, but the state government also had a heavy burden. Although operating expenses were not great, in 1785 interest on the state debt amounted to £94,000 out of a total state expense of £107,000; in addition Congress was requesting funds. Taxes were necessarily high, and there was so little money in circulation that collectors encountered a good deal of trouble, especially in the interior.[21]

These public and private problems resulted in much legislative action. The western delegates, representing small farmer constituencies, agitated for tax reform, paper money, and debtor relief legislation. The fact that so many planters felt the weight of taxes and debts assured the passage of a series of alleviating measures. Among them was a valuation law to protect debtors from undue property loss: property would be evaluated, and if, at the sheriffs' sales, there was no bid up to two-thirds of that value, the creditor must accept the property at the official evaluation.[22] In 1782 a stay law postponing action on debts was passed, and in 1785 a new law stopped suits for debt. When the latter act expired, another bill was passed which permitted payment of debts by installments.[23] In addition, the tax law was reformed so that land was taxed in accordance with its value instead of its extent.[24]

The most important legislation provided for an issue of paper money. The Senate, reflecting the influence of the merchants and the wealthiest planters, succeeded in blocking passage temporarily, but the bill had the support not only of the small farmers but of many large planters, and it could not long be postponed. What the Senate did accomplish was to moderate the law (moderation was perhaps also guaranteed by planter support), and the result was the issuance of £100,000 in currency to be loaned for five years at 7 per cent.[25] This money proved to be sound. The

20. *Columbian Herald* (Charleston), Oct. 3, 1785.

21. *Ibid.*, July 15, 1785; *Pa. Packet* (Phila.), Feb. 9, 1787.

22. Thomas Cooper, ed., *The Statutes at Large of South Carolina* (Columbia, S. C., 1838), IV, 710-12; *Charleston Evening Gazette*, Sept. 29, 1785.

23. Cooper, ed., *Statutes of S. C.*, IV, 513, 640-41, V, 36.

24. *Ibid.*, IV, 627-29.

25. *Ibid.*, 712-16.

relatively small amount and the high interest rate prevented any serious depreciation; moreover, both merchants and planters co-operated to maintain the money's value.[26] The total effect of paper money and debtor relief legislation was to mitigate the effects of economic conditions and avoid any uprisings such as occurred in Massachusetts or such as had threatened in South Carolina in 1785.[27]

Few roll-call votes were recorded on these issues, but there are two which reveal the alignment. The first occurred in March 1787, when an attempt was made to change the depreciation table by which the value of past transactions in depreciated currency was computed. The west favored the measure 48-14, but it lost when the eastern parishes all but unanimously rejected it (49-2). The transition region was divided.[28] The second vote was taken on February 22, 1788, when the House rejected a motion to pass a valuation bill which would have obliged creditors to accept the property of debtors at a price higher than the creditors preferred. Such measures were favored by the western delegates and by the delegates from the border area, but the eastern representatives were overwhelmingly opposed.[29]

The sectional alignment may be dramatized by extreme examples. The district of St. John's (Colleton) in 1790 contained 587 whites and 4,705 slaves, or about forty slaves for every adult white male. It had seven representatives in the lower house—one for every eighty-four whites. It cast a unanimous vote against changing the state constitution and against the laws favoring

26. *Columbian Herald* (Charleston), May 4, July 20, 1786; *Charleston Evening Gazette*, July 5, Aug. 14, 1786; *Charleston Morning Post*, Aug. 4, 1786; Samuel Wilcox to Jeremiah Wadsworth, Dec. 8, 1786, Wadsworth Papers, Box 137, Conn. Hist. Soc.; Cripps & Co. to Caleb Davis, Jan. 6, 1787, Caleb Davis Papers, XIVa, Mass. Hist. Soc.; Hugh McCall to Edward Carrington, June 20, 1788, Boston Pub. Lib.

27. "Appius," in the *Charleston Morning Post*, Feb. 15, 1787. An interesting discussion of the debt question is in *ibid.*, Feb. 19, 1787; see also A. Bryan to George Bryan, Apr. 9, 1788, Bryan Papers, Hist. Soc. Pa.

28. *State Gazette of S.-C.* (Charleston), Mar. 12, 1787. A depreciation table recognized the declining value of the various state and federal certificates of indebtedness by establishing legal rates of exchange which were less than par.

29. *Ibid.*, Feb. 25, 1788. See also a vote on a motion to consider an instalment bill, in the *City Gazette, and Daily Advertiser* (Charleston), Feb. 15, 1788.

debtors and poorer citizens. Camden County,[30] on the other hand, contained 29,400 whites and 8,865 slaves, yet had at most only 19 delegates—one for every 1,547. On the issues just mentioned, these delegates voted almost unanimously on the other side.

The course of politics in South Carolina reflected the general socio-economic divisions of the state. On one side was the city of Charleston and the wealthy rural parishes near the coast with their heavy concentration of slaves. At the other extreme was the major part of the state extending from a line some fifty miles inland to the western border. There were slaves here too, but the dominant economic unit was the small farm. Sometimes aided by delegates from the transition parishes, the westerners tried to democratize the state constitution and secure economic advantages for the rural majority of small property-holders. Their lack of political power prevented the westerners from securing their objectives unless their aims were also supported by elements of the dominant planter aristocracy. The basis of political parties in South Carolina can therefore be expressed as a division between large landowners and small farmers or, equally well, as a conflict between the east and the west.

In Virginia a simple contrast between east and west does not fully explain the situation. The traditional dichotomy of Tidewater versus Piedmont, while not actually false, is inaccurate. In reality the division was above all between those who dwelled near navigable streams and those who did not.[31] The great plantations, with their slaves and wealthy masters, developed along the rivers, not so much because of the alluvial soil as because of the transportation facilities. The Potomac and the James, the York, the Rappahannock, and the Pamunkey were loci of social prestige, economic power, and political control. As the planters became wealthy they reached farther west along the river valleys, securing fresh land for their own use, for future sale, or for cultivation

30. Camden County was so designated in the 1790 census. It had been known first as "The District between the Broad and Catawba"; by 1788 the districts of Fairfield and Chester had been set off.

31. This section is based on my two articles, "The Distribution of Property," *Miss. Valley Hist. Rev.*, 41 (1954-1955), 241-58, and "Sections and Politics in Virginia, 1781-1787," *Wm. and Mary Qtly.*, 3rd Ser., 12 (1955), 96-112. I have here omitted much detail and most of the references.

by tenants.[32] Land not easily accessible to these navigable streams was less valuable and therefore less apt to be developed into the "plantation" type of agriculture. It was occupied by small farmers, who were forced by circumstances to be more self-sufficient and less dependent upon foreign commerce. Had Virginia's rivers been navigable only a short way into the interior, there might have been simply an east-west sectional division, but this was not the case. In the north, the Potomac and the Rappahannock reached to the Blue Ridge and beyond. The whole area between these two great streams, the "Northern Neck," had become one huge speculative enterprise, and it continued to be the home of vast landed estates, of tenants, slaves, and planters. Although nowhere in Virginia was there to be found so high a concentration of slaves as in South Carolina,[33] the Northern Neck may be compared with the coastal parishes of that state.

The Northern Neck is the unique example; in no other part of Virginia were there so many tenants, slaves, and great planters. But regions of the same type existed near the other rivers, of which the most important was the James. Its wide valley extended far beyond the fall line, where, for example, Albemarle County contained some very large estates. Such counties had similar characteristics: a large number of wealthy planters, who held most of the property, especially in land;[34] a considerable slave population; a large proportion of landless whites; and fewer small farmers than elsewhere. Most of these counties were located in the Tidewater, and had been settled for many decades; but where favorable geographical conditions permitted, the economic development of an area might proceed very rapidly, so that it was possible for such Piedmont counties as Powhatan, Orange, and Albemarle to pass quickly through the frontier stage, produce a planter class, and reverse their political allegiance. It was not nearly so

32. Main, "The One Hundred," *ibid.*, 11 (1954), 354-84.

33. In St. Paul's Parish, South Carolina, there were about 50 slaves per white taxpayer, and in all of the eastern parishes the ratio was at least eleven to one and usually much more than that. The wealthiest section of Virginia contained fewer than ten slaves per taxpayer.

34. In Westmoreland (in the Northern Neck) the wealthiest 10 per cent of the taxpayers held over 61 per cent of the taxable property; the same proportion held about 42 per cent in Charlotte, in the southern Piedmont, and 36 per cent in Washington, in the extreme southwest.

much a matter of a county's age or location with respect to the
ocean, as it was the economic interest and related structure of
society, that determined political behavior.

The opposing element in Virginia politics consisted of the small
farmers, whose particular stronghold was the "Southside," the
extensive region south of the James. This section was not poverty-
stricken: it had more slaves than the South Carolina backcountry,
but it apparently harbored many debtors and was dominated by
small property-holders. Politically, it found allies in similar counties of the northern Piedmont and in parts of the Tidewater, particularly in those counties which lay at some distance from the
great rivers or which contained only a small proportion of valley
land. Such counties resembled the Southside in one or more
respects: they had an unusually large middle class, relatively few
great planters, and a more equal division of land.

The Northern Neck and the Southside represent the extremes.
Many counties belonged to neither type. Some of them contained
both valley and upland; others had recently been in the stage of
economic and social development characteristic of the Southside
but were now in the process of being occupied by large planters,
and their political allegiance was changing.[35] They therefore resembled the transition counties of South Carolina, except that in
Virginia the political poles were not east and west, but river valley
and upland.

Beyond the Blue Ridge, three sections had their own individuali-
ties. Both the Shenandoah Valley [36] and the "Alleghany" counties
now included in West Virginia, then a frontier region, resembled
the Southside in economic interests and social structure, having
an even larger middle class. But the Valley sent a large agricultural surplus down the Potomac to Alexandria or overland to
Baltimore and was therefore inclined to vote with the people of
the Northern Neck on commercial questions. Both areas looked
west for their future expansion and prosperity, and by the latter
part of the 1780's, they had become intensely interested in the

35. Examples are Chesterfield and Caroline. Compare the transition area
in South Carolina.

36. Freeman H. Hart, *The Valley of Virginia in the American Revolution,
1763-1789* (Chapel Hill, 1942).

Northwest Territory, where the Indians dwelt and the British still maintained trading posts. These two sections were led by their interests to support a strong government which would promote expansion. The third section, Kentucky, contained many small farmers and also many men of wealth. At this time its residents were concerned primarily with the free use of the Mississippi which would make possible more rapid growth.

Virginia's politics operated within the framework provided by the constitution of 1776. Although not so closely adapted to the large planter interest as South Carolina's constitution, it did favor the east over the west and the rich over the poor. Except for townsmen, the suffrage requirement was the possession of fifty acres or twenty-five acres and a house. In most of the counties only about half of the adult white males could meet these qualifications; the well-to-do Virginians, who in any case had great influence,[37] could therefore exert considerable weight if they were united. Since representation in the House was by counties rather than according to population, and since each county had two seats, the larger western counties were under-represented; however they had become so numerous by 1780 that they could over-rule the planter-dominated sections in the House. The Senate remained under the control of eastern men of wealth.

Economic problems gave rise to political issues. Virginia, like South Carolina, suffered from a post-war depression and a money shortage which injured everyone but most of all the debtors and less well-to-do farmers. The depression was aggravated by a number of factors: pre-Revolutionary debts owed to English and Scottish merchants; losses suffered during the war; very heavy buying after the war, which drained the state of cash and created new debts; further debts contracted for expansion; crop failures; and a state war debt which necessitated heavy taxation. State politics were also affected by frontier issues: westward expansion was being delayed by the Spanish, who closed the Mississippi, by the British, who retained fur-trading posts in the northwest, and by the Indians, who threatened the entire frontier.

37. Sydnor, *Gentlemen Freeholders, passim*; Jack P. Greene, "Foundations of Political Power in the Virginia House of Burgesses, 1720-1776," *Wm. and Mary Qtly.*, 3rd Ser., 16 (1959), 485-506.

The character of political alignments in Virginia may be illustrated by examining briefly a few of these issues. One series of problems revolved around the incidence and collection of taxes. During the depression years several efforts were made to postpone collection. In the fall of 1785, Northern Neck representatives almost unanimously opposed one such attempt, as did delegates from counties along the Tidewater areas of the Rappahannock, York, and James rivers (16-6). These lowland and valley delegates got the support of a few Piedmont counties, particularly along the upper James. The Southside delegates, on the other hand, overwhelmingly supported postponement (without success), as did the western delegates from the Shenandoah Valley, the Alleghany counties, and Kentucky.[38] Equally revealing were two votes taken on the question of whether all laws in conflict with the British treaty should be repealed. The most important of such laws were those which discriminated against loyalists and which impeded the collection of debts owed to British citizens. In 1784 a bill requiring the repeal of these acts was defeated by a wide margin.[39] It might have been expected that the Northern Neck planters, many of whom had pre-war debts, would oppose enforcement of the treaty. On the contrary, what support the bill received came mainly from this area and from other counties along the major rivers. The river valley planters were interested above all in re-establishing pre-war commercial ties, for which good credit was essential; moreover, they were often creditors of other Virginians, and therefore interested in prompt and full payment of debts.[40] It was the Southside and the west, more isolated from commercial considerations, which reflected the debtor (and anti-loyalist) point of view. In 1787, when the same question came up again, the Northern Neck continued to approve of the treaty; the Southside and its usual adherents east of the Blue Ridge, with minor exceptions, opposed it.[41] Farther west, however, opinions were now reversed; it had become clear that the

38. *Journal of the House of Delegates of the Commonwealth of Virginia,* Oct. Session, 1785, 46.

39. *Ibid.,* May Session, 1784, 41.

40. W. A. Low, "Merchant and Planter Relations in Post-Revolutionary Virginia, 1783-1789," *Virginia Magazine of History and Biography,* 61 (1953), 308-18.

41. *Journal of Va. House of Delegates,* Oct. Session, 1787, 52.

British would not evacuate the western posts unless the treaty was observed. In the Shenandoah Valley and the counties of present-day West Virginia, the frontier problem was the dominant consideration, and this area voted to enforce collection of pre-war debts.

Other illustrations would merely reaffirm the alignment described. On one side were those counties with a high concentration of property, in which the creditor group was strong, and where the suffrage was unusually restricted. On the other side were areas in which the middle class was more powerful and the debtors more numerous. These were the major sections which confronted each other throughout the Revolutionary era. Across the Blue Ridge were people whose allegiance shifted: on questions of financial policy they tended to support the Southside (with the exception of Kentucky), but on other issues they favored the Northern Neck. These western regions held the balance of power.

North Carolina differed from Virginia in that small farmers dominated state politics. Only in the northeastern counties, near Albemarle and Pamlico sounds, was there consistent opposition to their wishes. Yet even in this region, roughly enclosed by an arc drawn fifty miles from Edenton, the small farmer constituted the largest segment of the population. Of the adult white males inhabiting this area, more than 70 per cent were land-holders, and of these only one out of eight had a plantation-sized (500 acre) estate; thus perhaps 60 per cent fell into the category of small farmers, and their status is suggested by the fact that at least half of all land-holders owned no slaves. Although the well-to-do possessed most of the wealth in this second richest area of the state, property was more widely distributed than in other Tidewater regions of the South.[42]

The element that controlled the political behavior of the northeastern counties was probably the fact that the farmers were raising a sizable crop for export and were economically dependent on the commercial centers of New Bern and Edenton. These towns, and to a considerable extent the surrounding countryside, were represented year after year by businessmen—merchants,

42. Information on the social structure of North Carolina has been drawn from a study of tax lists on microfilm. See *n.* 9, chap. I.

lawyers, shipowners, and land speculators. The Blount papers[43] and the correspondence of James Iredell[44] introduce us to the personnel of this group, which included, among others, William R. Davie, Hugh Williamson, Archibald Maclaine, John Sitgreaves, Richard D. Spaight, Stephen Cabarrus, and Benjamin Hawkins. These men stood together on almost all of the political issues of the period and without exception supported the Constitution.[45] They were not democratically inclined. In the election of 1787, Sitgreaves found himself opposed in New Bern by a man who had "Influence with the most numerous Class of voters"—a fact which aroused him to assert that the greater part of mankind, "the Mobility," were "fickle, ungrateful & ungenerous." William Blount viewed "our Republican Governments as the Most intolerable of all Tyranny" and inquired, "Can any Man be safe in his house while the Legislature are setting?"[46]

These businessmen and planters of the northeast were opposed by the leaders of the rest of the state, including the entire Piedmont and part of the Tidewater. Except for the southeastern counties, there were few men of wealth in this extensive area, few slaves, and a distribution of property even more equal than in the east.[47] Farming was mostly for subsistence, because except in

43. Alice Barnwell Keith, ed., *The John Gray Blount Papers*, 2 vols. (Raleigh, 1952).

44. Griffith J. McRee, *Life and Correspondence of James Iredell, one of the Associate Justices of the Supreme Court of the United States*, 2 vols. (New York, 1858).

45. William H. Masterson, in his excellent biography *William Blount* (Baton Rouge, 1954), describes this group of men and concludes (p. 84), "The merchant-lawyer eastern group, generally creditors and loosely called Conservatives, supported all measures to strengthen the Congress; the western farming group, generally debtors and termed Radical, although not so cohesive a voting bloc as the Conservatives, on the whole supported few if any such measures." See also Blackwell P. Robinson, *William R. Davie* (Chapel Hill, 1957), 151-53.

46. Keith, ed., *Blount Papers*, I, 340, 338, 236.

47. To illustrate this point, Carteret and Hertford are to be compared with the western county of Surrey. The percentages of the total taxable property owned by the various percentiles of taxpayers are:

	Carteret	Hertford	Surrey
Wealthiest 10%	52%	37%	32%
Wealthiest 20%	70%	62%	54%
Remaining 80%	30%	38%	46%

a few areas transportation facilities were poor. The Piedmont interest was represented by a group of men, of whom some, like the Bloodworths, lived near the coast, and some, like Willie Jones of Halifax, were wealthy, but all of whom were connected with agriculture rather than commerce. They were all, as Maclaine observed to Iredell, popular with the "lower class of people," [48] and they all became Antifederalists.[49]

The controversies which divided the northeast from the rest of the state were much the same as those in South Carolina and Virginia. North Carolina also faced a shortage of money, a post-war depression, public and private debts, and difficulty in collecting taxes adequate to discharge the government's obligations.[50] The state's social structure, however, made it certain that the agricultural interest would prevail over the commercial, and debtor over creditor. On such issues as public finance and on matters pertaining to the British treaty and western lands, a number of roll-call votes were taken which show the sectional divisions.[51]

The votes reveal that the four eastern commercial towns and the northeast section[52] voted consistently together and that the

48. Aug. 25, 1783, McRee, *Iredell*, II, 69.

49. These men—who included also Thomas Person, James Galloway, Charles McDowell, David Caldwell, Matthew Locke, General Rutherford, William Lenoir, and William Goudy—have not left the correspondence which would encourage the writing of their biographies. See articles in Allen Johnson and Dumas Malone, eds., *Dictionary of American Biography*, 22 vols. (New York, 1928-1944); Louise Irby Trenholme, *The Ratification of the Federal Constitution in North Carolina* (New York, 1932); Blackwell Pierce Robinson, "Willie Jones of Halifax," *N. C. Hist. Rev.*, 18 (1941), 1-26, 133 70; Douglass, "Burke," in *ibid.*, 26 (1949), 150-86; Robinson, *Davie*, 153-55.

50. William Sharpe to James Madison, May 25, 1782, Madison Papers, II, Lib. Cong.; Burgwin, Jenkes & London to [unknown], July 8, 1785, Shepley Lib., II, 22, R. I. Hist. Soc.; Hugh Williamson to Charles Thomson, Jan. 14 and Feb. 3, 1786, Charles Thomson Correspondence, Gratz Coll., Case 1, Box 4, Hist. Soc. Pa.; Benjamin Hawkins to George Washington, June 10, 1784, *N. C. Hist. Rev.*, 12 (1935), 159.

51. For these votes see Walter Clark, ed., *The State Records of North Carolina* (Goldsboro, 1898-1905), XVI, 156-65, XVII, 364-65, 394, XVIII, 156, 346, 362, XIX, 115, 282, 487, 613, 622, 643-44, 674-75, 688, 824, XX, 82.

52. The northeast section is marked by a line from Carteret on the coast to the western border of Warren, except that it does not include Pitt or what was then Dobbs; it includes Nash but not Franklin.

west, including the towns of Hillsboro and Salisbury, voted just as consistently on the other side.[53] This is not surprising; but what does need to be explained is the fact that a group of counties in the southeast, which included the richest counties in the state, supported the west as often as they did the northeast. Thus small farmer domination of the state was upheld, and on close questions made possible, by the votes of wealthy planters.

Why the southeast so often aligned itself with the west is a mystery. Something might be attributed to Timothy Bloodworth, who, according to one historian, "organized the lower classes against the Conservatives."[54] But it is doubtful that Bloodworth could have controlled the vote of his own county (New Hanover) and of a half dozen others as well. A more tenable explanation may be inferred from other facts. First, the southeast delegates voted nearly unanimously for paper money, both in the House and the Senate; secondly, they favored a bill to allow purchase of confiscated British debts in depreciated currency. It appears, therefore, that the planters of this region constituted a debtor group, and so supported the debtor west, as, in fact, did many planters in South Carolina. Before the war Governor Martin referred to the people of the "Southern district" as "almost universally necessitous and in debt and whose policy it seems has been to overflow the province with paper money," as contrasted with "the minority from the Northern districts."[55] In any case, the position taken by the southeastern region was important because it often held the balance of power, and the continued dominance of the small farmers—perhaps it is better to say, the non-commercial

53. A partial exception to this alignment occurred when the east as well as the west opposed the repeal of laws in conflict with the peace treaty. Evidently feeling against the tories and hopes of evading debts were important everywhere. See the letter from Benjamin Hawkins to Washington, cited in *n.* 50, above.

54. Thomas Perkins Abernethy, *From Frontier to Plantation in Tennessee* (Chapel Hill, 1932), 46.

55. To Hillsborough, Dec. 26, 1771, W. L. Saunders, ed., *Colonial Records of North Carolina, 1662-1776* (Raleigh, 1886-90), IX, 76. These southeastern farmers were not so sympathetic with the commercial point of view as were the northeasterners. Wilmington, the only important town, often voted in opposition to its rural environs. Perhaps the northeast was better able to export its crops through the two sounds.

interest—was due to the support derived from Bloodworth and from wealthy planters.[56]

Two Southern states remain to be examined. The post-Revolutionary experience of Georgia was similar to that of other states, and Georgians too were divided in their opinions. There were the usual heated disputes over the treatment of loyalists;[57] and the democratic constitution, which established a unicameral legislature, came under fire. One critic believed that the addition of an upper house would "prevent a Legislature to be hurried on by the transient gusts of passion and prejudice."[58] Votes recorded on such issues as frontier expansion, land prices, and the creation of new western counties show that the state usually divided into two sections: the coast, including the counties near Savannah, controlled by merchants and large planters, opposed the interior, which consisted of the more recently settled counties near Augusta.[59] The first looked toward Charleston and thence overseas, the second faced west.

Georgia was confronted with financial problems similar to those of other states, and her reaction to them paralleled that of South Carolina. In 1786 a paper money bill was passed, and the increasing strength of the upcountry was probably reflected in a law which taxed land in proportion to its value.[60] Finally, on one subject at least Georgians were united. The prosperity not only of the upcountry but of Savannah depended ultimately upon the economic expansion of the state, and that in turn depended upon displacement of the Indians. Moreover, most of Georgia was still exposed to attack; the need for adequate defensive measures was vital.

Unlike Georgia, which was primarily a frontier state, Maryland

56. In the House the west had potentially 50 votes, the northeast 42, and the southeast, sixteen; the situation in the Senate was similar. Tennessee usually had only three delegates present and voting in the House.

57. *Gazette of the State of Georgia* (Savannah), Oct. 9, 16, Nov. 27, Dec. 18, 1783, July 15, 22, Aug. 12, 26, 1784.

58. *Ibid.*, Jan. 22, Feb. 5, 1784.

59. See especially Allen D. Candler, comp., *The Revolutionary Records of the State of Georgia* (Atlanta, 1908), III, 279, 423, 520-22; William W. Abbot, "The Structure of Politics in Georgia: 1782-1789," *Wm. and Mary Qtly.*, 3rd Ser., 14 (1957), 47-65.

60. Allen D. Candler, comp., *The Colonial Records of the State of Georgia* (Atlanta, 1911), XIX, pt. 2, 398-403.

was for the most part well populated, and resembled eastern Virginia rather than the Piedmont. Geographically, the dominant features in Maryland were the Chesapeake Bay and the Potomac River, which gave to almost the entire state easy access to domestic and foreign markets. Nearly all of the counties were in the Tidewater, and there was practically no "west," except for a sliver of land between the upper Potomac and Pennsylvania, which had little political influence.[61] Along the lower Potomac (St. Mary's, Charles, and Prince George's counties) was a region similar to Virginia's Northern Neck, with a very high proportion of landless whites and a relatively large number of planters with numerous slaves.[62] Another group of counties bordering the lower Chesapeake Bay, roughly from Baltimore south—Kent, Queen Anne's, Talbot, Dorchester, Calvert, and part of Anne Arundel—had similar characteristics. The remaining counties of the eastern shore, along with the upper Chesapeake and the upper Potomac, contained fewer slaves, a higher proportion of landowners, and fewer large planters.

The planter class continued to control the state as it had done during the colonial period and as it did also in 1776 when the new state constitution was adopted. Under this constitution the majority of the people had less control over their government than in any state except South Carolina, mainly because of very high property qualifications for holding office.[63] The western counties were seriously under-represented, but even had these faults been removed it might not have made much difference. It has been accurately observed that "the masses of inarticulate citizenry remained, on the whole, inarticulate." [64]

61. During most of the 1780's there were only two "backcountry" counties (Frederick and Washington). They had only eight votes out of the seventy-six. Montgomery County, part of Anne Arundel (present-day Howard) and most of Baltimore County (including present-day Carroll) were also west of the fall line and often voted with the west.

62. Barker, *Background of Revolution in Maryland*, Appendix I; *A Century of Population Growth*, 289.

63. £500 real or personal property for members of the House; £1,000 for sheriffs, councilors, and senators (who were indirectly selected by an electoral college); £5,000 for governors.

64. Philip A. Crowl, *Maryland During and After the Revolution: a Political and Economic Study* (Baltimore, 1943), 18.

Sectional and class alignments were discernible, however, even in the politics of this relatively homogeneous state. The most notable occasion was the dispute over paper money, which was by all odds the most important and exciting controversy of the Confederation period. The major contest occurred over the proposal to establish a land bank.[65] In the House the planters were divided. Hard-money advocates came mainly from the lower Potomac and lower Chesapeake—from the wealthiest counties, notably Dorchester, Charles, Somerset, and St. Mary's. On the other side were delegates from counties which contained fewer slaves and fewer large planters, including the three westernmost counties and those of the upper Chesapeake.[66] In 1785, for example, of the seven counties with the highest number of slaveholders and the most slaves, five voted against paper money; of the seven counties at the other end of the economic scale, all but one supported paper money.[67] The vote on this issue corresponds generally to socio-economic differences among the counties; however the correlation is not perfect—a fact illustrated by the position of Anne Arundel County, which though one of the richest in the state, was in 1787 a paper money stronghold.[68] The planter interest, it seems, was dominant in most Maryland counties. The small farmers favored paper money and debtor relief, but were politically effective only when the planters divided or when some of the wealthier citizens, probably those who would profit, lent their support.[69]

65. *Maryland Gazette* (Annapolis), Dec. 13, 1781.

66. For the financial difficulties confronting debtors at this time, see Crowl, *Maryland During the Revolution*, 89-90, 95. Courts were stopped by mob action on at least one occasion, and there were other riots in 1786 and 1787. *Ibid.*, 74, 92-94. The fact that the Senate steadily opposed paper money indicates that the division was partly along lines of wealth. Some contemporary observers made the same point. "A Citizen," in the *Md. Journal* (Baltimore), July 21, 1786; "Planter," Feb. 1, 1785, Broadside, Hist. Soc. Pa.

67. See the votes recorded by Crowl, *Maryland During the Revolution*, 91; *Md. Journal* (Baltimore), Jan. 19, 1787; *Md. Gazette* (Annapolis), Jan. 22, 1787; and note the correlation with data on percentage of slaveholding families, ratio of slaves to whites, and percentage of whites owning 20 or more slaves, given in *A Century of Population Growth*, 289.

68. Socio-economic alignments in Maryland are illustrated in Appendix F.

69. For the debts of well-to-do planters see Philip A. Crowl, "Anti-

In the South generally, we find broad patterns of political behavior well established by 1787, which are most adequately described in terms of sectional division. The accessibility to markets of certain areas permitted the rise of well-to-do or wealthy farmers who raised crops for export and who supported the commercial interest because they depended upon commerce. On the other side were the smaller farmers in regions more remote from transportation or on poorer soils, who were not able to specialize in the production of goods for market, and whose interests diverged from the wealthier, creditor, commercial sections. The small farmer areas were discriminated against, especially in Virginia, South Carolina, and Maryland, by under-representation in the lower house and virtual exclusion from the upper house of the state legislatures. Even in North Carolina, farmer control of the government depended upon frequent support from the planter-dominated southeast, and elsewhere the small farmers succeeded only when their objectives coincided with the interest of some, at least, of the planters. Ordinarily, they derived this planter support from transition areas which were changing from a subsistence to a commercial farming economy but which had not yet entirely changed their political orientation. Basically, the lines of conflict separated the wealthier sections and classes from the poorer ones, the areas of ports and navigable streams from the more distant upcountry.

Federalism in Maryland, 1787-1788," *Wm. and Mary Qtly.*, 3rd Ser., 4 (1947), 449, 465-68; Crowl, *Maryland During the Revolution*, 103; Max P. Allen, "William Pinkney's First Public Service," *Maryland Historical Magazine*, 39 (1944), 285.

Chapter III

SOCIETY AND POLITICS
IN THE NORTH

THE Northern states, like the Southern, were divided into regions based upon different economic interests and different social structures. Pennsylvania supplies a clear example of the way in which regional variation affected political alignments. Geographically, the state consisted of two major areas. In the first, two great rivers gave access to Chesapeake Bay and made parts of York, Lancaster, Chester, Montgomery, Bucks, Northampton, and Philadelphia counties nearly maritime. The second was defined by a line drawn from Hagerstown (Maryland) through Harrisburg to Easton, marking roughly the end of the plain and the beginning of the Appalachian mountains which dominated the remainder of the state. In Revolutionary times, this geographic pattern was reflected in social and economic differences. The mercantile and manufacturing classes were centered in Philadelphia, and in the southeastern counties farmers produced for urban consumption and for export. In the interior mountains and valleys the inhabitants were largely self-sufficient farmers, although a few western towns like Pittsburgh were allied to the commercial interest.

The Revolution sharply divided the people. Independence was enthusiastically supported by the artisans and western farmers under the leadership of new men who aggressively seized the initiative. The old established families, merchants and landholders, Quakers and Anglicans, were either loyalists or reluctant rebels. Their stronghold in the counties near Philadelphia also contained many prosperous farmers—often Quakers or pacifistic,

41

uninterested Germans—who tended to be loyalist or neutral. The conflicts created by the Revolution followed lines of class and sectional cleavage that existed in colonial times, but were greatly intensified by the events of 1774-76, which temporarily divested the Quaker-dominated east of its controlling power in state politics. Henceforth, elections were bitterly contested. The partisan line-up was clearly defined in the struggle over the Pennsylvania constitution and over such issues as the "test oath," the Bank of North America, and state finances.

The Pennsylvania constitution, more than any other of that time, embodied "radical" or "democratic" thought.[1] Its outstanding features were a unicameral legislature annually elected by taxpayers (and their sons, if of age); a supreme executive council, whose members served for three years, one-third being replaced annually; a president chosen annually from the council by that body and by the legislature; and a judiciary, appointed for only seven years. This document was produced by "mostly honest well-meaning Country men,"[2] and it was thereafter defended by the "Constitutionalists" and attacked by the "Republicans," who included the leading men of Philadelphia.

Throughout the years of the Revolution the question of revising the constitution was a major issue, and it came to a head during 1783-84 when a council of censors, provided for by the constitution, met to consider whether revision was needed. The Republican members, almost all of whom came from the southeastern counties, favored revision;[3] the Constitutionalists from the west,

1. The identification of the Pennsylvania constitution with democracy was as evident then as now. For example, Joseph Reed, one of its defenders, referred to a "junto" which was trying to "overthrow the *democracy* of our constitution." Robert L. Brunhouse, *The Counter-Revolution in Pennsylvania, 1776-1790* (Harrisburg, 1942), 96. So also the future Antifederalist John Smilie declared, "An honest man is the noblest work of God. A democratical government like ours admits of no superiority." Quoted in Charles Page Smith, *James Wilson: Founding Father, 1742-1798* (Chapel Hill, 1956), 156. On the other side of the political fence Benjamin Rush, the future Federalist, felt that the new constitution was "too much upon the democratical order." To Anthony Wayne, Sept. 24, 1776, in J. Paul Selsam, *The Pennsylvania Constitution of 1776* (Philadelphia, 1936), 209.

2. Rev. Francis Allison, quoted in Brunhouse, *Counter-Revolution in Pa.*, 13.

3. *Ibid.*, 278. The alignment is to be seen in votes which were taken; see the *Pennsylvania Gazette* (Phila.), Jan. 7, 21, 28, 1784.

led by future Antifederalists Robert Whitehill, John Smilie, and William Findley, defended the existing form. The political color of the Republicans may be demonstrated by the changes they sought in the constitution. Their program called for replacing the executive council with a governor who would exercise real power, including the right to veto bills and appoint officials, and who could be re-elected for an indefinite number of terms. They wished to establish an upper house, whose members might also be re-elected without limit, and to secure a life tenure for judges. These proposals were bitterly attacked by the Constitutionalists. The senate, they declared, would be an "aristocratic nobility" and would unite with the governor against the assembly—"the nobility will support the throne." Whereas the constitution of 1776 was founded on the authority of the people this one would be founded on the authority of the "wealthy and the great." [4]

The nature of the two parties is also revealed—indeed, was partly determined—by the so-called test oath. This law denied the suffrage to those who refused to take an oath of allegiance to the new constitution. It not only disenfranchised all loyalists, but barred neutral groups and those whose religious convictions prohibited oaths. Of the last, the Quakers were the most important. The law was in part an act of self-defense against potential enemies of the state, but since those who were affected would have voted with the Republicans, the test oath was also in part a device of the Constitutionalists to disbar their opponents. After the war, they exploited the general hostility against tories in order to retain it. The tories were accused of being wealthy creditors who would soon control the property of the state, dominate the government, and establish an aristocracy. The Quakers, since they had refused to fight, were considered identical with the tories. "We conceive it to be a dictate of reason and natural equity," the Constitutionalists averred, "that those who declined to participate in the toils, the sacrifices, and the hazard of the late revolution, should not enjoy all the benefit and advantages arising from that inestimable blessing." [5] In reply, the Republicans pointed out that "the good

4. *Pa. Packet* (Phila.), Feb. 12, 1784.
5. *Pa. Journal* (Phila.), Oct. 2, 1784. See also "A Friend," in *ibid.*, Oct. 10, 1781; "Fabricus" in *ibid.*, Apr. 10, 1782; "Sic Vos Non Vobis," in the

people injured by these laws are not only numerous, but wealthy," and turned the tables on their foes by asserting that the act, "by confining the power of the state to a little more than one half of its citizens, . . . creates a most alarming and oppressive *aristocracy*." [6]

The test oath was finally repealed in 1786 as a result of two factors. First, the Republicans secured enough political power to restore the Quakers to their previous position, first in Philadelphia, then in the whole state; [7] and secondly, even some Constitutionalists felt that the act was unfair. In 1786, at a time when that party had a majority, no less than fifteen representatives who had been elected as Constitutionalists changed sides on this question. [8]

Another issue of major importance concerned the Bank of North America. The bank was connected above all with the name of Robert Morris. [9] The political struggle in the state, and for that matter federal politics, cannot be fully understood without reference to the suspicion directed at Morris. His ability, wealth, position, and reputation made him a powerful leader in the state and in the Confederation. As superintendent of finance he controlled the finances of Congress for three years during the Revolution; he conducted profitable mercantile ventures while holding that office, and he had a dominant influence in the Bank of North America. He was suspected of profiting privately from his official position, of using the army for political purposes, and of holding aristocratical views; in short he was regarded as a threat to the existing system of government. Not only in Philadelphia but from Charleston to Boston, Morris's power, wealth, and political opin-

---

Independent Gazetteer (Phila.), Sept. 13, 1783; "A Hint," in the *Pa. Packet* (Phila.), Jan. 8, 1784; "A Consistent Whig," in *ibid.*, Oct. 6, 1784; Circular Letter No. 2, Philadelphia, Aug. 1783, Broadside, Hist. Soc. Pa.; Brunhouse, *Counter-Revolution in Pa.*, 274, *ns.* 79-82.

6. *Pa. Packet* (Phila.), Oct. 6, 1784, Jan. 1, 1785.

7. Edward Shippen to Joseph Shippen, Jr., Oct. 2, 1785, Shippen Papers, VIII, Hist. Soc. Pa.; for the repeal of the test oath, see Brunhouse, *Counter-Revolution in Pa.*, 180-81.

8. *Pa. Packet* (Phila.), Mar. 13, 14, 1786. See also the letter from David Jackson to George Bryan, quoted in Brunhouse, *Counter-Revolution in Pa.*, 169.

9. Janet Wilson, "The Bank of North America and Pennsylvania Politics, 1781-1787," *Pennsylvania Magazine of History and Biography*, 66 (1942), 3-28. For Morris's early connection with the bank, see Clarence L. Ver Steeg, *Robert Morris, Revolutionary Financier* (Philadelphia, 1954).

ions aroused hostility.[10] Since he was a leading Republican, many of the attacks upon him in Pennsylvania were inspired by party politics, and the measures he supported were automatically opposed by the Constitutionalists.

Morris's Bank of North America was created in 1781 as part of his general plan to overcome Congress's financial difficulties, but its connection with the government terminated with Morris's retirement in 1784, and it became a private company operating under a Pennsylvania charter. The Constitutionalists launched a drive to repeal the charter. The critics of the bank based their arguments on economic, social, and political grounds. They accused it of contributing to the depression because it promoted heavy importations which drained specie from the country. Since the bank was the only one of its kind, it had a financial monopoly, which, it was said, the directors employed to crush all opposition and to dominate trade. "The Junto have actually the command of all the money in the State, by means of their Bank." Moreover the bank paid dividends of 16 per cent, which its critics viewed as proof of their charge that it demanded excessively high interest rates, victimizing borrowers, especially farmers. "From the establishment of the bank," John Smilie asserted, "interest rose from six per cent. to the enormous degree at which we see it at present. Usury has been coeval with the bank." Even worse, according to the bank's adversaries, it promoted the concentration of wealth into a few hands, thus fostering the growth of aristocracy and the control of government by the few, rather than the many. Already, the Constitutionalists believed, the bank had acquired an undue influence over the state government, and Morris's wealth and position were dangerous.[11]

10. Examples of this hostility are to be found throughout the published and unpublished sources of the period. Typical are those in Burnett, ed., *Letters*, VI, 139, 390, 429, VII, 167, 263, 378-80, 398, 432.

11. Sample criticisms of the bank may be found in the *Pa. Herald* (Phila.), Sept. 8, 1785, Apr. 5, 1786 (Smilie), Apr. 15, 1786; *Pennsylvania Mercury and Universal Advertiser* (Phila.), Dec. 10, 1784; *Freeman's Journal* (Phila.), Mar. 10, 1784, Jan. 3, Feb. 7, Aug. 22, 1787; *Independent Gazetteer* (Phila.), Feb. 28, 1787; Joseph Reed to Charles Pettit, May 2, 1784, Reed Papers, N.Y. Hist. Soc. Morris's power in the bank was disliked even by some of its friends. John Chaloner to Jeremiah Wadsworth, Dec. 21, 1784 and Oct. 7, 1785, Wadsworth Papers, Box 136, Conn. Hist. Soc.

The Republicans, of course, rallied to Morris's support, and the contest raged for several years. The Constitutionalists endeavored to repeal the bank's charter and substitute a system of government loans at lower rates of interest. "Where ought credit to be placed for the public weal in a republican government?" asked "A Mechanic." "I will venture to answer, in government only. And the placing that credit any where else is of the most pernicious and destructive consequence; for it removes both power and credit out of the proper hands, and fixes them into those of individuals." [12] By 1785 the Constitutionalists had gained control of the government, and the repeal of the charter followed. Republican strength in the electoral contest was limited to the area immediately surrounding Philadelphia.[13] However, the bank's supporters were only temporarily worsted; they gained ground in the 1786 election and, aided by votes from new allies in the east and a few western representatives, managed to restore the charter in 1787. "Well then the Bank is reestablished," a Constitutionalist lamented, "and we may sit down and Groan under its Baneful Influence. Had the Friends to equal Liberty had a few more such Men as Finley in the House, this Monster never would again have raised its Head." [14]

Among various other issues which divided the two parties only the debt question, with its usual ramifications, was of major importance. On this controversy, however, the party lines were less clear because each party contained divergent groups. The major strength of the Constitutionalists lay in the west, where the farmers were unwilling to pay specie taxes for the discharge of the state and federal debts, of which they held but little. They preferred that payment be made in paper money, but they were primarily concerned with establishing a land bank that would issue currency on loan. The eastern wing of the party included many who were speculating in debt securities. They did not necessarily object to paper money, but their overriding consideration

12. *Independent Gazetteer* (Phila.), Mar. 13, 1784.
13. For the repeal see Brunhouse, *Counter-Revolution in Pa.*, 175. The vote is recorded in the *Pa. Packet* (Phila.), Apr. 4, 1786.
14. Joseph Hart to George Bryan, Jan. 2, 1787, Bryan Papers, Hist. Soc. Pa.

was that adequate provision be made for the payment of all debts, both state and federal, by the state. Similarly, the Republicans were divided. The party as a whole supported the demands of security holders, but some, perceiving that Congress was not able to meet its obligations, wanted the state to pay interest on federal securities; others, realizing that payment of state and federal debts was certain to entail an emission of paper money, were more alarmed at this prospect than that of non-payment; still others, who wished to give Congress more power, insisted that only the central government should discharge the federal debt, and that taxes must be granted to Congress for this purpose.

A compromise resolved this complex situation. The creditors were provided for when Pennsylvania assumed and began to pay off both state and federal debts; the westerners were placated by an issue of paper money; and those who sought power for Congress were pleased by the state's approval of the impost, which authorized Congress to levy import duties whenever all the states should make the same concession, and, on the same terms, a grant to Congress of power to regulate commerce.

Throughout these political controversies, the southeast and the west remained consistently opposed. During the 1780's the Republicans were usually in control of Philadelphia and of the nearby counties, and the Constitutionalists dominated the western area. The former represented "the property holders and the business men,"[15] often Anglican or Quaker, typified by Robert Morris, John Dickinson, William Bingham, and James Wilson; the latter represented above all the small western farmers, whose spokesmen were John Smilie, William Findley, and the Whitehills. Except possibly for New York, party lines were more evident than in any other state. Candidates for office openly affiliated with one or the other, and voted with unusual consistency in the legislature. By 1787 the Republicans were in firm control of the state.

In New York, as in Pennsylvania, a study of politics is greatly simplified by the existence of two loosely knit parties. One was primarily upstate and rural. Its principal strength lay in the agrarian counties of Orange, Dutchess, Ulster, Washington, and

15. Brunhouse, *Counter-Revolution in Pa.,* viii.

Montgomery, to which Albany was often added. It was frequently supported by the urban craftsmen. Its leader was George Clinton, governor during the entire Confederation period. Although men of distinguished family were to be found among the Clintonians, particularly some of the influential Livingston clan, most of the leaders were not of the wealthy elite. The party appealed primarily to middle-class farmers. The other party centered in New York City and the neighboring counties on Long Island (Kings, Queens, and Suffolk) and Staten Island (Richmond); it sometimes, though not always, got the support of Westchester, immediately to the north. This anti-Clintonian faction was associated with mercantile interests; it received the votes of the town of Albany and at times of Albany County, in addition to those of the southern towns; it had the allegiance also of the great land-owning families, whose interests were united economically and socially with those of the merchants, lawyers, and bankers. These included the Van Rensselaers, Livingstons, Cuylers, Bayards, Schuylers, Morrises, and Van Cortlandts. The party drew its leaders from these families and from merchants and lawyers such as John Jay, Alexander Hamilton, James Duane, Egbert Benson, and Abraham Ten Broeck.

Many of the issues which beset Pennsylvania also figured in New York politics. Although there were few Quakers, there were many loyalists in the state, and various punitive laws (one of which deprived them of the right to vote) were comparable in their effect to the Pennsylvania test oath.[16] To some extent the contest over treatment of loyalists was a conflict between classes, since the loyalists were defended by the larger property holders and attacked by the Clintonians. It was also sectional, since the British sympathizers were to be found in the south rather than in the north, and the struggle in the legislature aligned New York City and its allies against the up-river agricultural counties.[17] Another source of controversy was the Bank of New York, which incurred

16. Oscar Zeichner, "The Loyalist Problem in New York after the Revolution," *New York History*, 21 (1940), 284-302.

17. Spaulding, *New York in the Critical Period*, 118-33, 281; Thomas C. Cochran, *New York in the Confederation* (Philadelphia, 1932), 62-63. See also citations in Sidney I. Pomerantz, *New York, an American City, 1783-1803* (New York, 1938), 82-83.

criticism similar to that directed against the Bank of North America; however the issue did not become important.[18] The dominance of the Clintonians was so complete that the Bank of New York at first failed to secure a charter; attacks upon it were averted because the credit needs of the farmers were satisfied by the establishment of a land bank, which issued paper money on loan. It was the paper money issue which aroused the most determined struggle of all domestic questions, and the alignment on it reveals the general political situation.

The Clinton administration backed paper money legislation in 1784, 1785, and 1786. These were depression years, in which the state suffered from the same economic conditions that existed elsewhere. Paper money legislation appealed to a wide range of people. Since it would be loaned by the state at a low rate of interest, it benefited common men who needed credit—especially farmers, but also the smaller merchants, country storekeepers, and manufacturers.[19] Its advocates declared that it would permit the easier payment of taxes, arrest the decline of price levels, and furnish relief to debtors by providing a legal tender medium acceptable in discharge of past debts. Since this was a period of deflation, it was argued that paper money would restore proper relations between debtor and creditor, and that it would reduce distinctions between rich and poor. "A Spartan" declared:

it may be the means of counteracting the designs of a class of people who wish to advance the dignity of our government; maintaining that of all governments, the democratic is most contemptible [sic], too much power being lodged in the mob or lower class of people. That nothing is equal to a monarchical, . . . that therefore the greater distinction you can make in the wealth and affluent way of life, between the upper and lower class of people, the

18. "A True Friend to his Country" asserted that the bank might be "replete with ruin to thousands, and destructive to the prosperity and liberty of America." New York Gazetteer, and Country Journal (New York), Jan. 17, 1786. "Honestus" objected to "so powerful and uncontroulable a combination of property in private hands." N.Y. Packet, Mar. 27, 1786. See also Pomerantz, New York, an American City, 186.

19. N.Y. Packet, Mar. 6, 1786. A brief summary of the subject is in Merrill Jensen, The New Nation: a History of the United States During the Confederation, 1781-1789 (New York, 1950), 320-22.

sooner that desired event will take place That a scarcity of money [will] make the poor who want, wait upon the rich.[20]

All of these arguments were calculated to win wide popular support.

The alignment on the issue was in part one of large versus small property owners, and it also represented a division between the agricultural and the commercial areas of the state. On March 18, 1785, the Assembly voted (23-20), that a proposed issue of paper money should be legal tender for debts or taxes which had been owing prior to its issue. The proviso favored the debtors and was backed by all but six of the delegates from counties north of New York City. In the south the vote was solidly on the other side with but one exception—Goforth, a shoemaker.[21] One month later the vote was taken on the final bill. Although the southern counties were now joined by contiguous Westchester, the remaining counties carried the bill by their almost unanimous support (19-3).[22] In the following year a vote was again taken on a legal tender clause. The only negatives came from the extreme south, plus two from Albany and two from Westchester; and on a final vote the opposition shrank to nine, all from the south.[23]

The votes on these and other important issues reveal that the political division in New York was primarily north versus south, or agricultural versus commercial, although it must be remembered that even in the agricultural interior the largest landowners usually voted with the anti-Clinton groups. The same alignment also existed on issues connected with the state debt and New York's relations with the federal government.

Neither New Jersey nor Delaware produced Antifederalists; and therefore the domestic politics of those states need not be

20. *N.Y. Packet*, Feb. 16, 1786, quoted in Spaulding, *New York in the Critical Period*, 146-47. See also "Cassius," in the *Hudson Weekly Gazette*, (N.Y.), Dec. 14, 1786.

21. New York Assembly Journal, 8th Session, 1785, 98, N.Y. State Lib.; *N.Y. Packet*, Apr. 14, 1785.

22. New York Assembly Journal, 8th Session, 1785, 153, N.Y. State Lib.

23. *Ibid.*, 9th Session, 1786, 68, 71. See also *ibid.*, 1784, 51, 76; 1786, 57. For the 1786 bill, see Philip Schuyler to Abraham ten Broeck, Mar. 19, 1786, Accession No. 67, Box 2, No. 10354, N.Y. State Lib.; *Country Journal, and Poughkeepsie Advertiser*, Feb. 23, 1786.

examined at this point. In New England, on the other hand, internal disputes were of great importance in predisposing attitudes toward the Constitution. Connecticut is an exception to this generalization. In that state the only questions which aroused public emotion were those involving relations with Congress; otherwise, politics were relatively tranquil. The war had not generated the usual hatreds and suspicions, for the state had been nearly united on the issue of independence, except for Fairfield County in the southwest. No constitutional changes had occurred to arouse dissensions. There was no real trouble with the tories, and at the war's end they were accepted with little controversy.[24] Connecticut was affected by the post-war depression and the decline of commerce, which led creditors and debtors, merchants and farmers, to complain and to seek solutions in their different ways.[25] On the whole, however, one gets the impression that the state was relatively prosperous.[26] When Shays's Rebellion occurred in Massachusetts, it left Connecticut untouched, except for some slight

24. The only article published against them which I have seen was by "Philanthropos," in the *Connecticut Gazette; and Universal Intelligencer* (New London), Apr. 4, 1783. See also the *Connecticut Courant* (Hartford), Apr. 6, 1784 (supplement); David Humphreys to Henry Knox, Sept. 25, 1786, Knox Papers, XIX, No. 18, Mass. Hist. Soc.; Franklin Bowditch Dexter, ed., *The Literary Diary of Ezra Stiles* (New York, 1901), III, 111-12.

25. Peter Colt to Wadsworth & Church, July 14, 1784, Wadsworth Papers, Box 136, Conn. Hist. Soc.; Jeremiah Wadsworth to Nathanael Greene, Mar. 4, 1785, Wadsworth Papers, Conn. State Lib.; Hez[a] Bissell to Caleb Davis, July 27, 1787, Caleb Davis Papers, XIVa, Mass. Hist. Soc. The following is typical: "Business is very dull & languid—the people seem, either from Necessity or recollection, to be growing more prudent in their Call for foreign Articles." Jonathan Trumbull, Jr., to John Trumbull, Nov. 1, 1784, Jonathan Trumbull, Jr., Papers: Letters, Writs, and Miscellaneous, 1763-1808, Conn State Lib.

26. Stephen M. Mitchell to William S. Johnson, Aug. 9, 1786, William S. Johnson Papers, Conn. Hist. Soc.; David Humphreys to Thomas Jefferson, June 5, 1786, Frank Landon Humphreys, *Life and Times of David Humphreys*, 2 vols. (New York, 1917), I, 354; J. P. Brissot de Warville, *New Travels in the United States of America* (London, 1792), 132-36. Robert Hunter recorded in his diary the testimony of a Mr. Waring concerning Connecticut: "Talking about this state, he said in general the people were very happy. None of them are very rich, or very poor. They are mostly all farmers, who live comfortably within themselves upon the produce of their own ground, which consists chiefly of rye, barley, oats, Indian corn, potatoes, etc." Wright and Tinling, eds., *Quebec to Caroline*, 143.

disturbances in Litchfield County.[27] This harmony was due in part to the moderate policy pursued by the government, which did not levy taxes as high as those in Massachusetts.[28]

The fact that no paper money was issued suggests that most citizens were satisfied. In November of 1786 such a measure was defeated by a very large majority, and in the following year it was again rejected by a vote of 124 to 22.[29] Support of the bill came almost entirely from the northern tier of counties, especially from those towns not on the main arteries of trade. Here the citizens were having trouble finding enough money for taxes, let alone debts. They insisted that the shortage of money forced debtors to sell their property at a loss; the present laws, favoring the creditors, tended to concentrate property in the hands of the few.[30] Yet discontent seems to have been confined to a small minority; the majority of Connecticut's farmers were satisfied with the policies of the government.

Deeply indented by Narragansett Bay, Rhode Island depended for its prosperity upon the welfare of the commercial centers that stretched from Providence to Newport. The state produced little and could consume little. The merchants depended upon both the coastwise and foreign trade; the towns acted as entrepôts, carrying goods to other states. The exposed position of the ports resulted in their being seriously damaged during the war,[31] and Rhode Island was left with the usual heavy state debt. In the

27. *Weekly Monitor, and Litchfield Town and Country Recorder*, May 21, 1787; Uriah Tracy to Theodore Sedgwick, May 28, 1787, Sedgwick Papers, vol. A, Mass. Hist. Soc.

28. Richard Donald Hershcopf, The New England Farmers and Politics, 1785-1787 (unpub. M.A. thesis, Univ. of Wis., 1947), 208-15. For objections to a poll tax, see the *Weekly Monitor* (Litchfield), Sept. 10, 17, 1787; "Leonidas," in the *Middlesex Gazette* (Middletown), Mar. 19, 1787.

29. *New Haven Gazette*, Nov. 2, 9, 1786, June 28, 1787; *Conn. Courant* (Hartford), June 11, 1787.

30. *Ibid.*, Apr. 3, 1786, Mar. 19, May 28, 1787; "Nummarius," in the *Weekly Monitor* (Litchfield), Sept. 17, 1787; "A Farmer," in *ibid.*, Oct. 3, 1786; *Middlesex Gazette* (Middletown), June 18, 1787; *Conn. Gazette* (New London), Feb. 10, 1786.

31. Population declined by over 7,000, or about one-twelfth, between 1774 and 1782. Newport suffered half of this loss. *Providence Gazette*, Feb. 26, 1785. One legacy was anti-tory feeling. See for example, instructions of South Kingston, Apr. 16, 1783, of East Greenwich, Oct. 17, 1783, and of Newport, Oct. 27, 1783, Misc. MSS, R. I. Hist. Soc.

interior the farmers practiced a self-sufficient economy; there were many debtors and many poor—more, apparently, than in Connecticut.[32]

Until about 1785 there does not seem to have been any basic division in state politics, which had centered less in substantive issues than in the mere rivalry of competing personal factions. As will be seen, the federal impost aroused no disagreement, and it appears that there was no opposition to the policy of paying interest on the state debt by an impost of 2 per cent.[33] By the end of 1784, however, the economic depression was severely felt. Private debts owed to English merchants were exceedingly heavy —one English firm had over £100,000 due to it in the state—and local merchants suffered.[34] As usual, farmers, especially debtors, were injured by the currency shortage, and complaints were heard that taxes were too high, court and lawyer fees were excessive, the public security holders were receiving too much, and "some debtors committed to goal [sic], and others making over their land, stock &c. for want of money."[35] Petitions for paper money appeared, and although in March 1786 a paper money bill was defeated, the tide could not long be stayed. "The people are almost drove to desperation," one writer admitted; they were "like fire."[36] Property was being sold at a quarter of its real value. Paper money, it was asserted, would ease the strain, and the creditors, who benefited unduly by virtue of the appreciation of money since the debts were contracted, would receive their due, but not usurious profits. Moreover paper could be used to discharge the heavy

32. See, for example, the remarks in Robert Hunter's diary. Wright and Tinling, eds., *Quebec to Caroline*, 119, 126-28, and contrast with *ibid.*, 143, 147, 150.

33. John Brown to David Howell, Oct. 23, 1783, MS XIV, No. 27, R. I. Hist. Soc.; Jonathan Arnold to David Howell, Feb. 7, 1784, Frederick S. Peck Coll., VII, R. I. Hist. Soc.

34. Moses Brown to Champion and Dickason, June 25, 1785, Moses Brown Papers, V, No. 38, R. I. Hist. Soc.; Champion and Dickason to Moses Brown, Aug. 10, 1785, *ibid.*, No. 42; Nicholas Brown to David Howell, Mar. 26, 1785, MS XIV, No. 53, *ibid.*

35. "A Real Friend to the Public," in the *Newport Mercury*, Feb. 5, 1785; instructions of Smithfield, 1785, in Frank Greene Bates, *Rhode Island and the Formation of the Union* (New York, 1898), 120.

36. [Unknown] to Moses Brown, 1786, Moses Brown Papers, V, No. 83, R. I. Hist. Soc.

state debt which, if paid in full by taxation, would create an excessive burden; most Rhode Islanders were convinced that to pay off the debt in any other way would be unfair, for the securities had been bought at a low rate by the well-to-do.[37] In the spring elections of 1786 there was a political revolution in which the paper money forces secured control, and they maintained their power in 1787.[38] The result was the passage of a paper money bill. Although it met opposition from the commercial centers and ridicule from hard money men in other states, it acted as a stay law for the execution of debts, thus rescuing the farmers; the state debt, too, was rapidly retired, though not in such a way as to please the creditors.[39]

The paper money issue is the only one on which there is enough information to permit analysis of political divisions. Even in this case no record of votes is available, but enough petitions have survived to make certain conclusions possible.[40] It appears that the division was the familiar one of coastal towns versus the interior. Out of nine towns bordering the ocean or Narragansett Bay (all but one being along the bay), eight were opposed to the issue of paper money,[41] whereas out of ten interior towns, all but three favored the measure. The three exceptions lay in the southwest corner adjoining Connecticut. Despite the relative absence in Rhode Island of the pervasive divisions that characterized politics in some other states, we see in this instance the underlying dichotomy between commerce and agriculture.

37. *American Herald* (Boston), May 15, 1786; *Newport Mercury*, Aug. 7, Jan. 30, 1786 and subsequent issues. "Solon, jun." argued that only the freeholders would gain, since the poor could not borrow. *Providence Gazette*, Aug. 5, 1786. An eloquent defense of paper money by "A Farmer," is in the *Newport Mercury*, Apr. 16, 1787. See also Hillman Metcalf Bishop, "Why Rhode Island Opposed the Federal Constitution," *Rhode Island History*, 8 (1949), 34-38.

38. Bates, *Rhode Island and the Union*, 123; *New Haven Gazette*, May 31, 1787.

39. Channing-Ellery Papers, III, 153, R. I. Hist. Soc.; "A Real Farmer," in the *U.S. Chronicle* (Providence), Aug. 28, 1788; Bishop, "Rhode Island Opposed," *R. I. Hist.*, 8 (1949), 41-42.

40. For these petitions, see Bates, *Rhode Island and the Union*, 120-29, 147; *American Herald* (Boston), May 15, 1786; *New Haven Gazette*, Sept. 21, 1786.

41. The exception was Tiverton. Middletown favored paper in 1785 but changed three years later.

A line drawn some fifteen miles west of the Massachusetts coastline indicates the regional division of interests in that state. To the east were the major and minor commercial and fishing centers and the hinterland which furnished products for their consumption and export. This eastern area included almost all of Essex County, the eastern third of Middlesex, all of present-day Suffolk and two-thirds of Norfolk (then part of Suffolk), most of Plymouth, southern Bristol, and all of Barnstable (Cape Cod), Dukes (Martha's Vineyard), and Nantucket counties. To the west were the upland villages and little farms, producing principally for local use, and largely self-sufficient. One region in this extensive area, however, resembled the east economically: the commercial centers of the Connecticut River in Hampshire County, upstream as far as Hatfield, which was some twenty-five miles north of the Connecticut border. Another detached part of the state, the counties now comprising Maine, requires separate treatment.

The major political controversy during the 1780's concerned the payment of public and private debts. The conflict did not reach a climax until 1786, but it existed as early as 1781. As usual, private debts were burdensome, and a delinquent debtor might be forced to pay court costs equal to the labor of twenty days.[42] The very heavy state debt was concentrated in the east, and if it was to be paid at par value in specie, onerous taxes would have to be collected from the whole state for the benefit of eastern creditors.[43] Eastern Massachusetts supported the court system, urged the regular collection of debts, and tried to levy such taxes as would make possible the payment of the state debt at par, while the western part of the state tried to revise the court system, delay the

42. The expensive court system, which was unfair to debtors, is fully discussed by Robert J. Taylor, *Western Massachusetts*. This book is an excellent account of the period.

43. An annual tax of $1.75 per capita would pay the cost of government, including interest on the debt, and a tax of $2.50 would free the state of debt in 15 years. But Taylor points out that this meant a tax of at least $8.75 or $12.50 for the average farm household. Farmers especially in the west saw very little cash, and they also had local taxes and private debts to pay. Taylor, *Western Massachusetts*, 133.

collection of debts or render payment easier by increasing the money supply, and keep taxes low.[44]

The first indication of a serious division came in the early years of the decade. In 1781 a law which had made paper money legal tender was repealed. The repeal was opposed by many western towns because it favored the creditors; one town feared "that it originated from wicked and designing men, who either wish to ruin the cause we are engaged in, by spreading discord among the inhabitants of this State, or to build their own fortunes upon the ruin of the common people."[45] In the years immediately following, opposition to the court system, high taxes, collection of debts, and scarcity of money resulted in occasional riots and the protest of local conventions.[46]

During the mid-1780's, economic conditions in Massachusetts as elsewhere grew worse. The scarcity of money, due in part to heavy exportations of gold and silver to England, resulted in bankruptcies among merchants and caused high interest rates. "As Money has ever been considered the root of all evils," grumbled a contributor to the *Massachusetts Centinel*, "may we not presage happy times, as this source is almost done away."[47] The effects of this scarcity and of the commercial depression combined with heavy importations of British manufactures, caused much unrest among Boston mechanics. This often took the form of anti-

44. Dissatisfaction in the far west is illustrated by a convention in Berkshire County which threatened secession. It is interesting that the towns which favored secession were to be Antifederal whereas the towns opposed to it were to be Federal.

45. *Boston Gazette*, Feb. 5, 1781. See also the protest of East Sudbury (Middlesex) in *ibid.*, May 14, 1781 and East, "Massachusetts Conservatives," Morris, ed., *Era of American Revolution*, 360.

46. These early movements can be followed in the newspapers, especially *Thomas's Massachusetts Spy: Or, Worcester Gazette*, and the *Massachusetts Gazette* (Springfield), together with various volumes of the Massachusetts Archives. See Joseph Hawley to Ephraim Wright, Apr. 16, 1782, *Am. Hist. Rev.*, 36 (1930-1931), 776-78. There is a good summary in Anson Ely Morse, *The Federalist Party in Massachusetts to the Year 1800* (Princeton, 1909), 206-7.

47. Apr. 9, 1785. See Major Shaw to Henry Knox, Mar. 21, 1782, Knox Papers, VIII, 90, Mass. Hist. Soc.; Richard Cranch to James Elworthy, Jan. 1, 1785, Cranch Papers, Mass. Hist. Soc.; Benjamin Lincoln to Rufus King, Feb. 11, 1786, Charles R. King, ed., *The Life and Correspondence of Rufus King*, 4 vols. (New York, 1894-1897), I, 156.

tory feeling, which of course had other causes, and was to be found in the country as well as in the city.[48] But the principal economic hardship was suffered in the rural towns and country-side, not that heavier financial losses were sustained, but that the people were less able to bear them. The results were accurately and vividly described by the town of Athol:

That from the extreme scarcity of Cash in the interior Parts of this Commonwealth we are reduced to the most distressing Situation by Suits being Daily commenced against the Inhabitants of this, as well as many other Parts of this Commonwealth who have sufficient Property to discharge their Debts were it to be received in payment for the same; but as the Situation of our Affairs are at present our Property is torn from us & our Gaols filled & still our Debts are not discharged; but our Property daily diminishing greatly to the injury of the Debtors and in many Cases but little to the advantage of the Creditor.[49]

The rapacity of lawyers was regarded as contributing to the general distress, and it was suggested that the profession be abolished. "Like Drones they fatten on the Lab'rers toil/Defraud the Widow and the Orphans spoil."[50] At least one writer held the Massachusetts bank responsible in part for the hard times, but no assault upon it developed.[51]

48. *Boston Gazette*, Feb. 19, 1781, Mar. 31, Apr. 28, May 5, 1783, Apr. 4, 1785; *Boston Evening Post*, Apr. 19, 1783; *Independent Ledger, and American Advertiser* (Boston), Apr. 14, 1783, Jan. 5, 1784; *Pa. Journal* (Phila.), June 4, 1783; *Continental Journal* (Boston), Oct. 14, 1784; *Mass. Centinel* (Boston), Feb. 9, Apr. 6, 9, 13, 1785; James Sullivan to S. P. Savage, Apr. 3, 1785, S. P. Savage Papers, II, Mass. Hist. Soc.

49. May 1, 1786, Mass. towns, Force Transcripts, VI, Lib. Cong. For pre-Shays complaints see the instructions of Conway, in the *Mass. Gazette* (Springfield), Jan. 20, 1784; petitions from Windsor, Spencer, and Bristol, House Journals, VI, 282, 334, VII, 63, Mass. State Lib.

50. "Aristides," in the *Boston Gazette*, Apr. 17, 1786. See also *ibid.*, Mar. 27, 1786, Apr. 2, 1787; *Independent Ledger* (Boston), Apr. 28, 1783; *Mass. Centinel*, May 3, 1786 and other dates; *Independent Chronicle, and Universal Advertiser* (Boston), Mar. 9, 1786; petitions of Dedham and Stoughton, *Pa. Packet* (Phila.), June 22, 26, 1786; Caleb Strong to Theodore Sedgwick, June 24, 27, 1786, Sedgwick Papers, vol. A, Mass. Hist. Soc.; Samuel Breck to Henry Knox, July 14, 1787, Knox Papers, XX, 131, Mass. Hist. Soc.; other references in Samuel Bannister Harding, *The Contest over the Ratification of the Federal Constitution in the State of Massachusetts* (Cambridge, Mass., 1896), 9-10.

51. *Mass. Centinel* (Boston), Apr. 30, 1785.

A major solution offered by the discontented was to reduce taxes by curtailing payment of requisitions to Congress. Besides a federal impost, Congress in 1783 requested the grant of supplementary taxes which, in the case of Massachusetts, would return $224,427, to be paid into the federal treasury. The request was overwhelmingly defeated (96-33) in 1785. Even some of the eastern towns rejected it, although most of the support it did receive came from the east and from Maine. In June of the following year the grant was approved, but only after a provision for part payment in gold and silver had been eliminated.[52] The division on this measure was clearly sectional. The east, supported by the Connecticut River towns, favored the grant (44-9), but the west opposed it (41-14). The deciding vote on this as on many other occasions was cast by the delegates from Maine.

Even more important was the question as to what taxes should be levied to support the domestic debt of the state. Although the House journals do not reveal the alignment on this issue, it is clear that most of this debt had fallen into the hands of merchants, who had secured it at half-price or less. Interest on the face value of the debt was being paid, principally by means of an excise tax which, it was charged, had passed the House only after many farmer delegates had departed. Critics asserted that the mass of the people were being taxed to benefit the few, money was taken from the poor and given to the rich—at a time of economic depression.[53] Rufus King admitted that taxes were exceedingly heavy: the tax on polls and estates was equal to one-third of the rents or incomes of the estates of all inhabitants.[54] It is not surprising that the less well-to-do were resentful, and that many demanded some other mode of paying the debt. One solution was to revalue state securities at their market price, or accomplish much the same thing by levying taxes payable in securities.[55] Others suggested

52. House Journal, V, 335, VII, 150-54, Mass. State Lib.; *Mass. Spy* (Worcester), Mar. 31, 1785.

53. *Hampshire Herald* (Springfield), Feb. 14, Sept. 26, 1786. Of course the wealthy had to pay too, and some complained with reason: Elbridge Gerry had to pay a tax of £100 specie! Gerry to Rufus King, Mar. 28, Apr. 23, 1785, King, *King*, I, 84, 89-90.

54. To John Adams, Oct. 3, 1786, *ibid.*, 190.

55. *Hampshire Herald* (Springfield), May 17, 1785, Jan. 31, Feb. 7, 1786; *Boston Gazette*, June 19, 26, 1786; *N.Y. Packet*, Mar. 6, 1786; *Mass.*

that the solution lay in paper money. This proposal, however, does not seem to have won the full support of the west.[56]

After the protests of 1782-83, the interior towns for the most part contented themselves with petitions, but a convention was held in 1784, and the right to hold conventions was steadily affirmed.[57] In 1786-87, however, unrest exploded in the famous Shays's Rebellion. During the summer preceding the armed outbreak, conventions in the counties of Hampshire, Middlesex, and Worcester sent petitions to the General Court, supplemented by those of various towns. Western Massachusetts complained of heavy taxes, the method of handling the state debt, the shortage of money, private debts, the expenses of government, the high fees incident to court suits, and the activities of the Court of Common Pleas.[58] It was proposed that official salaries and lawyers' fees be reduced (at least eight towns and two counties requested that the legal profession be abolished or controlled); the Court of Common Pleas eliminated and the General Court removed from Boston; and taxes lowered or rendered easier of payment. Occasional suggestions were made that the Senate be abolished, the constitution revised, and imprisonment for debt limited.[59]

Shays's Rebellion further divided the state. The area in sympathy with the protest movement corresponded closely to that already defined as being "western." The Connecticut River towns were, as before, eastern in their political outlook. Berkshire County was rent by a bitter conflict, with important leaders on both sides.[60] Elsewhere in the west only a handful of towns failed to

---

Centinel (Boston), Feb. 8, 1786. Of particular interest are the instructions of West Springfield, *Hampshire Herald* (Springfield), Feb. 14, 1786.

56. Instructions of the town of Conway, *Mass. Gazette* (Springfield), Jan. 20, 1784; *Continental Journal* (Boston), July 28, 1785; many petitions. Paper money bills were defeated in the House 93-23 and 99-19. House Journal, VI, 280 (Nov. 9, 1785), VII, 143 (June 28, 1786), Mass. State Lib.

57. *Mass. Gazette* (Springfield), June 22, 1784.

58. The numerous unpublished petitions add little to that of the Hampshire County convention, which has been often reprinted for good reason.

59. On this last point see petitions of Bedford, Oct. 16, 1786, and Middlesex County, Aug. 23, Oct. 3, 1786, Mass. towns, Force Transcripts, Lib. Cong.; *American Recorder, and Charlestown Advertiser*, Sept. 1, 1786; *Worcester Magazine*, 4 vols. (1786-1788), 2 (1786-1787), 357-58.

60. Taylor's account of Shays's Rebellion in his *Western Massachusetts* is excellent, and is particularly thorough on the Berkshire County aspects.

support the rebels' principles, if not always the rebellion itself, and the disaffected included not only the less well-to-do but many of "property." [61] Southeastern Middlesex, most of Essex, Suffolk, and Plymouth counties were not in sympathy with the westerners, yet even here exceptions were to be found, especially in the rural areas.[62] Two votes in the General Court reveal the alignment. A bill which empowered the Supreme Court to try persons who were obstructing justice was passed by a close vote.[63] The east, supported by the three Connecticut River delegates, voted for the measure (40-10); the west opposed it (41-12). The measure passed with the help of the Maine counties. A similar division occurred on the question of stationing troops in the west.[64] Here the delegates from Berkshire County, now under the control of the anti-Shays forces, cast all twelve of their votes for the bill, but otherwise the west was against it.

The division is also indicated by the votes in the Bowdoin-Hancock election, which followed the uprising. Bowdoin's activity in crushing the rebellion made him highly popular among the

61. See for example, the *New Haven Gazette*, Mar. 1, 1787; Major North to Henry Knox, Feb. 19, 1787, Knox Papers, XVIII, 138, Mass. Hist. Soc. Noah Webster wrote to James Bowdoin, "People here have an idea that the opposition consists of a rabble; but I know it consists of the substantial yeomanry of the country. But *few* take arms, for they dread a civil war; the majority of the people are however with the insurgents in principle. They are *right* in their views of the domestic debt; altho' the insurgents are *wrong* to pursue violent measures." Mar. 15, 1787, Bowdoin and Temple Papers, pt. 2, Mass. Hist. Soc., *Collections*, 7th Ser., 6 (1907), 181. See also Jonathan Smith, "The Depression of 1785 and Daniel Shays' Rebellion," *Wm. and Mary Qtly.*, 3rd Ser., 5 (1948), 77-94. Smith errs in stating that Harvard was anti-Shays. R. T. Paine was informed that all but 15 of the residents there were opposed to the government including the justice of the peace, General Whitney. R. T. Paine Papers, XXIII, Mass. Hist. Soc. See also Henry S. Nourse, *History of the Town of Harvard, Massachusetts, 1732-1893* (Harvard, 1894), 346-47.

62. One observer declared that all but one of the selectmen in Newburyport were enemies to the government. Of course this is an absurd exaggeration, but it is significant that the statement could be made. Nicholas Pike to James Bowdoin, Newburyport, Feb. 12, 1787, Bowdoin-Temple Papers, IV, 87, Mass. Hist. Soc. My generalizations here are based on town histories, newspapers, petitions, and letters.

63. House Journal, VII, 328-29 (Nov. 8, 1786), Mass. State Lib. Actually the data here are drawn from a vote to reconsider passage, which failed 66-55.

64. *Ibid.*, VIII, 60-3 (June 13, 1787).

merchants and equally unpopular elsewhere. "Brutus" warned the people: "Rapidly are you dividing into two Classes—extreme Rich and extreme Poor"; the alliance of Bowdoin and Lincoln represented a "Union of the Military and Monied interests"; and Bowdoin's supporters were "Men of Property and Fortunes, who expect one Day to lord it over, impoverish and enslave, YOU." [65] Hancock's popularity was so great that Bowdoin, even under favorable circumstances, would have had no chance, and he was overwhelmingly defeated. Yet he barely lost in Boston and made a respectable showing elsewhere in the eastern port towns, actually carrying Salem and Gloucester. In contrast, Hancock was almost unanimously favored by the Worcester County towns of Sutton (179-9) and Harvard (100-4).[66] The repressive activities of the government probably only deepened the anger of the west. New Braintree, for example, asserted that yeomanry of good principles and large property groaned under distress, disapproved of the measures adopted, and demanded reform.[67]

The events surrounding Shays's Rebellion increased the antagonism of the farmers toward their eastern opponents, and it worked the other way with equal force and greater consequence. The New York *Daily Advertiser* had pointed out, in the summer of 1786 that "the people of property are in continual fears of such measures being adopted, either by a paper currency, tender law or some other visionary expedient, as will destroy all confidence not only in the state, but in one another." Many men of property were indeed worried. "Our affairs seem to lead to some crisis," wrote John Jay, "some revolution—something I cannot foresee or conjecture. I am uneasy and apprehensive; more so than during the war." Charles Pettit, merchant of Philadelphia, also foretold a "Crisis," but sagely remarked that "a Convulsion of some kind seems to be desirable," for it offers "the only chance we have of restoration to political health." [68]

Upon the outbreak of Shays's Rebellion, the almost universal

65. *Boston Gazette*, Apr. 2, 1787.
66. These and other votes can be found in the *Mass. Gazette* (Springfield), Apr. 3, 6, 10, 13, 1787.
67. Jan. 1, 1787, Mass. towns, Force Transcripts, Lib. Cong.
68. Jay to Washington, June 27, 1786, Johnston, *Jay*, III, 204; Pettit to Jeremiah Wadsworth, May 27, 1786, Burnett, ed., *Letters*, VIII, 371.

reaction among men of means was to crush it. There might be indeed a few genuine grievances, but essentially they thought, or said they thought, that it was an uprising of the poor against the rich, made possible by the absence of an army, and designed to control the government and to annihilate all debts. So wrote Henry Knox and David Humphreys; the latter commented also on "a licentious spirit prevailing among many of the people; a levelling principle; a desire of change."[69] Dangerous indeed, such ideas! Whether or not this interpretation was really believed in Boston, it became official elsewhere and was quickly disseminated and embellished. Rufus King reported that the rebels aimed at the very being of government (having earlier given an honest report to John Adams, in which he frankly blamed imprudently high taxes and the pressure of creditors, and warned that there might be exaggerations).[70] Somebody conceived the idea that the Shaysites had supporters in Vermont and therefore ultimately in Canada, while Henry Lee was soon informing Washington that the rebels sought a union with Britain—for this supposition there was, as usual, "good ground."[71] Either there was much hysteria

69. Knox to Washington, Oct. 23, 1786, *Documentary History of the Constitution of the United States of America,* 5 vols. (Washington, 1905), IV, 30-32; Humphreys to Washington, Nov. 9, 1786, Humphreys, *Humphreys,* I, 378.

70. To Gov. Bowdoin, Dec. 28, 1786, Emmett Coll., No. 527, N.Y. Pub. Lib.; to Adams, Oct. 3, 1786, King, *King,* I, 190-91.

71. To Washington, Nov. 11, 1786; Burnett, ed., *Letters,* VIII, 506. Subsequently other second-hand reports elaborated on this rumor. For example, *ibid.,* 487, 489; *Doc. Hist. of the Constitution,* IV, 39. Where the idea originated that all property was endangered I am not certain. The earliest such statement I have found concerned not the Massachusetts rioters but those in New Hampshire. William Plumer to John Hale, Exeter, Sept. 20, 1786, Col. Soc. Mass., *Transactions,* 11 (1906-1907), 392. It was repeated in the *New Hampshire Gazette* (Portsmouth), on Sept. 28. A couple of weeks later David Sewall wrote from York, Maine, which is very close to the New Hampshire line, to George Thatcher, who was in Congress, that some of the Hampshire County (Mass.) resolves, "if complied with, must end in an abolition of all public & private debts and then an equal distribution of Property may be demanded. The Constitution is not democratick enough in the Opinions of these Geniouses." *Historical Magazine,* 16 (1869), 257. Thereupon Knox, who early in Oct. had written Congress that the immediate cause for the trouble was the grant of supplementary funds, reported (Oct. 18) that rebels in both states sought to annihilate all debts. Ford, ed., *Journals of Congress,* XXXI, 752, 887. Soon thereafter this interpretation of the Massachusetts "rebellion" became generally accepted.

or deliberate falsification or both. Perhaps the French minister, Louis Otto, hit upon one cause for such exaggerations when he noted that the Shaysites were advocating the abolition of the Senate, a principle which, he wrote, "attacks the very basis of the constitution, and tends to establish, after the example of Pennsylvania, a perfect democracy." [72]

The aid of Congress was promptly sought, and Congress responded by calling for troops, ostensibly because of an Indian threat. The disguise was not a very good one and was easily pierced: [73] the Massachusetts farmers knew well who the "Indians" were and felt that the move was "only a political one to obtain a standing Army." Lafayette, in Paris, was also concerned that the result might be an alliance between Congress and the rich.[74] Probably the subterfuge did more harm than good. In any case, Henry Knox had suggested to the Boston merchant, Stephen Higginson, the proper approach: "Exertions must be made & something must be hazarded, by the Rich," since neither Congress nor the government of Massachusetts had money available for raising troops. Higginson replied that the attachment of the rich "to their beloved property" would render them willing to spend a little in order to save much; and so indeed it proved.[75]

All this excitement and all these fears, real or imaginary, worked a shift of opinion, the importance of which is well-known. Massachusetts men of property drew together, and many who had once doubted the value of a strong government now hailed the prospect, and applauded the Society of Cincinnati which might

72. To Vergennes, Sept. 20, 1786, in George Bancroft, *History of the Formation of the Constitution of the United States of America*, 2 vols. (New York, 1882), II, 395.

73. Charles Pettit to the President of Pennsylvania, Oct. 18, 1786, Burnett, ed., *Letters*, VIII, 487; James Swan to Knox, Oct. 1786, Knox Papers, XIX, 35, Mass. Hist. Soc.; Major North to Knox, Oct. 29, 1786, *ibid.*, 36; Stephen Higginson to Knox, Nov. 12, 1786, "Letters of Stephen Higginson, 1783-1804," Am. Hist. Assn., *Ann. Report*, 1896 (1897), 741. See also the excellent account in East, "Massachusetts Conservatives," Morris, ed., *Era of American Revolution*, 382-86.

74. Elbridge Gerry to King, Nov. 29, 1786, King, *King*, I, 197; LaFayette to William S. Smith, Jan. 16, 1787, DeWindt Coll., Mass. Hist. Soc.

75. Knox to Higginson, Oct. 22, 1786, Knox Papers, XIX, 31, Mass. Hist. Soc.; Higginson to Knox, Nov. 12, 1786, Am. Hist. Assn., *Ann. Report*, 1896 (1897), 741-42. The Knox Papers, XIX, contain information regarding the progress and success of the loan, which exceeded $20,000.

help to obtain it. Indeed the rebellion, once ended, seemed to them a blessing in disguise.[76] Ebenezer Wales wrote, "I beleave that the Tumults here, in this State will Alarm the other States; and by that Means Congress will Soon have Suffict Powers For the Benefitt of the Whole."[77] He was right. By means of newspapers and letters the gospel was quickly circulated, and the drive for a government which could suppress such threats to property was accelerated.[78] Meanwhile among the Massachusetts farmers, the knowledge that their legitimate grievances had been rejected, and that the wealth and property of the state had been mobilized against them, increased their antagonism and prejudiced them against any proposal which might emanate from the east.

Antagonism also existed between Massachusetts proper and her truly eastern counties, the detached district of Maine. Delegates from Maine frequently held the balance of power even though there were sometimes fewer than a dozen present in the legislature. In view of the maritime interest of the region, and the fact that most of the towns were located on or near the coast, it is not surprising that their influence was ordinarily exerted in support of Boston and its allies. Maine, to be sure, was not content with the court system, nor with the prevailing mode of taxation; it sought

76. For the reaction in Massachusetts see Am. Hist. Assn., *Ann. Report*, 1896 (1897), 168, 179, 743; East, "Mass. Conservatives," Morris, ed., *Era of American Revolution*, 389; *Independent Chronicle* (Boston), Jan. 11, 1787; *Conn. Courant* (Hartford), May 7, 1787. The obvious value of the rebellion in securing a national government occasioned some imputations that it had been deliberately planned for that purpose. George Bryan wrote that before the Philadelphia convention, "some Intimations" were made by members of the Cincinnati that a monarchy was planned, and "that the people of Massachusetts were driven into Rebellion for the very purpose of smoothing the way to this step by their Suppression." MS in Bryan Papers, Hist. Soc. Pa. Mercy Warren believed that the discontents had been "fomented" by a "class of men least suspected." To John Adams, Dec. 1786, Mass. Hist. Soc., *Proceedings*, 64 (1930-1932), 160. Certainly the rebellion served a very useful purpose and advantage was quickly taken of it. See George Richards Minot to Nathan Dane, Mar. 3, 1787, *ibid.*, 48 (1914-1915), 430.

77. To Caleb Davis, Nov. 4, 1786, Davis Papers, XIIIa, Mass. Hist. Soc. Wales was soon to vote for the Constitution in the Massachusetts ratifying convention.

78. *New Haven Gazette*, Oct. 18, 1787; *Virginia Journal, and Alexandria Advertiser*, Nov. 9, 1786; and many others. See Millard Hansen, "The Significance of Shays' Rebellion," *South Atlantic Quarterly*, 39 (1940), 305-17.

greater representation, and there was also resentment against the activities of land speculators.[79] A movement to make Maine independent existed, finding support in the eastern counties of Cumberland and Lincoln, which were farthest from Boston; but it was not popular in York.[80]

Yet the divisions among Maine delegates were not according to counties. The split came on certain economic questions which aligned the coastal towns against those of the interior. Not all issues created such a division, because the Maine delegates to the Massachusetts legislature had much in common and tended to vote as a bloc. On the whole, however, the mercantile seacoast towns supported eastern Massachusetts on nearly all questions, whereas those of the predominantly agricultural interior often voted with the west.[81]

New Hampshire, like Massachusetts, was divided along east-west lines, and also by differences between debtor and creditor interests which corresponded to some extent with geographical regions. Also like Massachusetts, the state contained a section which threatened to secede—in this case, the towns bordering Vermont. A dispute over the provisions of the state constitution found east and west opposed.[82] After 1783, however, these controversies ceased to be important.

New Hampshire nevertheless had its share of divisive issues. As early as the fall of 1783 suits for private debts were becoming burdensome in the agricultural interior. Twenty-three towns of southern Cheshire and Hillsboro counties (in the south-central

79. See the article by George Thatcher disguised as "Scribble-Scrabble," in the *Cumberland Gazette* (Falmouth), June 8, 1786, asserting that large tracts of land owned by individuals led to great social distinctions.

80. See issues of *ibid.*, and of the *Falmouth Gazette and Weekly Advertiser*; letter to Caleb Davis and Benjamin Hichbourn, Machias, May 22, 1786, Davis Papers, XIIIa, Mass. Hist. Soc.; James Avery to Caleb Davis, Machias, Nov. 14, 1786, *ibid.*; local histories; occasional notices in Boston newspapers.

81. See particularly the votes on the supplementary fund in 1785-86. Note, for instance, on many votes, the position taken by Sanford, New Gloucester, Newcastle, Warren, and Hallowell as opposed to Wells, Falmouth, North Yarmouth, Georgetown, Bath, and Boothbay. See also the instructions of Fryeburg, May 31, 1786, in John Stuart Barrows, *Fryeburg, Maine* (Fryeburg, 1938), 110-11, and later instructions in the *Cumberland Gazette* (Falmouth), Feb. 9, 1787.

82. Upton, *Revolutionary New Hampshire*, 183-85.

and western parts of the state) met in convention, complained about the multitude of lawsuits, and asked that debtors be given a reasonable time to pay.[83] The public debt also created problems. An effort was made to levy taxes which would pay the state debt at par, but as usual this policy encountered opposition from debtors who could pay neither debts nor taxes. Further murmurings of discontent were heard in 1785 and came to a head during 1786, paralleling Shays's Rebellion. Conventions were held in July, August, and September, and a riot occurred on September 20.[84] Most of the disturbances were in the central part of the state, but the mob acted in Exeter, far in the east, and it is clear that the unrest had as much to do with class as with sectional lines of divisions.

The debtor point of view was given ample expression in the press. The state debt, it was maintained, had been secured by the present holders at a depreciated rate, and they did not deserve full value in return—the masses ought not to be taxed for the benefit of a few. Moreover, in a time of money shortage creditors profited unjustly from specie payment, and debtors were discriminated against, for if they could not pay, their property could be sold only at a great loss. The solution was paper money, which the rich opposed because they wished to receive far more than they had loaned and to create an aristocracy which would ultimately be not only economic but political. The advocates of paper money, "A Tradesman" wrote, "Know the secret springs or moving causes of private plans which are calculated to raise certain classes of men to a state of nobility; men who have already engrossed so great a share of the public stocks by jobbing, that they dread the consequences of annihilation. [They want] an oligarchical government, which puts it in the power of a few rich men to speak, write, and even think for the multitude, whom they esteem but as asses of burthen. . . . [But] the people are not such fools as their hon-

83. A. S. Batchellor, ed., *Early State Papers of New Hampshire* (Manchester, 1891, Concord, 1892), XII, 762-66; See Chester's instructions to its representatives, *ibid.*, XI, 318.

84. *New Hampshire Gazette* (Portsmouth), May 20, Sept. 16, Oct. 17, 1785, Aug. 10, 24, Sept. 28, 1786; letters from William Plumer, June 6, July 22, Aug. 13, Sept. 18, 20, Col. Soc. Mass., *Transactions*, 11 (1906-1907), 384-392; the *Freeman's Oracle, and New Hampshire Advertiser* (Exeter), Aug. 29, 1786.

ours take them to be, which time will discover." [85] The court system, the fees charged by courts and lawyers, and the conduct of the latter also favored the rich, it was said, but "Hunger . . . will break through stone walls . . . necessity has no law, and is the mother of invention, the people cannot bear their burthen any longer. . . . Every day brings us nearer to extremity, when a paper medium can no longer be dispensed with." [86]

Those who uttered such sentiments were described by their opponents as "men in distress involved in debt and discontented," and the September riot was interpreted in much the same way as was Shays's Rebellion. It was reported that some were demanding "an equal distribution of property" or "the annihilation of debts," while "all of them exclaimed against law and government." [87]

Actually the demand for paper money of some sort was almost universal; only a handful of towns, most of them near the coast, were opposed to it, and at least three-fourths favored a paper issue. There was, however, much disagreement on how far the state should go. Some felt that only enough money should be issued to pay the state's creditors; others wanted a larger issue to be loaned at low rates of interest or even at no interest, and to be legal tender for all debts. The range of opinion can be readily illustrated from the many resolutions passed by town meetings during 1786. The town of Barrington, in Strafford County (presently to be Federalist), was impressed by the burden of the state debt but did not want paper money to be loaned to citizens. The town meeting suggested that enough bills of credit be issued to pay the entire debt and defray the expenses of the government; after one year, taxes would be levied annually for ten years to redeem the bills.[88] A more radical but not extreme position was taken by

85. *New-Hampshire Spy* (Portsmouth), Nov. 14, 1786.

86. "Rusticus," in the *New Hampshire Gazette* (Portsmouth), Aug. 10, 1786. For this point of view see also *ibid.*, Feb. 10, June 1, Aug. 30, 1786; *New Hampshire Mercury, and General Advertiser* (Portsmouth), Sept. 6, 1786; on the shortage of money, John Sullivan to Thomas Jefferson, Mar. 4, 1786, in Otis G. Hammond, ed., *Letters and Papers of Major General John Sullivan, 1779-1795* (N. Y. Hist. Soc., *Collections*, 15 [1939]), III, 448.

87. William Plumer to John Hale, Sept. 20, 1786, Col. Soc. Mass., *Transactions*, 11 (1906-1907), 392; *New Hampshire Gazette* (Portsmouth), Sept. 28, 1786.

88. Barrington town records, Nov. 18, 1786, N. H. Hist. Soc.

the town of Atkinson, which was also in the southeast, but which presently would be Antifederal. Its town meeting referred to "a labyrinth of difficulty and distress" and suggested the emission of £150,000 in paper. This money would be loaned at interest, and repayment would begin after three years. Meanwhile the bills could be used for taxes, private debts, and court fees.[89] Finally the future Antifederal town of Marlborough, in the interior, insisted that the borrowers pay no interest at all, that the paper should be legal tender, and that it remain in circulation for twenty years.[90]

Still other suggestions were made, and it was perhaps this lack of agreement which gave the hard money advocates their chance. A plan was submitted by the legislature which called for an issue of only £50,000. Part of this was to be used for the expenses of the government but not for the interest on the state debt. The remainder was to be loaned at 6 per cent on the security of improved lands. The loan would be payable in six years and the money was not to be legal tender.[91] This plan was certain to be rejected by the towns to which it was submitted—a fact which was probably counted upon. Few voted for it. Some opposed it because they wanted no money at all, while most of the others opposed it because it was too mild a measure. Many of such towns recommended more radical features. Yet when the legislature reconvened it was informed by a committee that a majority of the votes in the towns was against paper money! It may be that the committee added the votes of those opposing paper money on any terms to those which rejected this particular plan but made no precise recommendation, and thus falsified the real result of the poll. In any case, nothing was done, and during 1787 better times lessened the demand.[92]

89. Batchellor, ed., *New Hampshire State Papers*, XI, 122-27 (Aug. 21, 1786).
90. Marlborough town records, Dec. 8, 1786, N. H. Hist. Soc. See also the instructions of Antifederal Richmond, Sept. 4, 1786, Batchellor, ed., *New Hampshire State Papers*, XIII, 317.
91. *Ibid.*, XI, 127-30.
92. I have used the town records which have been published in the *State Papers* and those which have been partly copied in the New Hampshire Historical Society. The votes in the towns were taken on different questions; some just voted for or against the plan, others voted for or against paper in general, still others polled on detailed points. Judging from these, the

On paper money and on other issues, too, the state was divided, very roughly, along geographical lines. In New Hampshire scarcely a rule can be formulated that is not disproved by a majority of exceptions, but there were about two dozen towns which ordinarily followed the lead of Portsmouth.[93] Of these over half were in the southeast, another group was located along the Connecticut River, and the remaining few were scattered. Consistently opposed to these were two dozen other towns, of which about two-thirds were located near the center, the remainder scattered about the state. But well over half of the towns refused to follow any pattern at all, and it is only by the roughest of generalizations that one can project a division between the southeast and the interior. Ordinarily, the southeast was able to control the legislature, partly because a large proportion of the towns failed to send representatives, but mainly because the inland towns were divided.[94]

The preceding general survey of internal political issues in the Northern as well as the Southern states reveals certain consistent patterns of voting behavior which are distinct in some states, less consistent in others, but traceable in all. These patterns can be most simply described as the opposition of the commercial to the non-commercial interest. Each of these interests, especially the commercial, was divided into a number of lesser interests (to borrow Madison's phrase), and these interests were so numerous and their objectives so complex that generalization is hazardous. The commercial interest included, first, the various professions and classes in the towns. If our attention were to be centered on certain issues, such as the treatment of the loyalists, it would be nec-

---

plan was defeated by a four to one margin. A slightly smaller majority favored paper money of some sort, but probably the extreme demand that paper be legal tender for all debts would have failed.

93. The generalizations here are based on votes in Batchellor, ed., *New Hampshire State Papers*, VIII, 953-54, 979, XX, 434-35, 516, 656, 697-99, 761, XXI, 59, 75, 83, 117. They concern the treatment of debtors, tender laws, taxes, the state debt, and adherence to the treaty with England.

94. There were well over 100 towns or groups of towns entitled to send delegates, but usually only one-third and sometimes even one-half of the representatives were absent on these key votes. This applies to the southeastern towns as well as to those of the interior.

essary to emphasize the conflict between urban classes. But after 1783 the loyalist issue can be virtually ignored, partly because agreement upon many other issues healed the split between merchant and artisan, and partly because the conflict between them had been resolved, for the time being, in favor of the former.

The merchants and their allies were usually supported by those farmers who were producing for urban consumption or for export, and who recognized that their welfare depended upon commercial prosperity. The key here is not so much the size of the farm as its location with respect to the market or to transportation facilities connecting it with the market. The farmer of the Potomac, Connecticut, or Hudson valleys might be many miles from a major town, but he was nonetheless influenced by commercial factors. It is true of course that merchants and commercial farmers did not always agree, especially if the farmers were in debt. Yet the area of agreement was very large: witness, for example, the correlation between the voting behavior of Savannah, Charleston, New Bern, Edenton, Norfolk, Richmond, Alexandria, Philadelphia, New York, New Haven, New London, Boston, and Portsmouth with that of their environs. Agreement between town and adjacent country was further promoted by the fact that both were controlled by the well-to-do.

On the other side were farmers whose interest was not, or did not appear to be, so connected with commerce. Typically, they were unable to produce a large surplus either because the land was inferior, or because they lacked the means (were slaveless, for instance), or because they were too distant from a market. Since it was difficult to accumulate wealth under such circumstances, the vast majority were small property holders in a local society wherein wealth was, by comparison, equally distributed. Such people naturally subscribed to equalitarian, or "levelling" principles, and held economic ideas favorable to debtors and members of the "middling sort" generally. It was out of such ideas that Antifederalism grew.

Thus far political alignments have been described with reference to the internal issues within each state. It is now necessary to discover whether the same situation existed in regard to federal affairs. The principal division of opinion on national issues arose with respect to the payment of the federal debt and the granting of the power over taxation. The debate centered upon the so-called impost. The dispute over the impost not only presents an opportunity to re-examine political alignments but also makes possible a further description of Antifederal thought.

Chapter IV

ANTIFEDERALISTS VS. NATIONALISTS: THE IMPOST

A LTHOUGH Antifederalism is defined in relation to the Constitution, it originated as a political force during and after the Revolution when a decisive crystallization of opinion occurred. On one side were those who wanted a strong central or "national" government, and on the other side those who preferred the retention of power by the state governments. The location of sovereignty was constantly debated, but the issue which provoked most dispute was the impost. The volume of letters written and articles published relative to this question is great enough, and the votes recorded in state legislatures are numerous enough, to reveal the arguments on both sides rather fully, and to disclose the sources of opposition and support. Because the question was complex, future Antifederalists were far from unanimous in attitude, yet because the impost involved the distribution of authority between state and federal government, most of the opponents of centralization united against it, and their arguments foreshadowed the greater debate over the Constitution.

The effort to secure the adoption of the impost was part of the broader movement to strengthen the government under the Articles; this will be discussed more fully in the next chapter. The immediate effect of the impost would have been to confer a limited power of taxation upon Congress. Those who wished to strengthen the central government considered this reform fundamental. Without an independent income, Congress must defer to the states; it could not support an army, which must therefore look to the states for pay. Many reformers believed that an independent income and consequent control over the army would reconstitute the existing political structure and transfer effective sovereignty from the states to Congress. It was to prevent such centralization, of course, that the requisition system had been written into the Articles, and at first sight it would seem that the Antifederalists could easily block any such maneuver by defending the existing arrangement. But the situation was not that simple; a good case could be made for reform on the ground of necessity. The impost was advanced in response to serious military and financial difficulties for which, it could be plausibly argued, a federal tax was the solution.

Congress first recommended the impost in the early spring of 1781. It was a time of great stress. The military outlook was dark; Continental and state paper currency were seriously depreciated; Congress urgently needed money to pay the army and the interest on the debt. The states were having trouble supplying their troops and meeting their financial obligations and were unable to pay Congress's requisitions. Therefore on February 3, Congress requested that it be granted the power to collect a tax of 5 per cent of the value of almost all imported articles. The money would be used to pay the debt, and collections would continue until it was discharged. The credit of the government would thereby be re-established and more money could be borrowed. Although this request was not in the form of an amendment to the Articles, the states so regarded it, and their unanimous assent became necessary for its adoption.[1]

So urgent was Congress's need of revenue that success of the impost seemed assured; in 1781 it was approved by eight states.[2] Although Massachusetts, Rhode Island, Maryland, South Caro-

1. Ford, ed., *Journals of Congress*, XIX, 112-13.
2. Connecticut's act was at first deficient, but the necessary changes were made within a year. Charles J. Hoadly and Leonard W. Labaree, eds., *The Public Records of the State of Connecticut*, 6 vols. (Hartford, 1894-1945), III, 314-15, IV, 153-54. Other early impost acts are, Henry Harrison Metcalf, ed., *Laws of New Hampshire* (Bristol, 1916), IV, 379-80; James T. Mitchell and Henry Flanders, comps., *The Statutes at Large of Pennsylvania from 1682-1801* (Harrisburg, 1896-1908), X, 296-98; William Waller Hening, ed., *The Statutes at Large, being a Collection of all the Laws of Virginia, . . .* (Richmond, 1822-23), X, 409-10, 451; Clark, ed., *State Recs. of N. C.*, XXIV, 405-6; *Laws of the State of New York, 1777-1788*, 2 vols. (Albany, 1886), I, 347-49; Peter Wilson, ed., *Acts of New Jersey* (Trenton, 1784), 191-92; *Laws of the State of Delaware*, 2 vols. (New-Castle, 1797),

lina, and Georgia did not act upon it that year, no strenuous opposition was voiced by their citizens. By February 1782, however, serious criticism of the measure was raised in the Massachusetts legislature and spread into the newspapers; nevertheless Massachusetts reluctantly fell into line, as did Maryland and South Carolina. But Georgia failed to act, and in November Rhode Island definitely rejected the measure. At almost the same time Virginia repealed her earlier grant. Although the victory at Yorktown had lessened the emergency, the army was clamoring for pay and the debt still mounting. Congress tried again. Its impost request of April 1783 met two of the objections to the previous plan by providing that the collectors would be chosen by the states and that the grant would be limited to twenty-five years. Again unanimity was required.[3] The new recommendation was far more acceptable to the states, and it was assisted by Washington, who urged its passage in a circular letter. Much of the opposition it encountered arose from peripheral (though not irrelevant) objections to officers' pensions, fear of the army, and suspicion of Robert Morris.[4] Progress was slow, but by 1786 all of the states had accepted the measure. New York, however, required that the state retain control over the collection of the tax and that the state's paper money be taken in payment. These conditions were not accepted by Congress (although one Antifederal delegate thought that they ought to be[5]), and the impost failed.

II, 762. The fact that Georgia failed to pass the impost of 1781 was not emphasized at the time and has sometimes been overlooked since; Jensen even has Georgia acceding (*New Nation*, 58, 63). The result has been to put all of the stress on Rhode Island's action. Actually it is quite probable that Virginia would have repealed her act even had Rhode Island given in, and the impost still would have remained ungranted.

3. Ford, ed., *Journals of Congress*, XXIV, 257-61.

4. James Warren wrote to John Adams, "Morris is a King, and more than a King. He has the Keys of the Treasury at his Command, Appropriates Money as he pleases, and every Body must look up to him for Justice and for Favour." With the impost under his control, "he will have us all in his Pocket." Oct. 27, 1783, Mass. Hist. Soc., *Collections*, 73 (1925), 230. See also chap. III, *n.* 10.

5. Timothy Bloodworth to Gov. Richard Caswell, July 28, 1786, Dreer Coll., Letters of Members of the Old Congress, I, 49, Hist. Soc. Pa. Roger Sherman thought so too. To William S. Johnson, May 13, 1786, W. S. Johnson Papers, Letters to, 1760-1790, Conn. Hist. Soc.

The impost ran counter to particular economic interests, but it failed primarily because it offended those who feared a consolidation of power in the central government. For the study of Antifederalism, the economic objections are not as significant as the political; nevertheless they must be analyzed in order to display the nature of the issue.

Since the impost would enable Congress to pay its debts, it was certain to have a differential effect upon the interests of individuals and particular groups. Federal creditors were the most obvious beneficiaries, even if they had to bear part of the taxes. How persons who held no securities would fare depended upon the incidence of taxation. It was not clear who would pay most of the tax, and different economic groups tried to fathom where their interest lay. A few merchants, like Archibald Maclaine of North Carolina, considered the measure "big with destruction to the commercial interests." [6] Patrick Henry was convinced that the tax would be borne by the rich.[7] But in Connecticut "Agricola" argued that the burden would be borne by the farmers, not by merchants, who would merely add 5 per cent to the cost of goods. The tax, he believed, would have less effect upon wealthy farmers, who could provide their own materials for clothes, than upon middling farmers, mechanics, day-laborers, and the poor, who could not.[8] As will be seen, opposition to the impost centered among farmers, some of whom believed that they would suffer economically,[9] but on the whole farmers did not consistently base their protest on economic grounds: some of them did not expect to pay, while others preferred the impost, which was an indirect tax, to assessments on land or on polls. Benjamin Harrison remarked that although all duties would eventually come out of the pockets of consumers, "the people at large do not see it and

6. To George Hooper, Feb. 25, 1783, Clark, ed., State Recs. of N.C., XVI, 941. Maclaine was a lawyer but spoke for the merchants.
7. Edmund Randolph to Madison, May 24, 1783, Madison Papers, IV, Lib. Cong.
8. Conn. Courant (Hartford), Dec. 10, 1782.
9. Instructions of the town of Smithfield, Rhode Island, May 19, 1786, William R. Staples, Rhode Island in the Continental Congress (Providence, 1870), 558.

are therefore much better contented to pay money that way than in taxes on their landed and other property."[10]

The anticipated effect of the impost upon different groups or classes of the population was less instrumental in creating opposition than its likely effect upon the particular interests of certain states. Rhode Island, for example, depended upon commerce to an unusual degree, importing very heavily and then re-exporting commodities. The money she raised by her own tariff went into the state treasury; if the money went instead to Congress, it was contended, her citizens must contribute very heavily while receiving little in return, and furthermore her trade would be greatly handicapped.[11] New York also had a special interest in opposing the impost, for, as the French minister, Louis Otto, explained, "It collects a kind of impost from the states of New Jersey and Connecticut, which, not having large towns, have their chief market in the city of New York." In 1786 New York was drawing about one-third of its revenue from an import tax, the loss of which would require high land taxes.[12] States such as Virginia and South Carolina which lacked manufacturing and bought large quantities of foreign goods feared that they would pay more than their share. Other states, however, expected to benefit from the impost, and voted accordingly. The citizens of each state had to weigh a variety of advantages and disadvantages.

Such economic considerations are not to be discounted, yet they tended to cancel one another out; in any case, they were not of primary importance in shaping attitudes toward the impost. Explaining Virginia's reaction in detail, Edmund Randolph scarcely mentioned economic objections. So, too, a French observer believed that New York's opposition was entirely political, founded in a desire to adhere strictly to the Articles, fear of power in general and of the taxing power in particular, apprehen-

10. To Jefferson, Apr. 23, 1784, Boyd, ed., *Papers of Jefferson*, VII, 114.
11. "A Farmer," in the *Providence Gazette*, Mar. 23, 30, 1782; "A Freeholder," in *ibid.*, Oct. 26, 1782; speaker of the House of Representatives to the President of Congress, Nov. 30, 1782, Staples, *Rhode Island in Cont. Cong.*, 400; Nicholas Brown to David Howell, Mar. 26, 1785, MSS, XIV, No. 53, R. I. Hist. Soc.; Jonathan Arnold to David Howell, Feb. 7, 1784, Peck Coll., VII, *ibid.*
12. To Vergennes, Apr. 9, 1786, Bancroft, *History of the Constitution*, I, 498; Spaulding, *New York in the Critical Period*, 155-56, 171.

sion of what a future Congress might do, and finally the conviction that the grant would "put the capstone to aristocracy" ("On met le comble a l'aristocratie").[13] It was not money, but power, that mattered most.

For the impost was not just an economic, but a political, measure. Congress, for the first time, would be granted the power over taxation. The implications were enormous; they involved fundamental principles of government. In their attempt to defeat the plan, the opponents of the impost elaborated a body of political ideas which formed an important part of Antifederal thought and anticipated many of the arguments that were to be used later against the Constitution.

Defenders of the Articles of Confederation emphasized its virtues and insisted that any changes should be considered with great care. The existing form of government had been decided upon deliberately, by men of ability who carefully considered the country's needs. It had proved its efficiency, had "carri'd us Triumphantly thro' a long and Bloody war," and would now "bind us together as Freemen." [14] The impost grant would effect fundamental alterations, might "disturb the general Harmony, derange the elegant proportions and endanger the welfare of the whole building." [15] The result might be fatal to liberty.

One of the earliest anti-impost articles cited Burgh to prove that all power was arbitrary, and this fundamental doctrine became a major premise of the argument. Power begat power; once

13. Baron de Beelen Berthoff to [unknown], Apr. 14, 1786, Letters, Hist. Soc. Pa. For these economic factors see also Stephen Higginson to Theophilus Parsons, Apr. 1783, Burnett, ed., *Letters*, VII, 124; the North Carolina delegates to the governor of North Carolina, Sept. 26, 1783, *ibid.*, 312; Cochran, *New York*, 142-44; David Ramsay to William Gordon, June 23, 1784, Misc. Papers, N.Y. Pub. Lib.; Joseph Jones to Madison, June 8, 1783, in Worthington C. Ford, ed., *Letters of Joseph Jones of Virginia, 1777-1787* (Washington, 1889), 112; *Independent Chronicle* (Boston), Aug. 21, 1783.

14. Jabez Bowen to James Warren, Nov. 26, 1783, Warren-Adams Letters, Mass. Hist. Soc., *Collections*, 73 (1925), 235; "Verus," in the *Freeman's Journal* (Phila.), June 9, 1784; "Philo Patria," in the *Independent Gazetteer* (Phila.), Sept. 30, 1786, printed also in three other papers; "Argus," in the *Independent Chronicle* (Boston), Apr. 18, 1782 and in the *Providence Gazette*, Aug. 3, 1782.

15. The Rhode Island delegates to the governor of Rhode Island, Oct. 15, 1782, Burnett, ed., *Letters*, VI, 506; see also "Jonah," in the *Mass. Gazette* (Springfield), Jan. 14, 1783.

given, it was never abandoned but rather extended by its posses-
sors.[16] Although the present Congress might be able to resist
temptation, any authority, once granted, would ultimately be
abused; therefore it was essential to guard now against oppression
in the future. The foundations of arbitrary rule might be laid
while the people slept, and even to men of integrity, power
ought not to be given, lest their successors be less trustworthy.[17]
But, it was asked, was even the present Congress so virtuous? The
mere fact that a grant of power was requested demanded that the
question be raised. Perhaps the danger was not remote but immediate, and the impost was in fact begotten by a thirst for power in
the present rulers.[18] Congress's request, wrote James Warren, "will
excite Jealousy & destroy the necessary Confidence of the People
in their Wisdom & Integrity." [19] Abuses in many departments
during the war suggested that people should beware, lest power
be concentrated into the hands of a few and create an aristocracy.
One observer warned that the money raised by the impost might
"pay our debts" but that the power it created "might destroy our
liberties." [20] The fear of what might result from a change of government continued to be important throughout the decade.

16. "The Examiner," in *ibid.*, Sept. 10, 1782; "Argus," in the *Independent
Chronicle* (Boston), Apr. 18, 1782; "Rough Hewer" (Abraham Yates), in the
N.Y. Gazetteer, Mar. 22, 1785, also in the *Newport Mercury*, Apr. 9, 1785,
(where Yates again quotes Burgh); Richard Henry Lee to General William
Whipple, July 1, 1783, Ballagh, *Lee*, II, 284; Lee to Samuel Adams, Mar. 14,
1785, Burnett, ed., *Letters*, VIII, 66n.; Thomson Mason to John Francis
Mercer, June 22, 1783, Rowland, *Mason*, II, 59.
17. "A Countryman," in the *Providence Gazette*, Sept. 21, 1782; "Can-
did," in *ibid.*, Dec. 28, 1782 (and several other papers); "Jonah," in the
Mass. Gazette (Springfield), Jan. 7, 14, 1783; "An Honest Republican," in
the *Independent Chronicle* (Boston), Aug. 7, 1783; "Independens," in the
New Hampshire Gazette (Portsmouth), Aug. 23, 1783; William Gordon to
Washington, Aug. 13, 1783, Mass. Hist. Soc., *Proceedings*, 63 (1929-1930),
499-500; Nicholas Brown to David Howell, Mar. 26, 1785, MS, XIV, No. 53,
R. I. Hist. Soc.
18. "A Rough Hewer," in the *New York Gazetteer, or, Northern Intelligencer* (Albany), Aug. 4, 1783, reprinted in the *Newport Mercury*, Sept. 6,
1783 and in the *N.Y. Packet*, Mar. 18, 1784; "A. C.," in the *Providence
Gazette*, Jan. 25, 1783; *N.Y. Journal*, Jan. 25, 1787.
19. To Benjamin Lincoln, Apr. 28, 1783, Mercy Warren Papers, 1709-
1786, Mass. Hist. Soc.
20. "A Republican," in the *N.Y. Journal*, Oct. 19, 1786, also in the
Independent Gazetteer (Phila.), Oct. 24, 1786. See also "A Countryman," in
the *Independent Chronicle* (Boston), Jan. 30, 1782, and the *Providence*

The most dangerous of all powers, most serious in its consequences if abuse occurred, and most likely to change a free government into an oppressive one, was control over taxation, for, as "Democritus" wrote, "power, among people civilized as we are, is necessarily connected with the direction of the public money."[21] That the Articles of Confederation denied to Congress the right to raise money by taxation was no accident, nor a product of ignorance, but a recognition that control of the public's money could be "faithfully watched" only if the individual states had their separate treasuries. "Taxation is the necessary instrument of tyranny. There is no tyranny without it."[22] The location of the tax power had been vital in the dispute with Great Britain; and indeed all history proved, so Abraham Yates, Jr., declared, that "no important revolutions have taken place in any government, till the power of raising money from the people has been put into different hands. This power is the first, nay, I may say the only object of tyrants.... This power is the center of gravity, for it will eventually draw into its vortex all other powers."[23]

The critics warned that other grave dangers might be anticipated if the impost were passed. The grant, once made, would establish a precedent. If the Articles could be violated in this, so they could be violated in an infinity of ways. The time might

Gazette, Feb. 8, 1783; "Independens," in the New Hampshire Gazette (Portsmouth), Mar. 27, 1784; "Democritus," in the Freeman's Journal (Phila.), Mar. 26, 1783, also in the Providence Gazette, May 3, 1783.

21. Ibid.

22. "The Plain Dealer," in ibid., May 10, 1783. See also "Grotius," in the Boston Gazette, Feb. 10, 1783; "Hampden," in the S. C. Weekly Gazette (Charleston), Mar. 22, 1783; John Brown to David Howell, Oct. 23, 1783, MS, XIV, No. 7, R. I. Hist. Soc.

23. "Rough Hewer, Jr.," in the N.Y. Packet, Apr. 21, 1785; "Sidney," in ibid., Mar. 17, 1785. The "Sidney" series was originally printed in the Albany Gazette, Jan. 14, 21, 28, 1785. It also was written by Yates. See also South Carolina Senate Journals, Mar. 13, 1784, Microfilm Coll., Lib. Cong. Silas Deane to Simeon Deane, Apr. 1, 1783, in Worthington Chauncey Ford, ed., Correspondence and Journals of Samuel Blachley Webb, 3 vols. (New York, 1893-1894), III, 10; resolutions of a Suffolk County (Mass.) convention, in the Independent Chronicle (Boston), May 20, 1784; resolutions of a Middletown (Conn.) convention, in the Conn. Gazette (New London), Apr. 2, 1784 and the Connecticut Journal (New Haven), Apr. 7, 1784; "A Freeholder," in the Providence Gazette, Oct. 26, 1782; "S.A.," in ibid., Apr. 22, 1782; "Jonah," in the Mass. Gazette (Springfield), Jan. 7, 1783.

come when "the Liberties of this Country" might be sacrificed, for the *"power giving* System" might transmit to posterity the *"latent* seeds of future tyranny" and Congress might become "a *bunch of kings.*" [24] Abraham Yates, Jr., called upon Montesquieu and Beccaria to testify that republicanism could exist only in small states and pointed out that in both Switzerland and the Netherlands, local governments retained control over finances. [25] In a confederation of small states, the people could watch their representatives and pass laws to suit the needs of the area; democracy could be preserved. But in a great consolidated union, Congress's power could not be controlled; laws would be discriminatory, favoring one area over another, and some Caesar, finding absolute authority within his reach, would finally "start up in kingly shape." Each of the American states must therefore retain its sovereignty and independence, adhering to the form of government created by the Articles. If granted to Congress, the tax power would demolish state sovereignty; the states would become mere provinces; the people could no longer watch their rulers; and liberty would end. [26] The Virginia legislature asserted that to grant the tax power to any body other than the Assembly was "injurious to its sovereignty, may prove destructive of the rights and liberty of the people, and . . . is contravening the spirit of the confederation." [27]

24. "Candid," in the *Freeman's Journal* (Phila.), Dec. 4, 1782; "Democritus," in *ibid.*, Feb. 12, 1783; David Howell to Abraham Yates, Jr., July 12, 1785, Abraham Yates, Jr., Papers, N.Y. Pub. Lib.; "Letter from a gentleman in Massachusetts to a friend in Providence," in the *Providence Gazette*, Aug. 24, 1782; Arthur Fanner to David Howell, Nov. 5, 1782, Peck Coll., VII, R. I. Hist. Soc.; instructions to the delegates of Fairfax County, May 30, 1783, Rowland, *Mason*, II, 50-51; David Howell to the deputy governor of Rhode Island, Apr. 19, 1784, Burnett, ed., *Letters*, VII, 496; Dr. Solomon Drowne to David Howell, Nov. 4, 1782, *Hist. Mag.*, 12 (1867), 226.

25. "Rough Hewer, Jr.," in the *N.Y. Packet,* Apr. 21, 1785.

26. "Democritus," in the *Freeman's Journal* (Phila.), Mar. 26, 1783; "Jonathan of the Valley," in the *Independent Chronicle* (Boston), June 16, 1785; "Rough Hewer, Jr." in the *N.Y. Packet,* Apr. 21, 1785; "Grotius," in the *Boston Gazette*, Feb. 3, 1783; "Rough Hewer," in the *N. Y. Gazetteer* (Albany), Oct. 20, 1783; "Philo Patria," in the *Independent Gazetteer* (Phila.), Sept. 30, 1786; "A Farmer," in the *Providence Gazette*, Mar. 23, 1782; "A Countryman," in the *Continental Journal* (Boston), Jan. 30, 1783; Bartlett, ed., *Rhode Island Records*, IX, 612; William Gordon to Horatio Gates, Jan. 24, Feb. 26, 1783, Mass. Hist. Soc., *Proceedings*, 63 (1929-1930), 482, 487.

27. Hening, ed., *Statutes of Va.*, XI, 171 (Dec. 1782).

Thus the impost was opposed both by those who preferred a weak government to a strong and by those who demanded responsibility in their governors.

Criticism also focused on the fact that the collecting officers were to be the agents of Congress rather than of the states. "When Congress are empowered to grant pensions and salaries, and multiply their dependents," ran one complaint, "the Government of *America* becomes an *Aristocracy,* and the people loose their Majesty."[28] This power was "enormous and dangerous," and the states should retain control of the collection officers as a check upon Congress. This objection was the subject of much debate in state legislatures and was only partly removed by Congress in its request of 1783.[29]

As it had first been drafted in 1781, the impost was to continue indefinitely until the debt had been paid. Many feared that since Congress would continue to contract debts, the grant would be perpetual. "This grant is to be irrevocable," David Howell warned. Once passed, it would be "fixed as fate, and no more in the power of the respective legislatures of the several States than the elements, the seasons, or the planetary bodies: And whatever may be our wishes or prayers afterwards, when this important act is once passed, it will be like *Adam's fall,* unalterable, and affect not only ourselves, but all our posterity.—It will be like *Pandora's box,* once opened, never to close."[30] A state legislature, it was said, had no right to grant the money of posterity. Equipped with permanent revenues, Congress would be tempted to make its authority permanent, and with control over the army might well succeed. Once again, as in the dispute with Britain, "a degree of Jealousy is

28. "Independens," in the *New Hampshire Gazette* (Portsmouth), Aug. 24, 1783.

29. "Rough Hewer," in *N.Y. Gazetteer* (Albany), Oct. 6, 1783, *ibid.* (N.Y.), Mar. 22, 1785; "An Honest Republican," in *Independent Chronicle* (Boston), July 31, 1783; "A Correspondent," in the *N.Y. Journal,* Jan. 25, 1787. The legislative proceedings will be considered later, but see, for example, Edmund Pendleton to James Madison, May 4, 1783, Gratz Coll., Old Congress, Box 9, Hist. Soc. Pa. The importance of control over the collectors was of course clearly understood by the impost's supporters also. See Madison's notes on Hamilton's speech of Jan. 8, 1783, Ford, ed., *Journals of Congress,* XXV, 872.

30. "A Farmer," in the *Providence Gazette,* Apr. 13, 1782.

necessary, [for] where it is extinguished Liberty expires."[31] In 1783 Congress attempted to remove this objection by setting a time limit of twenty-five years, but many still remained dissatisfied, and insisted that "permanent funds, in Congress at present, would much endanger the liberties of the people."[32]

The opponents of the impost could not content themselves merely with criticism. Arguments would not pay the debt, and if the impost were to be rejected, some alternative way to preserve the government's credit had to be found. The impost's foes were almost unanimously convinced that the debt should be paid, and although many of the critics contented themselves with purely negative arguments, a large number suggested alternative means of payment.[33]

A few believed that Congress ought to pay the debt from collections under the requisition system. This idea was more plausible during the war years, when it could be argued that with the return of peace, payments by the states on requisitions would enable Congress to discharge the debt. This point of view became difficult to maintain during the post-war depression years, when collections still lagged.[34] In 1786 several critics suggested that the debt should be discharged at its depreciated value. The abilities of the people were insufficient to pay it in full; in any case, since the debt had depreciated, the present holders would benefit unduly at the expense of the people. Full justice would be done by paying the creditors what they had actually invested. This argument was important, but it was not used until the impost had become nearly a dead issue, and arose for the most part in con-

31. Jonathan Arnold and David Howell to the governor of Rhode Island, Oct. 15, 1782, Burnett, ed., *Letters*, VI, 504.

32. *Conn. Courant* (Hartford), Oct. 7, 1783. This objection was often expressed. Incidentally "Argus" found another danger, and hoped that "people will ever be so watchful and jealous of their liberties, as not to admit the exertion of *implied* powers." *Independent Chronicle* (Boston), Apr. 26, 1782.

33. There were a few who saw no danger in nonpayment. For example, the *N.Y. Packet*, Apr. 13, 1786, reprinted in the *American Herald* (Boston), Apr. 24, 1786, and "Grotius," in the *Boston Gazette*, Feb. 3, 1787. On the other hand about half of the newspaper articles and many private letters contained constructive proposals.

34. "Phileutherus," in the *Mass. Gazette* (Springfield), Aug. 19, 1783; *Conn. Journal* (New Haven), Sept. 10, 1783.

nection with payment by the states, not by Congress.[35] Still another proposal involved the use of public lands to retire the debt. One writer estimated that there were three hundred and sixty million acres of ungranted lands which, sold at a little over sixpence per acre, would retire the debt.[36]

Two other suggestions were more generally supported. All of the dangers inherent in the impost proposal might be avoided, it was said, if each state separately raised money and paid its own share of the debt. If Congress would but let each state know its proportion of the whole sum, the state could discharge its share in ways that would suit local conditions and impose the least burden. Besides, as some pointed out, the various certificates could be made receivable for taxes at a depreciated rate—an expedient which was indeed used. In this way the creditors could be paid, the Articles of Confederation retained intact, and the people satisfied.[37]

35. The following, however, referred to the impost: "Philolutheros," in the *Hudson Weekly Gazette* (N.Y.), Dec. 7, 1786; "Jus.," in the *American Herald* (Boston), June 12, 1786 ("The money holders and wealthy members, are strenuous for its establishment"; for they "have built castles in the air of princely fortunes"; but the debt should be paid in such a way as will not "beggar the greater part of the community"); the *American Recorder* (Charlestown), Aug. 18, 1786, in the same tone.

36. *Conn. Journal* (New Haven), July 30, 1783; "An Honest Republican," in the *Independent Chronicle* (Boston), June 26, 1783; "An Old Son of Liberty," in the *Newport Mercury*, Oct. 26, 1782; David Howell to the governor of Rhode Island, July 30, 1782, Dec. 24, 1783, Burnett, ed., *Letters*, VI, 402, VII, 397; Monroe to Madison, May 8, 1785, *ibid.*, VIII, 117; Richard Henry Lee to William Short, June 13, 1785, Ballagh, ed., *Lee*, II, 373.

37. "A Rough Hewer," in the *N.Y. Gazetteer* (Albany), Oct. 6, 1783; "Rough Hewer," in the *N.Y. Gazetteer* (New York), Mar. 11, 1785; "Cato," in the *Continental Journal* (Boston), Jan. 30, 1783; "A Freeholder," in the *Providence Gazette*, Nov. 9, 1782 (the fullest presentation, by Theodore Foster); "The Plain Dealer," in *ibid.*, May 10, 1783; "A Farmer," in *ibid.*, Mar. 30, Apr. 13, 1782 (also good); town of Killingworth, in the *Conn. Courant* (Hartford), Sept. 2, 1783; town of Smithfield, R. I., Apr. 19, 1786, in Staples, *Rhode Island in Cont. Cong.*, 558-59; Monroe to Jefferson, June 16, 1785, in Burnett, ed., *Letters*, VIII, 145; Stephen Higginson to Samuel Adams, May 20, 1783, *ibid.*, VII, 188; Silas Deane to Simeon Deane, Apr. 1, 1783, Ford, ed., *Correspondence of Webb*, III, 10; James Warren to Benjamin Lincoln, Apr. 28, 1783, Mercy Warren Papers, 1709-1786, Mass. Hist. Soc.; James Warren to John Adams, June 24, 1783, Warren-Adams Letters, Mass. Hist. Soc., *Collections*, 73 (1925), 220; Thomson Mason to the freeholders of Stafford County, June 10, 1783 and to John Francis Mercer, June

This procedure was always an imminent possibility during the Confederation, and it may be inquired why Congress did not in fact assign each state its proper share of the federal debt to discharge in its own way. Apart from certain technical difficulties, the failure can be accounted for in two ways. Public creditors in some states opposed it; they feared (with reason) that federal debt securities would then be redeemed by the states at a depreciated value—although their fear was tempered by the thought that it was better to receive something from the states than nothing from Congress. Nationalists also opposed a distribution of the federal debt among the states. The existence of a debt which inhered in Congress furnished them with a powerful argument in favor of granting Congress the right to tax; therefore they fought against an apportionment.

The final solution advanced by the anti-impost men countenanced a nation-wide duty on imports, but it was to be collected by the states rather than by Congress. Each state would levy an impost, collect it with state officers, pay it into a state treasury, and finally forward it to Congress. Congress would thus receive a revenue, and the debt would be paid, but the taxing power would be retained by the states.[38] Long after the impost had ceased to be an issue, it was observed that if Congress had submitted a plan for an impost which credited the proceeds to the state in which the articles were consumed and allowed collection by state officers, the measure would have been accepted.[39] In all probability this was correct.

It is now necessary to describe the fate of the impost in the states, with the primary object of discovering the sources of opposition to it. Because each state must be considered separately, it is

---

22, 1783, Rowland, *Mason*, II, 53, 60; Samuel Osgood, as reported in Rufus King to Elbridge Gerry, July 9, 1786, King, *King*, I, 187; petition of Plympton, Mass., Oct. 3, 1786, Mass. towns, Force Transcripts, Lib. Cong.

38. "Argus," in the *Independent Chronicle* (Boston), Apr. 26, 1782; "An Honest Republican," in *ibid.*, June 26, July 17, 1783; David Howell to the governor of Rhode Island, July 30, 1782, Burnett, ed., *Letters*, VI, 402; William Gordon to Washington, Aug. 13, 1783, Mass. Hist. Soc., *Proceedings*, 63 (1929-1930), 500; Edmund Pendleton to James Madison, May 4, 1783, Gratz Coll., Old Congress, Box 9, Hist. Soc. Pa.

39. *U. S. Chronicle* (Providence), June 12, 1788.

not possible to adhere to chronology altogether, but the New England states, where the earliest opposition appeared, will be considered first. The South, which did not accept the measure until 1786, will next be discussed, and the account will close with a description of the impost's defeat in New York.

The first opposition occurred where one might least have expected it: among the merchants of Boston. Early in 1781, shortly after Congress had adopted the impost, the Massachusetts legislature considered the grant and postponed action on it. The General Court explained that it was willing to contribute to federal expenses, but was afraid Massachusetts might pay more than her share; moreover the merchants felt that they would not be able to pass the burden on to consumers because they thought retail prices could not be raised any higher.[40] Evidently their influence was enough to delay action. Not until February of 1782 was a bill considered, and then it was introduced over the opposition of twenty-one representatives. Its progress was slow. A bare majority was persuaded to approve the words "permanent funds." The House refused to entrust Congress with complete power to collect the tax, and insisted that the proceeds should not be given to Congress "without passing to the Credit of this State." The legislature then recessed. Debate was renewed in April, and on May 1 the bill was finally passed (61-46) after a proviso had been inserted which made the grant revocable.[41] Governor Hancock kept the bill for ten days and then returned it with his objections, the nature of which is not known.[42] The House insisted that because of the time interval the bill had become law—an assertion which Hancock denied; the controversy was left unsettled until the next session

40. Resolves of the General Court of the Commonwealth of Massachusetts, 1780-1781, 153-54, Mass. State Lib.

41. House Journal, May 1781 to May 1782, 558, 560, 657-58, 714-16, Mass. State Lib.

42. Hancock to the House of Representatives, May 10, 1782, Adams Papers, N.Y. Pub. Lib.; John Lowell to Samuel Adams, Aug. 8, 1782, ibid.; Samuel Adams to John Lowell, May 15, June 4, 1782, Cushing, ed., Writings of Adams, IV, 272-75; House Journal, May 1781 to May 1782, 756-57, Mass. State Lib. That Hancock was opposed on principle is suggested by the fact that David Howell of Rhode Island wrote to him during the summer. Burnett, ed., Letters, VI, 404.

when on June 7 the House finally ruled against the Governor (58-46).[43]

The votes were recorded on this last ruling, on the proviso, and on the final passage. Analysis reveals that opposition to the impost came not from the interior, which favored passage by a three to one margin and voted to overrule the popular Hancock, but from the eastern section, supported by the Connecticut River towns. It was the commercial rather than the agricultural interest that delayed passage, although in both cases unanimity was lacking. Boston was divided, with merchants on both sides; other seacoast towns were slightly opposed. Of the forty-six votes cast against the measure on May 1, thirty-four came from the east.[44]

Why the alignment took this form is not positively revealed by the records. It appears, however, that the interior expected to escape the tax, perhaps because the farmers there purchased few foreign products, perhaps because they supposed that the merchants would bear the cost. The impost may have seemed an easier way of paying the federal debt than a system of state taxes which might be levied not only on imports but on land and polls.

In any event, the situation soon changed. As early as May 1782 a Worcester County convention expressed skepticism about entrusting Congress with power over the money,[45] and by 1783 the alignment was completely reversed. Congress's request of that year, although in some ways more acceptable, was handicapped by the fact that the end of the war had made the need for revenue less evident; also there was fear that the money would be used to pay a bonus to federal army officers. In March 1783, Congress had granted officers a bonus of five years full pay in lieu of life pensions promised them in 1780. The whole idea of military pensions was execrated in rural New England, and even the "commutation" of pensions into a cash payment was heartily disliked.[46] When the

43. House Journal, May 1782 to May 1783, 67-68, Mass. State Lib.
44. This includes two from the Maine coast.
45. The Mass. Spy (Worcester), May 23, 1782.
46. Joseph Pierce to Henry Knox, July 31, Oct. 7, 20, 1783, Knox Papers, XIII, 127, XV, 10, 83, Mass. Hist. Soc.; instructions of the town of Conway in the Mass. Gazette (Springfield), Jan. 20, 1784; Sidney Kaplan, "Veteran Officers and Politics in Massachusetts, 1783-1787," Wm. and Mary Qtly., 3rd Ser., 9 (1952), 37. Hatch writes that the House opposed half-pay four to one, support of it coming from the Senate and the seaport towns, opposition

Massachusetts legislature entertained Congress's impost request of 1783, its members merely sent a protest against the commutation to Congress, and then adjourned.[47] The question was revived, however, in the fall upon receipt of a letter from Financier Robert Morris enclosing a plea from John Adams. This time the supporters of the impost managed to beat down a provision forbidding Congress to use the money to pay the officers; they finally secured endorsement of the impost by a very close vote (72-65).[48] The vote revealed that the eastern towns supported by those along the Connecticut River now favored the grant by a large majority, whereas the rest of the state opposed it by a two to one margin. Worcester County delegates voted against it (18-2). This final alignment corresponded to the usual division on internal affairs.

Western Massachusetts continued to oppose the grant. In 1784 the towns of Franklin, Wrentham, Medway, and Bellingham proposed a Suffolk County convention to discuss the impost, commutation, and other grievances. The suggestion was rejected by Boston.[49] Suffolk County included Boston and other commercial centers, but the aforementioned towns, at the western end, were small agricultural villages which consistently supported the other interior communities against Boston and its allies. So also Rochester, a future Antifederal center, criticized the half-pay plan for officers, advocated a tax on luxuries instead of polls and estates, petitioned for an issue of legal tender paper money, and as late as 1786 opposed the impost on the ground that it "allmost annihilates the Constitutional Check which the General Court

---

from the interior, "where the financial distress was sharpest and where the dogmas of equality were pushed to their furthest extent." Louis Clinton Hatch, *The Administration of the American Revolutionary Army* (New York, 1904), 145.

47. House Journal, 1783-1784, 157-58 (July 9, 1783), Mass. State Lib.; Ford, ed., *Journals of Congress*, XXV, 607-9.

48. Stephen Higginson to Samuel Holten, Oct. 14, 1783, and to Arthur Lee, Oct. 23, 1783, Burnett, ed., *Letters*, VII, 334, 334n.; House Journals, 1783-1784, 201-2, 222, 224-25, 232, 236, 241, 251-54, 258-61, Mass. State Lib.

49. The *Conn. Journal* (New Haven), Apr. 7, 1784. Boston declared, "We are of opinion that if we ever mean to be a nation, we must give power to Congress, and funds too."

had on Congress." [50] But Massachusetts had approved the impost, and the contest was not reopened in that state.

Rhode Island resisted more obstinately. The decade witnessed a continual conflict between the towns lying on Narragansett Bay, especially Providence and Newport, and the agricultural communities which usually controlled the state. Criticism of the impost came first not from the dominant agrarian but from the commercial interest. Soon after the debate in Massachusetts had begun, the *Providence Gazette* published the first of an able series of anti-impost articles by David Howell,[51] and many critical writings soon followed. Howell, a professor at Brown University, was supported by other professional men such as Doctors Jonathan Arnold and Solomon Drowne, and Judge Theodore Foster, who were not speaking for a rural constituency; on the contrary, they represented powerful mercantile interests such as those of John and Nicholas Brown.[52] But resistance soon spread to include almost the entire state, and in the fall of 1782 the legislature rejected the impost by a unanimous vote. The foes of the measure rejoiced that liberty had been preserved, and the General Assembly sent Congress a vigorous defense of its action.[53] It is evident that the object was not merely to escape payment of the federal debt, for the state did try to furnish funds, despite difficulties of collection.[54] Rather, the merchants were convinced that Rhode Island, which depended to an unusual degree upon commerce, would be obliged to pay an excessive amount of money, most of which would not remain in the state but would go to public security holders elsewhere. They much preferred that the state collect its own impost

50. Mary Hall Leonard, "Revolutionary Records of a Country Town," *New England Magazine*, new Ser., 19 (1898-1899), 296-98.

51. "A Farmer," Mar. 23, 30, Apr. 13, 1782.

52. Hillman Bishop, in *R. I. Hist.*, 8 (1949), 5-6; James B. Hedges, *The Browns of Providence Plantations* (Cambridge, 1952), 324-25.

53. Royal Flint to Jeremiah Wadsworth, Aug. 26, 1782, Wadsworth Papers, Box 133, Conn. Hist. Soc.; Jonathan Arnold to David Howell, June 29, 1782, Peck Coll., VII, R. I. Hist. Soc.; Solomon Drowne to David Howell, Nov. 4, 1782, *ibid.*; Arthur Fenner to David Howell, Nov. 5, 1782, *ibid.*; Bartlett, ed., *Rhode Island Records*, IX, 612; Staples, *Rhode Island in Cont. Cong.*, 399-400.

54. *Rhode Island Acts and Resolves*, 14 (Oct. 1782), 29-30 (Nov. 1782), 45-53 (Feb. 1783), 29 (May 1783), 18-21, 26-31 (June 1783), 17 (Feb. 1784), 34-37 (June 1784).

and pay off the state and federal debts held by its citizens. The farmers were persuaded either by this argument or by the political objections which were forcibly urged.[55]

When Congress renewed its request in 1783, the legislature refused to act; but the merchants did not sustain their opposition indefinitely. Some, indeed, had favored the grant from the beginning, and by March 1785 Nicholas Brown, who held $50,000 in federal securities,[56] swung over because, as he said, federal creditors were being neglected. Others must have been similarly motivated, for in February the impost was ratified. Rural opposition to surrendering power to Congress was united with the federal creditor interest in the provisions of the act, which required collection by state officers, the assignment of £18,000 to Congress as the state's share of the interest on the American foreign debt, and the withholding of the remainder in order to pay interest on federal securities owned by citizens of the state.[57]

This act was not a full compliance with Congress's request, and the impost grant was reconsidered in 1786. By this time the political situation had changed. Suggestions were being made that the state issue paper money which would be used to pay both state and federal creditors. The prospect may have convinced federal creditors that they would fare better if Congress, rather than the state, controlled the impost. Opponents of paper money, moreover, now had reason to favor granting Congress the impost; the relinquishment of this duty would almost certainly preclude a currency emission, for it would alienate tax resources essential to its support. In any event, the legislature defeated a paper money bill, and duly granted the impost to Congress without restrictions.

No vote has been preserved on these questions; however the alignment seems clear. It is significant that the same number of votes were cast for paper money and against the impost—which suggests that the pro-paper party was anti-impost. This inference

55. John Brown to David Howell, Oct. 23, 1783, MS, XIV, No. 27, R. I. Hist. Soc.; Jabez Bowen to James Warren, Nov. 26, 1783, Mass. Hist. Soc., *Collections*, 73 (1925), 235.

56. To David Howell, Mar. 26, 1785, MS, XIV, No. 53, R. I. Hist. Soc. For Brown's securities see E. James Ferguson, *Power of the Purse* (Chapel Hill, 1961), 281-82.

57. Bartlett, ed., *Rhode Island Records*, X, 87-88.

is confirmed by the fact that when a new election brought about a reversal of political control and the passage of a paper money bill, it also resulted in a postponement of the impost grant. In addition, two petitions from interior towns exist: one favored the impost but only with serious qualifications, and the other suggested means of paying the federal debt which did not include the impost.[58] Finally, eight towns are known to have objected to commutation, which elsewhere resulted in anti-impost feeling; of these, seven were inland and the eighth was on the south coast, not on Narragansett Bay.[59] It is probable, then, that the division in Rhode Island eventually resembled that in Massachusetts, with the commercial interests favoring the grant and the agricultural opposing it. In both states the alignment on internal issues coincided with attitudes toward Congressional power.

In yet a third New England state the impost encountered opposition, and here also there were a number of complicating factors. Although Connecticut was the first state to approve the impost of 1781, her action was not in accord with Congress's proposal because it specified that collectors might be suspended by the legislature for misconduct and—a more serious restriction—that the grant was to last only for three years after the war.[60] Increasing opposition delayed a revision of the bill for over a year. When a new measure was finally approved in 1782, it retained state control of collectors and forbade Congress to use the money for officers' pensions.[61] Connecticut's reluctance is surprising, since the state had every selfish economic reason to favor the impost.[62] The explanation seems to lie in dislike of the promise to grant officers half-pay for life.

When the question was reopened in 1783, there was strong

58. Smithfield and Gloucester in Staples, *Rhode Island in Cont. Cong.*, 558-60 and Bates, *Rhode Island and the Union*, 120.

59. Misc. MSS, So 87, C 884, Ea 77, R. I. Hist. Soc.

60. Feb. 1781, Hoadly and Labaree, eds., *Public Records of Connecticut*, III, 314-15.

61. M. Tallcott to Jeremiah Wadsworth, Feb. 15, 1782, Wadsworth Papers, Box 133, Conn. Hist. Soc.; Benjamin Talmadge to Wadsworth, June 6, 1782, *ibid.*; Hoadly and Labaree, eds., *Public Records of Connecticut*, IV, 153-54.

62. Oliver Wolcott to Samuel Lyman, Apr. 3, 1781, Burnett, ed., *Letters*, VI, 44.

feeling that Congress had violated the Articles of Confederation in making concessions to the officers and as a result ought not to be trusted with money. When in November the governor recommended the grant, the legislature, which was determined to block it, refused to approve his message.[63] The following year supporters of the measure obtained the consent of the governor and the upper house, but the lower house refused to grant Congress "any Substantial Revenue" which would carry with it "Substantial Power, independent of the different assemblies." Mistrust of centralized authority and the indignation aroused by Congress's commutation of the officers' pensions, swayed the majority, and on February 27 the impost was overwhelmingly defeated (69-37).[64] Only one part of the state favored passage: Fairfield, the Episcopalian, loyalist, anti-paper, and future Federalist county, voted fourteen to one for the bill. Elsewhere the margin was three to one against it; even most coastal and river towns were opposed, although the measure did win votes from commercial centers such as New London and Norwich. Agricultural Connecticut was primarily responsible for rejecting the impost. The towns which had supported paper money were all but unanimously against it; towns which in the future were to be Antifederal also opposed it with but one exception.

But the tide was turning. Opinion began to change in regard to commutation, and as dislike of this measure subsided, so did opposition to the impost. It had not been a question of money or the payment of debts, for the lower house had passed a bill to pay both state and federal debts by a state impost. Later in the year an impost bill was introduced which specified that the money must be used only for the debt. This proviso apparently satisfied

63. Oliver Ellsworth to Samuel Holten, Oct. 28, 1783, Emmett Coll., No. 601, N.Y. Pub. Lib.; Jonathan Trumbull to Washington, Nov. 15, 1783, Jared Sparks, ed., *Correspondence of the American Revolution: Being Letters of Eminent Men to George Washington, from the Time of his Taking Command of the Army to the End of his Presidency*, 4 vols. (Boston, 1853), IV, 53.

64. Peter Colt to Jeremiah Wadsworth, Jan. 25, Feb. 28, 1784, Wadsworth Papers, Box 135, Conn. Hist. Soc.; Jonathan Trumbull to the Connecticut delegates in Congress, Feb. 3, 1784, Misc. letters, XVII, Mass. Hist. Soc.; *Conn. Gazette* (New London), Feb. 27, 1784; *Conn. Journal* (New Haven), Feb. 25, 1784.

most objections and the measure passed by a margin of ninety-three to twenty-four.[65]

Information is limited concerning the remaining New England state, New Hampshire. It had adopted the impost of 1781 promptly, but by 1783 some opposition had developed. "Independens" wrote against it,[66] and when Congress's request of 1783 was considered, the Assembly delayed, voting to send out an address to the people on the subject. This vote was reconsidered (42-31), and the impost eventually passed in January 1784.[67] The vote does not reveal any clear sectional division. Some of the interior towns still objected to the measure because it was associated with commutation, but in the fall of 1785 a convention of twenty-three towns from the south central section of the state announced in its favor.[68] Adoption would benefit the state economically, for it imported but little, and that fact may explain the relative lack of controversy.

New England was not alone in its suspicion of the impost. Opposition developed almost as soon, and lasted longer, in the South. Even had Rhode Island not rejected the 1781 request, it would have been defeated by Virginia, when in December 1782 she repealed her earlier grant.[69] Neither then nor later was a vote recorded. It seems, however, that at first support came largely from the Northern Neck and the James River areas, and that it was favored by most men who became Federalists, whereas future Antifederalists insisted upon limitations to the grant.[70]

---

65. *Independent Chronicle* (Boston), May 27, 1784; Hoadley and Labaree, eds., *Public Records of Connecticut*, V, 326-27.

66. *New Hampshire Gazette* (Portsmouth), Aug. 23, 1783.

67. Batchellor, ed., *New Hampshire State Papers*, VIII, 979; Metcalfe, ed., *Laws of New Hampshire*, IV, 537-39.

68. Batchellor, ed., *New Hampshire State Papers*, XI, 678, XII, 476, 762-76.

69. Hening, ed., *Statutes of Va.*, X, 409-10, XI, 171.

70. For the mixture of motives involved, see R. H. Lee to R. Wormley Carter, June 3, 1783, Ballagh, ed., *Lee*, II, 282: "With all the dangerous train of concealed circumstances, this system presents ease in paying taxes, and plausibility in other respects, that will be very apt to delude and take in those minds that trouble not themselves to investigate consequences, or trace effects in their causes. Besides the danger to liberty that it threatens, I much fear that it will strangle our infant commerce in its birth, make us pay more than our proportion, and sacrifice this country to its northern brethren."

The act ratifying the impost of 1781 had been passed at Staunton, where the Assembly had taken refuge from Tarleton, and was therefore enacted under exceptional, emergency conditions, and, as Randolph expressed it, "without thought, and amidst the alarms of war."[71] When the legislature met again, the next year, the fighting was over, the emergency ended, and measures taken in haste could be repented at leisure. That Congress had financial problems was conceded by everyone, but the danger of such a grant of power convinced some that it should not be made under any conditions, while the majority felt that a federal impost would be desirable only if it were safeguarded: the tax collected by state officials, the grant made revocable, and any surplus over the state's quota on requisitions passed to the credit of the state.[72] The legislature therefore repealed the earlier grant and enacted no substitute.

When the legislature met again in May 1783, the members must have been startled to find Patrick Henry in favor of the measure. Henry felt, according to Randolph, that the burden would fall on wealthy consumers, rather than on his small farmer constituents. His immediate reason for changing his mind, however, was his desire to secure postponement of tax collections.[73] If he succeeded, the backcountry would be relieved, but money would still have to be raised for Congress. Henry was willing to assign the impost to Congress for this purpose. However, he ultimately failed to postpone tax collections, and since his constituents were now to be taxed in the usual way, the grant of the impost to Congress became pointless. Henry therefore changed sides again, and when he did, opposition to the impost became almost universal. According to Joseph Jones, only two members of the House favored it without qualifications.[74] It was obvious that Virginia would gain financially by retaining control of her impost: she could collect duties on goods consumed not only by her large population, but

71. To Madison, Dec. 13, 1782, Jan. 3, 1783, Madison Papers, III, Lib. Cong.
72. Edmund Pendleton to Madison, May 4, 1783, Gratz Coll., Old Congress, Box 9, Hist. Soc. Pa.; Joseph Jones to Madison, May 25, June 8, 21, 1783, Ford, ed., *Letters of Jones*, 107, 112, 121.
73. Randolph to Madison, May 24, 1783, Madison Papers, IV, Lib. Cong.
74. Joseph Jones to Madison, June 8, 14, 21, 1783, Ford, ed., *Letters of Jones*, 112, 116, 121.

by North Carolinians, who imported large amounts by way of their northern neighbor. Hence, in response to Congress's request, a bill was drafted which in form granted the impost, but required that all the proceeds go to the credit of the state.

At this juncture the legislature received an urgent plea from George Washington. Although some members called it an "unsolicited intrusion," it favorably influenced others toward the impost, and near the end of the session a bill was introduced which nearly coincided with Congress's request.[75] By a slight majority it was ordered to lie on the table.[76] But the tide had definitely turned, and before the year's end the impost was accepted. It was for some "a bitter pill, but finding it must be swallowed, they ceased at length to make opposition."[77] Perhaps Henry had changed his mind again—his home county (Prince Edward) petitioned in favor of the impost in 1784. Another major opponent, George Mason, was now willing to accept it, and the contest was closed in Virginia.[78]

The course of events in South Carolina was somewhat similar. The impost of 1781 had been approved in February 1782, but a year later the grant was withdrawn. By that time both Rhode Island and Virginia had rejected it, and New York was changing her mind. The only anti-impost article to be published in the state presented the usual objections: "Hampden" referred to the sword and the purse, a permanent revenue, and a "charter of slavery."[79] In addition, there was such prejudice against Robert Morris that

75. Washington, Circular Letter to the States, June 8, 1783, John C. Fitzpatrick, ed., *The Writings of George Washington*, 37 vols. (Washington, 1931-1940), XXVI, 483-96; Randolph to Madison, June 28, 1783, Madison Papers, IV, Lib. Cong.; Joseph Jones to Madison, June 28, 1783, Ford, ed., *Letters of Jones*, 124.

76. Thomson Mason to John Francis Mercer, June 22, 1783, Rowland, *Mason*, II, 59; Mason to Mercer, June 27, 1783, Mercer Papers, Va. Hist. Soc.; R. H. Lee to William Whipple, June 1, 1783, Ballagh, ed., *Lee*, II, 285; the *Independent Chronicle* (Boston), Aug. 21, 1783.

77. Joseph Jones to Jefferson, Dec. 29, 1783, Ford, ed., *Letters of Jones*, 136-37; Hening, ed., *Statutes of Va.*, XI, 350-52. Jefferson also called it a "pill we were to swallow." To Madison, May 7, 1783, Boyd, ed., *Papers of Jefferson*, VI, 266.

78. Petition, June 1, 1784, Va. State Lib.; Madison to Jefferson, Dec. 10, 1783, Boyd, ed., *Papers of Jefferson*, VI, 377.

79. Cooper, ed., *Statutes of S.C.*, IV, 512-13; *S. C. Weekly Gazette* (Charleston), Mar. 22, 1783.

some were unwilling to grant any money he might control. General Greene had made himself unpopular and aroused suspicion of the army by interfering in state affairs, reminding some of the dangers of centralized authority.[80] In the summer of 1783 the legislature refused to approve Congress's request. According to David Ramsay, the state objected to permanent funds, and believed that collections ought to be made by the state and for the credit of the state.[81] Washington's circular letter caused some members to reverse themselves to the extent of conceding that Congress might appropriate the money from a 5 per cent tax, but they still held to the idea that it should be collected by state officials. Not until March 1784 did the legislature finally comply with Congress's wishes.[82] David Ramsay asserted that opposition to the impost in South Carolina was grounded in economic considerations rather than a philosophical reluctance to increase federal powers, but he himself had previously testified to the contrary; moreover a minority of the Senate published a report which criticized the grant in political as well as economic terms.[83]

The extent and source of the opposition in South Carolina can only be conjectured. The impost of 1781 was repealed in 1783 by so large a majority (61-23) as to prove that there must have been objectors both in the east and in the west. In 1784 the bill passed by a margin of three to one, which suggests a general change of heart.[84] The historian Charles Gregg Singer asserts that the upland regions were against the measure, and that they were joined in 1783 by many delegates from the east. That some eastern planters continued to criticize it is proved by Ralph Izard's observation in

80. Singer, *South Carolina in the Confederation*, 74; Greene to Washington, Mar. 16, 1783, Sparks, ed., *Correspondence of the Revolution*, IV, 5; Alexander Gillon to Arthur Lee, Nov. 29, 1783, Harv. Coll. Lib. (photostatic copy, Lee Papers, Univ. of Va. Lib.).

81. To Benjamin Rush, Aug. 22, 1783, Rush Papers, Phila. Lib. Co.; Madison to Randolph, Aug. 18, 1783, Burnett, ed., *Letters*, VII, 269.

82. Greene to Washington, Aug. 8, 1783, Sparks, ed., *Correspondence of the Revolution*, IV, 38; Cooper, ed., *Statutes of S.C.*, IV, 570, 594-96.

83. Ramsay to William Gordon, June 23, 1784, Misc. Papers, N.Y. Pub. Lib.; Senate Journal, 1784, 289-90, quoted in Singer, *South Carolina in the Confederation*, 84-85.

84. *Ibid.*, 72; *Gazette of State of S.-C.* (Charleston), Mar. 18, 1784.

1784 that "Considerable opposition was given to it by some of the ablest, and most respectable Men in this Country." [85] It seems most likely that opposition existed in all parts of the state, even in Charleston, but that the principal support came from the east and gradually extended westward.

Information concerning the other Southern states is scanty. Maryland approved the 1781 impost but did not formally ratify it until the spring of 1782—a delay which suggests that there was some opposition. But in 1783 the state granted Congress's second request promptly.[86] North Carolina, dominated by representatives of the small farmers, acted quickly in 1781 and again in 1783. The only opponents on record were a lawyer representing the merchants and a future Antifederalist (Thomas Person) who spoke for the farmers.[87] Most North Carolinians preferred a duty on imports to any other kind of federal tax, such as a tax on land, and they were quite willing to assign the impost to Congress, since Virginia and South Carolina levied and collected import duties which were ultimately paid by North Carolina consumers. Under existing circumstances, the state derived neither revenue nor credits from these taxes paid by her inhabitants, and was to this extent victimized by its neighbors.[88]

Georgia refused to pass the impost until 1786. Since all of the attention in Congress was centered on Rhode Island, there was little comment on Georgia's inaction, particularly since the state was unrepresented in Congress at crucial times and could not be called to account. It was well known however that the state's position was no mere oversight; Madison referred to "jealousy and delays." [89] The opposition was general: in February 1783 the Assembly postponed an impost grant by a wide margin (30-6). The

85. Singer, *South Carolina in the Confederation*, 73-75; Izard to Jefferson, Apr. 27, 1784, Boyd, ed., *Papers of Jefferson*, VII, 130.

86. William Kilty, ed., *The Laws of Maryland*, 2 vols. (Annapolis, 1799-1800), I, chap. 48 (June 15, 1782), chap. 26 (June 1, 1783).

87. Hon. A. Maclaine to George Hooper, Feb. 25, 1783, Clark, ed., *State Recs. of N.C.*, XVI, 941; *ibid.*, XVII, 944.

88. North Carolina delegates to Congress to the governor of North Carolina, Sept. 26, 1783, Burnett, ed., *Letters*, VII, 312; Hugh Williamson to Governor Martin, Sept. 30, 1784, Clark, ed., *State Recs. of N.C.*, XVII, 99.

89. To Randolph, July 2, 1782, Burnett, ed., *Letters*, VI, 378.

small minority was scattered about the state.[90] Not until three years later did Georgia finally yield, passing at the same time other measures supporting Congress, over "warm and violent opposition." [91]

Among the four middle states, three supported Congress without much dispute. In Delaware there is no evidence of any opposition to the impost, and the state agreed promptly to Congress's two requests. New Jersey favored a federal impost for reasons of economic self-interest: its citizens had large sums invested in federal certificates and expected to receive far more than they would pay; moreover if the impost were not ratified the state would continue to be taxed by New York's impost.[92] Pennsylvania readily granted the first impost in April 1781. Although critical articles presently appeared in the newspapers, and although two of the ablest were written by Pennsylvanians, the impost of 1783 also passed without delay. The state, which imported heavily, would surely pay a considerable share of the tax, but her citizens would collect a very large amount because they held a high proportion of the federal debt. It is perhaps this fact that accounts for the willingness of many Constitutionalists to acquiesce in payment of the debt by federal taxes which would operate throughout the Union rather than by individual state action. In any event, there was never much dispute over the impost in Pennsylvania.

Quite different was the fate of the impost in New York. Congress's first request of 1781 was accepted promptly and without debate.[93] If it is true, as has been stated, that Governor Clinton opposed it even then, neither he nor his supporters tried to block

90. Candler, comp., *Revolutionary Records of Georgia*, III, 274-75. A series of presentments of grand juries in 1785-86 which, copied in Northern papers, made it appear that Georgians were overwhelmingly in favor of the impost, are deceptive: actually they merely parroted George Walton, who presided. One jury failed to obey his injunction to present as a grievance the lack of an impost, and the response of another was vague, but most repeated what he had said, dutifully, word for word. *Gazette of State of Georgia* (Savannah), Mar. 10, 24, Apr. 7, 14, 21, 1785; *Pa. Packet* (Phila.), Jan. 24, 1786; *American Herald* (Boston), Feb. 13, 1786.

91. Abraham Baldwin to Charles Thomson, Feb. 14, 1786, Papers of Charles Thomson, N. Y. Hist. Soc., *Collections*, 1878, 202-23; Gen. Nathanael Greene to Thomson, Apr. 24, 1786, *ibid.*, 208; Candler, comp., *Colonial Records of Georgia*, XIX, pt. 2, 492-98, 552-53, 554-56.

92. McCormick, *New Jersey in the Critical Period*, 170-71, 233.

93. *Laws of N. Y., 1777-1784*, 347-49.

it, and it was favored by the merchants. It had been passed "hastily," so it was later said, and "without consideration, . . . at a time when the enemy were in possession of two-thirds of the state." [94] By 1783, however, a division had developed, not over the passage of an impost bill but over the extent of Congress's control. In March, a clause which provided that collectors must be approved by the governor and the Council of Appointment failed by a single vote. [95] The division revealed an alignment corresponding to that on other issues: supporters of Congressional power came from the south, near New York City, and they were aided by delegates of Albany. But opinion was swinging against the impost. When in April Congress renewed its request, the state refused to act.

The change of opinion that occurred with the end of the war was signalized by the publication, beginning in August, of a series of "Rough Hewer" articles written by the Clintonian, Abraham Yates. [96] Thenceforth, the Clintonians consistently refused to accede to the impost in the required form. In 1786 they defeated an attempt to give Congress control over collection by a vote of thirty-three to twenty-two, and, as we have seen, the grant they extended to Congress required that New York's paper money, which the Clintonians had forced through in 1784, be accepted in payment of duties. A year later they again defeated an attempt to make the impost grant conform with Congress's stipulation. The test vote in 1787 came on the old question of control over the collecting officers; by a vote of thirty-eight to nineteen the Assembly insisted upon retaining this authority in the state. [97]

The two votes just described demonstrate that the New York City and Albany merchants were anxious to grant Congress complete control over the impost. The only contrary votes registered

94. Cochran, *New York in the Confederation*, 136-37.

95. New York Assembly Journal, 1781-1783, 151, N. Y. State Lib.

96. *N.Y. Gazetteer* (Albany), Aug. 4, Oct. 6, 20, Nov. 3, 1783. Other articles originating in the state were "Casca," "Sidney," "Rough Hewer, Jr.," "Philo Patria," and "A Republican."

97. New York Assembly Journal, 1786, 134, 1787, 52, N. Y. State Lib.; *Laws of N. Y.*, *1785-1788*, 320-22. See the map in Spaulding, *New York in the Critical Period*, 280.

by delegates from the towns were those cast by representatives of mechanics, although a majority even of these were allied with the merchants. The city was supported also by the southern counties of Suffolk and Richmond; Westchester was divided. The upstate counties, on the other hand, insisted that the state retain control over taxation, voting forty-six to four on these two roll calls.[98] These counties were the paper money stronghold. The relationship between the two issues is to be found in the act itself and in the fact that the delegates who favored paper money opposed the impost, and those who disliked the impost supported paper money. The exceptions to this generalization were mainly the delegates from Kings, Queens, Westchester, and Albany— counties which were the battleground between opposing sides on this as on other questions.

From what has been said, it is evident that no generalizations concerning the division over the impost can be made without serious qualification and without taking cognizance of changes in attitude that occurred with the passage of time. Until the victory at Yorktown, the impost had the character of emergency legislation, for Congress could not successfully wage war without money. When the emergency passed in 1782 and peace negotiations were opened with England, the unlimited grant of power and the complete control demanded by Congress inspired a reversal of opinion. By the spring of 1783, the request was encountering heavy opposition in Massachusetts, Rhode Island, Virginia, South Carolina, New York, and Georgia, and had been ratified by Connecticut only with qualifications. Congress's revised edition of the impost, adopted in April 1783, was less objectionable to the states, but dislike of commutation, fear of the army, and suspicion of Robert Morris for a time impeded its progress. These underlying objections could not be altogether overcome by Washington's appeals, nor by the discharge of the Continental army.

Merchants had been prominent among those who opposed Congress's first request for an impost in 1781. In Rhode Island, in Massachusetts to a large degree, and quite possibly in other states,

98. These were the counties of Dutchess, Ulster, Washington, and Montgomery,

they were first to elaborate the anti-impost argument. In doing so they merely invoked political ideas in common circulation and adapted them to the needs of the moment. The chief reasons for their objections, however, were local and personal economic interests. Some felt that the impost would be a burdensome tax on commerce; others thought they would be unable to pass the tax on to consumers. Still others were angered by the dominance of Robert Morris, jealous of his power, and suspicious that any measure he favored would benefit him at their expense. But except in Rhode Island, where opposition persisted longer, their attitude soon changed. It now appeared that the tax could indeed be passed on to consumers. Morris faded from the scene. The impost was no longer a fund to back Congress's applications for foreign loans, but a source of income which might enable Congress to pay its domestic debts. To security-holders, the impost represented specie payment, and to all merchants, it symbolized financial regularity. By the middle of 1783, if not before, the commercial interest was pro-impost, and the cities had become centers of agitation in behalf of the grant.

The attitude of farmers went through a similar process of increasing definition. It was at first conceivable, perhaps, that the impost would be paid by the city dwellers, or, as Henry thought, by the "wealthy consumer," but either this notion faded or other factors became paramount, for after the first months the center of opposition shifted to the agricultural interior. In Massachusetts, Rhode Island, Connecticut, and New York, the division on the impost followed the familiar lines of sectional cleavage that ranged non-commercial against commercial interests on other issues of state politics. In Virginia, and probably in South Carolina, anti-impost sentiment was strongest in the Piedmont, in regions farthest from the ocean and the major rivers. Generally speaking, the adherents of paper money were hostile to the grant.

It should be stressed that farmers were not unanimous in their opposition. As consumers, their interest would perhaps be adversely affected by the impost, and the grant of power violated their preference for weak central government; but these considerations were often balanced by other factors. The few farmers who held securities could expect to benefit from federal funding of the debt.[99] More important in shaping attitudes, however, was a calculation of the general gain or loss to the state, in which the farmers as citizens would share. New Hampshire, for example, did not consume many imported goods, and hence would pay little of the tax. The unequal distribution of the federal debt was a factor: citizens of Pennsylvania and New Jersey had exceptionally large holdings, and if Congress funded the debt, more money would flow into these states as interest payments than their citizens would pay towards the impost. Certainly the tax could be expected to benefit states like New Jersey, which imported goods through New York and thus paid import duties collected by her neighbor. Finally, in all states there was a considerable number of completely or nearly self-sufficient farmers who would pay almost nothing toward the impost, whereas if each state discharged its own share of the federal debt, they would surely be forced to contribute. Generally speaking, only a few states—Massachusetts, Rhode Island, New York, Virginia, and perhaps South Carolina—had any substantial economic reason to reject the impost, and within these states whole sections and socio-economic groups stood to benefit in some way from its adoption. Doubtless this fact explains why the non-commercial, soon to be Antifederal, groups were divided—why the Clintonians and the inland Rhode Islanders objected to the impost but the Constitutionalists of Pennsylvania did not, why western Massachusetts stood with Virginians against it but all of North Carolina was on the other side.

The complexity of the alignment was increased by the fact that, whatever the economic interests involved, opposition was not so much to *an* impost as to *the* impost—in the form recommended and insisted upon by Congress. It has been previously observed that the objection was not to the money but to the power, and in state after state the real controversy was not over granting Congress the revenue from a 5 per cent duty but whether the grant should be hedged about with restrictions. By 1786 every state had offered the grant under various limitations. While it is obvious that objections on purely political grounds cannot fully account for the opposition, it is also obvious that objections based solely

99. For evidence that few farmers held federal securities, see Ferguson, *Power of the Purse*, 274, 281.

upon economic factors do not explain the situation. Where the measure was expected to be an economic benefit, it was accepted— sometimes reluctantly; where it was thought to be a desirable political reform, it was also supported; where it was considered to be neither, it was rejected or revised. It was rejected above all in those areas and by those persons who were to become Antifederalists, and the arguments they developed in opposition to the impost were soon to be employed in a greater debate.

Chapter V

ANTIFEDERALISTS VS. NATIONALISTS: COMMUTATION, COMMERCE, AND THE CONVENTION

WHILE the final battles over the impost were being fought in 1786, the attention of Congress was already turning toward more extensive reforms. The opponents of centralization were not unwilling to strengthen the government under the Articles of Confederation, but they continued to be skeptical of any radical change and suspected the motives of those who advocated it. This suspicious attitude was illustrated in 1785, when the Massachusetts legislature forwarded resolutions to its delegates in Congress recommending a convention to revise the Articles.[1] The delegates replied that a convention would be dangerous, for "plans have been artfully laid, and vigorously pursued, which had they been successful, We think would inevitably have changed our republican Governments into baleful Aristocracies. . . . We are apprehensive and it is our Duty to declare it, that such a Measure would produce thro'out the Union, an Exertion of the Friends of an Aristocracy, to send Members who would promote a Change of Government: and We can form some Judgment of the plan, which such members would report to Congress."[2]

The authors of this reply were neither ignorant nor extremists. Elbridge Gerry, future Antifederalist leader, was a well-to-do merchant; Samuel Holten, Antifederal doctor, ultimately ceased his opposition and withheld his vote in the Massachusetts ratifying

1. *Acts and Resolves, Public and Private, of the Province of the Massachusetts Bay* (Boston, 1869-1922), 1784-1785, 666-68, 706-11.
2. Sept. 3, 1785, Burnett, ed., *Letters*, VIII, 208.

convention; and Rufus King was soon to become an ardent Federalist. There were others who shared their opinion. Samuel Osgood had informed John Adams the year before of the danger "that if permanent Funds are given to Congress, the aristocratical Influence, which predominates in more than a Major Part of the United States will finally establish an arbitrary Government in the United States."[3] The same idea often recurs in Stephen Higginson's letters, and in 1787, after he was beginning to change his mind, he wrote, "I sometimes almost lament that the Aristocracy in 1783 was suppressed."[4] This conviction on the part of some well-informed individuals that attempts had been and would be made to establish an aristocracy was shared by a large number of people, and it became a fundamental assumption of the Antifederalists.

To what extent this idea was justified is irrelevant; the significant fact is its existence. Yet the Antifederal position is better understood if some of the evidence for the conviction is described. The Antifederalists were well aware that there were in all of the states many men who wanted to change the form of government,[5] that most of them were too skeptical of the common man's judgment to have any faith in a democratic system unless it was much modified, and that they preferred either an aristocracy—that is, government by the better sort of people, meaning themselves—or (a small minority) monarchy.[6] Such views were expressed in the newspapers and magazines, sometimes quite openly, as in this comment from the New York *Daily Advertiser*: "Of all the evils which attend the republican form of government, there are none

3. Jan. 14, 1784, *ibid.*, VII, 414.
4. To Samuel Osgood, Feb. 7, 1787, Osgood Papers, N.Y. Hist. Soc.
5. See especially Merrill Jensen, "The Idea of a National Government During the American Revolution," *Political Science Qtly.*, 58 (1943), 356-79.
6. One favorable reference to democracy by a strong Federalist is Henry Knox to Theophilus Parsons, Mar. 29, 1785: "A social compact so constituted, that a very small minority shall operate to check the great Majority cannot be upon durable principles. . . . When one considers the inestimable value of Liberty he cannot hesitate to prefer a democracy to every other form of government." Knox Papers, XVIII, 14, Mass. Hist. Soc. This statement is almost unique. On monarchy see Louise Burnham Dunbar, *A Study of "Monarchical" Tendencies in the United States, from 1776 to 1801* (n.p., 1920).

that seem to have more pernicious effects than the *insolence* which liberty implants into the lower orders of society." [7]

The Articles of Confederation had located power in the state governments, and many opposed this from the first; to others, who might otherwise have opposed it, the situation was satisfactory so long as they could control those governments. The trouble was that, in John Lloyd's words, "Gentlemen of property" too frequently lost electoral contests to men from the "lower classes"; [8] moreover things were getting worse rather than better as these lower classes demanded economic and political concessions. Shays's Rebellion frightened the gentlemen badly. One worried citizen warned that the rebel demands, if granted, "must end in an abolition of all public & private debts and then an equal distribution of Property may be demanded. The Constitution is not democratick enough in the Opinions of these Geniouses." [9] The trouble, as Edmund Randolph put it, lay in "the turbulence and follies of democracy." [10] One obvious solution was to transfer power from the states and construct a national government in which the well-to-do would have, at least, a veto power. In a widely circulated article, "Harrington" insisted that "the more we abridge the states of their sovereignty, . . . the more safety, liberty, and prosperity will be enjoyed by each of the states." [11] Such a highly centralized government could then be freed from popular control, for were all power held by the people, "disorder and tyranny must ensue." [12] Antifederalists reasoned from much the same premises, but their value judgments were different. To them,

7. July 15, 1786. See also "A Citizen of America," in the *Columbian Herald* (Charleston), Mar. 24, 1788; *ibid.*, Jan. 11, 1787; *U. S. Chronicle* (Providence), Mar. 13, 1788; *Virginia Independent Chronicle* (Richmond), Dec. 5, 1787; *New Haven Gazette*, Nov. 30, 1786; *Conn. Courant* (Hartford), Aug. 6, 1787; "Nestor," in the *Independent Gazetteer* (Phila.), June 3, 1786, reprinted in many other papers; *ibid.*, June 20, 1787; "A Bostonian," in the *American Museum*, 1 (1787), 294-306; "Pro Republica," in the *Columbian Magazine*, 1 (1786-1787), 171-74.

8. To T. B. Smith, Dec. 7, 1784, in Phillips, "South Carolina Federalists," *Am. Hist. Rev.*, 14 (1908-1909), 537.

9. David Sewall to George Thatcher, Oct. 16, 1786, *Hist. Mag.*, 16 (1869), 257.

10. Farrand, ed., *Records of the Federal Convention*, I, 51.

11. *American Museum*, 1 (1786), 494.

12. "Sidney," in *ibid.*, 2 (1787), 81.

the attempt to strengthen the central government was identical with the attempt to solidify upper class rule, and this they opposed.

Efforts to establish a strong central government had taken various forms. One was the impost amendment. When that failed, it had been argued that Congress might simply assume powers implied in the Articles or inherent in the nature of any government, and during the last months of the war, some of the Nationalists had tried to use the army to gain their ends.[13] This conspiracy, perhaps more than anything else, excited the fears of future Antifederalists and aroused suspicion of attempts to increase Congress's powers—the argument over half-pay and commutation must be considered in the light of these apprehensions. Finally, the question of constitutional revision was involved in the debate over giving Congress the power to regulate trade. The last two issues require fuller discussion.

The Articles of Confederation registered the general fear of standing armies. Congress was prohibited from maintaining a peacetime force except for internal defense. In war, Congress requested the states to provide troops, which were taken under Congressional direction, but all officers below the rank of general were appointed by the states, and the taxes necessary to support an army were, of course, levied by the states.[14] Even this degree of restriction was not enough to appease some foes of centralization, and their fears were aroused in 1780, when, in order to forestall a mass resignation of military officers, Congress promised half-pay pensions for life to those who would remain in service for the war's duration. This act was widely censured, particularly in New England, and Congress did nothing to redeem the promise until 1783, when, as we have seen, the half-pay for life was "commuted" into a grant of five years' full pay.[15] Congress lacked

13. Jensen's account is excellent. See *The New Nation*, 69-82.

14. "Cato," in the *Continental Journal* (Boston), Jan. 30, 1783; letter of Arthur Lee, Feb. 21, 1783, in Bancroft, *History of the Constitution*, I, 91; "Sidney" in the *N.Y. Packet*, Mar. 17, 1785, often republished elsewhere. The union of "purse and sword" was a danger frequently emphasized even when the army had almost ceased to exist after the war.

15. See the discussion by Jensen, *The New Nation*, 72-73. For the original grant of half-pay, see Hatch, *Revolutionary Army*, 79-85.

funds to honor this commitment, but the impost of 1783, along with a supplementary fund to be raised by state taxes, which Congress also requested at this time, was expected to provide the money to take care of all federal debts. The impost and the whole question of increasing federal powers therefore became entangled with the dispute over commutation, and matters were further complicated by the formation of the Society of Cincinnati, an hereditary, secret organization of veteran army officers. The Cincinnati was widely suspected of a design to create a permanent nobility and exert political influence [16]—Antifederalists were later to accuse the Society of deliberately fomenting Shays's Rebellion as part of a deep plot to overturn the government.[17] It was known, at least, that in 1783 some of the officers of the army had conspired with members of Congress in an attempt to force the states to grant federal taxes.

Future Antifederalists were prominent among those who feared the army's political power and opposed military pensions or any other measure which would differentiate the army from the general body of the population and perhaps contribute to the formation of a military caste. In South Carolina, Judge Aedanus Burke led the attack on the Cincinnati. In Massachusetts, half-pay and commutation were supported by the seacoast towns, but the interior was so much opposed that passage of the impost was greatly delayed.

The most extensive and interesting controversy occurred in Connecticut, where the officers were accused of attempting to profit at the expense of the people, who had contributed as much as they had to the war and were suffering equally from the depression.[18] In 1783 the citizens of Killingworth took note of the dangerous game which some of the Nationalists had been playing with the

16. Jensen, *The New Nation*, 261-65.
17. See *n.* 76, chap. III.
18. Resolutions of Farmington, in the *Conn. Courant* (Hartford), Aug. 12, 1783. Connecticut had opposed the half-pay proposal from the beginning. See especially Samuel Huntington to the governor of Connecticut, Oct. 26, 1780, Burnett, ed., *Letters*, V, 429 and *ibid.*, 430n.; Wallace E. Davies, "The Society of the Cincinnati in New England, 1783-1800," *Wm. and Mary Qtly.*, 3rd Ser., 5 (1948), 4-7. There is an account of the affair in William H. Glasson, *Federal Military Pensions in the United States* (New York, 1918), 44-47.

army: "every one must naturally infer that Congress were greatly engaged to get funds . . . in some way and manner, not fixed and established by the articles of confederation—and for that reason, were disposed to secure the interest and influence of the army to effect it."[19] It was argued that Congress did not have power to grant pensions, and that to permit it to assume such a power would establish a dangerous precedent. Powers not specifically granted to Congress remained with the people, from whose ultimate authority there was no appeal, and for Congress to grant a pension was "unconstitutional, unjust and oppressive."[20] The town of Norwich warned its delegates that the people could not escape God's "Just Resentment" if they delegated such control over property to men "so far out of our Reach."[21] Most comprehensive of all was the protest of Farmington. After noting the expense and the unfair discrimination in favor of officers, the town condemned commutation:

Because it is founded on Principles Subertive of a Republican Government Tending to Destroy that Equallity among the citisans which [is] the only permanent foundation on which it can be supported to throw an excessive Power, the constant attendent of property into the Hands of the Few, to cherish those anti-republican Principles & feelings which are now predominent in many of the states. and finally to dissolve our present Happy and Benev-

19. *Conn. Courant* (Hartford), Sept. 2, 1783.

20. Torrington, *ibid.*, July 29, 1783. See also resolutions of Canaan, in *ibid.*, Oct. 14, 1783; "Civis," in *ibid.*, July 24, 1783; town of Lebanon, in the *Conn. Gazette* (New London), May 2, 1783. The following instructions of Hartford to its delegates (Sept. 16, 1783) were copied almost word for word by Ashford (Oct. 3), Wallingford (Sept. 29), and probably by others: "And first (Gentlemen) Wee desire and expresly instruct you strenuously to oppose, all Encroachments of the American Congress, upon the Sovereignty and Jurisdiction of the seperate States, and every assumption of Power not expresly vested in them by the articles of Confederation. And in particular, Wee desire and instruct you to move, or pursue, a strict and Thorough Investigation of the great and interesting Question (to wit) Whether Congress were authorized by the federal Constitution to grant half pay for life to the Officers of the Army, or five years full Pay, as an Equivalent, and how and in what Manner it was obtained. That if upon due Enquirey an Examination, the measure shall appear to be unfounded, and come into by Surprize—That then you attempt, every constitutional method for its Removal." Extracts from the Hartford town records, Conn. State Lib.

21. Extract from Norwich Revolutionary Records, May 1, 1783, *ibid.*

olent Constitution & to erect on the Ruins, a proper Aristocracy: wherein the Body of the People are excluded from all share in the Government, and the Direction & mannagement of the state is committed to the Great & Powerful alone.[22]

Unwilling to trust their legislature, the anti-commutation men resorted to the familiar method of a convention, which met in Middletown in September 1783. The convention stated its purpose to conduct "the most candid and thorough enquiry into the nature, extent and power of Congress" and to determine whether those powers had been exceeded. Since representatives of only twenty-eight towns appeared, it was decided to adjourn in order to give other towns more time to appoint delegates.[23] The convention reassembled in November with a majority of towns in the state present. A petition condemning commutation was sent to the legislature, and a standing committee appointed which was headed by Captain Hugh Ledlie of Hartford and composed, incidentally, mostly of officers.[24] Another meeting was held in March 1784. The delegates repeated their criticism of commutation, attacked the Cincinnati, and favored passage of a bill to pay the state and federal debts by a state impost.[25] The convention planned to meet again, but now opinion was changing. Newspapers were almost universally hostile to further conventions; Samuel Adams responded to an appeal to speak out against them; the impost passed, and the controversy came to an end.[26] In Connecticut, as elsewhere in New England, the anti-commutation feeling was strongest in the interior of the state, in the agricultural upland villages, so many of which were soon to oppose the Constitution.

22. Extracts from Farmington Revolutionary Records, May 6, 1783, *ibid.*
23. *Conn. Gazette* (New London), Aug. 29, Sept. 12, 1783.
24. *Conn. Courant* (Hartford), Nov. 4, Dec. 23, 1783. Ledlie had served as a captain in the French and Indian War, and later was one of the Windham Sons of Liberty. He eventually moved to Hartford and became a rabid Antifederalist. Hoadly and Labaree, eds., *Public Records of Connecticut,* XI, 485, XII, 232, 444; Leake, *Lamb,* 4.
25. *Conn. Journal* (New Haven), Apr. 7, 1784; *Conn. Gazette* (New London), Mar. 5, Apr. 2, 1784.
26. Peter Colt to Jeremiah Wadsworth, Mar. 28, 1784, Wadsworth Papers, Box 135, Conn. Hist. Soc.; *Conn. Courant* (Hartford), Apr. 20, 1784; *Conn. Journal* (New Haven), Apr. 7, 21, 28, 1784; Noah Webster to Samuel Adams, Mar. 24, 1784, Samuel Adams Papers, N.Y.

The controversy over the nature of the Union complicated the dispute as to whether Congress should be given power to regulate trade. It is often difficult to say whether the hostility aroused by the suggestion stemmed from Southern fears of Northern commercial domination, agrarian distrust of merchants, or the Antifederal determination to limit Congressional powers. The last argument, to be sure, was no doubt often used to conceal the existence of the others; nevertheless the foes of the commerce grant nearly always defined the issue in terms of principle. In Georgia, "Agricola" observed: "The high sounding terms of sovereignty and independence have caught and inflamed the minds of some, and the dread of losing our liberty, by giving power to Congress, has intoxicated and alarmed those of others."[27] Abraham Yates, Jr., of New York wrote to David Howell, "I ... agree with you *that the power giving system* is not abandoned. ... I am rather suspitious that the advocates for augmenting the powers of Congress will try to make Commercial Regulations—I think this question should be *watched*."[28] In Massachusetts, "Jonathan of the Valley" likewise warned against a general power to regulate trade; he admitted the existence of a commercial "crisis" but insisted that only a limited grant should be made.[29] Samuel Bryan, son of the Pennsylvania Constitutionalist leader, also felt that Congressional regulation of commerce was necessary, but believed that in order "to prevent Congress in that event absorbing all power and influence within their vortex" the duties should be collected by state officers and paid into the state treasuries. He

---

Pub. Lib.; Samuel Adams to Noah Webster, Apr. 30, 1784, Cushing, ed., *Writings of Adams*, IV, 305-6. Adams had previously refused to support Ledlie's campaign against half-pay and commutation. Ledlie to Adams, Sept. 9, 1783, Adams to Ledlie, Sept. 25, 1783, Adams Papers (photostatic copy), XVI, Lib. Cong. In a letter to John Adams he expressed the belief that conventions were "not only useless but dangerous." Apr. 16, 1784, Cushing, ed., *Writings of Adams*, IV, 296. See an article reviewing the controversy in Connecticut by "A Farmer," in the *Weekly Monitor* (Litchfield), Oct. 3, 1786. An exceedingly interesting account of commutation, the Cincinnati, and other questions, not friendly to the Antifederalists, is in the *Conn. Courant* (Hartford), Nov. 20, 1786, and the *Middlesex Gazette* (Middletown), Nov. 27, 1786.

27. *Gazette of State of Georgia* (Savannah), Sept. 29, 1785.
28. Aug. 29, 1785, Abraham Yates, Jr., Papers, N.Y. Pub. Lib.
29. *Independent Chronicle* (Boston), June 16, 1785.

concluded, "I am apprehensive that Congress will seize the present moment to obtain dangerous powers."[30] Elbridge Gerry similarly felt that any such powers ought to be temporary.[31]

In 1785 Congress proposed an amendment to the Articles which would give it the authority to impose taxes on trade, without a time limit, but under certain restrictions, including the proviso that duties were to be collected and expended by the states.[32] Although this proposal did not invade state control of taxation, it met strong opposition and finally failed. It is evident, however, that the limitations on its authority which Congress wrote into this proposal owed something to ideas forming part of Antifederal thought, as well as to Southern fears. Indeed, the commerce amendment of 1785 was not opposed by the Antifederalists, some of whom had been instrumental in drawing up the plan.

What the Antifederalists actually opposed was an unlimited, not a restricted, grant of the commercial power. Unfortunately, there is not enough evidence to permit a state-by-state analysis of the alignment. However in Virginia a vote was taken in 1785 on the question of giving Congress unlimited power to regulate trade. Support of the proposal came from the Northern Neck and from the James and York valleys, which included the commercial towns and the creditors. Opposed were the delegates from the Southside—the area west of the fall line and south of the James. The same alignment had been registered in a vote taken in 1784 on the question as to whether Virginia should conduct foreign affairs independently or only with the approval of Congress—if the state could disregard Congress, she indeed retained her sovereignty, as the Articles of Confederation declared.[33] The division on this issue, which is a pretty clear test case, was identical with that just described: the Northern Neck delegates and their allies supported Congress; the Southside stood for state authority.[34]

These votes indicate the alignment on Congressional powers

30. To George Bryan, May 1785, Bryan Papers, Box A24, Hist. Soc. Pa.
31. To Samuel Adams, Sept. 30, 1785, Burnett, ed., *Letters*, VIII, 224. See also "Fidelity," in the *Conn. Courant* (Hartford), Sept. 12, 1785.
32. Ford, ed., *Journals of Congress*, XXVI, 321-22, XXVIII, 201-5.
33. Journal of the House of Delegates, May Session, 1784, 74, Va. State Lib.
34. Northern Neck, 10-4, James-York group, 6-1, Southside, 4-17.

which underlies the history of the post-war years in Virginia and, as analysis of the whole range of federal issues suggests, in other states as well. The strongholds of resistance to federal powers were regions in which small, self-sufficient, and often debtor farmers were most numerous. Nathan Dane of Massachusetts testified at this time that opposition to stronger government came from "the yeomanry or the body of the people." [35] In a well-known passage, this point was elaborated by the French minister to the United States, Louis Otto, who observed that the people were aware that an increase of power in the central government would mean "a regular collection of taxes, a strict administration of justice, extraordinary duties on imports, rigorous executions against debtors—in short, a marked preponderance of rich men and of large proprietors." [36]

Objections on socio-economic grounds were mixed in with the traditional fear of centralized authority and suspicion of the motives of persons who were eager to extend federal powers. As early as 1782 the future Antifederalist Abraham Yates had his doubts amply confirmed in a conversation with Alexander Hamilton, who asked him:

Wether if the Financier appointed me [Yates] Receiver of Taxes I would promiss on Every Occasion to promote the view of the Financier [Morris] tho it should be against my oppinion & should Even I conceive it to be against the Intrest of the State. I got a little out of Temper I told him I was an Honest Man and Acted agreeable to the Dictate of my Conscience. He farther in Conversation told me he looked upon the Loan Office as useless that it ought to be put in the Hand, of the Receiver of Taxes or such other Person as was under the Immediate Direction of the Financier. I told him I thought the Financier had too much Power already and that Congress had better Curtail him—but I thought Congress could not now take it up as he had done Congress such Essential Service. [37]

Such suspicions as those of Abraham Yates were not without apparent foundation. An article written by "Nestor" in 1786 and

35. To Rufus King, Oct. 8, 1785, King, *King*, I, 69.
36. To Vergennes, Oct. 10, 1786, Bancroft, *Constitution*, II, 399.
37. To James Duane and Ezra L'Hommedieu, Oct. 19, 1782, Yates, Jr., Papers, N.Y. Pub. Lib.

widely reprinted projected a vision of the future that must have sounded ominous indeed to many people.[38] Not content with advocating Congressional power over commerce, he declared that a coercive power was necessary, that the one-house legislature was bad, that frequent rotation in office was undesirable, that the power to emit money should be restricted to Congress, and that the country was endangered by the existence of too much waste land: the westward movement should be controlled by requiring that one new state at a time be opened for settlement, and land offices closed until every part was populated.

Despite what seemed to many people the sinister auspices under which centralization was sometimes put forward, Antifederalist leaders could not oppose all changes in the Articles of Confederation, because they believed that some were needed. We have already seen that the impost—with proper safeguards, and the commercial power—with due restrictions, were both supported by many who looked with disfavor on a highly centralized government. An impressive number of Antifederal leaders favored some degree of stronger government before 1787, among them William Grayson, Timothy Bloodworth, Joseph Jones, James Monroe, James Warren, James Mercer, Elbridge Gerry, Benjamin Harrison, George Mason, Patrick Henry, John Francis Mercer, and George Clinton.[39]

38. *Independent Gazetteer* (Phila.), June 3, 1786; *American Herald* (Boston), June 19, 1786; *N.Y. Packet*, June 15, 1786; *Charleston Morning Post*, July 7, 1786; *American Museum*, 1 (1786), 9-13.

39. Grayson to Madison, May 28, 1786, to William Short, Apr. 16, 1787, Burnett, ed., *Letters*, VIII, 374, 581; Bloodworth to Richard Caswell, Sept. 4, 1786, *ibid.*, 462, and in Elliot, ed., *Debates*, IV, 70 (where he asserts that it was a well-known fact that he had favored granting Congress power over commerce); Jones to Madison, June 12, 1785, Ford, ed., *Letters of Jones*, 145; Monroe to Jefferson, June 16, 1785, Burnett, ed., *Letters*, VIII, 143-45 (and other letters in *ibid.*); James Warren to Washington, Sept. 2, 1785, Sparks, ed., *Correspondence of the Revolution*, IV, 114-15; James Mercer to John Francis Mercer, July 15, 1783, *Va. Mag. of Hist. and Biog.*, 59 (1951), 189; Gerry to Samuel Adams, Sept. 30, 1785, Adams Papers, N.Y. Pub. Lib.; Benjamin Harrison to the Virginia delegates, Dec. 21, 1782, in Burnett, ed., *Letters*, VI, 570n.; Mason in Madison to Jefferson, Dec. 10, 1783, Hunt, ed., *Writings of Madison*, II, 27-28; Henry in William Short to Jefferson, May 14, 1784, Boyd, ed., *Papers of Jefferson*, VII, 257 ("He saw Ruin inevitable unless something was done to give Congress a compulsory Process on delinquent States &c."); John Francis Mercer to James Madison, Nov. 12, 26,

When, therefore, the call for a convention was first issued at Annapolis, the opponents of major change were in a dilemma. Admitting that the Articles were imperfect, and acknowledging that amendments were almost impossible to obtain by the prescribed mode, they could not consistently reject the idea of a meeting, as long as that meeting was authorized only to recommend reforms within the existing constitutional framework. They therefore permitted Congress to endorse the convention, and hoped for the best. George Bryan, reminiscing some time after ratification, recalled the circumstances which had influenced the Antifederalists' decision:

Previous to the Appointment of the Convention there seemed to be in Pennsylvania a general Wish for a more efficient Confederation. The public Debt was unpaid & unfunded. We were deluged with foreign goods, which it was evident might have paid large Sums to the Continental Treasury, if Duties could have been generally laid & collected, & at the same time the levying such Duties would have checked the extravagant Consumption. Whilst Congress could only recommend Measures & the States individually could refuse to execute them it was obvious that we were in Danger of falling to pieces.[40]

At the same time, however, it was impossible to overlook the potentially evil consequences of the movement to revise the Articles. Mercy Warren, like Bryan, believed that "every man of sense is convinced a strong efficient government is necessary," but whereas "old patriots wish to see a form established on the pure principles of republicanism," others preferred an aristocracy or a monarchy and called for a standing army to suppress the few who still cherished the spirit of freedom.[41] Similarly "Amicus Patriae" wrote that there was no need to annihilate the state governments, for the situation required only that Congress be given the power to regulate trade and collect duties. This degree of authority

---

1784, Burnett, ed., *Letters*, VII, 609-10, 616; Clinton to Washington, Oct. 14, 1783, Washington Papers, CCXXVI, No. 11, Lib. Cong. The same also applies to men who were at first Antifederal and then changed, such as Nathan Dane and Samuel Osgood.

40. MS, no date, Bryan Papers, Hist. Soc. Pa.

41. To Mrs. Catherine Macauley, Aug. 2, 1787, Mercy Warren Letter Book 22, Mass. Hist. Soc.

should be tried for a few years, he thought, and if it proved mischievous, it could be repealed. No other powers were needed.[42] "Legion" agreed that everyone felt the powers of Congress should be increased "with great caution and circumspection," and he continued, "perhaps it would be best to grant the additional powers to Congress for a certain limited time, until it could be observed how they operated and answered the purpose. If they did, continue them—if not sufficient, enlarge them, until found adequate to the government of a great commercial people."[43] So also Samuel Adams, who approved of granting commercial power, was dubious about the Constitutional Convention, and in the Massachusetts legislature he tried to limit the authority of the state's delegates.[44] Perhaps his influence may be seen in the instructions which stated that the delegates were being sent "for the sole and express purpose of revising the Articles of Confederation."[45]

Such men as these were torn between their desire for change and their skepticism of Nationalist objectives, but they did not oppose the Convention. There were some others, to be sure, who altogether disapproved of it. "A.B." warned that it threatened liberty and freedom; people should guard against those who loved power.[46] "Jonathan of the Valley" had earlier warned that "some of the men who would compose the convention would be men of design, and intrigue," so that "a system of slavery would probably be the consequence."[47] In the Connecticut legislature a delegate from Enfield feared that "the state would send men that had been delicately bred, and who were in affluent circumstances, that could not feel for the people in this day of distress."[48]

42. *Continental Journal* (Boston), May 31, 1787.
43. *Independent Gazetteer* (Phila.), Apr. 13, 1787.
44. Gorham to Knox, Feb. 18, 1787, Knox Papers, XIX, 172, Mass. Hist. Soc.
45. Farrand, ed., *Records of the Federal Convention*, III, 584.
46. *Newport Mercury*, Jan. 29, 1787.
47. *Independent Chronicle* (Boston), Oct. 20, 1785.
48. *Conn. Courant* (Hartford), May 21, 1787, and other papers; David Humphreys to Washington, Jan. 20, 1787, Humphreys, *Humphreys*, I, 395; see the report of Louis Otto, June 10, 1787, quoted in Charles Warren, *The Making of the Constitution* (Boston, 1928), 206-7. Fear of what a convention might do was part of the general fear of delegated power. "Cassius" had

How large this group of total objectors was cannot be determined. The majority of Rhode Islanders certainly held this view, since they refused to send delegates to the Convention. But elsewhere future Antifederalists did participate.[49] New York sent Robert Yates and John Lansing (perhaps to keep an eye on Hamilton). The Antifederal state of North Carolina did not hesitate to appoint delegates, and in Massachusetts the Shaysite Antifederalist, Phanuel Bishop, declared, "We have long been sensible of the imbecility of the Confederation of the United States, and of the Consequences of that Imbecility, and therefore appointed delegates."[50] Probably the majority hoped that the Convention would succeed in finding a solution of the nation's problems within the framework of the Articles. The composition of that body, however, rendered it unlikely that any such moderate plan would be adopted.

The Convention which assembled at Philadelphia in the late spring of 1787 contained only a small handful of men who were opposed to a strong government and none who spoke out clearly for democracy. The proceedings do not therefore require an analysis from the point of view of Antifederalism, except for a criticism of their results, which will be the theme of the following chapters. But a few points may be made. The Antifederalists who attended did not represent the rank and file of the party but the propertied minority. George Mason of Virginia was one of the richest planters in the state. Edmund Randolph, also of Virginia, who began and ended as a Federalist with a brief Antifederal stage in between, was also an exceedingly wealthy man. Elbridge Gerry was a prosperous merchant of Massachusetts. John Lansing of Albany was a wealthy lawyer with commercial interests; Robert Yates of the same city was also a prominent lawyer, though with somewhat less property. John Francis Mercer, a young Virginian

---

expressed this feeling: "the investing any man or body of men with any degree of legislative authority, who are not under the immediate controul of the people, is contrary to every idea of a republican government." *Hudson Weekly Gazette* (N.Y.), Dec. 14, 1786.

49. Outside the convention, even R. H. Lee was now prepared for a stronger government. To Thomas Lee Shippen, July 22, 1787, and to John Adams, Sept. 5, 1787, Ballagh, ed., *Lee*, II, 427, 434.

50. Harding, *Ratification in Massachusetts*, 111n.

who had moved to Maryland, was personally in debt but he belonged to an important and wealthy family. Even Luther Martin, the only possible exception, was a prominent lawyer and politician.

When the Convention opened not one of this group made any objections to the initial statements of purpose; Mason and Gerry actually joined in the attack on democracy.[51] But as the delegates made clear the intent to establish a strong national government, the Antifederalists, one by one, drew back. The famous New Jersey plan, put forward to counter the Virginia plan—which represented the Nationalists' ideas—was supported not only by some of the delegates from small states but by Lansing and Yates of New York and by Martin (although not by Mason, who favored a strong government). This plan accorded with Antifederal ideas in that the Articles were retained as the fundamental basis of government. Congress would be given the right to lay duties on imports, to regulate trade, and to enforce the collection of requisitions; a plural executive with limited authority and a supreme court were added. The laws of Congress and treaties were declared to be supreme, and obedience to them compulsory. This plan certainly met the major criticisms of the Articles, and would have been acceptable to many, if not most Antifederalists; but the majority in the Convention rejected it, and from the Antifederal point of view, the defeat of the New Jersey plan was the turning point. Lansing, Yates, and Mercer withdrew. Gerry and Mason, who remained, found themselves half attracted, half repelled by the developments. Both came to feel that the democratic principle was not being sufficiently recognized,[52] and both joined Luther Martin in objecting to various aspects of the emerging plan,[53] although they approved of much that was being done. In the end, of course, all refused to sign. Randolph issued a list of objections, but presently reversed himself, while Mason, Gerry, Martin, Lansing, and Yates also justified their positions publicly and at length. The Constitution did not, therefore, represent the views or the influence even of the moderate Antifederalists, to say

51. Farrand, ed., *Records of the Federal Convention*, I, 48.
52. *Ibid.*, 101, 132, 134, 359, 364; II, 388.
53. For example, *ibid.*, I, 165, 233, 340-41, 437; II, 330, 362, 478.

nothing of the majority, and the hope that the Convention would produce a plan acceptable to them was disappointed.

While the Antifederalists within the Convention were being gradually disillusioned, those outside viewed the assemblage with mingled optimism and apprehension. Perhaps the attitude of David Redick of Pennsylvania fairly summarizes the ambivalent position of many. Redick, who became a severe critic of the Constitution, wrote while the Convention was holding its secret sessions, that "every plan for confederating a number of Sovereignties should be liberal in giving up partial conveniences, in order to bring them into as compact a body as possable, or at least, as close a body as Necessary: but [the "but" is typically Antifederal] it should be verry niggardly in giveing up any the least right of maintaining and Supporting such forms of internal Governments as the genius of the people is fited for." Moreover, the government should be made more democratic as the people became fitted for it. Redick was hopeful that the Convention might be a success, but he added, "I acknowledge I have still my fears whilst such as Guvero [Gouverneur Morris] and Turner the caledonian [James Wilson] are in the council, not that I think they lack knowledge: but that they are artfull, plausable men of influence, and I fear they may not be lovers of mankind."[54] Hopeful of moderate change, fearful of a radical one, the Antifederalists awaited the decision of the Convention. They were not reassured when Governor Clinton, doubtless acting on information from Lansing and Yates, let it be known that the outcome might be undesirable.[55] Their fears were to be realized.

54. To General William Irvine, Aug. 29, Sept. 10, 1787, Irvine Papers, IX, Hist. Soc. Pa.
55. In the *Daily Advertiser* (N. Y.), July 21, 1787, Hamilton denounced Clinton. See articles supporting the latter in the *N.Y. Journal*, Sept. 20, 1787 and the *Freeman's Journal* (Phila.), Aug. 22, 1787.

Chapter VI

ANTIFEDERAL OBJECTIONS
TO THE CONSTITUTION
PART I

WE have seen that the Antifederalists were divided as to whether the Convention was desirable. This difference of opinion is important, for it reveals the fact that the Antifederalists were far from united in their political ideas. By definition, an Antifederalist was anyone who opposed the ratification of the Constitution, and the word therefore included some who would have been satisfied with a few changes in the new plan and those who would not accept it under any conditions. Yet it is possible to exaggerate these differences, which after all existed among the Federalists too. Some Federalists who approved of the Constitution felt that the new government was too strong and needed amending once ratification had taken place; others believed that the new government was too weak. Some thought that the President should be replaced by a king, others that he should serve for life, still others that he was already too strong;[1] many wanted the states to retain varying degrees of power; a few wanted to abolish the states.[2]

1. David Humphreys to Hamilton, Sept. 16, 1787, Humphreys, *Humphreys*, I, 422; Washington to Madison, Mar. 31, 1787, Fitzpatrick, ed., *Writings of Washington*, XXIX, 190-91; Uriah Forrest to Jefferson, Dec. 11, 1787, Boyd, ed., *Papers of Jefferson*, XII, 416.

2. Edward Carrington to Jefferson, June 9, 1787, Mass. Hist. Soc., *Proceedings*, 2nd Ser., 17 (1903), 464-65; Hamilton memorandum on the Constitution, Hamilton Papers, 1st Ser., VII, Lib. Cong.; John Jay to John Adams, May 4, 1786, Johnston, *Jay*, III, 195; Knox to Washington, Aug. 14, 1786, Sparks, ed., *Correspondence of the Revolution*, IV, 176.

Other Federalists had a variety of objections.[3] All these differences emerge from the records of the Federal Convention and are disclosed in numerous letters, yet they existed within a broad area of agreement.

Like their opponents, the Antifederalists differed in opinion, but they too concurred in a few primary ideas. All of them, for example, believed that the Constitution created too strong a government.[4] The diversity in their attitudes was important and will presently be described, but it should not obscure the fact that the majority was in basic agreement on certain principles.

A fundamental conviction of nearly all Antifederalists was that the Constitution established a national, not a federal, government, a consolidation of previously independent states into one, a transfer of sovereignty in which the states, once sovereign, would retain but a shadow of their former power.[5] Whether this was

3. Henry Laurens to William Bell, Nov. 29, 1787, Laurens Papers, Letter Book No. 13, S. C. Hist. Soc.; "An Old Soldier," in the *Conn. Gazette* (New London), Jan. 4, 1788; Washington to David Humphreys, Oct. 10, 1787, Fitzpatrick, ed., *Writings of Washington*, XXIX, 287; Edmund Pendleton to [unknown], June 14, 1788, Emmett Coll., No. 1133, N.Y. Pub. Lib.; James McClurg to Madison, Oct. 31, 1787, Hunt, ed., *Writings of Madison*, V, 48n.; Jonathan Roberts in Moses Auge, *Lives of the Eminent Dead and Biographical Notes of Prominent Living Citizens of Montgomery County, Pa.* (Norristown, 1879), 67-68; George Nicholas to David Stewart, Apr. 9, 1788, C. E. French Coll., Mass. Hist. Soc.; Randolph in Farrand, ed., *Records of the Federal Convention*, II, 563-64; Abraham Clark to Thomas Sinnickson, July 23, 1788, Burnett, ed., *Letters*, VIII, 764; James Madison to Thomas Madison, Oct. 1, 1787, quoted in Abernethy, *Western Lands*, 361. William Plumer thought that the executive was too weak and Congress's powers too restricted. William Plumer, Jr., *Life of William Plumer* (Boston, 1857), 97.

4. Grayson of Virginia is sometimes cited as an Antifederalist who believed that the Constitution was too weak, but he made the contrary clear during the Virginia Convention (Elliot, ed., *Debates*, III, 283).

5. At that time a federal government meant one such as that established by the Articles, in which sovereignty remained with the federated units. In a national, or "consolidated" government the central authority was supreme, so that although the states might still exist, they would have only local, limited functions. In the Philadelphia Convention, Gouverneur Morris "explained the distinction between a *federal* and a *national, supreme*, Govt.; the former being a mere compact resting on the good faith of the parties; the latter having a compleat and *compulsive* operation. He contended that in all communities there must be one supreme power, and one only." Madison's notes, in Farrand, ed., *Records of the Federal Convention*, I, 34. For other references in the Convention, see *ibid.*, 24, 30, 37, 40, 41, 53, 136, 141, 158, 186, 242, 249, 294, 463. See also Irving Brant, *James Madison, Father of the Constitution* (New York, 1950), chaps. 2-4.

actually the case is, of course, still warmly debated, too frequently with reference to what the Constitution has become, or what the debaters wish it were. The Federalists met this attack by an attempt to deny the accusation in public, but it seems from their private statements that they intended to create a national government, although prevailing opinion obliged them to compromise. The records of the debates in the Philadelphia Convention are convincing evidence of this intention; the real convictions of the Federalist delegates can also be discovered in letters and journals. When George Richards Minot, a Massachusetts Federalist, referred in his journal to "the new federal, or rather *national* constitution," he expressed the secret thoughts of his party.[6]

The protestations of the Constitution's supporters did not convince the Antifederalists, who were certain that state sovereignty would be annihilated and that this would be evil—good government demanded a confederation. They were therefore at pains to prove that a consolidation was intended. If they had been able to cite the private letters and communications of their opponents, they would have been better able to persuade the people of this.[7] But although they did have the testimony of Gerry, Yates, Lansing, Mason, Martin, and Mercer, who attended the Convention, they were obliged to rest their case primarily on an analysis of the Constitution itself. Antifederalists everywhere, north and south, high and low, examined the distinction between national and federal government. In Virginia the wealthy planter George Mason asserted that "it is a national government and no longer a Confederation." In Massachusetts, the little Shaysite town of Harvard advised its delegate that the Constitution would "effectually destroy the sovereignty of the States, and establish a National

6. George Richards Minot Journal, 1787, Mass. Hist. Soc. It is extraordinary that there is no full account of Federalist thought. A few other references concerning their belief that the Constitution established a national government are, "Americanus," in the *Daily Advertiser* (N.Y.), Nov. 23, 1787; Henry Knox, notes, Knox Papers, XX, 176, Mass. Hist. Soc.; article in William Irvine's handwriting, Irvine Papers, IX, Hist. Soc. Pa.; William Gardner to Nicholas Gilman, June 14, 1788, Misc. MSS, N.Y. Hist. Soc.; Randolph in Elliot, ed., *Debates*, III, 64-65, 71.

7. Once in a while an incautious Federalist did help his critics, as when Benjamin Rush defended a national government in the Pennsylvania convention. McMaster and Stone, *Pennsylvania and the Constitution*, 771.

Government," while Elbridge Gerry, merchant, was informing the Massachusetts legislature that "the constitution proposed has few federal features, but is rather a system of national government." And in Pennsylvania, "A Farmer" lectured the public on the difference between a federal republic and a consolidated or national government.[8]

Consolidation was proved to the satisfaction of the Antifederalists by evidence drawn from all parts of the new plan. The opening words, "We, the People" at once disclosed the intent—in Samuel Adams's metaphor, "as I enter the Building I stumble at the Threshhold." [9] Surely if the object were federal it should read, "We, the States"; from the outset, then, it was "proven" that this was not to be a compact among the states.[10] Yet the proof arising from the plain implication of this phrase, though logical, was produced only occasionally, and it was not very effective in arousing opposition to the plan, for after all, who could object to a government's being made by the people? Besides there were more convincing evidences of consolidation.

If this were truly a federation still, as the Federalists claimed, then sovereignty must remain in the states. In that case the vital powers of government must be exercised by the states, and Congress must be granted only limited authority. What was the effect of the Constitution? Congress was given unlimited power—power which, as the little Maine town of Fryeburg warned, "will in its consequences entirely vacate the Constitutions of the respective states." [11] It was not so much any particular power which proved the danger, but the combination of control over taxation and the army together with the judicial powers, the significant words "necessary and proper," "General welfare," "supreme law of the

8. Elliot, ed., *Debates*, III, 29; *American Herald* (Boston), Jan. 21, 1788; *Debates and Proceedings in the Convention of the Commonwealth of Massachusetts, held in the Year 1788, and which finally ratified the Constitution of the United States* (Boston, 1856), 25, hereafter cited as *Mass. Debates; Freeman's Journal* (Phila.), Apr. 23, 1788.

9. Samuel Adams to R. H. Lee, Dec. 3, 1787, Cushing, ed., *Writings of Samuel Adams*, IV, 324.

10. Dench and Nasson in *Mass. Debates*, 200, 236; Henry in Elliot, ed., *Debates*, III, 22, 44; Caldwell and Taylor (North Carolina) in *ibid.*, IV, 15-16, 24; Findley in the *N.Y. Journal*, Dec. 11, 1787; "Cincinnatus," in *ibid.*, Nov. 29, 1787, and the *Independent Gazetteer* (Phila.), Dec. 15, 1787.

11. Barrows, *Fryeburg*, 112.

land," and the ominous omission of a clause reserving powers. What remained to the states? They could never resist so potent a rival—one which would become ever more powerful. Therefore the state governments must ultimately become extinct, or, if they survived, they would be to the general government only as the counties to a state.[12] Point by point the Constitution was examined to prove that this consolidation was inevitable.

The crucial importance of the tax power had long been an axiom of political thought, and the Antifederalists now re-emphasized the significance of the change which would be wrought by the Constitution. George Mason informed the Virginia convention, "Mr. Chairman, whether the Constitution be good or bad, the present clause clearly discovers that it is a national government, and no longer a Confederation. I mean that clause which gives the first hint of the general government laying direct taxes. The assumption of this power ... does ... entirely change the confederation of the states into one consolidated government."[13] No limits had been set to the exercise of this authority; therefore it would reach everyone, affect all property. Since governments spend as much as they can raise, Congress and the states would compete for the money of their citizens, and in the contest the former would emerge supreme. Without some restrictions on Congress's power to tax, the critics insisted, consolidation must result, for taxation is the most basic of powers: where it resides, sovereignty exists, and when it is transferred to Congress, sovereignty also is transferred. Where then is the federation?[14] Moreover, if a state should try to resist this all-engrossing power, it

12. Smilie in McMaster and Stone, *Pennsylvania and the Constitution*, 270; R. H. Lee in Ford, ed., *Pamphlets*, 282, 292; "Brutus," in the *N.Y. Journal*, Oct. 18, 1787; Whitehill in *ibid.*, Dec. 26, 1787; Findley in *ibid.*, Dec. 11, 1787; Dench in *Mass. Debates*, 199; Dawson in Elliot, ed., *Debates*, III, 607; Tredwell in *ibid.*, II, 402-3.

13. *Ibid.*, III, 29.

14. "Brutus," in the *N.Y. Journal*, Dec. 27, 1787; Williams in Elliot, ed., *Debates*, II, 330-31, 338-41; Smith in *ibid.*, 332-37; summary of the objections in Connecticut by Ellsworth, in Hoadly and Labaree, eds., *Public Records of Connecticut*, VI, 559; "Centinel," in the *Independent Gazetteer* (Phila.), Oct. 5, 1787; Whitehill in the *Pa. Herald* (Phila.), Dec. 15, 1787; Findley in McMaster and Stone, *Pennsylvania and the Constitution*, 770, 772, 775; William Symmes to Capt. Peter Osgood, Nov. 15, 1787, *Historical Collections of the Essex Institute*, 4 (1862), 211-17.

would be in vain, for Congress could send an army to enforce collection: "Congress, with the purse-strings in their hands, will use the sword with a witness." [15] How could it be argued that this was no national government, when "the last Resource of a free People" was taken away? [16]

Still other evidence of an intended transfer of sovereignty was the clause which declared the Constitution, the laws of Congress, and treaties to be the supreme law of the land. In the Pennsylvania ratifying convention Robert Whitehill asserted, "This Article *eradicates* every Vestige of State govt—and was *intended* so —it was *deliberated*." [17] "This new system, with one sweeping clause, bears down every constitution in the union," declared "Cincinnatus." [18] Since the powers of Congress were so extensive, state and general governments would frequently legislate on the same subject, and in any such conflict of interest the new national judiciary would assert the supremacy of the national law or treaty.[19] The result might be eventual abolition of the state governments; at the very least the grant of such powers proved the intent to make the national government supreme.[20] This clause, said the Antifederalists, must be considered in connection with the other broad grants of power, especially the "general welfare" and the "necessary and proper" clauses. What was left ungranted?

The critics then turned to the failure to reserve any powers to the states. Considered in connection with the elastic clauses, this omission seemed highly significant. If it were not clearly stated

15. Bodman in *Mass. Debates*, 159-60.
16. White in *ibid.*, 156. See also Smilie in McMaster and Stone, *Pennsylvania and the Constitution*, 778; R. H. Lee in Ford, ed., *Pamphlets*, 293; Whitehill in the *Pa. Herald* (Phila.), Dec. 15, 1787; "A Democratic Federalist," in *ibid.*, Oct. 17, 1787.
17. McMaster and Stone, *Pennsylvania and the Constitution*, 780.
18. *N.Y. Journal*, Nov. 8, 1787, and the *Independent Gazetteer* (Phila.), Nov. 16, 1787.
19. "Samuel," in the *U.S. Chronicle* (Providence), Jan. 24, 1788.
20. Bloodworth in Elliot, ed., *Debates*, IV, 179; "The Impartial Examiner," in the *Va. Independent Chronicle* (Richmond), Feb. 20, 1788; "Letter from a countryman," in the *Independent Gazetteer* (Phila.), Feb. 28, 1788; "Centinel," in the *Md. Journal* (Baltimore), Nov. 2, 1787 and in the *Freeman's Journal* (Phila.), Nov. 2, 1787; Lowndes of South Carolina in the *Daily Advertiser* (Charleston), Jan. 19, 1788; "A Countryman," in the *N. Y. Journal*, Dec. 15, 1787, Jan. 10, 1788. Here and elsewhere the footnotes do not cite every mention of an objection.

that all powers not granted were reserved, then it certainly seemed that Congress might exercise such powers through interpretation. In order to collect taxes, Congress might find it "necessary and proper" to infringe upon the right of trial by jury, or the freedom of the press, or any other right; in order to legislate for the "general welfare," Congress might do anything it pleased, for nothing was specifically forbidden. The time might come, George Mason warned, when Congress would oppress the people; and if anyone dared to defend them could not Congress, pretending to act for the general welfare, construe their action as sedition? Could not Congress thereupon restrict the press, and try cases arising from that restriction within its own ten-mile jurisdiction? The implications were enormous.[21] Obviously an amendment to the Constitution was required to make it clear that this was a government on which at least a few limits were to be set—unless indeed to reserve powers was useless when the important ones had been surrendered. Certainly the absence of such a restriction proved that the Federalists intended not a federal but a national government—a consolidation.[22]

The final evidence that the proposed government would be supreme lay in the power of the judiciary. If any state should challenge an act of Congress, the decision would be made by the Supreme Court, and the Court surely would support Congress. Congress and the Court together would make of the Constitution what they chose, and in practice, therefore, Congress could legislate on every possible subject.[23] The fullest discussion of this point (which was by no means universally made) was by Robert Yates, disguised as "Brutus." He observed that most of the powers were granted "in general and indefinite terms, which are either equiv-

21. Elliot, ed., *Debates*, III, 441-42.

22. Samuel Osgood to Samuel Adams, Jan. 5, 1788, Adams Papers, N. Y. Pub. Lib.; Monroe and Henry in Elliot, ed., *Debates*, III, 218, 422; Spencer and Lenoir in *ibid.*, IV, 152, 206; "Letter from a Hermit," in the *U. S. Chronicle* (Providence), Mar. 27, 1788; "An Officer of the Late Continental Army," in the *Independent Gazetteer* (Phila.), Nov. 6, 1787, and elsewhere; John Francis Mercer, address in the Etting Coll., VI, Hist. Soc. Pa. The amendment was suggested by all of the conventions which recommended changes.

23. Samuel Osgood to Samuel Adams, Jan. 5, 1788, Adams Papers, N. Y. Pub. Lib.

ocal, ambiguous, or which require long definitions to unfold the extent of their meaning." The meaning of the Constitution would be decided by the Supreme Court, and therefore the judges could "mould the government, into almost any shape they please." From the decision of the Court there was no appeal. The result surely would be that Congress's power would become unlimited, to the total subversion of the states.[24]

All of these things taken together, the Antifederalists asserted, proved that the Constitution created not a federation but a consolidated government,[25] and if this were so, the members of the Philadelphia Convention had violated their instructions. The vast changes which the Constitution represented were authorized neither by the letter nor the spirit of these instructions; indeed, to alter the general frame of government was precisely what many of the delegates had been forbidden to do. Here was no mere revision, no mere reform of the old, but the imposition of "a new political fabric, essentially and fundamentally distinct," no federation of states, but "a consolidation of them into one government." The convention had acted illegally.[26]

At this point it is reasonable to inquire whether and in what way the Federalists defended themselves. To investigate their

24. N. Y. Journal, Jan. 31, Feb. 7, 1788.

25. In addition to the above sources, many others objected to this centralization. See especially Mrs. Warren to Mrs. Macauley, May 1788, Mass. Hist. Soc., Proceedings, 64 (1930-1932), 158; Findley in the Pa. Packet (Phila.), Dec. 6, 1787; Tench Coxe to Madison, Jan. 23, 1788, Doc. Hist. of the Constitution, IV, 457; "Agrippa" in Ford, ed., Essays, 64-65; John Francis Mercer to Jefferson, Oct. 27, 1804, Md. Hist. Mag., 2 (1907), 210; Martin in Farrand, ed., Records of the Federal Convention, III, 192; "Helvidius Priscus,"in the Independent Chronicle (Boston), Dec. 27, 1787; "Sidney," in the N.Y. Journal, Oct. 18, 1787; Lowndes in the Daily Advertiser (Charleston), Jan. 25, 1787.

26. "Cato," in Ford, ed., Essays, 253; Charles J. Taylor, History of Great Barrington, (Berkshire County,) Massachusetts (Great Barrington, 1882), 317; Address of the minority members of the Pennsylvania House of Representatives, in the Pa. Packet (Phila.), Oct. 4, 1787; Mrs. Warren in Ford, ed., Pamphlets, 14; Whitehill in the Pa. Herald (Phila.), Dec. 15, 1787; "A Republican Federalist," in the Mass. Centinel (Boston), Dec. 29, 1787; Lansing and Yates in the Daily Advertiser (N.Y.), Jan. 14, 1788; Lenoir in Elliot, ed., Debates, IV, 203. Most of the delegates were authorized to make alterations in and additions to the Articles; the wording varied somewhat, often being quite general, but the New York and Massachusetts instructions explicitly limited the changes to revisions in the Articles. Farrand, ed., Records of the Federal Convention, III, 560-86.

views would require a separate book, and the student would be obliged to examine not merely the familiar published apologia but the private letters. In public the Federalists sometimes argued that the Convention had been authorized to solve the problems of the time: to supply the deficiencies of the Confederation. The solution required a new government. They also argued—and this was the more significant answer—that the Convention had not created a consolidated government, but a federal one with national features.[27] Surely some Federalists had their tongues in their cheeks when they used this argument, but others really believed that such a government had been created. Among the latter were many who followed Madison in his change from Federalist to Jeffersonian.

Be that as it may, the Antifederalists were certain that a national government had been intended. Why did they regard this as so serious a fault? The answer to this question brings us to the core of Antifederal thought, to certain key assumptions and their implications, of which the first was the danger of granting power. That "every man has a natural propensity to power,"[28] was no new observation. Its wide acceptance before the Revolution and its importance in the controversy over the impost have been demonstrated, and it was natural that nearly every Antifederal writer should emphasize it in the new debate. A sampling will suffice: "We know that private interest governs mankind generally. Power belongs originally to the people; but if rulers be not well guarded, that power may be usurped from them. People ought to be cautious in giving away power" (William Goudy of North Carolina). "It is natural for men to aspire to power—it is the nature of mankind to be tyrannical" (William Lenoir of North Carolina). "Power was never given ... but it was exercised, nor ever exer-

27. Washington's letter which was sent forth with the Constitution read, "In all our deliberations on this subject we kept steadily in our view, that which appears to us the greatest interest of every true American, the consolidation of our Union," Ford, ed., *Journals of Congress*, XXXIII, 502. The word may have been innocently used, in the sense of merely making more firm, but it certainly was impolitic, and naturally it was noted. For example, "A Republican Federalist," in the *Mass. Centinel* (Boston), Jan. 2, 1788.

28. "The Impartial Examiner," in the *Va. Independent Chronicle* (Richmond), Mar. 5, 1787.

cised but it was finally abused" (William Symmes of Massachusetts).[29]

This point established—and the Federalists were not disposed to contest it, at least in principle—the Antifederalists asserted that the Constitution granted power to a dangerous extent and did not restrain the wielders of that power. It was obvious, they admitted, that the people must delegate some degree of authority to their rulers, but preferably in the form of limited, stipulated powers, as under the Articles of Confederation. But the ultimate sovereignty of the people must be safeguarded; to vest total power in a national government was unnecessary and dangerous.

For many Antifederalists, all their objections were comprehended in this idea. They proved by numerous examples that power had been surrendered, and asserted that the ultimate result must be oppression. The minority of the Massachusetts ratifying convention was not very articulate, but when Captain Snow said, "I think power the hinge on which the whole Constitution turns," his thought was clear enough. So was General Thompson when he declared, "Sir, the question is, whether Congress shall have power."[30] The town of Wilbraham did not bother with a long list of objections but only noted that "the constitution took too much power from the State and gave it to the nation."[31] John Lansing explained that the people must delegate powers, "but, as the state governments will always possess a better representation of the feelings and interests of the people at large, it is obvious that

29. Elliot, ed., *Debates*, IV, 10, 93, 203; *Mass. Debates*, 173; see also for example Tredwell of New York in Elliot, ed., *Debates*, II, 393; "Deliberator," in the *Freeman's Journal* (Phila.), Mar. 26, 1788; Whitehill in the *N.Y. Journal*, Dec. 26, 1787; Nathaniel Barrell to George Thatcher, Jan. 15, 1788, *Hist. Mag.*, 16 (1869), 265; Clinton in Ford, ed., *Essays*, 278; "Agrippa" in *ibid.*, 107; "Centinel," in McMaster and Stone, *Pennsylvania and the Constitution*, 581, 616-618.

30. *Mass. Debates*, 132, 180.

31. Rufus P. Stebbins, *An Historical Address, delivered at the Centennial Celebration of the incorporation of the Town of Wilbraham, June 15, 1863* (Boston, 1864), 133. For other examples, see Dollard, in the *Daily Advertiser* (Charleston), May 29, 1788; "Brutus," in the *N.Y. Journal*, Jan. 17, 1788; "Common Sense," in *ibid.*, Apr. 21, 1788; Albany Antifederal Committee, "Objections to the Adoption of the Constitution," Apr. 10, 1788, in *ibid.*, Apr. 26, 1788, reprinted in the *Worcester Mag.*, 4 (1788) and in Joel Munsell, *The Annals of Albany*, 10 vols. (Albany, 1850-1859), IV, 336-43.

those powers can be deposited with much greater safety with the state than the general government." [32]

There was still another reason why consolidation was evil. Not only did it entrust men with excessive power, but it violated history's lesson that freedom could be maintained only by local governments. "The vast Continent of America cannot be long subjected to a Democracy if consolidated into one Government," wrote Thomas Wait of Portland. "You might as well attempt to rule Hell by Prayer." [33] On this point Antifederalists and Federalists engaged in lengthy discussions of history and its lessons. The former argued that a free republic could exist only in a small territory: if a state included a large area, the representatives could not know the minds of the people, the local conditions and needs. Moreover, within a large territory the various regions would strive against one another; different climates, products, interests, manners, habits, laws, would lead to discord. How legislate uniformly for a land so diverse? A law which suited one part might oppress another. Therefore the major functions of government must be exercised at the local or state levels, and a confederation alone would preserve freedom. A pure democracy, "Brutus" observed, was that in which the people were sovereign and ruled themselves by assembling together. For this a small territory was essential. With every step away from this ideal, government becomes more likely to oppress; to create a strong national government, with power transferred from the people to the state, was to create tyranny.[34] The outcome would be loss of liberty, ending in aristocracy, monarchy, or some other form of despotism.

Actually the position of the Antifederalists cannot be understood solely with reference to constitutional theory, which they

32. Elliot, ed., *Debates*, II, 217.
33. To George Thatcher, Nov. 22, 1787, *Hist. Mag.*, 16 (1869), 258.
34. "Brutus," in the *N.Y. Journal*, Oct. 18, 1787; Albany Antifederal Committee in *ibid.*, Apr. 26, 1788; Thomas Person to John Lamb, Aug. 6, 1788, Lamb Papers, N.Y. Hist. Soc.; Mason, Henry, and Monroe in Elliot, ed., *Debates*, III, 31-32, 161, 216; R. H. Lee in Ford, ed., *Pamphlets*, 288; "Cato," in Ford, ed., *Essays*, 255-56, 259; Martin in Farrand, ed., *Records of the Federal Convention*, III, 195; minority of the Pennsylvania ratifying convention, in the *Pa. Packet* (Phila.), Dec. 18, 1787; "Centinel," in the *Md. Journal* (Baltimore), Oct. 30, 1787; "An Old Whig," in the *Independent Gazetteer* (Phila.), Oct. 27, 1787; Findley in McMaster and Stone, *Pennsylvania and the Constitution*, 769.

often used as a rationalization. What they feared was not just the abstract transfer of authority from state to national government but the concrete transfer of power from the people to the well born. They were convinced that governments were usually run by an aristocracy, and that this government in particular was so constructed as to be certainly controlled by the few. Therefore they wanted power to be widely distributed among the states. Power concentrated led to aristocracy; power diffused, to democratic rule.

This democratic point of view was not shared by all of the Antifederalists, for reasons which will later be discussed; nor was it always openly expressed by those who did believe it. It is not often found in the debates in the ratifying conventions, where one would expect to discover so serious a criticism of the Constitution, and because it is not prominent in the most available published source it can be underestimated as a factor. Yet the reason for this omission is very simple. In the conventions, the Antifederalists were face to face with their opponents, and one did not (in those days) lightly tell one's fellow delegate that he was involved in an aristocratic conspiracy to create a government designedly removed from popular control. Most of the delegates who did the talking on both sides were themselves of the "better sort," and they conducted themselves, as a rule, with gentlemanly restraint. When one transgressed the boundary of polite behavior he was called to order; anything that resembled a personal affront was quickly resented and apologized for. The Antifederalists, therefore, were in this position: if they wished to imply that the Constitution was aristocratic, benefiting the few rather than the many, they had to speak in the most general terms, so as to exempt all of the Federalists present from the least suspicion of wrong doing.

The result was that in the conventions the argument was seldom used and the implication, when raised, was never pushed very far. In North Carolina, when it was suggested that the members of the Convention did not have at heart the best interests of the people, the Federalists promptly protested. Joseph M'Dowall insisted that "some were very imperious, aristocratical, despotic, and monarchical," but then abandoned that line of argument.[35] In

35. Elliot, ed., *Debates*, IV, 57.

New York, Melancton Smith asserted only that the new government "will fall into the hands of the few and the great. This will be a government of oppression." [36] John Smilie in Pennsylvania also suggested that some members of the convention were the sort of men who "could not bear to be on the same Footing with other Citizens," but did not directly accuse any of the Pennsylvania delegates; indeed, the remark was made only on the last day, when he was angered at the impolite behavior of the galleries.[37]

In Virginia, after Mason, Monroe, and Henry had all insinuated that democracy was to be impaired, and the last had referred to a difference of opinion between the "middle and lower ranks of people" and the "well born," John Marshall merely replied that everybody wanted a democracy and that the Constitution established one. Randolph had already angrily defended the members of the Convention against the charge of aristocratic designs.[38] In Massachusetts the most extreme public statement by an Antifederalist occurred when Amos Singletary stated frankly that the "lawyers, and men of learning, and moneyed men" expected to control the government, and having secured "all the power and all the money" would "swallow up all us little folks." [39] The records do not reveal how this was received by the Federalists. For the most part the argument is to be found in letters or in the newspapers, where the anonymous writer was not obliged to be as polite as the delegates.

It should be observed also that some Antifederalists were not opposed to a government with aristocratic features, agreeing with the Federalists that the country had suffered from too much democracy.[40] The relation between Antifederalism and democracy will be considered later. Here it will only be observed that some of the Antifederalist leaders were restrained by their own social attitudes from objecting publicly to an excess of aristocracy.

36. *Ibid.*, II, 246-47. Outside of the convention Smith was more frank, asserting that some members of the Federal Convention were guilty of peculation and fraud. Ford, ed., *Pamphlets*, 115.
37. McMaster and Stone, *Pennsylvania and the Constitution*, 785.
38. Elliot, ed., *Debates*, III, 27-30, 44, 50, 140, 211, 222.
39. *Mass. Debates*, 203.
40. For an article critical of the Antifederalists see Cecelia M. Kenyon, "Men of Little Faith: The Anti-Federalists on the Nature of Representative Government," *Wm. and Mary Qtly.*, 3rd Ser., 12 (1955), 3-43.

Nevertheless, the criticism that the Constitution favored the few at the expense of the many was almost universal.[41]

What the Antifederalists feared, then, was that the power given to a national government would be wielded by an upper class. The easiest way of avoiding such dominance would have been to concede no power at all, but if some had to be granted, it should not be so much as to enable the few to oppress the many. The Philadelphia Convention, they believed, had gone too far. William Findley, having asserted that the Constitution established a national government, remarked that "The natural Course of Power is to make the many Slaves to the few." [42] Samuel Chase wrote to John Lamb that he objected to the Constitution chiefly because "the bulk of the people can have nothing to say to it. The government is *not* a government of the people." [43] In the Maryland convention he said (or planned to say) that only the rich and well-born would be chosen to Congress.[44] Most Antifederalists were convinced of this, and had little doubt what would happen under the proposed system. Once in the "Aristocratical Saddle," the riding would be easy, with the army as a whip.[45] The "men of Fortune" would not feel for the "Common People"—not for their sakes were the "rich and well born" so intent on ratification.[46] An "aristocratical tyranny" would arise, in which (as Timothy Bloodworth wrote) "the great will struggle for power, honor and wealth,

41. There were almost 40 lengthy presentations of the Antifederal view; of these at least 30 stated that the Constitution was aristocratic, and over half were emphatic on the subject; almost all of the more severe critics were writing in newspapers or in private letters.

42. McMaster and Stone, *Pennsylvania and the Constitution,* 769.

43. June 13, 1788, Leake, *Lamb,* 310. Samuel Chase certainly was no democrat later in life, but at this time he was taking the popular side. When in 1788 James McHenry criticized Maryland's constitution because it granted the people the right to instruct their representatives (a right which, he wrote, "brings every thing back to that chaos which existed before the compact"), Chase defended the provision. *American Museum,* 4 (1788), 332-34.

44. Crowl, "Anti-Federalism," *Wm. and Mary Qtly.,* 3rd Ser., 9 (1947), 464. These were notes for a speech to be delivered, but whether he gave it is unknown.

45. William Smith to Abraham Yates, Jr., June 12, 1788, Yates, Jr., Papers, N. Y. Pub. Lib.

46. Col. Barton, in Robert C. Cotner, ed., *Theodore Foster's Minutes of the Convention held at South Kingston, Rhode Island, in March, 1790, which failed to adopt the Constitution of the United States* (Providence, 1929), 54; Albany Antifederal Committee, in the *N.Y. Journal,* Apr. 26, 1788.

the poor become a prey to avarice, insolence, and oppression."[47] John Quincy Adams noted in his diary that the Constitution was "calculated to increase the influence, power and wealth of those who have any already," and he concluded mournfully that "it is hard to give up a system which I have always been taught to cherish, and to confess that a free government is inconsistent with human nature."[48]

For surely under an aristocracy the liberty of the common people would vanish. Mercy Warren wrote of liberty, aristocracy, tyranny, "*dark, secret*, and *profound intrigues*," of "the rapacious . . . growing rich by oppression" while the "philosophic lovers of freedom" could only weep at her exit.[49] In South Carolina, James Lincoln warned that democracy was being replaced by aristocracy and added, "What have you been contending for these ten years past? Liberty! What is liberty? The power of governing yourselves. If you adopt this constitution have you this power?" And everywhere the Antifederalists answered, "No."[50] In the same state, Aedanus Burke informed Lamb that when the backcountry learned of the ratification:

in some places the people had a Coffin painted black, which borne in funeral procession, was solemnly buried, as an emblem of the dissolution and internment of publick Liberty. . . . They feel that

47. To Lamb, June 23, 1788, Lamb Papers, N.Y. Hist. Soc. See also "Philanthropos," in the *Va. Journal* (Alexandria), Dec. 6, 1787; "Philadelphiensis," in the *Independent Gazetteer* (Phila.), Feb. 21, 1787; "An Old Constitutionalist," in *ibid.*, Oct. 26, 1787; "John Humble," in *ibid.*, Oct. 29, 1787; "Brutus," in the *N.Y. Journal*, Oct. 18, 1787; "John DeWitt," in the *American Herald* (Boston), Oct. 29, Nov. 5, 9, 1787. Timothy Hoadly of Branford, Conn. voted against ratification "because he regarded the Constitution as calculated to create an aristocratical form of government." Francis Bacon Trowbridge, *The Hoadley Genealogy* (New Haven, 1894), 27-28. One last example will be more than enough. The town of Simsbury, Conn. adopted the following resolution (Nov. 12, 1787): "that to adopt s^d proposed Constitution would institute & erect an Aristocracy which they fear would end in Despotism and Tyranny & Extinguish or nearly absorb our antient Charter Priveledges ever sacred & Dear to us & that instead of lessning our Taxes & Burdens it would greatly Increase & Augment them and finally prove destructive to our most invaluable Liberties and Priveledges." Lucius I. Barber, *A Record and Documentary History of Simsbury* (Simsbury, 1931), 329-30.
48. Mass. Hist. Soc., *Proceedings*, 2nd Ser., 16 (1902), 331.
49. Ford, ed., *Pamphlets*, 6, 7, 23.
50. *Daily Advertiser* (Charleston), Feb. 1, 1788.

they are the very men, who, as mere Militia, half-armed and half-clothed have fought and defeated the British regulars in sundry encounters. They think that after having disputed and gained the Laurel under the banners of Liberty, now, that they are likely to be robbed both of the honour and the fruits of it, by a Revolution purposely contrived for it. I know some able Men among us or such as are thought so, affect to despise the general opinion of the Multitude. For my own part I think that that Government rests on a very sandy foundation, the Subjects whereof are convinced that it is a bad one.[51]

The members of the Convention, the Antifederalists declared, had no reluctance to trample on the most sacred rights of the people, and now, springing from that convention was "a monstrous aristocracy," which would "swallow up the democratic rights of the union, and sacrifice the liberties of the people to the power and domination of a few." [52]

Working from these general principles, the Antifederalists examined every part of the Constitution for proofs of consolidation, excessive grants of power, tendencies toward aristocracy, and infringements of liberty. In this scrutiny, in which each examiner tried perhaps to discover some new danger, it was inevitable that a large number of criticisms would be made which were felt only by a few individuals, and others which were intended only for propaganda. Most of these will be ignored in favor of the objections which were frequently stated and believed. There was no dearth of these; the Antifederalists found much to criticize in the Presidency, the judiciary, and the legislative branches.

The supreme importance of the House of Representatives was obvious to men who had upheld commons against lords and king, and assemblies against councils and governors. Those who had supported the popular cause in the Revolution had insisted that

51. June 23, 1788, Lamb Papers, N.Y. Hist. Soc.
52. "Rusticus," in the *N.Y. Journal*, Sept. 13, 1787; "Cincinnatus," in *ibid.*, Nov. 1, 1787. For the infringement on liberty see also Tredwell in Elliot, ed., *Debates*, II, 405; Lansing and Yates in *ibid.*, I, 481; Luther Martin in Ford, ed., *Essays*, 366; Rufus King to Madison, Jan. 27, 1788, King, *King*, I, 316-17; Lowndes in the *Daily Advertiser* (Charleston), Jan. 21, 1788; R. H. Lee to William Shippen, Jr., Oct. 21, 1787, and to Samuel Adams, Oct. 27, 1787, Ballagh, ed., *Lee*, II, 441-42, 458; "Cato Uticensis," in the *Va. Independent Chronicle* (Richmond), Oct. 17, 1787.

the lower house should be dominant, controlling not only the legislative process but the executive as well.[53] The principle had been expressed in the new state constitutions, sometimes by the elimination of the senate, usually by the elevation of the legislative at the expense of the executive authority. The Antifederalists believed that the House ought to be democratic—indeed it had better be, for as Timothy Bloodworth remarked it was "the only democratic branch."[54] Therefore it ought to be truly representative of public opinion and kept continually responsive to that opinion by frequent elections. For the former purpose, the delegates should be numerous enough so that their constituencies were small—so that they would be intimately known by the electors and intimately acquainted with the popular will.

These premises were the basis of widespread criticism of the proposed House of Representatives. State legislatures, it was said, had a large enough membership for truly representative government, but this was not true of Congress. The House would represent only a minority of the people, and this minority would be (as Melancton Smith expressed it) the *"natural aristocracy"* rather than "the middling class."[55] The House thus might become nothing but an "assistant Aristocratical Branch."[56] The solution was to increase the number of representatives, but there was a limit beyond which it was impractical. Altogether, the nature of the House was, as George Mason remarked, "a conclusive reason"

53. For example, during New Hampshire's constitutional convention of 1778, Samuel Philbrick had written to Josiah Bartlett, "[It was] Voted that the Suprem Executive Authority Shall not be wholly Seprate from the Legislative—this was argued all most two half days: a Large number Insisting upon having the Supreem Executive Authority Lodged in one man with the advice of a Prive Counsel—and Some few thought it most Proper to be Lodged in one man only; he to be Elected Annually: but the Greater Part thought it most Safe in the Hands of the Counsil and Assembly." Upton, *Revolutionary New Hampshire*, 181. See also the resolution passed by Concord, N.H., quoted in *ibid.*, 185.

54. Elliot, ed., *Debates*, IV, 55. See also the remark by Mason in Farrand, ed., *Records of the Federal Convention*, I, 359, 364.

55. Elliot, ed., *Debates*, II, 242, 246, 227-29; Farrand, ed., *Records of the Federal Convention*, II, 386.

56. "John DeWitt," in the *American Herald* (Boston), Nov. 9, 1787. See also "Brutus," in the *N.Y. Journal*, Nov. 15, 29, 1787; "A Republican Federalist," in the *Mass. Centinel* (Boston), Jan. 30, 1788; *Mass. Debates*, 134; Lansing and Clinton in Elliot, ed., *Debates*, III, 260-62.

for limiting Congress's powers to such "as were absolutely indispensable, and these to be most cautiously guarded."[57]

Annual elections had also been defended by some of the colonials, and guaranteed by all of the new constitutions, including the Articles of Confederation. There were, however, good arguments in favor of longer terms, and the Antifederalists were not united on the question. In the South especially there was relatively little criticism of the biennial provision. Critics in several northern states, however, insisted that biennial elections were "a departure from safe democratic principles of annual ones."[58] In the Massachusetts ratifying convention, annual elections were defended by some of the delegates, one of whom remarked that if the people had not been able to get rid of the Bowdoin administration after one year, "our liberties would have been lost."[59] The Pennsylvania minority also preferred the shorter term, believing with William Findley that annual elections were "an annual Recognition of the Sovereignty of the People." Yet in that state alone did the desired amendments include this point.[60] It is clear that although the Antifederalists did support shorter terms and rotation in office, this particular criticism was not of major significance.

Far more important and more frequently expressed were objections concerning the Senate. Before examination of them it is necessary to take note of certain criticisms which were not made, for the omission may seem to imply an inconsistency. Antifederalists did not desire the elimination of the Senate in favor of a unicameral legislature.[61] This does not mean that they were devoted to the principle of checks and balances in government, nor that they approved of two houses in the state governments. On the contrary, many defended the unicameral principle, and three state con-

57. *Ibid.*, III, 402.
58. George Clinton, in Ford, ed., *Essays*, 267. See also Williams, in Elliot, ed., *Debates*, II, 242.
59. *Mass. Debates*, 101-2.
60. McMaster and Stone, *Pennsylvania and the Constitution*, 776; *Pa. Packet* (Phila.), Dec. 12, 1787.
61. Smilie of Pennsylvania argued in favor of a single house, but he abandoned that ground because, he admitted, the situation in Pennsylvania was exceptional. McMaster and Stone, *Pennsylvania and the Constitution*, 773.

stitutions had established a single house. But the situation in regard to the national Congress was entirely different. There was reason for the Senate to be welcomed, not rejected. After all, the Antifederalists believed in a confederation, and there was little trace of any such thing in the plan now proposed. The states, as such, did not choose the lower house, nor the President; important powers had been taken from them; their economic role was reduced, and so (as it seemed) the only trace of a federation was to be found in the Senate—this body alone forecast the continued existence of the states. The Antifederalists were not merely willing to suffer a Senate—they were glad to see it, because it was a federal feature.[62] However they did not intend that it should be a more aristocratic body than the House, represent different interests in society, or have vastly greater powers.

This fact also explains why a significant characteristic of the Senate was so seldom criticized. A century later, the indirect election of senators was considered undemocratic, condemned as one of the least desirable features of the Constitution. It has therefore been assumed that it was singled out for objection in 1787-88. Actually the Antifederalists could not see anything wrong with having the senators represent the states. This was to them, if anything, a virtue. It is true that some writers pointed out that the Senate would be an aristocratic body, not responsible to the people, because of the method of selection.[63] "Cincinnatus" went much further than most critics when he remarked that the Senate was far removed from the people, "and exactly in the ratio of their removal from the people, do aristocratic principles constantly infect the minds of men." [64] But not even he, nor anyone else, came out clearly for popular elections.

The Antifederalists, then, were willing to accept a national Senate, especially if it represented the states. However, they did object to the term of office, the failure to assure rotation, and the exceptional powers granted to the upper house. An objection

62. See Luther Martin in Farrand, ed., *Records of the Federal Convention*, III, 193.
63. Especially the Albany Antifederal Committee, the town of Fryeburg, Maine, the Pennsylvania minority, Monroe, Mason, Lowndes, George Clinton, "A Tenant," "Algernon Sidney," and "An Old Constitutionalist."
64. *N.Y. Journal*, Nov. 22, 1787.

frequently, though not universally, made was to the six-year term, which violated the basic doctrine that a representative must be kept responsible to his constituents.[65] The six-year term had to be considered also in conjunction with the lack of a provision for recall and the failure to limit re-eligibility. The Articles of Confederation were superior, the Antifederalists asserted, because the annually elected delegates to Congress served for only three years out of six, and each state had the power, as the Articles specified, "to recal its delegates, or any of them, at any time within the year, and to send others in their stead, for the remainder of the Year." [66] In contrast, the senators, no longer responsible to the legislatures which had elected them, would become independent and uncontrollable; the danger was especially great because the Senate would be an aristocratic body. "What," asked George Clinton, "is there left to resist and repel this host of influence and power?" [67] There was no agreement as to the ideal term, but it was generally felt that some restriction was essential, and Melancton Smith expressed a widespread feeling when he declared, "I think a *rotation* in the government is a very important and truly republican institution." [68] Without any popular control, the outcome was inevitable. William Findley remarked that he could not have contrived a better plan for creating an aristocracy.[69]

Antifederalists also disliked the special powers which had been given to the aristocratic Senate. That which aroused the most

65. Col. Jones of Bristol in *Mass. Debates*, 144.

66. Quotations from the Articles and from the Constitution are in the form printed in Henry Steele Commager, ed., *Documents of American History* (New York, 1934), 111-15, 139-45.

67. Ford, ed., *Essays*, 273. Clinton never used one word where two would do.

68. Elliot, ed., *Debates*, II, 310.

69. McMaster and Stone, *Pennsylvania and the Constitution*, 778. For sample objections see Jones, Taylor, and Singletary in *Mass. Debates*, 147, 305; M'Dowall and Bloodworth in Elliot, ed., *Debates*, IV, 87, 135; G. Livingston and Lansing in *ibid.*, II, 286-90; Mason in *ibid.*, III, 493-94; Martin in Farrand, ed., *Records of the Federal Convention*, III, 194; "John DeWitt," in the *American Herald* (Boston), Nov. 9, 1787; "An Officer of the Late Continental Army," in the *Independent Gazetteer* (Phila.), Nov. 6, 1787; "Republicus," in the *Kentucky Gazette* (Lexington), Mar. 1, 1788; "A Countryman," in the *N.Y. Journal*, Jan. 22, 1788; town of Providence, in the *Providence Gazette*, May 29, 1788; town of Fryeburg, Maine, in Barrows, *Fryeburg*, 112.

comment was its control over treaties, for many Antifederalists felt that both houses of Congress ought to ratify them, especially since they were to be the supreme law of the land. The Virginians became most excited about this, partly because Antifederalists in the Old Dominion were insisting that the navigation of the Mississippi would be traded away by Northerners in exchange for commercial concessions, and that Northern commerce in general would be favored over Southern interests; but other Southerners [70] and at least a few Northerners also objected to this special power.[71] Other characteristics of the Senate were occasionally singled out for disapproval, such as its right to alter money bills,[72] the fact that the senators would be impeached by their own house instead of by some special tribunal,[73] and its share in appointments.[74]

Usually, however, it was merely noted as a passing objection that the Senate, or the Senate and President combined, had too much power; the primary emphasis was placed on the Senate's lack of responsibility to the people. It is significant that so detailed an analysis of the Constitution as that issued by the Albany Antifederal Committee made no particular objection to the Senate's power, but only to its independence of public opinion. The objections against the Senate usually had the primary purpose of demonstrating that powers should be withheld from a government so constructed.

The office of President also came under attack. The major criti-

---

70. Elliot, ed., *Debates*, III, 61, 221, 292-93, 340, 366, 499, 501-2, 609; IV, 115, 116, 119, 131, 135; John Francis Mercer, draft letter in Etting Coll., Hist. Soc. Pa.; Rev. Leeland in Joseph Spencer to Madison, Feb. 28, 1788, *Doc. Hist. of the Constitution*, IV, 527; Joseph Jones to Madison, Oct. 29, 1787, Mass. Hist. Soc., *Proceedings*, 2nd Ser., 17 (1903), 487.

71. Barrows, *Fryeburg*, 112; Whitehill and Smilie in McMaster and Stone, *Pennsylvania and the Constitution*, 773; "Many Customers," in the *Independent Gazetteer* (Phila.), Dec. 1, 1787.

72. "Cincinnatus," in the *N.Y. Journal*, Nov. 22, 1787; "Algernon Sidney," in *ibid.*, Feb. 23, 1788; Grayson in Elliot, ed., *Debates*, III, 375; Mason in Ford, ed., *Pamphlets*, 329.

73. "Cincinnatus" and "Algernon Sidney," cited above; R. H. Lee in Ford, ed., *Pamphlets*, 300; Monroe and Mason in Elliot, ed., *Debates*, III, 220, 402; Taylor in *ibid.*, IV, 32.

74. Clinton in Ford, ed., *Essays*, 273; Mason in Ford, ed., *Pamphlets*, 329; R. H. Lee to the governor of Virginia, Oct. 16, 1787, Ballagh, ed., *Lee*, II, 451; "Cincinnatus," in the *N.Y. Journal*, Nov. 22, 1787; "A Georgian," in the *Gazette of State of Georgia* (Savannah), Nov. 15, 1787.

cism was not directed at the mode of his election nor his term of office. Less than a dozen Antifederalist writers registered a protest against the electoral college. Evidently there was some disagreement as to how it would function. James Monroe thought that most elections would be thrown into the House of Representatives, where the vote would be by states, and therefore the President would owe his election to the state governments, not to the people.[75] On the other hand Mercy Warren believed that the choice would be made by the electoral college, which she called "an aristocratic junto." [76] There were a few other scattered complaints about the failure to provide for popular elections, but the vast majority of critics did not even mention the subject.[77] Probably this was so because no substitute seemed any more acceptable. Direct election would be a national rather than a federal feature (as was understood in the Philadelphia Convention), while election by the legislature was no more democratic than by the electoral college.

Only a handful of Antifederalists objected to the four-year term for the President.[78] A much larger number felt that there should be some limit on his re-eligibility. Thus in South Carolina, a western representative remarked that the President could use his power for four years and be re-elected without restraint, and continued, "You dont even put the same check on him that you do

75. Elliot, ed., *Debates*, III, 488. If so, then this would be a "federal" feature, and as such acceptable to many Antifederalists. The reader will recall that each elector voted for two men, and the candidate securing the largest number of votes became President, if he had a majority; if not, the decision would be made by the House, each state having one vote.

76. Ford, ed., *Pamphlets*, 12.

77. See also "Candidus," in the *Independent Chronicle* (Boston), Dec. 6, 1787; "A Tenant," in the *N.Y. Journal*, Apr. 29, 1788; "Republicus," in the *Kentucky Gazette* (Lexington), Mar. 1, 1788; Clinton in Ford, ed., *Essays*, 263; "An Old Constitutionalist," in the *Independent Gazetteer* (Phila.), Oct. 26, 1787; John Francis Mercer, letter cited in Etting Coll., Hist. Soc. Pa.; Monroe in Elliot, ed., *Debates*, III, 220, 488; Mason in *ibid.*, 464, 493.

78. Richard Henry Lee wrote that the terms of president and senators meant that an oligarchy would develop; in the House alone was to be found a "check" in favor of the "democratic principle." To Edmund Randolph, Oct. 16, 1787, Ballagh, ed., *Lee*, II, 452. It was reported that a New Hampshire delegate voted against ratification because "Presidents would prove nothing less than four-year-old kings, and finally kings for life." Frederick Kidder and Augustus A. Gould, *The History of New Ipswich, from its first grant in MDCCXXXVI to the present time*: . . . (Boston, 1852), 116.

on your own state governor; a man from and bred among you—a man over whom you have a continual and watchful eye—a man who from the very nature of his situation, it is almost impossible can do you any injury; this man you say shall not be elected for more than four years, and yet this mighty—this omnipotent governor general may be elected for years and years." [79] But even this point was made by a minority of the critics. The relative lack of concern over the President's term is surprising, when there was so much criticism of the Senate on this score, and when the governments established by the Articles and the state constitutions were so different in this regard. Perhaps the reason lay in the popularity of Washington: most people agreed that he would be President, did not care how long he served, and could not see that it made any difference how he was chosen. [80]

The principal objection of most Antifederalists to the executive branch was that the President had been given too much power. He was, they asserted, an elective king, a prince under a republican cloak, "vested with power dangerous to a free people." [81] Various critics objected to every power that he had been given— his right to make appointments and treaties, his influence over the army, his right to pardon, and most of all his veto. [82] Yet there were many Antifederalists who did not raise any serious criticism whatever, and the amendments that were suggested in the state conventions did not call for radical change. New York proposed a council to help in appointments; it proposed also that the President should not exercise his power over the armed forces nor grant

79. *Daily Advertiser* (Charleston), Feb. 1, 1788.
80. Not everyone failed to look to the future. Hugh Ledlie wrote to Lamb that he had heard that Hamilton, meeting Lamb on the street, asked "how you could be so much against the New Constitution, for it was pretty certain your old good friend Genl Washington would in all probability be the first president under it; to which you reply'd that in that case all might be well, but perhaps after him Genl Slushington might be the next or second president." Jan. 15, 1788, Lamb Papers, N.Y. Hist. Soc.
81. "Philadelphiensis," in the *Independent Gazetteer* (Phila.), Feb. 21, 1788; Aedanus Burke in the *Daily Advertiser* (Charleston), May 21, 1788; town of Harvard in the *American Herald* (Boston), Jan. 21, 1788.
82. Published sources amply illustrate these points. See also especially "An Old Whig," in the *Independent Gazetteer* (Phila.), Nov. 1, 1787; "Lycurgus," in *ibid.*, Oct. 17, 1787; "Tamony," in the *Va. Independent Chronicle* (Richmond), Jan. 9, 1788; "Impartial Examiner," in *ibid.*, June 11, 1788; "A Countryman," in the *N.Y. Journal*, Dec. 6, 1787.

pardons without the consent of Congress, and finally that he should serve only eight years. The amendments introduced by Robert Whitehill in Pennsylvania also called for an executive council and limited in certain respects the President's power and control over the army. Virginia and North Carolina endorsed the principle of rotation in office but suggested no other changes, while the Maryland minority agreed with New York in limiting the President's control over the army and furnishing him with a council, but said nothing about rotation. Altogether it is evident that the Antifederalists were ready to accept a stronger executive than that provided by the Articles of Confederation, although they were not prepared to concentrate so much authority as the Constitution gave. Royal governors were still remembered.

It should be noted, in conclusion, that many Antifederalists contemplated the possibility of a union of interest between the Senate and the President, concluding that if it should occur the result would be despotism: a king and a House of Lords equaled an oligarchy.[83] The House of Representatives was nothing but a "pretended concession to democracy," and would be unable to contend with such vast superiority of power.[84] Perhaps taken singly, individual parts of the Constitution might be justified, but as a whole it could lead only to tyranny. Some observers had mixed emotions as they viewed the prospects. A South Carolinian asked that his family seal be traced in England, "for as our steps toward monarchy are very obvious, I would wish my Children to have all the Rights to rank, & distinction, which is to be claimed from Ancestry. . . . We are getting back fast to the system we destroyed some years ago." [85]

83. Arthur Lee to John Adams, Oct. 3, 1787, Charles Francis Adams, ed., *The Works of John Adams*, 10 vols. (Boston, 1850-1856), IX, 554; "1st Book of Samuel, Chap. VIII," in the *Va. Independent Chronicle* (Richmond), Oct. 31, 1787.

84. "Lycurgus," in the *Independent Gazetteer* (Phila.), Oct. 17, 1787.

85. Francis Kinlock to Thomas Boone, May 26, 1788, Felix Gilbert, ed., "Letters of Francis Kinlock to Thomas Boone, 1782-1788," *Journal of Southern History*, 8 (1942), 104-5.

Chapter VII

ANTIFEDERAL OBJECTIONS
TO THE CONSTITUTION
PART II

A^{NTIFEDERALISTS} viewed a strong national government as a
threat to liberty. From this standpoint a vital part of the
proposed structure of power to be erected by the Constitution was
section eight of the first Article, which endowed Congress with
the powers once held by the states. This section was studded with
such ominous words as "taxes," "general welfare," "Commerce,"
"Armies," "necessary and proper." Of them all, it was the first
which attracted the most attention.

There were, indeed, a handful of Antifederalists who were
willing to grant Congress unlimited power to tax; at the other
extreme were a few who thought this power should inhere solely
in the states. The vast majority conceded that some federal taxation was necessary, but they were convinced that the Constitution
had gone too far; the very principles for which the Revolutionary
War had been fought were endangered. The new government,
said one critic, seemed "to verge too much towards the British
plan, laid by Lord North, for enslaving America before the late
war." In former times, Americans had fought against the "iron
yoke of British bondage" but now, he warned, we were "bending
our necks to as heavy a one of our own make." [1] Americans did not
have to be reminded that control over taxation was the key to
power, and that it had in the past and might now again result in

1. Deacon Winn of Woburn, Mass., in the *Independent Chronicle*
(Boston), Mar. 27, 1788.

despotism. The series of remarks reported from the Massachusetts ratifying convention illustrate the arguments usually employed. Amos Singletary reminded the delegates that the Revolution had been fought primarily over the issue of taxation. William Bodman asserted that the power granted was unlimited and therefore dangerous; he inquired how anyone could say that state sovereignty would survive when Congress could send an army to collect taxes, and further warned that people ought to be jealous of their rulers. Abraham White believed that "Congress, with the purse-strings in their hands, will use the sword with a witness." Dr. Samuel Willard traced the historical consequences of entrusting men with power. And, finally, Mr. Randal "feared a consolidation."[2] Elsewhere, Antifederalists itemized at length the possible objects of taxation and noted that national laws would override those of the state; such a power would certainly mean the death of the state governments. Melancton Smith expressed a generally held conviction when he declared it an axiom, that the body which "has all power and both *purse* and *Sword* has the absolute Gov't of all other Bodies and they must exist at the will and pleasure of the *Superior*."[3]

Particularly obnoxious was the power to levy direct taxes.[4] Some Antifederalists indeed still had faith in the requisition system, although most of these were now prepared to admit that if the states failed to pay, Congress should have the right to enforce collection.[5] The majority, however, felt that the requisition system should be supplemented by specific taxes granted to Congress. In conceding this point, they made a distinction between import taxes and internal or direct taxes. The former (the impost) could be granted to Congress, perhaps with restrictions concerning the

2. *Mass. Debates*, 156-69.

3. Notes on the debates in the New York ratifying convention, McKesson Papers, N.Y. Hist. Soc.

4. Of the 38 individuals or groups who produced fairly complete criticisms, 6 evidently approved of the clause. Fourteen objected in general terms and with varying degrees of vigor, but did not discriminate among different types of taxation. Eighteen singled out direct or internal taxes for special notice.

5. Examples are, "Many Customers," in the *Independent Gazetteer* (Phila.), Dec. 1, 1787; Williams and Lansing in Elliot, ed., *Debates*, II, 217, 331-32, 371-76; Mason in *ibid.*, III, 31.

method of collection,[6] just as it had been proposed with limitations earlier. Such a specific, limited, and indirect tax could be granted without too much danger to liberty. It could be collected without the use of force and without invasion of state authority, whereas to collect direct taxes Congress must go into the states, operate upon individuals, and compete with the states for control.[7] Moreover, it would be impossible for Congress to propose direct taxes which would not discriminate between states or groups—a poll tax, as several remarked, was especially dangerous to the majority of the less well-to-do,[8] and direct taxes such as those on cider or ale might operate unequally—yet neither individuals nor states could resist. The solution was for the states themselves to control their internal taxes. Congress, after all, could get along very well on the revenue from import duties, since the major expense, the payment of the federal debt, might be discharged by each state separately, as best suited its citizens.[9] If more funds were needed, requisitions would provide a supplementary revenue. Only if the states refused to pay the requisition should Congress have the right to intervene.

The force of these criticisms was recognized in the amendments which were suggested by the state ratifying conventions. Even in the nine Federalist-inspired resolutions which Massachusetts and New Hampshire adopted, Congress was forbidden to levy direct taxes unless imposts and excises were insufficient, and then only if a state failed to pay a requisition.[10] Virginia and North Carolina permitted Congress to levy direct and excise taxes only if the requisition system did not work.[11] The Maryland minority wanted the same stipulation in regard to direct taxes and also prohibited a poll tax, while in Pennsylvania, the minority allowed Congress

6. Conceded, for example, by the Bryans, James Warren, Benjamin Workman, William Findley, George Clinton, R. H. Lee, James Monroe, and John Lamb.

7. See, for example, Smith's remarks in Elliot, ed., *Debates*, II, 332-37.

8. Williams in Elliot, ed., *Debates*, II, 340; "A Son of Liberty," in the *New Hampshire Recorder, and Weekly Advertiser* (Keene), Jan. 2, 1788; "A Countryman," in the *N. Y. Journal*, Dec. 20, 1787.

9. "Cincinnatus," in the *N.Y. Journal*, Dec. 6, 1787.

10. *Mass. Debates*, 83; *New Hampshire State Papers*, X, 20.

11. Elliot, ed., *Debates*, III, 659, IV, 245.

to levy only import and export taxes.[12] The conventions of Rhode Island forbade the poll tax, insisted that a requisition be tried before direct taxes were levied, and demanded that three-fourths of the states must agree to any direct tax.[13] Finally, the New York convention also prohibited the poll tax and any excise on an article of domestic growth or manufacture; Congress could levy direct taxes only if other revenues failed and if a state refused to pay a requisition.[14] Thus the Antifederalists tried to make sure that the states would retain at least partial control over this critical power, and that the people would be safe from the union of purse and sword.[15]

Second in importance among the powers of Congress was its control over the army. Once again, the wording of the Constitution was very general[16] and left to the states little more than the appointment of militia officers. It was obvious, the critics declared, that the states had no strength to resist federal encroachments. Moreover, the President was to be commander-in-chief both of the regular army and of the militia when it was serving under the United States. The attention of the Antifederalists was especially drawn to the authorization given Congress to raise an army even when the country was at peace, without limits as to time; it might

12. Ibid., II, 522-23; *Pa. Packet* (Phila.), Dec. 17, 1787.
13. Staples, *Rhode Island in Cont. Cong.*, 654, 679.
14. Elliot, ed., *Debates*, II, 331-32.
15. Arguments on this point are easily accessible and research into familiar published sources provides all the evidence needed. Among unpublished references not listed above are, "Candidus," in the *Independent Chronicle* (Boston), Dec. 6, 1787 (especially for the danger from direct taxes); "Deliberator," in the *Freeman's Journal* (Phila.), Mar. 26, 1788; "Philadelphiensis," in *ibid.*, Dec. 12, 1787; "A Watchman," in the *Worcester Mag.*, 4 (1788), 242; "A Georgian," in the *Gazette of State of Georgia* (Savannah), Nov. 15, 1787; "Hampden," in the *Mass. Centinel* (Boston), Jan. 26, 1788; "Impartial Examiner," in the *Va. Independent Chronicle* 'Richmond), Feb. 20, June 18, 1788; "A Farmer," in the *Independent Gazetteer* (Phila.), Apr. 15, 27, 1788; "John DeWitt," in the *American Herald* (Boston), Nov. 19, 1787; John Lamb, article in his handwriting, Feb. 16, 1788, Lamb Papers, N.Y. Hist. Soc.
16. "To raise and support Armies, ... To make Rules for the Government and Regulation of the land and naval Forces; To provide for calling forth the Militia to execute the Laws of the Union, suppress Insurrections and repel Invasions; To provide for organizing, arming, and disciplining, the Militia and for governing such Part of them as may be employed in the Service of the United States."

even control the militia. Obviously Congress could enforce the most oppressive of laws, and if its own army did not suffice, militia from one end of the nation might be marched to dominate another. "In a free Government," said John Smilie, "there never will be Need of standing Armies, for it depends on the Confidence of the People. If it does not so depend, it is not free." Moreover, he pointed out, not only would Congress have its own army, but it could also command the militia: "the last Resource of a free People is taken away"; how then could the people resist? [17]

The danger of this was obvious to the student of history: standing armies had always resulted in oppression. "By far the greater part of the different nations, who have fallen from the glorious state of liberty, owe their ruin to standing armies." [18] In the United States, where liberty had its home, was it to be surrendered? "It is yet much too early to set it down for a fact, that mankind cannot be governed, but by force." [19] The temptations of power were well known; why now make it possible for "some ambitious man to step up into the throne, and to seize absolute power," or alternatively to "enable a few proud, intriguing, aristocratical men" to trample upon the people.[20] Moreover, to realize the true danger it must be remembered that Congress also had the power to tax. The two went together: taxes would be collected by the army which in turn would be supported by taxes. One power might be granted, perhaps, but not both, and that this had been done was revelatory of the framers' intent, and prophetic of the future. "The Convention," said Smilie, "knew this was not a free government; otherwise, they would not have asked the powers of the purse and sword." [21] Benjamin Harrison had the courage to warn Washington that "the sword, and such powers will; nay in the nature of things they must sooner or later, establish a tyranny,

17. McMaster and Stone, *Pennsylvania and the Constitution*, 777.
18. "Impartial Examiner," in the *Va. Independent Chronicle* (Richmond), Feb. 27, 1788.
19. *American Herald* (Boston), Dec. 3, 1787. The minority of the Pennsylvania convention also warned that the new government would be executed by force. McMaster and Stone, *Pennsylvania and the Constitution*, 480.
20. "Centinel," in the *Freeman's Journal* (Phila.), Oct. 24, 1787; "Cincinnatus," in the *N.Y. Journal*, Nov. 29, 1787.
21. Elliot, ed., *Debates*, II, 522.

not inferior to the triumvirate, or centum viri of Rome." [22] Similarly George Clinton warned that one day the people would try to resist the burdens placed on them, and that the government would use force; this in turn would require more money, and "add fuel to the fire." Here was unlimited power in the hands of those who might not be responsive to the public will—power which surely proved that the states were no longer independent, especially when it was considered in relation to the other great powers.[23]

But just as the Antifederalists, while criticizing the extent of Congress's control over taxation, did not intend to deny revenue entirely, so too the objections leveled against an excessive authority over the military did not deny the need for a national army. This would have been absurd indeed in a people who had just won a war with the use of federal troops. The Antifederalists did not seek to withhold essential powers, only the means to pervert them. In wartime an army was obviously necessary. What they did wish to avoid was an army that existed continuously. Yet even then most of the state conventions which suggested amendments accepted the principle that a standing army in time of peace might be justifiable if a two-thirds majority of both houses agreed.[24] It was also clear that under certain circumstances Congress ought to have power over the militia. No state convention denied this, but several did limit the degree of control. In brief, the Antifederalists tried to make sure that the army could not be used against the will of the majority. The fact that the Constitution failed to include such a safeguard seemed not merely careless but deliberate and ominous.

22. Oct. 4, 1787. Mass. Hist. Soc., *Proceedings*, 2nd Ser., 17 (1903), 477.
23. Ford, ed., *Essays*, 272. See also for these objections, the Albany Antifederal Committee, in the *N.Y. Journal*, Apr. 26, 1788; "Tamony," in *ibid.*, Feb. 8, 1788 (stressing the President's authority); "Cincinnatus," in *ibid.*, Nov. 15, 1787; "A Federal Republican," in the *Norfolk Journal*, Mar. 5, 1788; "A Democratic Federalist," in the *Pa. Herald* (Phila.), Oct. 17, 1787 (where he cites Burgh); "Philadelphiensis," in the *Freeman's Journal* (Phila.), Dec. 12, 1787 and in the *Independent Gazetteer* (Phila.), Dec. 12, 1787, and in *ibid.*, Feb. 7, 1787 (especially good); Luther Martin in Ford, ed., *Essays*, 358. Elliot's *Debates* of course contain many references.
24. This was suggested by Virginia, North Carolina, Maryland (the convention minority), New York, and New Hampshire (which preferred three-fourths of both Houses). Rhode Island and Pennsylvania wanted no standing army at all.

The power over commerce, on the other hand, was not a major issue. Despite past controversy over giving Congress the power to regulate trade, the sweeping grant of authority conferred by the Constitution met with only scattered opposition. Northern Antifederalists did not oppose it—indeed many were emphatic that Congress should be granted this control. In the South there were some objections. Benjamin Harrison feared "that if the constitution is carried into effect, the states south of Potowmac, will be little more than appendages to those to the northward of it," and Rawlins Lowndes warned the South Carolina legislature that the Northern states could levy high freight charges upon the South.[25] Yet most Southerners failed to mention the matter at all[26] and several stated that they were willing to accept the clause.[27] A middle position was taken by George Mason[28] and expressed in amendments adopted by the conventions of Virginia and North Carolina and those advanced by the minority of the Maryland convention. These granted the power to Congress but protected the peculiar interests of the South by providing that a two-thirds majority would be required for the passage of a commerce act. Perhaps most Southern Antifederalists favored some such restriction, but in the North the power over commerce, far from being disliked, was one of the admired features.

Another objection of great importance, judging from the number of times it was introduced, was the danger inherent in that clause which gave Congress power to control the time, place, and manner of holding elections.[29] What might seem a frivolous criti-

25. To Washington, Oct. 4, 1787, Mass. Hist. Soc., *Proceedings*, 2nd Ser., 17 (1903), 477; *Daily Advertiser* (Charleston), Jan. 25, 1788.

26. For instance George Lee Turberville, listing all of the objections which he had heard in Virginia, did not include federal control of commerce except as to export taxes. To Madison, Dec. 11, 1787, Madison Papers, N.Y. Pub. Lib.

27. Monroe and Grayson in Elliot, ed., *Debates*, III, 214, 278; "An Impartial Examiner," in the *Va. Independent Chronicle* (Richmond), June 18, 1788; "A Georgian," in the *Gazette of State of Georgia* (Savannah), Nov. 15, 1787; "A Federal Republican," in the *Norfolk Journal*, Mar. 5, 1788; Bloodworth in Elliot, ed., *Debates*, IV, 70.

28. Ford, ed., *Pamphlets*, 330.

29. "The Times, Places and Manner of holding Elections for Senators and Representatives, shall be prescribed in each State by the Legislature thereof; but the Congress may at any time by Law make or alter such Regulations, except as to the Places of chusing Senators."

cism becomes explicable when considered in its proper setting. The Antifederalists believed that many of the Federalists sought to create an aristocracy. Their examination of the Constitution—of the construction of Senate and Presidency, of the extensive powers granted to Congress, of the principles on which the whole was based—led them to fear that such was intended. They expected power to be abused, and it was the duty of those framing a government, which might control the destiny of future generations, to guard against even the bare possibility of future tyranny. The constitution, as Spencer Roane put it, should be like Caesar's wife —not merely good, but unsuspected.[30] Was there danger to be apprehended in this clause? Nearly everyone who examined the Constitution with a critical eye thought there was, and to the reply that the power over elections would be used only in cases of invasion, they inquired why the wording was then so general as to admit the application at any time.

Various fearful possibilities were fancied. The members of Congress, by using this power, might make their terms perpetual. The clause, it was observed, would allow Congress to decree the holding of elections at places where certain interests would be discriminated against.[31] "By altering the time," wrote James Winthrop, "they may continue a representative during his whole life; by altering the manner, they may fill up the vacancies by their own votes without the consent of the people; and by altering the place, all the elections may be made at the seat of the federal government."[32] "It apparently looks foward to a consolidation of the government of the United States," objected Samuel Spencer of North Carolina, "when the state legislatures may entirely decay away."[33] This clause, when considered in conjunction with the rest of the Constitution, re-emphasized the dubious nature of the whole. William Goudy of North Carolina declared, "Mr. Chairman, the invasion of these states is urged as a reason for this clause. But why did they not mention that it should be only in

---

30. "The Plain Dealer," in the *Va. Independent Chronicle* (Richmond), Feb. 13, 1788.

31. For example, "Cornelius," quoted in Harding, *Ratification in Massachusetts*, 121-24; Elliot, ed., *Debates*, II, 441.

32. Ford, ed., *Essays*, 105.

33. Elliot, ed., *Debates*, IV, 51.

cases of invasion? But that was not the reason, in my humble opinion. I fear it was a combination against our liberties. I ask, when we give them the purse in one hand, and the sword in another, what power have we left? It will lead to an aristocratical government, and establish tyranny over us. We are freemen, and we ought to have the privileges of such." [34] The Federalists were able to make it clear that some such power was needed in case the state legislatures were unable or unwilling to hold elections; the Antifederalists insisted that if such were the intent, it should be clearly stated. Every convention suggesting amendments included one which limited this power. [35]

The origins of this criticism by the Antifederalists can be readily understood, and certainly Congress did have power to abuse the elections clause; the objection was seriously meant and is to be regarded with respect. It is not so easy to take seriously, however, the criticism directed against Congress's control over a ten-mile square area. [36] This argument was made only occasionally, by not over one-third of those who made an extensive analysis of the Constitution. At times the debate became frivolous, as when a North Carolinian asserted that the area would be a fort from which fifty or a hundred thousand men would sally forth to enslave the people, [37] and when Gilbert Livingston referred to "an impenetrable wall of adamant and gold, the wealth of the whole country flowing into it." [38] Yet George Mason is not to be regarded as a frivolous speaker. He pointed out that if Con-

34. *Ibid.*, 56.

35. Yet the Federalists did not always favor a definition of Congressional control over elections. In Maryland it was not the majority but only the minority which favored the passage of the following, which is given as typical of the amendments suggested: "That the Congress shall have no power to alter or change the time, place, or manner of holding elections for senators or representatives, unless a state shall negelect to make regulations, or to execute its regulation, or shall be prevented by invasion or rebellion; in which cases only, Congress may interfere, until the cause be removed." Elliot, ed., *Debates*, II, 552.

36. "To exercise exclusive Legislation in all Cases whatsoever, over such District (not exceeding ten Miles square) as may ... become the Seat of the Government of the United States."

37. Winslow C. Watson, ed., *Men and Times of the Revolution; or, Memoirs of Elkanah Watson ...* (New York, 1856), 263.

38. Elliot, ed., *Debates*, II, 287.

gress did endeavor to establish a tyranny—and precautions ought to be taken against the possibility—then government officials could find in that area a safe base from which to oppress the people, beyond the reach of state law, under the protection of the central government with its army. Mason's objection was not against Congress's power to legislate within the area, but that this power was exclusive.[39] Others emphasized the same point. Although in most cases the arguments were made publicly, and therefore can be suspected of ulterior motive, Samuel Osgood, writing privately to Samuel Adams, felt that this clause might be abused unless precautions were taken.[40] Joshua Atherton also lamented in a letter that New Hampshire had failed to adopt an amendment on the subject.[41] Indeed only three states (New York, Virginia, and North Carolina) did so. The objection was not of major importance, but by some Antifederalists it was sincerely made.[42]

Another criticism, even less frequently offered, and then only in passing, was that the new government would be more expensive than the old; that the people could not support both state and federal governments.[43] It was argued that the more extensive powers granted by the Constitution would require far more federal officers; other critics feared that the federal debt would be paid at par and that heavy taxes would be levied for that purpose. The latter possibility, which had significant implications, will be discussed later. A few other objections were occasionally expressed, such as the possibility that Congress might create

39. *Ibid.*, III, 431.
40. Jan. 5, 1788, Adams Papers, N.Y. Pub. Lib.
41. To the Federal Republican Committee, June 23, 1788, Lamb Papers, N.Y. Hist. Soc.
42. For other objections, see Lenoir of North Carolina in Elliot, ed., *Debates*, IV, 203; Grayson, Henry, and Tyler of Virginia in *ibid.*, III, 431, 455; Tredwell of New York in *ibid.*, II, 402; Taylor in *Mass. Debates*, 199-200; Clinton in Ford., *Essays*, 262; Harrisburg convention in McMaster and Stone, *Pennsylvania and the Constitution*, 563; "A Columbian Patriot," in the *N.Y. Journal*, Apr. 5, 1788; *New-Hampshire Spy* (Portsmouth), June 21, 1788; *Hampshire Gazette* (Northampton, Mass.), Apr. 9, 1788. Yet such exhaustive discussions as those of the Albany Antifederal Committee, "An Officer of the Late Continental Army," "John DeWitt," "Cincinnatus," "Centinel," "Brutus," R. H. Lee and others did not mention this.
43. See, for example, Elliot, ed., *Debates*, II, 519, IV, 239.

monopolies,[44] or that Congress ought to be required to publish its journal more regularly than "from time to time."[45] Both of these ideas were supported in a demand for amendments. Still another minor criticism, but more often mentioned than the foregoing, was that instead of being paid by the states as under the Articles of Confederation members of Congress would now be paid out of national funds and would therefore be independent of state control. This might result in an abuse of the powers granted to the legislative branch.[46]

Such objections were insignificant compared with those concerning the ambiguities of the Constitution and the so-called "implied powers." Of particular interest is the fact that the arguments on these points anticipated subsequent developments. Suspicious as they were of the intent of the framers, the Antifederalists regarded with great mistrust the vague wording which might permit tyranny to enter on an implication. "There is," wrote Thomas B. Wait of Maine, "a certain darkness, duplicity and studied ambiguity of expression running through the whole Constitution. . . . As it now stands but very few individuals do or ever will understand it, consequently Congress will be its own interpreter."[47] Such extensive undefined powers over the lives and properties of the citizens were "capable of being interpreted to answer the most ambitious and arbitrary purposes."[48] The idea that powers, even when not granted, might be exercised by interpretation had been maintained in regard to the Articles; now, when so much more power had been given, it was even more to be feared.

It was not reassuring to discover that spokesmen for the Federalists argued in favor of implied powers. Madison wrote in the *Federalist Papers* that "No axiom is more clearly established in laws, or in reason, than that wherever the end is required, the

44. *Ibid.*, 407, III, 291; "A Son of Liberty," in the *N.Y Journal*, Nov. 8, 1788.

45. Elliot, ed., *Debates*, III, 60, 404, 459, 659-70.

46. See, for example, "Candidus," in the *Independent Chronicle* (Boston), Dec. 6, 1787; "A Georgian," in the *Gazette of State of Georgia* (Savannah), Nov. 15, 1787; amendments of Virginia and North Carolina.

47. To George Thatcher, Jan. 8, 1788, *Hist. Mag.*, 16 (1869), 262.

48. Albany Antifederal Committee, in the *N.Y. Journal*, Apr. 26, 1787; Henry and Dawson in Elliot, ed., *Debates*, III, 589-90, 612.

means are authorized; wherever a general power to do a thing is given, every particular power necessary for doing it is included." [49] Attempts of the Federalists to placate their opponents were therefore not very successful. William Findley remarked that "the System ought to speak for itself; and not need Explanations." [50] The wording of the Constitution as a whole was cited, and particular attention was paid to the "necessary and proper" and "general welfare" clauses. [51] "No terms," wrote "Brutus," "can be more indefinite than these, and it is obvious, that the legislature alone must judge what laws are proper and necessary for the purpose." What powers, therefore, did the Constitution actually withhold from Congress? The new government would be omnipotent. [52] Similarly the words "general welfare" might be interpreted to extend to every possible subject. Silas Lee, like George Mason, suggested that Congress might silence criticism of the administration. [53] "Timoleon" asked his reader to imagine that a ruler of the country found the rights of conscience and freedom of the press to be troublesome, and that the ruler therefore inquired of a justice of the Supreme Court whether a law could be passed to restrict these rights. The judge replied:

In the 8th section of the first article of the new Constitution, the Congress have power given *to lay and collect taxes for the general welfare of the United States.* By this power, the right of taxing is

49. *The Federalist,* No. 44.
50. McMaster and Stone, *Pennsylvania and the Constitution,* 776.
51. The first occurs at the end of the section describing Congress's powers: "To make all Laws which shall be necessary and proper for carrying into Execution the foregoing Powers, and all other Powers vested by this Constitution in the Government of the United States, or in any Department or Office thereof." There are two clauses containing the words "General Welfare." One occurs in connection with the power to collect taxes; the other is in the preamble, where the purpose of establishing the Constitution includes: "to promote the general Welfare."
52. No. 5, in the *N.Y. Journal,* Dec. 13, 1787; Gen. William Russell to Col. William Fleming, Jan. 25, 1788, Emmett Coll., No. 8945, N.Y. Pub. Lib.; "A Republican Federalist," in the *Mass. Centinel* (Boston), Feb. 2, 1788; R. H. Lee in Ford, ed., *Pamphlets,* 312; "Brutus," in the *N.Y. Journal,* Oct. 18, 1787; Monroe and Mason in Elliot, ed., *Debates,* III, 218, 441-42; Smilie in the *Pa. Herald* (Phila.), Dec. 19, 1787; Whitehill in McMaster and Stone, *Pennsylvania and the Constitution,* 285.
53. To George Thatcher, Jan. 23, 1788, *Hist. Mag.,* 16 (1869), 267.

co-extensive with the *general welfare*, and the *general welfare* is as unlimited as actions and things are that may disturb or benefit the general welfare. A right being given to *tax* for the general welfare, and a right of judging what is for the general welfare, as *necessarily* includes a power of protecting, defending, and promoting it by all such laws and means as are fitted to that end; for, . . . who gives the end gives the means necessary to obtain the end. . . .

From hence it clearly results, that, if *preachers* and *printers* are troublesome to the new government, and that in the opinion of its rulers, it shall be for the general welfare to restrain or suppress both the one and the other, it may be done consistently with the new Constitution.[54]

In short, it was argued that the general welfare and the necessary and proper clauses were indefinite and indefinable. The state governments had no check on the powers that they would confer by interpretation upon Congress. If the Constitution truly established a government of limited powers, then some restrictions were obviously essential. An amendment must be added which definitely reserved to the states all ungranted powers.[55] As a result of this argument all of the states which proposed amendments included one similar to that which became the tenth amendment to the Constitution.

One branch of the new government and its authority remains to be considered. It is no surprise that, in a land where lawyers played an important role, the judiciary stimulated a considerable amount of thought and an even greater amount of verbiage.

---

54. *N.Y. Journal*, Nov. 1, 1787.

55. Williams of New York in Elliot, ed., *Debates*, II, 338; "A Countryman," in the *N.Y. Journal*, Jan. 17, 1788; "An Old Whig," in *ibid.*, Nov. 28, 1787; "Brutus," in *ibid.*, Dec. 27, 1787; "Letter from a Hermit to a Friend," in the *U.S. Chronicle* (Providence), Mar. 27, 1788; R. H. Lee to the governor of Virginia, Oct. 16, 1787, Ballagh, ed., *Lee*, II, 453. The historian of Durham, Conn., writing at the time of the Civil War, asserts that he "was often told by those who knew" that the town voted against ratification "from the apprehension and fear felt by the people of the town, that the Federal Government to be created by it, would take advantage of the powers delegated to it, to assume other powers not delegated." William Chauncey Fowler, *History of Durham, Connecticut, from the first grant of land in 1662 to 1866* (Hartford, 1866), 27-28.

Probably had this section of the new plan been copied from the Bible, it would still have been closely scrutinized and warmly debated. Small wonder therefore that over two-thirds of the Antifederalists found something wrong. Nor is it surprising that they did not all discover the same faults.

They engaged in much generalizing and speculating, some of it wild, some (as events transpired) very much to the point. It has previously been noted that the great authority of the Supreme Court was cited as evidence of consolidation. "It appears to me," wrote Melancton Smith to Abraham Yates, Jr., that "this part of the system is so framed as to *clinch* all the other powers, and to extend them in a silent and imperceptible manner to any thing and everything, while the Court who are vested with these powers are totally independent, uncontroulable and not amenable to any other power in any decisions they may make." [56] Several Antifederalists believed that the Supreme Court would decide the meaning of the Constitution, and would extend the jurisdiction of the federal government. [57] Robert Whitehill echoed the opinions of some when he warned that "Appeals will be to the Supreme Court, which will put it in the Power of the wealthy to oppress the poor," and "A Georgian" agreed. "Lycurgus" believed that the court would help to put down uprisings, and "John Humble" was equally suspicious. [58] Only one critic, however, objected that the appointment of the judges would free them from popular control, [59] and the argument which developed a hundred years later, that the Court was undemocratic because of its lack of responsibility, and that it was biased against changes desired by the majority, while implied by a few writers, was never clearly stated.

56. Jan. 23, 1788, Yates, Jr., Papers, N.Y. Pub. Lib.
57. "Brutus," in the *N.Y. Journal,* Jan. 31, Feb. 7, 14, 21, 1788; Mason in Elliot, ed., *Debates,* III, 521-22; *ibid.,* II, 490; Samuel Osgood to Samuel Adams, Jan. 5, 1788, Samuel Adams Papers, N.Y. Pub. Lib.
58. McMaster and Stone, *Pennsylvania and the Constitution,* 779; *Gazette of State of Georgia* (Savannah), Nov. 15, 1787; *Independent Gazetteer* (Phila.), Oct. 17, 1787; *ibid.,* Oct. 29, 1787.
59. "A Watchman" wrote that the article "deprives the inhabitants of each state of the power of choosing their superiour and inferiour judges." *Worcester Mag.,* 4 (1788), 243.

Aside from these objections to the general power of the judiciary,[60] a few other detailed criticisms were expressed with some frequency. The federal courts had power over cases between citizens of different states, with appellate jurisdiction both as to law and fact. For this, some of the Antifederalists asserted, there was no need whatever, though a few felt that the Supreme Court might be given appellate jurisdiction as to law, but not as to fact.[61] Modifications in this section of the Constitution were recommended by the conventions of Massachusetts, New Hampshire, New York, Pennsylvania, Maryland, Virginia, and North Carolina. Also criticized was the clause giving the new courts authority over cases between a state and the citizens of other states, of foreign countries, and even, under certain conditions, of the state itself. The Antifederalists pointed out that this meant that a state might be sued against its will. What then became of state sovereignty? The state judiciary was annihilated, and the state legislature prostrated by such a provision.[62] Joshua Atherton of New Hampshire was worried about another possibility: might the scope of federal jurisdiction not "expose every State to be sued in the New Court, on their public Securities holden by Citizens of other States?"[63] Federalists argued that there was no such danger: the states would not be sued. Their assurances evidently satisfied almost everyone, since only the New York convention came out clearly in favor of an amendment on the subject; yet the future proved that the fear had been well founded.

60. See also "Impartial Examiner," in the *Va. Independent Chronicle* (Richmond), Feb. 27, 1788; R. H. Lee in Ford, ed., *Pamphlets*, 307; Mason in *ibid.*, 329; Martin in Farrand, ed., *Records of the Federal Convention*, III, 222; Henry and Grayson in Elliot, ed., *Debates*, III, 539-41, 563-70; Spencer and Locke in *ibid.*, IV, 136, 168-69; *ibid.*, II, 445.

61. Lancaster in *ibid.*, IV, 214; Mason in *ibid.*, III, 526; "Many Customers," in the *Independent Gazetteer* (Phila.), Dec. 4, 1787; minority of the Pennsylvania House of Representatives, in the *Pa. Packet* (Phila.), Oct. 4, 1787; "John DeWitt," in the *American Herald* (Boston), Oct. 29, 1787; "Agrippa," in Ford, ed., *Essays*, 118; Arthur Lee to John Adams, Oct. 3, 1787, Adams, ed., *Works of Adams*, IX, 555; Joseph Jones to James Madison, Oct. 29, 1787, Mass. Hist. Soc., *Proceedings*, 2nd Ser., 17 (1903), 488.

62. Mason in Elliot, ed., *Debates*, III, 527.

63. To the Federal Republican Committee, June 23, 1788, Lamb Papers, N.Y. Hist. Soc.

On the whole, most Antifederalists were satisfied with all or with the greater part of the judiciary article; the need for a national court system was nowhere challenged and most of its powers were accepted without question. It should be added that only a few foresaw what the Supreme Court was to become, and the protests of these few were barely heard.

If the Antifederalists failed to predict the future role of the Supreme Court, they did anticipate the concentration of power in the federal government, and they were alarmed. The rights and liberties of all Americans were in danger from encroachments from above. Such powers, wrote John Francis Mercer, "tempt the avarice and ambition of men to a violation of the rights of their fellow Citizens . . . in Government what may be done will be done." [64] How could these rights be protected? Obviously by rejecting the Constitution; but if that were not done, then evils must be averted by amendment, and the liberties of the citizens preserved by a bill of rights. Why was there none in the Constitution? Were the people to have no rights? [65] The Federalists replied that the Constitution established a government of limited powers in which those not granted were reserved, so that freedom of speech, press, trial by jury, and religion, with all other rights, were reserved to the people. The Antifederalists pointed out in rebuttal that the framers had seen fit specifically to reserve the rights of habeas corpus and trial by jury in criminal cases; it looked very much as if only these were to be guaranteed. Furthermore it was essential to remember the danger inherent in so strong a government. As John Smilie put it, "When we further consider the extensive, the undefined powers vested in the administrators of this system, when we consider the system itself as a great political compact between the governors and the governed, a plain, strong, and accurate criterion by which the people might at once determine when, and in what instance their rights were violated, is a preliminary, without which, this plan ought not to be adopted." [66] The vast majority of Antifederalists and some of the Federalists became convinced that a bill of rights was essen-

---

64. MS in Etting Coll., Autograph Letters, VI, Hist. Soc. Pa.
65. *Daily Advertiser* (Charleston), Feb. 1, 1788.
66. McMaster and Stone, *Pennsylvania and the Constitution*, 255.

tial.[67] Three "rights" were especially emphasized: freedom of religion, or conscience; the right to a trial by jury; and freedom of the press.

The first of these was least mentioned. Antifederalists were not greatly concerned about religious freedom under the Constitution, apparently because there was nothing that threatened it and no special safeguards were deemed necessary. A prominent Virginia Baptist thought religious freedom was "not sufficiently secured," [68] and a few individuals in the North felt that it should be expressly guaranteed; [69] but most opinion voiced in New England was animated by desire to exclude non-Protestants from public office—not by toleration but by intolerance.[70] Generally, when the ratifying conventions drafted bills of rights, they included provision for religious freedom as a matter of course, but other amendments were felt to be far more important.[71]

The need for protecting the right to trial by jury seemed of much greater consequence. The Constitution guaranteed that "the Trial of all Crimes, except in Cases of Impeachment, shall be by Jury." Why only crimes? Did this mean that there was no guarantee of trial by jury in civil cases? Moreover, the Supreme Court had appellate jurisdiction which enabled it to decide facts; here was a concrete example of what was to be expected, for there

67. Of Antifederal statements which made a fairly complete analysis of the Constitution, 31 out of 38 stressed the need for a bill of rights. Actually the proportion was even higher. The nature of the articles by "Cato Uticensis" and "A Tenant" precluded the statement that these amendments were wanted, but the tone of the objections implies that they were. Melancton Smith, George Clinton, and R. H. Lee do not seem to have spoken or written clearly in favor of a bill of rights, yet they may have desired one; the remaining two exceptions were articles written before the idea of amendments had taken hold. It would be safe to say that at least nine out of ten Antifederalists wanted a bill of rights.

68. Rev. John Leeland, as reported by Joseph Spencer to James Madison, Feb. 28, 1788, in *Doc. Hist. of the Constitution*, IV, 528.

69. The New Hampshire convention advocated religious freedom. But the Massachusetts convention did not propose such an amendment. *New Hampshire State Papers*, X, 21.

70. Jeremiah Libbey to Jeremy Belknap, Feb. 22, 1788, "The Belknap Papers," Mass. Hist. Soc., *Collections*, 6th Ser., 4 (1891), 390; *Mass. Debates*, 143, 222, 251.

71. In Maryland the Federalist convention majority felt it unnecessary.

would be no jury in such trials. The absence of this ancient right was lamented by nearly everyone who commented in any detail on the Constitution.[72] Every ratifying convention which considered amendments adopted one or more similar to the present Articles V, VI, and VII.

The Antifederalists were also concerned about the absence of a clause protecting freedom of the press, with which freedom of speech was occasionally—but not often—associated. The omission was ordinarily noted in general terms, but there were some specific statements. The author of "1st Book of Samuel, Chap. VIII" warned that those in control of the new government "will cause the scribes of the people to be brought bound into the distant land, where they assemble; and be there cast into prison, under the pretence of their having transcribed seditious papers against the King and the rulers."[73] Smilie feared that the right to criticize would suffer from an undemocratic government. Congress, he believed, could pass a law for the punishment of libels, and there would be no security for a printer tried in federal courts. He warned that "an aristocratical Govt cannot bear the Liberty of the Press."[74] Silas Lee also feared that Congress might punish a man who published statements criticizing the administration. Citing the Zenger case, "Cincinnatus" asserted that the judges could prosecute the press without being hampered by a jury. Why, asked Lincoln of South Carolina, was liberty of the press not secured? The omission must have been purposeful.[75] George Mason, as we have seen, feared that Congress would enforce oppressive laws by restricting the press and trying violators in federal courts, and "Timoleon" and Richard Henry Lee held the same opinion. Even when no such dire result was

72. As, for example, "Cincinnatus," in the *N. Y. Journal*, Nov. 8, 15, 1787; "Algernon Sidney," in the *Independent Gazetteer* (Phila.), Mar. 4, 1788. Findley believed that without jury trial the "Lower Class of People" would be oppressed. McMaster and Stone, *Pennsylvania and the Constitution*, 782.

73. *Va. Independent Chronicle* (Richmond), Oct. 31, 1787.

74. McMaster and Stone, *Pennsylvania and the Constitution*, 770.

75. George Thatcher, Jan. 23, 1788, *Hist. Mag.*, 16 (1869), 267; *Independent Gazetteer* (Phila.), Nov. 16, 1787, and the *N. Y. Journal*, Nov. 1, 1787; *Daily Advertiser* (Charleston), Feb. 1, 1788.

anticipated, Antifederalists generally felt that the "Enestimable Provilege" of a free press should be secured.[76]

Still another section of the Constitution which concerned the Antifederalists was the provision for amendment. Their fear was not that amendment would be too easy, but that it would be too difficult. Under the government of the Confederation, the obstacles placed in the way of amendment had safeguarded liberty. The Confederation Congress could not abuse control over taxation and the army, for it had no such powers. But now these powers were granted by the Constitution and were susceptible to abuse. Formerly, amendments threatened liberty, and to forestall them was the object; now they were essential to liberty's defense. But could such changes be obtained, once the Constitution had been ratified? Would three-fourths of the states agree to the thorough overhauling which was needed? The Antifederalists thought not.[77] It might be easy enough to add powers to a free government, but it would be impossible to subtract them from an arbitrary one. Once Congress gained power, would it be abandoned? No, for "People once possessed of power are always loth to part with it." [78] The nature of mankind must undergo a revolution not to be expected this side of eternity, wrote George Bryan, before amendments would be granted. Similarly, William Findley warned, "There is no Security for such Amendments as we want. If we don't obtain them now, we shall probably never procure them." The idea of later amendments, then, was a "delusion"; the few could block the efforts of the many.[79] Although some were willing to trust the Federalists' promise that amendments would be made after ratification, most Antifederalists felt that to ratify first would

76. Elliot, ed., *Debates*, III, 441-42; *N. Y. Journal*, Nov. 1, 1787; Lee to Samuel Adams, Oct. 5, 1787, Ballagh, ed., *Lee*, II, 446; Taylor, *Great Barrington*, 318. See also "A Republican," in the *N. Y. Journal*, Oct. 25, 1787.

77. For example, "John DeWitt," in the *American Herald* (Boston), Oct. 29, 1787; "Algernon Sidney," in the *Independent Gazetteer* (Phila.), Nov. 21, 1787; "An Old Whig," in *ibid.*, Feb. 6, 1788.

78. *Freeman's Journal* (Phila.), Mar. 5, 1788; *N. Y. Journal*, Nov. 27, 1787.

79. "Centinel," in the *Freeman's Journal* (Phila.), Oct. 24, 1787; McMaster and Stone, *Pennsylvania and the Constitution*, 776; R. H. Lee to Patrick Henry, Sept. 14, 1789, Ballagh, ed., *Lee*, II, 502; Lee in Ford, ed., *Pamphlets*, 317; Martin in Ford, ed., *Essays*, 375; *Mass. Debates*, 240, 242, 243, 249-50; Elliot, ed., *Debates*, III, 49, 291, 595, 639.

be, as Joshua Atherton expressed it, "to surrender our all, and then to ask our new masters, if they will be so gracious as to return to us some, or any part of our most important rights and privileges." [80]

Another category of objections to the new plan has so far been only parenthetically considered, namely, the belief that the Constitution would be beneficial to certain economic groups but detrimental to others. One may approach this general subject in several ways. First, it is possible to begin with the economic results which flowed from ratification and the establishment of the new government, relate these to certain articles of the Constitution, and conclude that there was an intentional, causal relationship. Interesting as such a procedure may be, it does not furnish decisive proof, nor is it good evidence of the ideas or intent of the framers and their critics. More appropriate to this study is a second sort of evidence: the beliefs of the Antifederalists. As historical evidence such material is of course biased, and that part of it published for public consumption is deliberately one-sided; it tells us more about the Antifederalists than about the Constitution. Yet, lest it be concluded that these hostile critics were totally wrong, a third type of evidence should be examined; for it appears that many of the supporters of the Constitution likewise viewed it as an economic document, at least in part. They, as well as the Antifederalists, were especially concerned about the effect of the plan on public debts, both state and federal, on private debts, on paper money, and on the various matters related to these.

The division of opinion concerning the Constitution may be explained in part, as we have seen, in terms of a debtor-creditor alignment. That the interest of the public or private creditor differed from the interest of the non-security holder or debtor is obvious now and was a commonplace then. Before the Philadelphia Convention met, "Plato" had pointed out that the people were divided into two great classes, one consisting of "all the holders of the Public Securities," the other including the "substantial yeomanry," who held few or none of the securities, and "whose interest it is to have the public debt discharged in the easiest manner." [81] Before the Convention had adjourned it had

80. To Lamb, June 11, 1788, Leake, *Lamb*, 312.
81. *U. S. Chronicle* (Providence), Apr. 19, 1787.

been predicted that its work would be favorable to the first class, in that the federal securities would probably appreciate in value.[82] In the Convention itself, Oliver Ellsworth referred to the anxiety of New Englanders to get rid of the public debt and observed that "the idea of strengthening the Natl. Govt. carries with it that of strengthening the public debt." [83] Upon reading the finished product, many thought that the prediction was justified, and hastened to act. From New Hampshire Jeremiah Libbey assured Jeremy Belknap that his continental securities had been kept safely, and that they would rise, with the national character, after ratification; similarly, in Virginia, Alexander Stuart reported general agreement that the state ought to buy public securities because they would appreciate under the new government.[84] The same principle applied to the debts of some states: when Henry Knox proposed to sell some of his Massachusetts securities he was informed that "from the appearance of the proposed Constitution being adopted . . . all public Securities would raise much higher." [85] Other observers were of like opinion, and in Canada, Guy Carleton, Lord Dorchester, learned that these ideas influenced the alignment on ratification. "Many wealthy individuals have taken a decided part in favor of the new plan," he was informed, "from the hope that the domestic debt of the Union may be funded, & that the various paper securities, of which they are holders to a great amount, purchased for a trifle, may rise to their value." [86]

82. Joseph Jones to Madison, June 7, 1787, Madison Papers, VII, Lib. Cong. The following article was widely reprinted, e.g., *Independent Gazetteer* (Phila.), Aug. 22, 1787; *Daily Advertiser* (N. Y.), Aug. 29, 1787; *Virginia Gazette, and Weekly Advertiser* (Richmond), Sept. 6, 1787: "One of the first objects with the national government to be elected under the new constitution, it is said, will be to provide funds for the payment of the national debt, and thereby to restore the credit of the United States, which has been so much impaired by the individual states. Every holder of a public security of any kind is, therefore, deeply interested in the cordial reception, and speedy establishment of a vigorous continental government."

83. Farrand, ed., *Records of the Federal Convention*, II, 91.

84. Oct. 24, 1787, "The Belknap Papers," Mass. Hist. Soc., *Collections*, 6th Ser., 4 (1891), 341; Alexander Stuart to Madison, Dec. 2, 1787, Madison Papers, VIII, Lib. Cong.

85. Henry Jackson to Knox, Oct. 21, 1787, Knox Papers, XXI, 23, Mass. Hist. Soc.

86. To Lord Sydney, Oct. 1788, in Douglas Brymner, *Report on Canadian Archives, 1890* (Ottawa, 1891), 101. Winthrop wrote, "The federalists,

This belief that the securities would appreciate in value was often expressed (indeed, the rise was fairly predictable), and Federalists were accused—for the most part by anonymous writers—of being motivated by this fact. Thus "A Federalist" wrote that those who favored the ratification (in Massachusetts) of the "gilded pill" were the "NOBLE order of C[incinnatu]s, holders of public securities, men of great wealth and expectation of public office, B[an]k[er]s and L[aw]y[er]s: these with their train of dependents from the Aristocratic combination."[87]

The Federalists also believed that private creditors would benefit. The difficulties which creditors had encountered in collecting debts, threatened as they were with installment and tender laws, paper money, and even rebellion, have been sufficiently noted. The Constitution was, they hoped, calculated to *make* men honest;[88] and indeed some of them explained the opposition to the Constitution on this basis.[89] The prospect that creditors could sue in the federal courts and recover claims in real money was particularly pleasing at a time when the collection of debts was exceptionally difficult and the number of suits in state courts

---

indeed, tell us that the state debts will all be incorporated with the continental debt, and all paid out of one fund." Ford, ed., *Essays*, 78. During the Federal Convention several of the delegates had spoken in favor of the assumption of state debts. Farrand, ed., *Records of the Federal Convention*, II, 327-28. See also Samuel Phillips Savage to George Thatcher, Feb. 17, Mar. 7, 1788, Thatcher to Pierse Long, Apr. 23, 1788, *Hist. Mag.*, 16 (1869), 339, 344, 348; *Pa. Gazette* (Phila.), Oct. 3, 1787; Andrew Craigie to D. Parker, July 27, 1788, quoted in Nathan Schachner, *Alexander Hamilton* (New York, 1946), 227; letters quoted in Nathan Schachner, *The Founding Fathers* (New York, 1954), 84-87.

87. *Boston Gazette*, Nov. 26, 1787. See also, "A *real* Federalist," in the *U.S. Chronicle* (Providence), Mar. 27, 1788; "Lycurgus," in *ibid.*, Apr. 3, 1788; Hugh Ledlie to John Lamb, Jan. 15, 1788, Lamb Papers, N.Y. Hist. Soc.; J. Galloway in Elliot, ed., *Debates*, IV, 190-91.

88. Henry Laurens to Edward Bridgen, Oct. 8, 1787, Laurens Papers, Letter Book No. 13, S. C. Hist. Soc.; Christopher Richmond to Horatio Gates, Feb. 13, 1788, Gates Papers, N.Y. Pub. Lib.; Jeremiah Libbey to Jeremy Belknap, Oct. 24, 1787, "The Belknap Papers," Mass. Hist. Soc., *Collections*, 6th Ser., 4 (1891), 341 ("it will make them honest, & put it out of their power to cheat every body by tender laws & paper money.").

89. For example, Madison to Jefferson, Oct. 17, 1788, Hunt, ed., *Writings of Madison*, V, 271.

extraordinarily high.[90] The long struggle against state issues of paper money would finally be won.[91]

The Antifederalists, or some of them, also felt that the Constitution discriminated in favor of the creditor interest in a variety of other ways. One prophesied: "They will order you, as yet smarting under the effects of thy bondage, to pay immediately all the debts due to the Britannites, yea, even the interest during the war; and they will order you to make good the plunder of the usurers and the speculators, the abomination of the land: and all these men will rejoice exceedingly." [92] "Cincinnatus" warned of unendurable taxes; he reminded his readers that the interest on the domestic debt was being paid in paper, at a cost, he stated, of $1,800,000 yearly. If the new government should raise the sum in specie, "it will certainly support public credit, but it will overwhelm the people. It will give immense fortunes to the speculators, but it will grind the poor to dust." [93] It would be impossible to avoid this burden, for now creditors of the states as well as of Congress could sue in federal courts for the payment of the securities at par.[94] Others could make use of the federal courts to collect money owed them. Southerners especially were warned that British merchants could collect old debts with interest, and it was

90. W. R. Davie of North Carolina in Elliot, ed., *Debates*, IV, 169; Henry Lee of Virginia in *ibid.*, III, 179; Hugh McCall to Edward Carrington, June 20, 1788, Boston Pub. Lib.; Arthur Bryan to George Bryan, Apr. 9, 1788, Bryan Papers, Box A24, Hist. Soc. Pa.; letters quoted in Albert J. Beveridge, *The Life of John Marshall*, 4 vols. (Boston, 1916-1919), I, 313, 445, 453.

91. Christopher Gadsden to Jefferson, Oct. 29, 1787, *Doc. Hist. of the Constitution*, IV, 356. The use of the Constitution as an economic instrument began quite early. In November of 1788 there was a "protest against the bill to regulate the recovery and payment of debts" signed by five South Carolinians—four of them Federalists—on the ground that it conflicted with the Constitution; they referred to the obligation of contracts and supreme law of the land clauses and warned that judges must give their decisions accordingly. Gratz Coll., Old Congress, Box 4, Hist. Soc. Pa.

92. "1st Book of Samuel, Chap. VIII," in the *Va. Independent Chronicle* (Richmond), Oct. 31, 1787.

93. *N.Y. Journal*, Dec. 6, 1787, and the *Freeman's Journal* (Phila.), Dec. 12, 1787.

94. Elliot, ed., *Debates*, III, 322, 473-75, IV, 205-6; *American Herald* (Boston), Nov. 19, 1787; Silas Lee to George Thatcher, Jan. 23, 1788, *Hist. Mag.*, 16 (1869), 268; Joshua Atherton to John Lamb, June 23, 1788, Lamb Papers, N.Y. Hist. Soc.

noted that states could no longer pass tender laws, installment bills, valuation and stay laws, to ease the lot of the unfortunate debtors.[95] George Tucker wrote to his heirs after the Constitution had been ratified in Virginia, "The recovery of British debts can no longer be postponed, and there now seems to be a moral certainty that your patrimony will all go to satisfy the unjust debt from your papa to the Hanburys." [96]

It seems obvious from all this that the clause prohibiting state issues of paper money was extremely important, if indeed the history of the preceding years did not furnish evidence enough of the fact. The curbing of state legislatures was a principal objective of the Federalists. One of them, speaking of a member of the New Hampshire legislature whom he disliked, wrote that "after the much wish'd for federal government is in motion it will not matter much who are sent to our Court, as their wings will be pretty well clip'd." [97] One of the wings thus sheared was that which upheld paper money issues. A number of Antifederalists, especially the well-to-do leaders, applauded this change, and because these men did most of the talking in conventions and writing for publication, there were few who openly defended paper money, and some indeed testified against it. Perhaps to defend it had become not quite *comme il faut*. Yet it had defenders. In Virginia Patrick Henry asserted, "It sounds mighty prettily to gentlemen, to curse paper money and honestly pay debts. But apply to the situation of America, and you will find there are thousands and thousands of contracts, whereof equity forbids an exact literal performance." Henry was assuredly correct in this, and he spoke for many besides himself when he inquired, "Let me

95. Article I, sec. 10: "No State shall . . . make any Thing but gold and silver Coin a Tender in Payment of Debts; pass any . . . Law impairing the Obligation of Contract, . . ." See the *Independent Gazetteer* (Phila.), Feb. 21, 1788; Elliot, ed., *Debates*, III, 566; Trenholme, *Ratification in N.C.*, 143; quotation and references in Robert L. Brunhouse, ed., "David Ramsay on the Ratification of the Constitution in South Carolina, 1787-1788," *Journal of So. Hist.*, 9 (1943), 554.

96. June 29, 1788, quoted in Moncure Daniel Conway, *Omitted Chapters of History Disclosed in the Life and Papers of Edmund Randolph* (New York, 1888), 106.

97. William Gardner to Nicholas Gilman, June 14, 1788, Misc. MSS, N. Y. Hist. Soc.

appeal to the candor of the committee, if the want of money be not the source of all our misfortunes. . . . This want of money cannot be supplied by changes in government." [98] In South Carolina, Rawlins Lowndes; in Maryland, John Francis Mercer and Luther Martin; in Massachusetts, William Symmes; and in North Carolina, Matthew Locke all agreed that states had in the past benefitted from paper money and ought to be permitted to do so again.[99] In most of the states the Federalists accused their opponents of being motivated by a desire for paper money. Many of them certainly had been in the past, and it is evident that this issue was extremely important in spite of the fact that Antifederalists did not make much of it openly.

It is impossible to determine how important economic motivations were in Antifederal thought, partly because it is so difficult to discover what makes men act, and partly because the Antifederalists themselves were so diverse in their interests that different factors operated unequally. What they wanted, whether they were interested primarily in blocking political centralization or in protecting the debtors, depended upon who they were. These differences in point of view will become clearer as we inquire what the Antifederalists desired as a substitute for the Constitution.

98. Elliot, ed., *Debates*, III, 161, 318-19.
99. *Daily Advertiser* (Charleston), Jan. 25, 1788; Farrand, ed., *Records of the Federal Convention*, II, 309, III, 214; Symmes to Osgood, Nov. 15, 1787, *Hist. Colls. of Essex Inst.*, 4 (1862), 214; Elliot, ed., *Debates*, IV, 169. The agitation for paper money was subsiding in 1787. Probably this clause would have attracted far more attention in 1785 or 1786.

Chapter VIII

THE ANTIFEDERAL SOLUTION

IN 1787 there were, politically, a number of different courses which the United States might follow. The choice was a serious one, for it would influence the fate of millions yet unborn. Neither monarchy nor the total abolition of the states was seriously considered; such extreme centralization was not acceptable to the vast majority of the people. So also the elimination of the central government was not to be thought of, although a few men did propose a division into separate confederacies, loosely associated.[1] The range of practicable solutions was in fact much narrower. Those who wanted a strong national government offered the Constitution, which was as far as they dared go. The Antifederalists were forced on the defensive by the overriding necessity of defeating the Constitution, but they were bound to consider what they wanted in its stead: if not ratification, then what? While most of them concentrated their attention on the immediate issue of defeating ratification, a number did make clear what they proposed as an alternative.[2]

It must be re-emphasized, to begin with, that the solutions which the Antifederalists advanced varied greatly. Nowhere is this more plain than in their attitude toward democratic ideas.

1. To divide the country into separate confederacies would do nothing to solve the nature of the central government, since the issue would have to be fought out in each of the three or four new nations. As a matter of fact the proponents of this idea were almost all Federalists, not Antifederalists (see Appendix A).

2. By "a number" is meant 15 or 16. Another 36 or so indicated their general position in a few words. Much can be inferred, also, from the objections made and the amendments suggested.

The relationship of Antifederalism to democracy, a matter so important to an understanding of the period, is a difficult subject to discuss with assurance. The word "Democracy" was used only occasionally, but it was known. It was employed in writing and in speaking, in letters, pamphlets, and newspaper articles, anonymous and signed. It was referred to with distaste and with praise, condemned or condoned or commended, by men as diverse as the rich South Carolina planter Ralph Izard, who did not like it, and the members of the Rhode Island legislature, who did.[3]

The meaning of the word was not always made clear; indeed it sometimes signified different things to different men. James Winthrop, for example, said that he preferred a "democratick" to an "aristocratick" republic, and defined the latter as one in which the state was governed by an order of nobles. Under this concept one could defend democracy and also believe in rule by the elite, as long as no nobles existed.[4] Sometimes a democracy was identified with a republic, as when Mercy Warren wrote that the Constitution did not erect a "Democratick or Republican" government[5]—the Antifederalists not infrequently used the word in this sense. Sometimes the word denoted a government which the people themselves ran, such as a town meeting. In such cases there was usually a modifying adjective, as when Samuel Adams referred to the "simple Democracies" in the towns,[6] and an anonymous writer wrote of the "airy phantoms of a pure democracy."[7] Some writers alluded to "the democracy," which was defined by Richard Henry Lee: it consisted, he said, of "the great body of the people, the middle and lower classes," as contrasted with "the few men of wealth and abilities" who comprised the "natural aristocracy."[8] In the same way Henry Knox wrote that "the democracy"

3. Ralph Izard to Jefferson, June 10, 1785, Boyd, ed., *Papers of Jefferson*, VIII, 196; Staples, *Rhode Island in Cont. Cong.*, 622.
4. Ford, ed., *Essays*, 106.
5. Ford, ed., *Pamphlets*, 8.
6. To Noah Webster, Apr. 30, 1784, Ford, ed., *Correspondence of Webb*, III, 37. For another example see "A Native," in Force, ed., *American Archives*, 4th Ser., VI, 750-51. Here again democratic and republican governments are considered identical.
7. *Independent Gazetteer* (Phila.), June 20, 1787.
8. Ford, ed., *Pamphlets*, 295.

might be managed.[9] This sense of the word comes close to modern usage, indeed the most common meaning of the term, if not always its implication, was much the same as today: fundamentally, a democracy was a government controlled by the people as a whole. It is not necessary to go into further detail here,[10] but it might be noted that the government of Pennsylvania was frequently described as democratic, and the Constitutionalists in that state as the democratic party.[11]

Although the word was understood, it was usually not employed even when democratic ideas were being discussed, possibly because some people were certain to react negatively to it, and its use would invite attack. The words "popular," [12] or "free," [13] were substituted. "Centinel," for example, wrote: "A republican, or free government, can only exist where the body of the people are virtuous, and where property is pretty equally divided. In such a government the people are the sovereign and their sense or opinion is the criterion of every public measure; for when this ceases to be the case, the nature of the government is changed, and an aristocracy, monarchy or despotism will rise on its ruin." [14] Sometimes, indeed, no identifying word at all was used, as in this passage, familiar to many of the Antifederal leaders:

If the persons to whom the trust of government is committed hold their places for short terms; if they are chosen by the unbiassed voices of a majority of the states, and subject to their instruction; Liberty will be enjoyed in its highest degree. But if they are chosen for long terms by a part only of the state; and if during that term they are subject to no controul from their constituents; the very idea of Liberty will be lost, and the power of chusing constituents becomes nothing but a power, lodged in a *few*, to chuse

9. To Rufus King, quoted in Harding, *Ratification in Massachusetts*, 12.

10. The development of democratic thought in the early months of the Revolution is described in Merrill Jensen, "Democracy and the American Revolution," *Hunt. Lib. Qtly.*, 20 (1957), 321-41.

11. See Benjamin Rush to Anthony Wayne, Sept. 24, 1776, quoted in Selsam, *Pennsylvania Constitution*, 209; Thomas McKean to John Adams, Apr. 30, 1787, McKean Papers, II, Hist. Soc. Pa.

12. For example, Joseph Reed to Anthony Wayne, June 13, 1781, in Roche, *Reed*, 187; Joseph Hawley to Elbridge Gerry, in Brown, *Hawley*, 170.

13. James Winthrop and George Clinton in Ford, ed., *Essays*, 59, 273.

14. *Independent Gazetteer* (Phila.), Oct. 5, 1787.

at certain periods, a body of *Masters* for themselves and for the
rest of the Community.[15]

Today democracy is a sacred word, but in the Revolutionary
era it aroused different emotions in different individuals. Rarely
indeed did any nationalist, any Federalist, refer to it approvingly.
Typically, what it represented was condemned, as Edmund Randolph condemned it in the Federal Convention.[16] Thus Jonathan
Jackson lamented the popular proneness to the idea; William
Hooper termed it "execrable"; Rufus King wrote of the "madness"
of it; and Theodore Sedgwick opposed "democratic equality." [17]
On the Antifederalist side, the word was almost always used with
approval. George Mason, indeed, said in the Federal Convention
that the country had experienced too much of it, but he presently
reminded the Convention that the people were in favor of it, and
ended by observing that though democratic principles were inconvenient they were the only security for the rights of the people.[18]
Thereafter he was to argue against the Constitution because it
was not democratic.[19] Elbridge Gerry also referred to the excess
of democracy, but he also warned the same body against depart-
ing too far from it; those of "a more democratic cast," he believed,
would oppose a general government.[20] With these possible exceptions, Antifederalists invariably used the word in a favorable
sense. Significant also is the fact that both sides agreed that the
people wanted it. The opinions of Jackson, Mason, and Gerry
have just been noted. Similarly Patrick Calhoun of South Carolina
opposed a convention in that state because "the general mass of
the people were so much bent for a democratical government"
that it might be dangerous.[21] Ralph Izard attributed democratic

15. Richard Price, *Observations on the Nature of Civil Liberty, the
Principles of Government, and the Justice and Policy of the War with
America* (Dublin, 1776), 14.
16. Farrand, ed., *Records of the Federal Convention*, I, 26-27, 51, 218.
17. Harding, *Ratification in Massachusetts*, 12-13n.; Douglas, "Burke,"
N. C. Hist. Rev., 26 (1949), 158; East, "Massachusetts Conservatives," in
Morris, ed., *Era of the American Revolution*, 378; Sedgwick to King, June
18, 1787, King Papers, N.Y. Hist. Soc.
18. Farrand, ed., *Records of the Federal Convention*, I, 48, 101, 134,
359.
19. Elliot, ed., *Debates*, III, 44.
20. Farrand, ed., *Records of the Federal Convention*, I, 48, II, 388.
21. *Charleston Evening Gazette*, Feb. 21, 1786.

convictions to the "Back Countrymen" of the same state;[22] Nathan Dane warned that the Constitution would be considered undemocratic,[23] and Richard Henry Lee also believed that whereas the people were democratic, the Constitution was not.[24]

From all this it may be concluded, first, that democratic ideas were quite often expressed, though the word was infrequently used; second, that insofar as democratic ideas were held, they were defended by the Antifederalists rather than the Federalists, and by the many, not the few.

It still remains to be inquired, how many of the Antifederalists were democratic and to what extent the Constitution was criticized from a democratic point of view. Two of the difficulties confronting such an inquiry have already been suggested. If the word was seldom used, how is it possible to judge whether the concept was believed? What evidence can be accepted as adequate to prove that democratic convictions existed? Here is an example: "a free government, I mean one in which the power frequently returns to the body of the people, is in principle the most stable and efficient of any kind." The writer is James Winthrop, who on the whole was probably not a democrat.[25] When Timothy Bloodworth said, "The House of Representatives is the only democratical branch," may we assume that he recognized the implications of the word and set him down as a democrat?[26] In view of the evidence presented above, in which camp was George Mason? All things considered, out of the thirty-eight lengthy discussions of the Constitution, about a third, for one reason or another, cannot be certainly placed with respect to attitudes toward democracy; probably most of these should be assigned to the undemocratic group. Of the remainder, all but half a dozen or so seem to have inclined toward, or to have clearly presented, a democratic view.

The second difficulty is that the most articulate leaders of the Antifederalists were, for the most part, members of the upper

22. To Jefferson, June 10, 1785, Boyd, ed., *Papers of Jefferson*, VIII, 196.
23. To Knox, Beverley, Dec. 27, 1787, Knox Papers, XXI, 88, Mass. Hist. Soc.
24. Ford, ed., *Pamphlets*, 295.
25. Ford, ed., *Essays*, 59.
26. Elliot, ed., *Debates*, IV, 55.

class, and therefore somewhat less likely than the majority of the people to approve of popular rule. To be sure, they inclined more in that direction than the Federalist leaders, but they went only a little way. Exactly how their ideas should be characterized is perhaps a matter of individual prejudice; to read the expositions of Richard Henry Lee, Samuel Bryan ("Centinel"), James Warren ("A Republican Federalist"), and George Clinton ("Cato") is to gain a good cross-section. The probable conclusion will be that less than half had democratic inclinations, and that these were muted. Democratic thought among the Antifederalists is therefore to be found expressed not so much in open debate or in the publications of the most prominent leaders as in the newspaper articles or occasional remarks of the more obscure and the less well-to-do.

The substance of criticism of the Constitution from the democratic point of view is summarized in the argument that the new government would be controlled by the upper class, not the "democracy," and therefore it would favor the rich, not the common man. For reasons previously explained, the argument was seldom pressed in open debate or signed articles.[27] The Albany Antifederal Committee may be considered an exception (perhaps there was safety in numbers); its members inquired whether it was "for the sake of the *poor* and common people, that the rich and well born" worked so hard for ratification.[28] Their protest was signed by twenty-six individuals. Otherwise, this point was elaborated only in private correspondence or in anonymous articles.

The most unequivocal printed criticism of the Constitution from the democratic point of view was that of "Lycurgus," who posed as an aristocrat defending the Constitution. The House, he declared, was a pretended concession to democracy, but in reality it had little power, since it was checked by the Senate and by the President. It was elected for two years, with no provision

27. But see Findley in McMaster and Stone, *Pennsylvania and the Constitution*, 778; Tredwell and Smith in Elliot, ed., *Debates*, II, 396, 246-47; Singletary in *Mass. Debates*, 203; Col. Barton in Cotner, ed., *Foster's Minutes*, 54.
28. *N.Y. Journal*, Apr. 26, 1788.

for rotation, so the members would not have to mix with the citizens but would be under the eye of the aristocracy and would come to act like the aristocrats. The Senate was a house of gentlemen, serving for long terms, while the power of the President over the army, treaties, and appointments was appropriate to an aristocratic system. The states, left with little power, would be absorbed, while the Supreme Court would hear almost all questions and would help put down any uprising. Finally, freedom of the press, of speech, and the right of habeas corpus would be denied. Altogether, for the aristocrats, the Constitution was ideal.[29]

The closest approach to this unique article was the "Cincinnatus" series, which thoroughly analyzed the Constitution. The author declared that the House of Representatives, the only democratic part of the government, was weak, while the Senate was removed from popular control; "and exactly in the ratio of their removal from the people, do aristocratic principles constantly infect the minds of men." The structure of the government and the powers given to it would enable the rich to "grind the poor to dust." [30] As a rule the point was made only briefly, as when "Philanthropos" warned that "the great will struggle for power, honor and wealth, the poor become a prey to avarice, insolence and oppression." [31] "Agrarius" predicted that: "The substantial yeomanry of America, the most valuable part of the community, will give place to lawyers and statesmen, who, in time, will engross all property, and thus the inhabitants of America will consist of two classes, the very rich and the very poor." [32] Two other examples will suffice. Before the text of the Constitution was released, "Rusticus" countered Federalist articles by asserting that some members of the Convention would trample on the "most sacred rights of the people," for they believed that "Heaven hath formed the bulk of mankind, to be mere slaves and vassals, to men of their superior genius, birth, and fortune." [33] A few months later John

29. *Independent Gazetteer* (Phila.), Oct. 17, 1787.
30. *N.Y. Journal,* Nov. 1, 8, 15, 22, 29, Dec. 6, 1787.
31. *Virginia Journal and Alexandria Gazette,* Dec. 6, 1787.
32. *Independent Gazetteer* (Phila.), Feb. 29, 1788.
33. *N.Y. Journal,* Sept. 13, 1787.

Quincy Adams noted in his diary that the Constitution was calculated to make the rich richer, and would bring free government to an end.[34]

That government under the Constitution would be by the few and therefore in favor of the rich was an argument sometimes employed by men who were not themselves democrats. Was it because they knew the democratic bias of the people and catered to it? A possible case in point is Samuel Chase of Maryland. This future Federalist asserted in the Maryland ratifying convention that Congress would represent not the farmers or planters or mechanics but only a few rich men in each state.[35] Perhaps he spoke for effect and did not express his real views, yet he wrote to John Lamb, "I consider the Constitution as radically defective in this essential: the bulk of the people can have nothing to say to it. The government is *not* a government of the people. It is *not* a government of representation."[36] John Francis Mercer probably expressed his convictions sincerely in a letter he wrote (but may never have sent) to the conventions of New York and Virginia. In nine-tenths of the world, he asserted, the many were unable to defend themselves from the few, and the people had constantly to guard against oppression by the wealthy. The Constitution established a government "in which the Interest of the *few* is preferred to the Rights of the *Many*"; unless amendments were made, "the great body of Yeomanry" would lose their liberty.[37] Still another man of wealth spoke in a similar fashion: "Every man of reflection must see, that the change now proposed, is a transfer of power from the many to the few,"[38] and George Mason pointed out that the Constitution was "not a democracy, wherein the people retain all their rights securely."[39] In New York, a Clintonian asserted that the Federalists "evidently aim at nothing but the elevation and aggrandisement of a few over the many. The

34. Mass. Hist. Soc., *Proceedings*, 2nd Ser., 16 (1902), 331.
35. Crowl, "Antifederalism," *Wm. and Mary Qtly.*, 3rd Ser., 4 (1947), 464.
36. June 13, 1788, Leake, *Lamb*, 310.
37. Etting Coll., VI, Hist. Soc. Pa.
38. R. H. Lee in Ford, ed., *Pamphlets*, 317.
39. Elliot, ed., *Debates*, III, 44.

liberty, property, and every social comfort in the life of the yeomanry in America, are to be sacrificed at the altar of tyranny." [40]
The belief that the Constitution was not democratic was shared
by David Redick. Perhaps, he meditated, the people were not yet
fitted for a democracy, but at least the government ought to become
more democratic as people were found to be fit for it; the Constitution reversed the process.[41] Finally, the democratic reaction to
the whole movement for the Constitution was recorded, if not
immortalized, in literary form by whoever wrote "1st Book of
Samuel, Chap. VIII":

And it came to pass, that in the eleventh year after the deliver-
ance of the people from bondage, the wise men and the rulers did
gather themselves together, and say, we have been sorely deceived, we would have more honor and reverence shewed unto us
under a King.
We must, said they one to the other, repress the insolence and
abominations of the people; we must make ourselves masters over
them. . . .
And the congregation of the wise men, and of the rulers did
decree, that all the country round about, . . . should be subject
unto one King, and unto one council.[42]

It appears that Nathan Dane was correct when he wrote to Henry
Knox that the new plan might not have "monarchy enough for some
nor democracy enough for others." [43]

While democratic ideas were an important part of Antifederal
thought, it is of course apparent that not all Antifederalists
regarded the Constitution from the sole standpoint of whether
it served the interests of democracy. Attitudes in regard to its
potential value also differed. A few Antifederalists were willing

40. E. Wilder Spaulding, *His Excellency George Clinton* (New York,
1938), 177.
41. To William Irvine, Sept. 10, 1787, Irvine Papers, IX, Hist. Soc. Pa.
42. *Va. Independent Chronicle* (Richmond), Oct. 31, 1787.
43. Dec. 27, 1787, Knox Papers, XXI, 88, Mass. Hist. Soc. Some other
sources in which criticisms based on the lack of democracy appear are, Henry
in Elliot, ed., *Debates*, III, 50, 140; Williams in *ibid.*, II, 242; Melancton
Smith in Ford, ed., *Pamphlets*, 109; "John Humble," in the *Independent
Gazetteer* (Phila.), Oct. 29, 1787; "John Wilkes," in *ibid.*, Jan. 27, 1788;
Bloodworth to Lamb, June 23, July 1, Lamb Papers, N.Y. Hist. Soc. Other
citations to democratic ideas have been furnished in previous footnotes.

to accept the Constitution if some minor amendments were made. They did not defend the Articles, evidently agreeing with the Federalists that the old government was beyond help, or at least that the Articles would have to be radically amended. They pressed enthusiastically for those amendments which they felt would transform the Constitution into a good government; some of them finally voted for ratification. Not numerous, this group included not over one-sixth of those who spoke and wrote on the subject, and all or very nearly all represented the well-to-do wing of Antifederalism, from which came so many of the men who changed their vote at the last minute, such as Nathaniel Barrell and Charles Turner of Massachusetts, Gilbert Livingston and Robert Yates of New York. Some of the best-known Antifederalists were among this group—Elbridge Gerry, Joseph Jones, George Mason, and perhaps Richard Henry Lee—men whose works have been published and studied as though they typified Antifederal thought but who in reality were moderates, influential perhaps because of their ability and prestige, but small in number. The overwhelming majority of the Antifederalists were of a different opinion.[44]

To the majority of Antifederalists, there was no need for so drastic a cure as the Constitution. The Federalists were trying to bring about a major political change and were therefore insisting that this change was essential. To justify the Constitution, it had to be proved that conditions were desperate and that extensive alterations in the government were imperative. Accordingly, they insisted that a serious commercial depression existed, that the credit of the United States and of the several states was endan-

44. For the ideas of these moderates, see Gerry's address in *Mass. Debates*, 25; Joseph Jones to Madison, Nov. 22, 1787, Mass. Hist. Soc., *Proceedings*, 2nd Ser., 17 (1903), 491; R. H. Lee to the governor of Virginia, Oct. 16, 1787, Ballagh, ed., *Lee*, II, 455 and in Ford, ed., *Pamphlets*, 286-87 (but see to Samuel Adams, Oct. 5, 1787, in Ballagh, ed., *Lee*, II, 447, where he suggests that it may be possible simply to amend the Articles); Williams in Elliot, ed., *Debates*, II, 242; Monroe in *ibid.*, III, 214, 217; Samuel Osgood to Samuel Adams, Jan. 5, 1788, Adams Papers, N.Y. Pub. Lib.; Barrell, Turner, and Symmes in *Mass. Debates*, 262-65, 274, 277-78; for Mason see Farrand, ed., *Records of the Federal Convention, passim*, and Henry Lee to Madison, Dec. 1787, Hunt, ed., *Writings of Madison*, V, 88-89n.

gered, that property rights were in jeopardy, that the states were disunited and weak, and that if the country were to become prosperous, respected, respectable, and safe, the Articles must be replaced by the Constitution. Indeed, so great was the emergency they conjured up that amendments could scarcely be contemplated, to say nothing of a new convention. This was not only viewing with alarm but with terror—what might be called the Federalist party line. It is not always easy to tell whether they really believed all they professed, but in any case, this was the argument which the Antifederalists had to refute.

They understood very well, of course, that the Federalists were exaggerating. The French minister Louis Otto had previously observed that the commercial depression had "happily arisen" and given the Federalists "a pretext for innovation"; [45] William Findley remarked that it was "like persuading a Man in Health that [he] is sick." [46] Actually the country faced no such emergency.[47] The idea that there was any danger from a foreign country was absurd, the Antifederalists declared; there was none to attack. If the country ever did become involved in war, the difficulties would be no greater than those overcome during the Revolution,[48] and there was no potential domestic conflict which could not easily be solved. The Federalists, wrote James Winthrop, did not fear that insurrections would occur, but that the government would "prove superiour to their assaults." [49] Moreover there was no economic crisis; despite Federalist cries of alarm the country was once again

45. To Vergennes, Oct. 10, 1786, Bancroft, *History of the Constitution*, II, 399.

46. McMaster and Stone, *Pennsylvania and the Constitution*, 770; see also R. H. Lee in Ford, ed., *Pamphlets*, 281; Williams in Elliot, ed., *Debates*, II, 240.

47. Before the Federalist party line was firmly established, their newspapers sometimes wrote about the good condition of the country which would be made even better by a change. See for example, "Senex," in the *S.C. Gazette and Public Advertiser* (Charleston), May 21, 1785; *Pa. Packet* (Phila.), May 17, July 19, 1787; *Conn. Gazette* (New London), June 29, Aug. 17, 1787; *Md. Journal* (Baltimore), Nov. 23, 1787.

48. Lowndes in the *Daily Advertiser* (Charleston), Jan. 21, 1788; Henry and Grayson in Elliot, ed., *Debates*, III, 46, 277; Tredwell in *ibid.*, II, 396-97; Melancton Smith in Ford, ed., *Pamphlets*, 96; "Brutus Jr.," in the *N.Y. Journal*, Nov. 8, 1787.

49. Ford, ed., *Essays*, 62.

becoming prosperous, and as prosperity returned, temporary difficulties would vanish. A few Antifederalists actually denied that there was any trouble at all[50] (on the other hand one or two went nearly as far as did the Federalists),[51] but the usual argument was that the depression, though real, was transient, so that no change of government was needed to secure the happiness of the people—at most a few slight modifications would suffice. As a nautical Bostonian expressed it:

Yesterday a select body of real federalists examined the ship Old Confederation, as she now lies hauled up in Congress dock-yard. —They report, she is sound bottom, and strong built; and that no farther repairs are wanting, than a thorough calking; which might be done in a few weeks—provided the owners would unite to set the workmen about the business:—They are wholly averse to breaking her up, as they think it a needless expense to put another on the stocks upon a new-construction, whilst they are in possession of one of good seasoned timber, which might be compleatly fitted to answer every purpose.[52]

Certainly as the depression lifted, the states would be able to pay their debts—indeed they were already doing it, as "Cincinnatus" and others pointed out.[53] The fact that the Dutch were still willing to loan money indicated that there was no danger of bankruptcy.[54] If, then, taxes were soon to be regularly paid, and the country would shortly be prosperous and safe, where was the emergency? Even if it were conceded that the Articles were imperfect the flaws could be easily repaired. On the whole, wrote "John DeWitt," the people were living "under a government of our own choice,

50. Henry in Elliot, ed., *Debates*, III, 54; "Alfred," in the *N.Y. Journal*, Dec. 25, 1787.

51. "Brutus," in *ibid.*, Oct. 18, 1787.

52. *Ibid.*, Feb. 11, 1788. See also Melancton Smith in Elliot, ed., *Debates*, II, 336; "Deliberator," in the *Freeman's Journal* (Phila.), Mar. 26, 1788; "A REAL Federalist," in the *Mass. Centinel* (Boston), Jan. 12, 1788; "Agrippa," in Ford, ed., *Essays*, 57-60; *Independent Gazetteer* (Phila.), Jan. 11, 1788.

53. *N. Y. Journal*, Dec. 6, 1787; "Agrippa," in Ford, ed., *Essays*, 60; R. H. Lee in Ford, ed., *Pamphlets*, 280-81. See E. James Ferguson, "State Assumption of the Federal Debt During the Confederation," *Miss. Valley Hist. Rev.*, 38 (1951-52), 403-24.

54. "A Newport Man," in the *Newport Mercury*, Mar. 17, 1788; *American Herald* (Boston), Dec. 10, 1787.

constructed by ourselves, upon unequivocal principles, and [it] requires but to be well administered to make us as happy under it as generally falls to the lot of humanity." [55]

But while the Antifederalists denied that the Articles of Confederation had completely failed, they nonetheless admitted the need for reform. Nearly every individual who dealt with the problem believed that changes were necessary. The question arises whether these recorded opinions were held by the rank and file; perhaps it was only the vocal element that admitted imperfections in the existing system—the upper-class leaders. While it is true that evidence is lacking concerning the opinion of the majority, it is probably safe to say that the body of Antifederalists concurred in the need for some reform. Logically, Antifederalists should have insisted that changes were unnecessary. To admit that alterations were essential weakened their case; it gave their opponents too much of an advantage and was politically unwise. That they did so can be explained only by the fact that no one could deny that changes were required. Then too, those Antifederalists who did speak for the rank and file were not content with the Articles. William Findley of Pennsylvania was one such, and we find him admitting that Congress should be given additional powers.[56] In the same state "Philadelphiensis," who was probably Benjamin Workman, agreed.[57] "A Farmer" went into considerable detail on the point, and James Wilson stated that his Antifederal opponents in the ratifying convention believed "that the present Confederation should have been continued, but that additional powers should have been given to it." [58] In Massachusetts, the determined Antifederalist General Thompson of Topsham, Maine, is reported to have said, "The Confederation wants amendments —shall we not amend it?" while the town of Harvard, in the Shaysite country, agreed "that amendments may be made upon the Confederation of the United States, by vesting Congress with

55. *Ibid.*, Oct. 22, 1787; Lowndes in Elliot, ed., *Debates*, IV, 290; Melancton Smith in Ford, ed., *Pamphlets*, 94.

56. To William Irvine, Mar. 12, 1788, Irvine Papers, X, Hist. Soc. Pa.; McMaster and Stone, *Pennsylvania and the Constitution*, 300, 770.

57. *Freeman's Journal* (Phila.), Dec. 12, 1787.

58. McMaster and Stone, *Pennsylvania and the Constitution*, 537; Elliot, ed., *Debates*, II, 449.

greater Powers, without so totally changing and altering the same, as the proposed Constitution has a tendency to."[59] In New York, Thomas Tredwell asserted, "It is on all hands acknowledged that the federal government is not adequate to the purposes of the union." John Lamb believed the same, and the Albany Antifederal Committee also admitted that the Articles were defective.[60] In North Carolina, James Galloway, Samuel Spencer, and Timothy Bloodworth, who were reputed to express the popular view, all conceded that changes were needed; Galloway noted that "a sense of this induced the different states to send delegates to Philadelphia."[61] Luther Martin in Maryland and Patrick Dollard in South Carolina made the same observation.[62] The fact is that it is difficult to find any other opinion being expressed; even Patrick Henry was willing to make a concession.[63] A few Antifederalists, of course, were so well satisfied with the status quo that they denied the need for any change. Probably many in Rhode Island felt that way, and occasional examples can be found elsewhere.[64] But they were a small minority—perhaps one in ten of those who wrote or spoke on the subject. Most Antifederalists, while denying that the Articles had failed, felt that something should be done. Of these a few, as we have seen, went a long way toward the Federal position, but the greatest number—the typical Antifederalist—wished to retain the Articles and to strengthen the Confederation.

One power which most Antifederalists were willing to concede to Congress was control over commerce. It has been noted previously that there was only scattered objection to the commerce clause. Actually, whatever opposition there had been to amending

59. *Mass. Centinel* (Boston), Jan. 30, 1788; *American Herald* (Boston), Jan. 21, 1788.
60. Elliot, ed., *Debates*, II, 358; Lamb Papers, article dated Feb. 16, 1788, N.Y. Hist. Soc.; *N. Y. Journal*, Apr. 26, 1788.
61. Elliot, ed., *Debates*, IV, 25, 77; Bloodworth to Lamb, July 1, 1788, Lamb Papers, N.Y. Hist. Soc.
62. Farrand, ed., *Records of the Federal Convention*, I, 347; *Daily Advertiser* (Charleston), May 29, 1788.
63. Elliot, ed., *Debates*, III, 56-57. See also the discussion in chap. V, especially the references to Bryan, Bishop, Redick, "Amicus Patriae," and "Legion."
64. For one, Granger, as reported in the *Conn. Courant* (Hartford), May 21, 1787.

the Articles in this regard seems to have almost vanished. Even in the South, James Monroe, William Grayson, Timothy Bloodworth, "Impartial Examiner," "A Federal Republican," and "A Georgian" all admitted that the Articles were defective in this respect,[65] and none of the ratifying conventions denied this power to Congress, though a few suggested limitations. In the North there was universal approval. None of the Antifederalists went into much detail on the subject—the Federalists were taking care of that—but merely remarked that the power ought to be granted. "Agrippa," for example, observed that ships' carpenters found business dull, "but as nobody objects against a system of commercial regulations for the whole continent, that business may be relieved without subverting all the ancient foundations and laws which have the respect of the people." [66] Were this done, "Centinel" declared, and a revenue granted, it would be "all that is wanting to render America as prosperous as it is in the power of any form of government to render her; this properly understood would meet the views of all the honest and well-meaning." [67]

The discussion over the tax power was much more detailed and must be considered in relation to the preceding debate over the impost. It was admitted by nearly everybody that the government needed a greater and more certain revenue than it had been receiving. A few of the Antifederalists believed no change was necessary, but by 1787 this was clearly a minority opinion—the fact was that the requisition system was not working properly. The best argument that could be made in its favor was that it was now providing Congress with some money, and that current defaults in state payments arose from economic difficulties and could be expected to cease as these difficulties subsided.[68] But it was possible that a state might refuse to pay (New Jersey had done so), and there was no real guarantee of the future success of

65. See chap. VII, n. 27.

66. Ford, ed., *Essays*, 61.

67. McMaster and Stone, *Pennsylvania and the Constitution*, 604. See also "A Farmer," in *ibid.*, 537; "An Old Constitutionalist," in the *Independent Gazetteer* (Phila.), Oct. 26, 1787; "Cornelius," in Harding, *Ratification in Massachusetts*, 125-26; "Brutus Junior," in the *N.Y. Journal*, Nov. 8, 1787; "An Old Whig," in the *New Haven Gazette*, Dec. 6, 1787.

68. See, for example, Melancton Smith in Elliot, ed., *Debates*, II, 356.

requisitions. Admitting this, some Antifederalists concluded that the general government ought to be given the power to compel collection from a delinquent state.[69] No one explained exactly how this was to be done; perhaps the threat was supposed to suffice; in any case, all drew back from the obvious implications. The fact is that this point of view could not be, and therefore was not, seriously maintained. Rather, the majority of Antifederalists presented this plan: the impost was to be granted; requisitions would continue, but if they were not paid Congress might then impose direct taxes.

In 1786 the federal impost had failed when Congress refused to accept the limitations demanded by New York. By that time opposition had come to be limited not to the tax, but to Congress's control over the collection, and in the debate over the Constitution most Antifederalists freely conceded the government's need for such a revenue. Indeed, some revenue from import duties would be incidental to the regulation of trade, if that power were granted. Some Antifederalists continued to feel that the money ought to be collected by the states and used by those states in which the revenue accrued, except for a specific amount granted to Congress.[70] One or two, at least, felt that the impost should be given only for a limited time.[71] But most believed that the power should be granted without qualifications.[72] They were unwilling, however, to grant any further power over taxation. Rather, it was felt that Congress should be authorized to levy additional taxes

69. This seems to have been the opinion of "The Impartial Examiner," in the *Va. Independent Chronicle* (Richmond), Feb. 27, 1788, and of "Many Customers," in the *Independent Gazetteer* (Phila.), Dec. 1, 1787. See also "A Farmer," in McMaster and Stone, *Pennsylvania and the Constitution*, 537; "A Georgian," in the *Gazette of State of Georgia* (Savannah), Nov. 15, 1787; Spencer in Elliot, ed., *Debates*, IV, 74-77; Lansing in *ibid.*, II, 217, 273-74; Martin in Farrand, ed., *Records of the Federal Convention*, III, 203-4.

70. "Agrippa," in Ford, ed., *Essays*, 100; Clinton and Lansing in Elliot, ed., *Debates*, II, 359, 371-76.

71. "Philadelphiensis," in the *Freeman's Journal* (Phila.), Dec. 12, 1787; R. H. Lee to Samuel Adams, Oct. 5, 1787, Ballagh, ed., *Lee*, II, 447.

72. "Brutus," in the *N.Y. Journal*, Jan. 3, 1788; "Deliberator," in the *Freeman's Journal* (Phila.), Mar. 26, 1788; Findley in McMaster and Stone, *Pennsylvania and the Constitution*, 771; "Cornelius," in Harding, *Ratification in Massachusetts*, 126; "An Old Constitutionalist," in the *Independent Gazetteer* (Phila.), Oct. 26, 1787.

only if the requisition system failed; direct taxes, in particular, should be imposed only as a last resort. Congress ought first to request money, but if a state refused, then Congress must be allowed to levy and collect a direct tax from the inhabitants—better that than force exerted on the state governments! Even Patrick Henry conceded this much.[73]

We may conclude, then, that if the Antifederalists had dominated the Philadelphia Convention, the government of the nation would have continued to be a confederation of sovereign states, and that the democratic principle of local self-government would have been emphasized. There would have been more attention paid to the doctrine of responsibility in officials through shorter terms of office, rotation, and perhaps, as in the Articles, recall. The powers of the general government would have been increased. The states would have given Congress the power to regulate commerce, to collect duties on imports, and to levy direct taxes in states which did not comply with requisitions. How much farther they would have gone toward a compromise with the Federalist position is uncertain, but in general the Antifederalist position on other issues could probably be stated as follows:

(1) No objection would have been made to the creation of a stronger President with at least some measure of independence, though he would not have been granted all of the powers bestowed on him by the Constitution, and his term of office would have been limited.

(2) Although the Antifederalists probably preferred a unicameral Congress, the two-house legislature would have been accepted. The Senate, however, would have been made more responsible to the state legislatures.

(3) A federal judiciary would have been accepted, but its jurisdiction would have been much restricted; it certainly would have been denied jurisdiction over cases between states, or between citizens and states, except as provided by the Articles.

(4) The government might (but this is dubious) have been given some such power as was expressed in the "supreme law of the land" clause, to be enforced perhaps by a judiciary, or perhaps

73. Elliot, ed., *Debates*, III, 56-57; Mason in *ibid.*, 31; see also Bodman in *Mass. Debates*, 311.

as a last resort by the army. This particular problem, it need hardly be said, was not solved by anyone, Federalists included.

Naturally some of the Antifederalists would have favored the grant of powers beyond those we have mentioned—"A *REAL Federalist*" was not alone in wishing that Congress would be given the exclusive power of coining and issuing money[74]—but the arrangements just described are very probably as far as the majority would have gone. The amendments proposed by the convention minorities in Maryland and Virginia and the convention majorities of North Carolina and New York testify to this, as do the pronouncements of leading spokesmen.[75] All the evidence suggests that the changes in the Articles which the Antifederalists themselves would have wrought are almost precisely those of the Paterson, or New Jersey Plan, which represented not merely the ideas of the small state delegates but those of the Antifederalists.

Why did not the Antifederalists make a definite proposal along these lines, in order to place before the country a concrete alternative to the Constitution? There were several reasons. Perhaps most important was the fact that the Federalists had seized the initiative, and the Antifederalists were never able to grasp it or even to cope with it; their attempts at co-operation came too late. Secondly, they were basically loyal to the concept of government represented by the Articles of Confederation, and therefore they needed only to refer to this, without having to explain their doctrine in detail. Finally, they were placed in the difficult position of being convinced that the situation required a change, and yet they were opposed to the only fully developed program of change which was being offered, while time, distance, and circumstance

74. *Mass. Centinel* (Boston), Jan. 12, 1788.
75. See especially R. H. Lee in Ford, ed., *Pamphlets*, 287; "Agrippa," in Ford, ed., *Essays*, 98-100, 118-19; Joseph Jones to Madison, Oct. 29, Nov. 22, 1787, Mass. Hist. Soc., *Proceedings*, 2nd Ser., 17 (1903), 487-88, 491; "A Farmer," in McMaster and Stone, *Pennsylvania and the Constitution*, 537; "Cornelius," in Harding, *Ratification in Massachusetts*, 126-27; the minority of the Pennsylvania Assembly, in the *Pa. Packet* (Phila.), Oct. 4, 1787; George Mason to Samuel Griffin, Sept. 8, 1789, Mason Papers, Lib. Cong. The following Antifederal articles are also particularly significant because of their implications: Albany Antifederal Committee, in the *N.Y. Journal*, Apr. 27, 1788; "An Officer of the Late Continental Army," in the *Independent Gazetteer* (Phila.), Nov. 6, 1787.

prevented them from formulating a counter-proposal. As a result they found themselves in a dilemma: at once accepting the necessity of change and denying the changes suggested, fearing to grant powers so great as those demanded by the Constitution, yet fearful of a total rejection. Many agreed with Mercy Warren when she confided, "Our situation is truly delicate and critical. On the one hand, we stand in need of a strong federal government, founded on principles that will support the prosperity and union of the Colonies. On the other, we have struggled for liberty and made costly sacrifices at her shrine and there are still many among us who revere her name too much to relinquish, beyond a certain medium, the rights of man for the dignity of government." [76] The ambivalent position of the Antifederalists placed them at a grave disadvantage. The Massachusetts Federalist George Richards Minot noted in his journal, "The people, as Mr. Dane observed to me when he returned from Congress, *were fairly committed.* The exigencies of the nation made it necessary for them to give something, and vastly more was asked than was necessary; and they were told that their rulers would have that or nothing." [77] The Antifederalists were never quite able to resolve the dilemma.

76. To Mrs. Macauley, Sept. 28, 1787, Mass. Hist. Soc., *Proceedings*, 64 (1930-32), 162.
77. Minot Papers, Mass. Hist. Soc.

Chapter IX

RATIFICATION: NOVEMBER TO MAY

THE full text of the Constitution had scarcely been published, and was not yet generally available, when the Pennsylvania legislature acted upon it. The Federalists were in haste. Opposition had appeared, first in the Convention when Mason, Randolph, and Gerry refused to sign (Lansing, Yates, Martin, and Mercer had previously withdrawn) and then in Congress; the best policy seemed to be to secure quick approval in as many states as possible, to build up a momentum which might overwhelm the antagonists before they could organize against it. The Constitution was therefore hurried out of Congress and actually presented to the Pennsylvania House before Congress had officially acted upon it. Richard Henry Lee complained, "It was ... this or nothing, and this urged with a most extreme intemperance." [1] The almost desperate haste is well described by David Redick:

I cannot imagine why the people in this city are so verry anxious to have it adopted instantly before it can be digested or deliberately considered. If you were only here to see and hear these people, to observe the Means they are using to effect this purpose, to hear the tories declare they will draw the Sword in its defence, to see the Quaquers runing about signing declarations and Petitions in favor of it before the[y] have time to examine it, to see gentlemen runing into the Country and neibouring towns haranguering the rabble. I say were you to see and hear these things as I do you would say with me that the verry Soul of confidence itself ought to change into distrust. . . . I think the measures pursued here is a strong evidence that these people know it will not bear

1. To George Mason, Oct. 1, 1787, Ballagh, ed., *Lee*, II, 438.

an examination and therefor wishes to adopt it first and consider it afterward.[2]

What gave the Federalists their opportunity was the large majority which they temporarily enjoyed in the state. All of the Republicans supported ratification, and since a few eastern members of the opposing party (the "Constitutionalists") were Federal, the legislature was firmly controlled by those who favored quick action. On the 28th of September a bill was introduced which provided for elections to be held in early November—that is, in less than six weeks; when some of the Constitutionalists tried to prevent a quorum by staying away, two of them were unceremoniously hauled back to their seats by a mob.[3] This unseemly haste angered the minority, which protested that the Federalists' unwillingness to permit full discussion proved that the Constitution was a bad one and asserted that it would be defeated if time were granted for full debate.[4]

The Federalists did indeed hope to prevent any adverse information from reaching the people. In Luzerne County, Timothy Pickering's campaign manager "carefully avoided letting them know that any objections were made to the Constitution" since the people were "prone to opposition."[5] Everywhere pro-Constitution articles predominated in the newepapers. In the few weeks before the election was held, the *Independent Gazetteer* published the first two numbers of the "Centinel" series, the first five by "An Old Whig," and a few other articles; but very few criticisms were printed by other newspapers. The *Freeman's Journal* began its attack too late to be of service. Probably only the eastern residents of the state were well-informed on the subject, and here the Federalists were in any case a majority. Outside of Philadelphia, the *Carlisle Gazette* published a few Antifederal articles but

2. To Gen. William Irvine, Phila., Sept. 24, 1787, Irvine Papers, IX, Hist. Soc. Pa.

3. Tench Coxe to Madison, Sept. 29, 1787, Madison Papers, VIII, Lib. Cong.; Robert Waln to his cousin, Oct. 8, 1787, *Pa. Mag. of Hist. and Biog.*, 38 (1914), 503; *Pa. Packet* (Phila.), Oct. 4, 1787.

4. *Md. Journal* (Baltimore), Nov. 18, 1787; *Pa. Packet* (Phila.), Oct. 4, Dec. 11, 1787; *Carlisle Gazette, and Western Repository of Knowledge*, Mar. 5, 1788; *Independent Gazetteer* (Phila.), Jan. 9, 1788.

5. Ebenezer Bauman to Timothy Pickering, Wilkesborough, Nov. 12, 1787, Pickering Papers, LVII, 339, Mass. Hist. Soc.

many more on the other side, while the *Pittsburgh Gazette* was strongly Federal. Undoubtedly the inability of the Antifederalists to communicate their ideas adequately contributed to the overwhelming victory of the Federalists, who won forty-six out of the sixty-nine seats in the convention.

It is almost certain that the Antifederalists would have gained considerably more strength had the convention met at a later date. Unrest over the outcome continued in Huntingdon County until the following fall, and in Northumberland the Federalists may have been in the minority, for they were outvoted in the fall elections.[6] Both counties had sent delegates who favored ratification. The later elections also went against the Federalists in Franklin and Washington counties, although they had captured three of the delegates of these counties to the convention. There were occasional riots in protest against the ratification, especially in Carlisle,[7] and strong support for a new general convention continued in other parts of the state for several months.[8] If more time had been allowed, it is likely that the Federalist majority would have been reduced by half a dozen votes at the least; it is doubtful, however, that the final result would have been altered.

The division of opinion in Pennsylvania may be described in several ways. Antifederalism here can be studied by examining the background of political conflicts, by determining the geographical distribution of votes, by investigating the division along socio-economic lines, or finally by describing the individuals who

6. Thomas McKean to Franklin, Sept. 5, 1787, Gratz Coll., Articles of Confederation, Hist. Soc. Pa.; Milton Scott Lytle, *History of Huntingdon County, in the State of Pennsylvania* (Lancaster, 1876), 101-9; Brunhouse, *Counter-Revolution* in Pa., 295, 343-44.

7. Arthur Campbell to George Bryan, Washington County, Mar. 8, 1788, Bryan Papers, Hist. Soc. Pa.; *Carlisle Gazette*, Jan. 9, 1788; *N.Y. Journal*, Apr. 18, 1788; *Pa. Packet* (Phila.), Jan. 10, 1788; John Shippen to Col. Joseph Shippen, Carlisle, Mar. 3, 1788, in Thomas Balch, *Letters and Papers relating chiefly to the Provincial History of Pennsylvania* (Philadelphia, 1855), 289; John Armstrong to Gen. William Irvine, Carlisle, Jan. 9, 1788, Irvine Papers, IX, Hist. Soc. Pa.; Brunhouse, *Counterrevolution in Pa.*, 210-211, 343-44.

8. *Ibid.*, 213-14; Paul Leicester Ford, *The Origin, Purpose and Result of the Harrisburg Convention of 1788: A Study in Popular Government* (Brooklyn, 1890); E. P. Smith, "The Movement for a Second Convention in 1788," in James Franklin Jameson, ed., *Essays in the Constitutional History of the United States in the Formative Period, 1775-1789* (Boston, 1889).

opposed ratification. To limit the analysis to one method permits easy generalization, but to utilize all is to approach nearer to the truth.

It is evident, first of all, that the two political parties which had long struggled for control of the state took opposite sides on this as on so many other issues. The Republican leaders had been foremost among those who favored a stronger government; they sent their own men to the Federal Convention, and the Constitution reflected their views. The Constitutionalists were almost forced into opposition, simply on political grounds; however the new plan contradicted the principles expressed in their own frame of government. In the ratifying convention the vote was strictly in accord with party lines. Yet this is not quite the whole story, for one wing of the Constitutionalist party did favor ratification: that which was based on the Philadelphia mechanics and artisans, who hoped that a stronger government would protect them against the competition of British manufactured goods and encourage exports. Therefore in the city, where the Federalist candidates, including Benjamin Rush and James Wilson, received over 1,200 votes each, Franklin got but 235 and David Rittenhouse only 148.[9] The city was Federalist.

Indeed, divisions within the state were to a great extent along sectional lines. Geographically, the Antifederal vote came exclusively from the "west," as previously defined in Chapter III, but whereas earlier the Constitutionalists had won some support in the east, now only John Whitehill of Lancaster and the delegation from Berks, a border county, remained Antifederal. It is true that leaders of the Philadelphia wing such as George Bryan, Benjamin Workman, and David Rittenhouse worked against ratification, but in that city the Republicans' overwhelming victory proved that the rank and file were Federal. Thus the east was almost solidly Federalist. The sectional lines were broken, however, by scattered Federalist victories in the west: the delegates from Luzerne and Huntingdon were Federal (though neither may have reflected the ultimate wishes of the people); Northumberland, previously a Constitutionalist stronghold, now shifted; one of the two delegates from Franklin and two of the four from Washington also

9. *Independent Gazetteer* (Phila.), Nov. 8, 1787.

voted for ratification. Clearly there was a sectional division, but just as clearly it does not entirely account for the alignment. A different approach will help to explain the situation.

An analysis of the social antecedents and economic interests of the delegates affords some light. The fact that the Antifederalists were Constitutionalists, and with a few exceptions westerners, suggests something of their backgrounds. About half of all the delegates to the convention had seen some military service during the war, almost all of them as officers, but of the Antifederalists only one had held a rank higher than captain, whereas among the Federalists there were at least sixteen field officers. The ten members of the convention who belonged to the Society of the Cincinnati were Federalists. Such facts as these imply that the Federalists came from higher social strata. This is suggested also by their superior education, for all of the college men in the ratifying convention were Federalists. The professions of the members also indicate the differences between parties. The great majority of the merchants, large manufacturers, lawyers, judges, and those with extensive holdings in land voted for the Constitution.[10] Moreover (as George Bryan put it) "monied men, and particularly the stockholders in the bank were in favor of it."[11] Clearly the businessmen were Federal, and most of the creditors, too, were on that side. In the case of public security holders there was little difference among the delegates, but outside the convention the greater part of the debt was concentrated in Federal hands. On the other side, about half of the Antifederalists were farmers, though it should be added that not all farmers were Antifederalists, for some eastern agricultural counties favored ratification. Almost no artisans or mechanics attended the convention, but the evidence is decisive that the vast majority of them favored ratification. Indeed most inhabitants of the towns, of whatever economic or other group, were united: Philadelphia, as has been noted, was overwhelm-

10. Just half of the Federal delegates fall in categories of higher status as contrasted with less than a fourth of the Antifederalists. For the occupational alignment see Appendix E.

11. Undated statement by George Bryan, Bryan Papers, Hist. Soc. Pa. The analysis, which is exceedingly valuable, has been printed in part in Burton Alva Konkle, *George Bryan and the Constitution of Pennsylvania, 1731-1791* (Philadelphia, 1922), 300-7.

ingly Federal; the smaller towns such as Bethlehem, Easton, Lancaster, and, in the far west, Pittsburgh, also helped to secure ratification.[12]

Other contrasts can be drawn. The Federalists held far more property, which is to be expected in view of the east versus west, rural versus urban nature of the division. In the convention were twelve men of wealth, of whom ten were Federalists; another half-dozen were well-to-do, of whom all but one were Federalists. The remainder, which included almost all the Antifederalists, had only moderate property. The published tax records reveal a considerable difference in property, for the average Federalist had half again as much land, horses, cattle, and sheep, and more than twice as many servants, as did the average Antifederalist.[13] As to religious affiliation, the Episcopalians and the Quakers in the convention supported the Constitution unanimously. All of these delegates, however, came from the east and had business interests which partly account for their votes; moreover members of these churches were Republicans, and it is likely that such political factors were more significant than religious doctrine. The Presbyterians were evenly divided: the eastern merchants, such as William Wilson, were Federal, whereas the western farmer politicians, such as the Whitehills, were Antifederal. Judge Samuel Ashmead of Philadelphia, a Federalist, was a Baptist. Delegates whose names reveal an English origin were mostly pro-Constitution, the exceptions being westerners; Germans divided two to one for the Constitution because most of them lived in the east, and a majority of the Scotch-Irish were opposed, reflecting western political opinion.[14] There was no significant difference in age, nor is any contrast in political experience apparent.

12. *Pa. Packet* (Phila.), Oct. 27, Dec. 13, 1787, Jan. 3, 31, 1788; *N.Y. Journal*, Apr. 18, 1788, Bryan's statement, cited in *n*. 11, above.

13. Wealthy or well-to-do Federalists: Ashmead, Baker, Barclay, Bull, Coleman, Graff, Gray, Latimer, McKean, Neville, Rush, Scott, J. Wilson, Wynkoop, Yeates. Antifederalists: Bishop, Breading, Heister. See the *Pennsylvania Archives*, 3rd Ser., XII, XIII, XV-XXII. In the case of land (excluding some speculative holdings) the average for 23 Antifederalists was about 310 acres and the median was 280; for 35 Federalists the figures were about 560 and 380.

14. See Andreas Dorpalen, "The Political Influence of the German Element in Colonial America," *Pennsylvania History*, 6 (1939), 233; Russell J. Ferguson, *Early Western Pennsylvania Politics* (Pittsburgh, 1938).

Certain generalizations emerge from these details. The Antifederal opposition certainly must be interpreted in the light of the long political controversies and the fundamental differences which had created the Constitutionalists and the Republicans, except that now the urban wing of the Constitutionalists was Federal. The upper classes (however measured) were undoubtedly Federal, but the artisans and mechanics were too; so, for that matter, were the city dwellers, regardless of status. The east was for ratification and the west against—but the town of Pittsburgh was a Federal island in an Antifederal sea. The most significant fact is certainly the Federalism of the commercial centers and of the area dependent on them. Had the Antifederalists won the support of all the farmers they must surely have conquered, but even if it be admitted that their strength was increasing, and that the Federalists' maneuvers obtained a deceptively large majority for the Constitution, it is unlikely that the outcome could have been reversed, because many rural counties were influenced by commerce. Antifederal strength was concentrated only in those districts which were isolated from the mercantile influence. George Bryan accurately pointed out that "the counties nearest the navigation were in favor of it generally; those more remote, in opposition." The keys to the ratification in Pennsylvania are not so much the rich and the poor, or the east and the west, but the Appalachians, the Delaware, the Susquehanna, and the Ohio.

The speed with which action was taken in Pennsylvania was equalled in Delaware. Here the Assembly met on October 4 and called for elections to be held during the third week of November. No opposition to this early date is recorded. By the time the convention met the election results in Pennsylvania were known; Delaware, however, did not wait for her neighbor to take final action, but ratified without delay—unanimously.

Almost nothing is known concerning Delaware's reaction to the Constitution, and it seems unlikely that further information will be forthcoming. Any comments on possible Antifederalism must therefore be speculative. It is well known, and will presently be demonstrated, that opposition to the Constitution was most intense among paper money advocates, not necessarily because the Constitution threatened the inflationists (although it did), but because these men were often small farmers who held political, social, and economic ideas which contrasted with those of the Federalists. With these factors in mind, one might expect an Antifederal party in the state. No paper money bill had been passed, but during 1787 petitions were received which criticized speculators in public securities, called for paper money, and asked for more lenient treatment of debtors by the courts. At least one newspaper article advocated the payment of the state debt on a depreciated scale. There are indications, too, that the elections to the ratifying convention were not everywhere unanimous, and we know of at least one citizen of the state who did not favor the Constitution.[15] This is indeed slender evidence on which to predicate the existence of Antifederalism, and it must be concluded that there was in fact little opposition to the Constitution.

Undoubtedly the speed with which ratification was accomplished and the almost total absence of newspaper articles critical of the Constitution had the same effect in Delaware as in Pennsylvania. The Constitution, to be sure, did have certain advantages for a small state; moreover most of the state's residents lived within reach of good transportation facilities. A historian of the state, John A. Munroe, emphasizing the influence of the Delaware River and of commercial relations with Philadelphia in promoting Federalism, continues: "The economic and cultural connections of the counties in three states and on both shores of the Delaware must have prepared their people for closer union."[16] Since the mercantile interest was so important in Pennsylvania, it is reasonable to suppose that it operated here, and no leaders emerged to arouse opposition. There may have been a few Antifederalists, but there was never an organized movement.

The situation in New Jersey, which in some respects resembled that in Delaware, has been carefully investigated and fully described by Richard N. McCormick.[17] He finds that there was

15. *Delaware Gazette, or the Faithful Centinel* (Wilmington), Nov. 22, 1786, July 4, Aug. 8, 1787; *Delaware Courant, and Wilmington Advertiser*, May 5, 26, July 21, 1787; George H. Ryden, *Delaware—the First State in the Union* (Wilmington, 1938), 30-33; Joseph Dorfman, *The Economic Mind in American Civilization*, 3 vols. (New York, 1946-49), I, 282n.

16. John A. Munroe, *Federalist Delaware, 1775-1815* (Brunswick, N. J., 1954), 108-9.

17. McCormick, ed., *New Jersey in the Critical Period*, chap. X.

almost no opposition to the Constitution (Abraham Clark being an exception), even among the numerous advocates of paper money.[18] Little criticism of the plan appeared in the newspapers, and McCormick points out that the legislature which called the convention included a strong agrarian party which might have fought ratification had it wished. He gives several reasons for the failure of Antifederalism to develop. Here as elsewhere there existed "the strong desire of influential conservatives to see curbs placed on the power of the state legislature to the end that property rights might be safeguarded."[19] But the paramount explanation lies in the peculiar economic interest of the state. It had a very large debt and had been obliged to levy heavy taxes on land. Were the Constitution adopted, the burden of much of this debt would be assumed by the central government, and funds would be raised by general duties on imports and by the sale of western lands. New Jersey would therefore contribute little and receive much, for her numerous public creditors would profit, and land taxes could be lowered. It was for this reason that the state had consistently supported measures, such as the impost, which would strengthen the central government.

This economic motive does not preclude the possibility that certain political aspects of the Constitution might have been found distasteful. Indeed objections were raised in the convention,[20] and Abraham Clark's criticisms were of this sort. Perhaps if the convention had met at a later date and Antifederal propaganda been distributed, an opposition might have developed. McCormick makes it clear, however, that the economic motive was so compelling that no movement to defeat the Constitution was likely to succeed.

Three states—Pennsylvania, Delaware, and New Jersey—ratified before the year 1787 ended; two more quickly followed. In one of these, Georgia, as in Delaware and New Jersey, the vote in the

18. Abraham Clark to Thomas Sinnickson, July 23, 1788, Burnett, ed., *Letters*, VIII, 764. Uriah Forrest, who was in England at the time, also opposed ratification at first. To Jefferson, Dec. 11, 1787, Boyd, ed., *Papers of Jefferson*, XII, 416-17. A few at least among the debtors were Antifederal. McCormick, *New Jersey in the Critical Period*, 264.

19. *Ibid.*, 272.

20. "Many supposed exceptions were agitated." *Ibid.*, 270.

ratifying convention was unanimous; even more than in the two northern states, the fact demands explanation.

It will be recalled that Georgia was divided into two sections. One of them was comparable to the adjacent lowland of South Carolina, sustaining a plantation society based upon the culture of staple crops which were sold abroad. Since tidewater South Carolina was strongly Federal, it is not surprising that the areas of Georgia lying along the coast and the lower Savannah River also supported the new plan. Moreover the Savannah provided transportation for practically everyone in the state, for the small farmers of the interior still resided close to its banks. They were thus bound in a commercial nexus. On the other hand, many settlers of the upcountry looked west rather than east, or were self-sufficient rather than surplus-producing, and one might have expected the development of Antifederalism there. Actually there does seem to have been at least a little of it in the state. A recent writer is of the opinion that the only surviving record of a vote for delegates shows a sizeable Antifederal minority in the Savannah district.[21] An article in the only local newspaper criticized the Constitution mildly—the author was roundly condemned for it—and Joseph Habersham testified that during the convention not all of the delegates were at first in favor of ratification.[22] However, it is perfectly clear that the great majority of Georgians approved of the Constitution, and this was true not only of those in and near Savannah but of those in the interior.

This coalescing of the opposing forces in Georgia had begun in 1786 when the two sections at last united on granting Congress the impost and commercial powers. Even allowing for the interest of the planters and the influence of the Savannah River, the Fed-

21. Forrest McDonald, *We The People: The Economic Origins of the Constitution* (Chicago, 1958), 130.

22. *Gazette of State of Georgia* (Savannah), Nov. 15, Dec. 6, 1787. Habersham wrote during the convention that the Constitution was "read over Paragraph by Paragraph with a great deal of temper and if it had not been thought rather too precipate [*sic*] I beleive woud have been assented to as it stands *by a very great majority*, on the whole you may conclude that it will be adopted in the course of a few days." To John Habersham, Augusta, Dec. 29, 1787, Dreer Coll., Letters of Members of the Old Congress, II, 68, Hist. Soc. Pa. Italics mine. No debates have been preserved. "Minutes of the Georgia Convention Ratifying the Federal Constitution," *Georgia Historical Quarterly*, 10 (1926), 224-37.

eralism of the upcountry requires explanation. All sources then and historians since have pointed to one decisive factor. It was expressed in a toast reported from Savannah: "May the State of Georgia ever respect the Union as the only method to preserve herself."[23] There was urgent need for a strong government which could repel the Indians. This necessity controlled Georgia's stand, as the Mississippi question controlled that of Kentucky, and problems in the northwest that of Virginia's "Allegheny" counties. The situation in Georgia is well described in a letter written a few months after ratification:

The situation of this State, at this time is truely alarming. Many of our most Valuable Settlements, and one of them among the first ever made, have been interrupted in their planting, and are likely to be entirely broke up, by the Indians. They have spread Terror thro every part of the State, and we have neither numbers, or resources sufficient to oppose their ravages. We have made overtures, thro the Commissioners appointed under the last Regulation of Congress, but as they are sensible of our feeble condition, and the weakness of the whole Union, I expect they will be treated with Scorn.[24]

The importance of the Indian question was well understood outside of the state. The Antifederalist George Bryan wrote that Georgia ratified because it needed immediate aid against the Indians, and Washington pointed out that "if a weak State with the Indians on its back and the Spaniards on its flank does not see the necessity of a General Government there must I think be wickedness or insanity in the way."[25] Not all Georgians may have been virtuous, but clearly they were not insane.

23. *Pa. Packet* (Phila.), Aug. 8, 1787.

24. Nathaniel Pendleton to Jeremiah Wadsworth, Savannah, May 10, 1788, Wadsworth Papers, Box 138, Conn. Hist. Soc.; see also J. Sumner to Henry Knox, Savannah, Dec. 12, 1788, Knox Papers, XXII, 36, Mass. Hist. Soc.

25. *N.Y. Journal*, Apr. 18, 1786; Washington to Samuel Powel, Jan. 18, 1788, Fitzpatrick, ed., *Writings of Washington*, XXIX, 386; see also John Jay to Jefferson, Nov. 3, 1787, Boyd, ed., *Papers of Jefferson*, XII, 317; Ulrich B. Phillips, "Georgia and States Rights," Amer. Hist. Assn., *Ann. Report*, 1901, II, 15-16. The most recent study confirms this conclusion. Kenneth Coleman, *The American Revolution in Georgia, 1763-1789* (Athens, Ga., 1958), 253, 270-71.

The Federalists of Connecticut, unlike those of Pennsylvania, waited until the Constitution had been officially received from Congress before they acted, but they risked no further delay and held elections in November. During the interval very little information hostile to ratification reached the public; instead the newspapers were crowded with favorable articles. The *Middlesex Gazette,* which had previously contained articles expressing the debtor point of view, published no word against the Constitution and, indeed, added "Foederal" to its masthead; the *Connecticut Courant* printed the objections of Elbridge Gerry and Richard Henry Lee but accompanied them with articles in refutation; the *Connecticut Gazette* and the *New Haven Gazette* were also strongly Federal. Lee's "Federal Farmer" was sent into the state from New York City, but it did not arrive until the election was over.[26]

Once again, therefore, the Antifederalists did not have a fair chance. Even so, in September the Federalists had feared the worst. Jeremiah Wadsworth reported to Rufus King: "there is a strong party forming against the Convention and much reason to fear the new Government will not go down—if the Massachusetts rebellion had continued we might [succeed]—here there is many of our Leading Men who dread the lessening of their own power & they will[,] joined with the little Polliticians form a great Majority in this State—but if Massachusetts adopt it I shall still hope for its adoption here in time."[27] However Shays's Rebellion had the desired result, it would seem, and the Federalists had nothing to fear; indeed other factors were also working in their favor. The clergy, who in Connecticut were unusually influential, favored ratification.[28] Most of the prominent political figures were Federalists, as were the higher ranking army officers and the merchants.

26. Jeremiah Wadsworth to Rufus King, Dec. 16, 1787, King, *King,* I, 264; Wadsworth to Henry Knox, Dec. 23, 1787, Knox Papers, XXI, 82, Mass. Hist. Soc.

27. Sept. 23, 1787, *ibid.,* 13.

28. David Humphreys to Washington, Sept. 28, 1787, *Doc. Hist. of the Constitution,* IV, 302; *New Haven Gazette,* Oct. 25, 1787; Edward Frank Humphrey, *Nationalism and Religion in America, 1774-1789* (Boston, 1924), 451. Benjamin Austin, in his book *Constitutional Republicanism* (Boston, 1803), 108, quoted Jedidiah Morse's *American Geography* as observing of Connecticut, "The clergy, who are numerous, and as a body very respectable,

The commercial centers and the areas near them, including towns along the coast and up the principal rivers, especially the Connecticut, favored ratification. In the southwest, Fairfield County continued its traditional policy and was solidly Federal.

An irate letter written by Hugh Ledlie described the situation before and during the ratifying convention in Connecticut.[29] He remarked upon the prejudice of the newspapers which greatly injured the Antifederalists. The Federalists, he wrote, "have got almost all the best Writers (as well as speakers) on their side." These men, he asserted, threatened that delegates who did not vote for ratification could not expect any political preferment. Newspapers also reported that threats had been made.[30] The entire convention, said Ledlie, was conducted "with a high hand" by those who wanted offices under the Constitution and who expected great profit from their public securities. Thus those of "Superior rank" bore down what he insisted would be an Antifederal majority, were a new election held.

The Antifederalists were weakened, during the sessions, by the defection of two of their few able leaders—William Williams (the Signer) of Lebanon and Joseph Hopkins of Waterbury.[31] But whether the "Wrong heads," as their opponents called them, would ever have secured a majority is doubtful, though probably the margin of 128-40 against them in the ratifying convention could have been reduced. The history of Connecticut during the 1780's demonstrates that the sources from which Federalism sprang were too strong for the opposition. The pro-impost, anti-paper money group had retained control, and had followed a policy sufficiently moderate so that only echoes of Shays's Rebellion were heard. In 1788 they succeeded in limiting Antifederalism to the rural, more isolated areas.[32]

Among the former anti-impost towns in Connecticut, more

---

have hitherto preserved a kind of *aristocratical balance in the democratical government* of the State, which has *happily* operated as a check to the *overbearing spirit of republicanism.*"

29. To John Lamb, Jan. 15, 1788, Lamb Papers, Box 5, No. 1, N.Y. Hist. Soc.

30. *N.Y. Journal,* Nov. 8, 1787, Mar. 10, 1788.

31. *Daily Advertiser* (N.Y.), Feb. 9, 1788.

32. For the vote, Hoadly and Labaree, eds., *Public Records of Connecticut,* VI, 549-52.

voted for than against the Constitution, though it was from these towns that the Antifederal vote was derived (twenty-five of the forty negative votes came from towns which had opposed the impost in 1784, thirteen from towns not represented then, only two from a pro-impost town). The towns which had supported the paper money movement tended to oppose the Constitution. Yet only in the northern half of the state, in the more isolated sections, was the Antifederal strength nearly equal to that of the Federalists. Once again, as in Pennsylvania, geography played an important role, and in Connecticut as elsewhere the more well-to-do, and the higher social orders, were Federalist. This was the opinion of Ledlie and of Humphreys, and it is indicated also by the status of the delegates to the ratifying convention and their votes. Almost all of the merchants, lawyers, and large landowners present favored ratification. Twenty-two out of twenty-three known college men, and nearly the same proportion of large property holders, were Federal. Out of twenty living members of the upper house of the state legislature, fifteen sat in the convention, only one of whom was an Antifederalist. Judges, members of Congress, and high-ranking army officers also favored ratification with scarcely an exception. But delegates who were farmers or obscure men were more evenly divided.[33] It may be concluded, then, that the alignment in Connecticut was strikingly similar to that in Pennsylvania, and that many of the same reasons accounted for the success of the Federalists.

The early victories of the Federalists, which have so far been described, were important but not decisive. Antifederalists were strong in Rhode Island, North Carolina, New York, Virginia, and New Hampshire, and in these states the outcome was certain to be profoundly affected, and probably determined, by the action of Massachusetts. Here lay the decisive conflict; had the Constitution lost in Massachusetts, it would never have been ratified.[34]

33. Slightly over half of the Federalists had a title, the majority that of an army officer; only one-fifth of the Antifederalists were given one. In Connecticut, the title "Honorable" was reserved for members of the upper house. As to property held, published records reveal at least twenty Federalists who were wealthy or well-to-do, but only one Antifederalist was wealthy (James Wadsworth). For the occupational analysis see Appendix E.

34. James Manning to the Rev. Dr. Smith, Feb. 11, 1788, Reuben Albridge Guild, *Life, Times, and Correspondence of James Manning, and*

The bitterness which accompanied Shays's Rebellion combined with the success of Shaysite sympathizers in the 1787 election ensured that the Constitution would be strongly opposed in Massachusetts, for whatever the eastern commercial group supported would be unpopular elsewhere. As usual, the newspapers published little except Federalist arguments before the election,[35] but the statement of Elbridge Gerry opposing ratification could not be suppressed, and it was printed in most of the papers. Its effect was very great. One Federalist wrote: *"damn him—damn him*—every thing look'd well and had the most favorable appearance in this State, previous to this—and now I have my doubts—...I cannot leave him without once more *damn'g him.*" Subsequently he reiterated, "Every thing went on *firm & well* untill that *damn'd* Letter."[36] Moreover, other respected leaders were also at first against ratification, including Samuel Adams,[37] James Warren, Nathan Dane, James Winthrop, Benjamin Austin, and Samuel Osgood. John Hancock remained silent.

The Federalists tried to have the convention called for early December, but this move was defeated, and the date was set for January. The delay may have given the Antifederalists more time to arouse the backcountry, and although the Federalists too made good use of it, the odds turned against ratification. Indeed, the

---

the Early History of Brown University (Boston, 1864), 406; Edward Carrington to Madison, Feb. 10, 1788, Madison Papers, VIII, Lib. Cong.; Edward Carrington to Henry Knox, Mar. 13, 1788, Knox Papers, XXI, 167, Mass. Hist. Soc.; James Dawson to Madison, Feb. 18, 1788, *Doc. Hist of the Constitution,* IV, 509-10; Melancton Smith to Abraham Yates, Jr., Jan. 23, 1788, Yates, Jr., Papers, N.Y. Pub. Lib.; Abraham G. Lansing to Yates, *ibid.;* Harding, *Ratification in Massachusetts,* 114-15.

35. Harding, (*ibid.,* 17-18), notes that many Antifederal articles were published, especially in the *American Herald* (Boston). This is true, but very few were printed before the election.

36. Henry Jackson to Henry Knox, Nov. 5, 1787, Boston Pub. Lib.; Jackson to Knox, Nov. 11, 18, Knox Papers, XXI, 47, 49, Mass. Hist. Soc.

37. Adams was reputed to have written the Antifederal "Helvidius Priscus" articles in the *Hampshire Gazette* (Portsmouth), Dec. 9, *Independent Chronicle* (Boston), Dec. 27, 1787. See Christopher Gore to King, Dec. 30, 1787, King, *King,* I, 266. But Warren shows that the author was really James Warren. "Gerry, James and Mercy Warren and Ratification," Mass. Hist. Soc., *Proceedings,* 64 (1930-32), 155. On the various articles written in Massachusetts see Harding, *Ratification in Massachusetts,* 21-23, and Warren's article.

Federalists had to struggle desperately to avert irreparable defeat in the elections. George Richards Minot noted in his journal that the Federalists were obliged "to *pack* a Convention whose sense would be different from that of the people." [38] Their tactics came to light in Berkshire County. The Federalists published a report that the popular leader in Stockbridge, John Bacon, had been won over by Theodore Sedgwick, and was supporting the Federalist candidate. Bacon's denial was printed too late to influence the elections.[39] Referring to this episode in his journal, Minot describes Bacon as "a real advocate for the rights of the people" and obviously disapproves of the Federalists' trickery. Indeed Minot makes it clear that the Federalists employed unethical means: his account of the affair is entered under the heading, "*Bad* measures in a *good* cause." In the same county petitions received by the convention suggest that the Federalist victories in Sheffield and Great Barrington were illegal; [40] and Minot, in describing the effort made to see that Antifederal leaders in the east were not elected, notes that Rufus King was chosen from Newburyport although he was no longer a resident. It was unfortunate for the Antifederalists that their leaders were residents of the eastern part of the state which was strongly pro-Constitution; it did not require much manipulation to assure their defeat. The result of all this was that the Antifederalists were deprived of their most articulate spokesmen in the convention. The Federalists won still another victory when Minot was made secretary of the convention. In November he had asked for Timothy Dwight's help in securing the post. "There are," he wrote, "many reasons for my attempting to procure this appointment which are improper to commit to paper, but which you will judge of much importance when you hear them." [41]

Nevertheless, when the convention assembled the Antifeder-

38.   This Journal, in the Massachusetts Historical Society, contains a long and very revealing entry describing the ratification. The evidence given by Minot is particularly impressive because he was a Federalist.

39.   *American Herald* (Boston), Dec. 17, 24, 1787; *Mass. Centinel* (Boston), Jan. 12, 1788; Jeremiah Wadsworth to Rufus King, Dec. 16, 1787, King, *King*, I, 264.

40.   *Mass. Debates*, 52-54.

41.   Nov. 30, 1787, Dreer Coll., American Lawyers, IV, Hist. Soc. Pa.

alists had a clear majority, which some of their own number claimed was forty or more.[42] The exact strength of the two sides cannot be determined, but it is known with certainty that a dozen members, elected as Antifederalists, voted for ratification or refrained from voting, and there are less definite indications that other changes occurred. At the outset the Antifederal majority was probably about twenty. The Federalists were pessimistic and had to labor for converts.[43] One major weapon was "influence." "The *better sort*," remarked Melancton Smith of New York, "have means of *convincing* those who differ from them." [44] Although Minot's journal does not reveal specific cases, it makes clear that the influence of the better sort was used in ways of which he did not approve. The early withdrawal of Oliver Phelps of Berkshire was a case in point. The Federalists gave out that he retired because he felt opposition to be futile, since a majority of his fellow delegates from Berkshire would support ratification. This story is clearly false—even on the final roll call that county was Antifederal, seventeen to five. According to East, who regards this incident as a turning point in the convention's history, Phelps was actually influenced by Samuel Osgood, to whom he owed money, and perhaps by Nathaniel Gorham, with whom he engaged in land speculation.[45] A different sort of influence prevailed with Nathaniel Barrell, of York. Barrell, who had married the daughter of a wealthy judge and ex-tory, received some hot letters which informed him that he was opposing the wishes of his father-in-law. Certainly the discovery that the Constitution was opposed by the "Multitude" and supported by the well-to-do and respectable, whom Barrell admired, must have had a great effect on his

42. Samuel Nayson to George Thatcher, Jan. 22, 1788, Matthew Cobb to Thatcher, Jan. 24, *Hist. Mag.*, 16 (1869), 266, 268.
43. Nathaniel Gorham to Rufus King, Dec. 29, 1787, King to Madison, Jan. 20, 1788, King, *King*, I, 266, 314; Gorham to Knox, Jan. 16, 1788, Knox Papers, XXI, 110, Mass. Hist. Soc.
44. To Abraham Yates, Jr., Jan. 28, 1788, Yates, Jr., Papers, N. Y. Pub. Lib.
45. Christopher Gore to King, Dec. 30, 1787, Phelps to King, Apr. 5, 1788, Gorham to King, Apr. 6, 1788, King, *King*, I, 266, 323, 325; East, "Massachusetts Conservatives," Morris, ed., *Era of the American Revolution*, 363*n*., 376-377*n*.; Gorham to [unknown], Mar. 25, 1788, Emmett Coll., No. 9444, N. Y. Pub. Lib. But in January Osgood was still opposed to the Constitution, so that Gorham's was probably the more important influence.

decision to vote for ratification.[46] Others must have had a like reaction.

Perhaps the superiority of the Federalists in debate had some effect upon the outcome. It may be that the debates as published do less than justice to the Antifederalists. The Federalists naturally wanted their own views to be fully recorded and the ideas of their opponents repressed for the effect in other states. Perhaps it was for this reason that Minot had been so anxious to secure the post of secretary—just as in Pennsylvania, newspaper accounts of debates consisted largely of Federalist speeches. Be that as it may, there is no doubt that the Antifederalists lacked the talent to express their objections forcibly, whereas the Federalists were able (as Minot admitted) to argue away many criticisms.[47] The Federalists, moreover, were in communication with their friends elsewhere, and could anticipate the objections that would be made; their speeches show careful preparation whereas the Antifederalists seem to be improvising.[48]

Toward the end of the convention the poverty of the Antifederalists was used against them. According to Henry Jackson, they could not leave without being paid, but when they applied to the Treasury they were informed that no money was available. So, wrote Jackson, "We have circulated, If the Constitution is adopted, there will be no difficulty respecting the Pay—If it *is not* they must look to the Treasurer for it." [49]

46. Joseph Barrell to Nathaniel Barrell, Dec. 20, 1787, Apr. 1, 1788, Sandeman-Barrell Papers, Mass. Hist. Soc.; David Sewall to George Thatcher, Jan. 5, Feb. 11, 1788, *Hist. Mag.*, 16 (1869), 261, 271. Sewall refers to Barrell's conversion by means of letters "and other matters."

47. David Sewall to George Thatcher, Mar. 4, 1788, Samuel Nayson to George Thatcher, Mar. 23, 1788, *ibid.*, 343, 347. Minot noted that "the most serious principles in government were argued away to nothing by able casuists, & the mouths of the opponents being shut, they were ashamed to say that they were not convinced. Annual elections, rotation in office, qualifications of officers, standing armies, & declarations of rights, were all shewn to be too trivial to be insisted upon. And it was demonstrated that to withhold any powers of taxation, or of any other kind from a government, lest they should abuse them, was an unreasonable principle of jealousy which would prevent any government at all."

48. Christopher Gore requested information from Rufus King regarding several criticisms. Dec. 23, 1787, King, *King*, I, 265.

49. To Knox, Feb. 3, 1788, Knox Papers, XXI, 131, Mass. Hist. Soc.

Still another technique was used to win Samuel Adams. A meeting of the Boston townspeople was instigated by the Federalists to express approval of the Constitution. The incident probably did not actually convert Adams, but he felt obliged to vote as his constituents wished. The meeting may also have swayed Hancock, as well as Charles Jarvis and John Winthrop of Boston. It may even have influenced opinion in some nearby towns.[50]

In spite of all these efforts, a majority of the convention still opposed ratification, and the Federalists were forced to make concessions. Toward the end of January they concluded that a few members might be won over by submitting amendments, not as a condition of ratification, but as mere recommendations. A few days later an article was published in the *Massachusetts Centinel* in which an Antifederalist (James Sullivan?) also advocated acceptance with amendments. Previously such an idea had been rejected, but it was now apparent that a few of the moderate Antifederalists were wavering, a fact which made it likely that a majority for the Constitution could be secured.[51] The adoption of amendments would furnish members who had been elected as Antifederalists with the necessary excuse to their constituents, and at least one town had authorized its delegates to ratify if amendments were adopted.[52]

With the trend moving in their favor, the Federalists were at last able to deal with John Hancock, whose support was vital. He was to present the amendments as his own; his influence would prevail among the wavering delegates. In return, he was promised Federalist support for governor, and was informed that if Virginia did not ratify the Constitution, he would probably be

50. Biographers of Adams have discussed this fully. For the nearby towns, see the *Mass. Centinel* (Boston), Jan. 9, 1788. Minot says that Adams "was personally insulted in such a manner as not to admit of his speaking or thinking with freedom upon this subject."

51. King to Madison, Jan. 23, 1788, King, *King*, I, 316; King to Knox, Boston, Jan. 27, 1788, Gorham to Knox, Jan. 30, 1788, Knox Papers, XXI, 121, 124; Mass. Hist. Soc.; "Hampden," in the *Mass. Centinel* (Boston), Jan. 26, 1788.

52. William Widgery to George Thatcher, Feb. 8, 1788, *Hist. Mag.*, 16 (1869), 270; George Augustus and Henry Warren Wheeler, *History of Brunswick, Topsham, and Harpswell, Maine* (Boston, 1878), 171.

President.[53] Accordingly, Hancock, who had pleaded the gout, made a remarkable recovery and presented the amendments. There followed a decisive shift of perhaps a score of delegates. Since the names of a dozen or so of these men are known, two generalizations concerning them may be made. The majority of them came from the area near the coast. Also, they had more money, and were of higher prestige than most of the Antifederalists because of professional or political achievements.[54]

The struggle over ratification climaxed a series of political and economic conflicts in Massachusetts, and the alignment of groups on this issue was identical with that in the previous controversies. It has already been observed that the state was divided politically into two areas: the region near the coast, plus the Connecticut River towns; and the interior. The first favored the Constitution by an overwhelming majority of 131 to 29. The latter rejected it by 139 to 56, and the margin had been even greater at the beginning of the convention. Two illustrations will serve. Towns along the Connecticut River, as far north as Hatfield, unanimously favored ratification.[55] In Maine, seacoast towns supported the Constitution twenty-two to five whereas the interior was against it, seventeen to two when the convention met and sixteen to three

53. Belknap to Hazard, Feb. 3, 1788, Mass. Hist. Soc., *Collections*, 5th Ser., 3 (1877), 15; John Avery, Jr., to George Thatcher, Feb. 13, 1788, *Hist. Mag.*, 16 (1869), 338; King to Knox, Feb. 3, 1788, Knox Papers, XXI, 127, Mass. Hist. Soc.; Harding, *Ratification in Massachusetts*, 85-87; Minot Journal, Mass. Hist. Soc. In the long run, though the Federalists did live up to their bargain, Hancock probably lost from it. Minot wrote in his journal (entry of January, 1789) that Hancock had alienated a large number of the popular leaders while the Federalists, who never had liked him, were ready to discard him. He therefore broke with them, claiming that he had been deceived at the time of ratification.

54. Known or suspected: Samuel Adams, Dr. Jarvis, and John Winthrop, wealthy merchant of Boston; Dr. Samuel Holten of Danvers, prominent and well-to-do; the lawyer William Symmes of Andover; John Sprague of Lancaster, a well-to-do, Anti-Shays lawyer; Charles Turner of Scituate, a prominent Congregational minister; Barrell of York, referred to above; Isaac Snow of Harpswell, a shipowner; Samuel Curtis of Worcester and James Nichols of Brookfield, neither of whom voted; James Williams of Taunton, Captain Samuel Grant of Vassalborough, Thomas Rice, doctor, and David Sylvester, merchant, of Pownalborough.

55. Perhaps these towns were influenced by the outcome in Connecticut, where, as Christopher Gore pointed out, "their local circumstances, their habits, & connections are so nearly related to our state." To Jeremiah Wadsworth, Jan. 9, 1788, Emmett Coll., No. 5047, N.Y. Pub. Lib.

on the final vote.[56] The Antifederalists, therefore, included those who favored lower taxes, paper money, and in general the objectives expressed in the petitions of 1786-87. For example, when the critical vote on stationing troops in western Massachusetts was taken in 1786, the areas which were Antifederalist in 1788 had opposed it by a margin of nearly three to one, whereas Federalist areas of 1788 had supported it by a majority of four and one-half to one. In the Antifederal ranks at the convention were at least twenty-nine delegates who had actively participated in Shays's Rebellion and several others who had attended county conventions. Indeed, a map showing the towns sympathetic with the Rebellion is almost identical with one outlining the Antifederal area.[57]

All of this evidence suggests that the Federalists and Antifederalists represented different socio-economic interests. Both Rufus King and Henry Knox observed that the well-to-do, well-educated, mercantile, and professional classes were to be found exclusively among the Federalists.[58] Minot is even more explicit in describing a difference in class: "Those of the learned professions, and the men of property were almost unanimously in favour of the constitution. But the great body of middling land holders were opposed to it." Jackson referred to the Antifederal delegates as "*poor* devils" who could not afford to pay their own way home. Of Lincoln County in Maine, George Thatcher, a Federalist, was informed: "The most reputable characters in that County are, I

56. It might seem logical that Maine towns favoring separation were Antifederal; this is the factor usually emphasized. Probably this interpretation stems from the belief that Antifederalism is to be equated with opposition to the Union, which as has been seen was far from the case. Also, Christopher Gore attributed the Antifederalism of Wedgery (New Gloucester) and Rice (Pownalborough) to their belief that ratification would delay separation. To Rufus King, Jan. 6, 1788, King, *King*, I, 312. Actually there is no positive correlation between attitudes toward separation and toward the Constitution, and no reason why there should have been.

57. See especially the black list in the Paine Papers, XXIII, Mass. Hist. Soc., and the *Worcester Mag.*, 3 (1787), 76. Local sources supplement these lists of Shaysites. Two Shaysites voted for the Constitution, one of whom had previously shifted sides and had testified against the "rebels." Towns which expressed Shaysite ideas voted against the Constitution, 90-7; towns known to have opposed the rebellion were Federalist, 85-12. See petitions in the Massachusetts Archives, town records, and published materials.

58. King to Madison, Jan. 20, 27, 1788, King, *King*, I, 314, 316-17; Knox to Washington, Jan. 14, 1788, *Doc. Hist. of the Constitution*, IV, 442-43.

believe, on what *you will call the right* side of the question—but the middling & common sort are on the opposite." In York the Antifederalists were described as such that "it would degrade a man of Sensibility and Integrity, if it was known and realized that he was a *genuine* Representative of them," and as "the lower class of Citizens." [59] The observation that men of property were on the Federalist side was also made during the convention. [60]

These remarks can be supported by other evidence. Tax lists reveal that the Federal towns were wealthier than Antifederal towns. This fact is not surprising, in view of the geographical division, but it also holds true within counties, especially in Suffolk, Worcester, Berkshire, Hampshire, and Plymouth. [61] Of the delegates to the convention, very few Antifederalists were well-to-do, whereas many Federalists were men of wealth. Almost all of the public securities were held by Federalists. [62] Merchants, shipowners, bankers, manufacturers, lawyers, and judges were Federalists by a very large majority, as were generals, naval captains, and members of the Cincinnati; most college men were Federalists, and most ministers. Thus wealth, talent, and position supported the Constitution. On the other hand, lower ranking army officers and men of lesser economic and social distinction tended to be Antifederal; doctors were to be found on both sides. Something— perhaps not very much—may be inferred from the titles that preceded or followed the names of delegates. The title "Esquire" was held by seventy-five Federalists and only fourteen Antifederalists, whereas the appellation of "Mr." was given to thirty-four Federalists and eighty-nine Antifederalists. Combining all of this

59. From Silas Lee, Jan. 23, 1788, *Hist. Mag.*, 16 (1869), 267; David Sewall to George Thatcher, Jan. 5, Feb. 11, 1788, *ibid.*, 261, 271.

60. *Mass. Debates*, 138, 203. See also Lewis B. Morris to General Webb, Springfield, Vermont, Feb. 7, 1788: "I doubt not that wisdom as well as the Property of the State are in favor of it, but unfortunately every Blockhead and Bankrupt in the State has as good a Vote as a better Man." Ford, ed., *Correspondence of Webb*, III, 93.

61. Joseph B. Felt, "Statistics of Taxation in Massachusetts, including Valuation and Population," American Statistical Assn., *Collections*, 1 (Boston, 1847), 454-73.

62. Treasury Department, vol. 1119, National Archives, contains the names of 28 men of known political convictions, of whom 24 were Federalists. McDonald has made a much more detailed analysis, to the same effect. *We The People*, 199-201.

personal information, a division can be made as follows: men of high social, military, or economic position [63] voted 107 to 34 for ratification, while those of lower status voted 126 to 61 against it.

It seems clear that a majority, though not a large one, of the citizens of Massachusetts opposed the Constitution when it was ratified, and it is probable that a majority continued to oppose it. Minot observed in his journal that as late as January 1789, Antifederalists controlled the House. This majority reflected the preponderance of the smaller property-holders and the greater political representation of the relatively self-sufficient interior towns as contrasted with the commercial centers and their satellite areas. The victory of the Federalists had been due to a number of factors. First, a large number of the towns (over fifty) did not send delegates to the convention, and of these two-thirds would probably have been Antifederal. Their absence gave the Federalists a better chance to bring about the necessary shift of votes. During the campaign, the Federalists had the advantage arising from their domination over the press [64] and their superior prestige, organization, and resources. During the convention, the fact that the best speakers and those of high social and economic position supported the Constitution influenced some, while the winning over of Hancock quieted the consciences of other members. Previous ratification by five states may have been important. The result was a shift of perhaps twenty delegates, most of whom came from the eastern towns of above average wealth, who were themselves of superior socio-economic position, and who ultimately turned to the party of their peers.

63. Esq., Gen., Col., men well-to-do or wealthy, merchants, lawyers, judges, shipowners, and large manufacturers. To put the matter differently: 40 per cent of the Federal and 12 per cent of the Antifederal delegates were merchants, lawyers, large landowners, doctors, or ministers, while 38 per cent of the Federalists and 58 per cent of the Antifederalists were farmers or of unknown occupation. McDonald has identified some individuals whom I missed (*We The People*, 191-99) and a more thorough research would surely reveal others, but no significant change is to be expected in the proportions.

64. Minot wrote, "The press was kept under the most shameful license. A combination was entered into by ye Printers not to publish any piece for or against the constitution, without knowing ye writers name, by which means all freedom of writing was taken away, as ye mechanicks had been worked up to such a degree of rage, that it was unsafe to be known to oppose it, in Boston."

By mid-February of 1788, six states had ratified the Constitution, and the Antifederal cause suffered accordingly. Five states must reject the Constitution in order to defeat ratification. Little help could be expected from South Carolina, but Rhode Island, New York, and North Carolina could be counted as Antifederalist strongholds. There remained three states, of which the Antifederalists must carry two: Virginia, Maryland, and New Hampshire. In the last the Antifederalists at first gained an inconclusive victory; the state did not absolutely reject the Constitution, but neither did it accept it.

The New Hampshire convention was called for mid-February, which permitted time for thought. As usual, the newspapers were not very helpful to the Antifederalists, publishing only half a dozen articles opposed to ratification and a large number in favor of it. A few Antifederal pamphlets were circulated but not, evidently, until the convention was in session.[65] Nevertheless out of over one hundred delegates (107, by one account) only thirty favored ratification. According to one Federalist, about twenty opponents were persuaded to change their minds; another claimed a larger number of converts. In any case the Antifederalists were unable to maintain sufficient control to reject the Constitution, nor were the Federalists able to induce a majority to accept it. In the end the convention voted to adjourn (56-51).[66] The burden of decision was therefore passed to the other states, and the ultimate result in New Hampshire was, in effect, left to the determination of events elsewhere, especially in Massachusetts.

Although the outcome was not a clear-cut victory for the Antifederalists, they had administered a setback to the Federalists and encouraged opposition elsewhere. Nicholas Gilman wrote of the surprise and chagrin in New York City and added, "Much is to be apprehended from this unfortunate check to the tide of our plitical prosperity. . . . this unfortunate affair will at least give a

65. Jeremiah Libbey to Jeremy Belknap, Feb. 26, 1788, "The Belknap Papers," Mass. Hist. Soc., *Collections*, 6th Ser., 4 (1891), 396.
66. *Ibid.*; John Sullivan to Jeremy Belknap, Feb. 26, 1788, *ibid.*, 393-94; Sullivan to John Gilman, Feb. 28, 1788, Gratz Coll., Old Congress, XI, Hist. Soc. Pa.; *Conn. Courant* (Hartford), Mar. 3, 1788; *Worcester Mag.*, 4 (1788), 300.

temporary spring to the opposition and I fear its effects in other States."[67] In Virginia, Washington was afraid that the Federal cause had been injured, since now people saw that the Constitution was not so popular "as they had been taught to believe."[68]

Unfortunately, no record has been preserved of the New Hampshire vote in February. The results in June, when the Constitution was ratified (57-47) are recorded, however, and presumably those towns which were Antifederal then were also opposed earlier. In addition, Epping, Salisbury, Peterborough, Meredith-New Hampton, and Hancock-Antrim-Deering, which in June cast no votes, had previously been Antifederal, while Derryfield and Hopkinton opposed ratification in February but supported it in June. Charleston also was apparently Antifederal at first.[69] Of these towns, one was in the southeast—the Federal stronghold—and one was on the Connecticut; the remainder were near the center of the state. This suggests that Antifederal strength in the interior was stronger at the time of the early convention than in June, and, although it was admitted that there were "some good men" among the Antifederalists, the usual uncomplimentary allusions of the Federalists indicate that they were debtors or poor farmers. Madison wrote to Washington: "the opposition, I understand, is composed precisely of the same description of characters with that of Massa-

67. To John Langdon, Mar. 6, 1788, Dreer Coll., Letters to Members of the Federal Convention, Hist. Soc. Pa.; Gilman to Sullivan, Mar. 23, 1788, N. H. Hist. Soc., *Collections*, 15 (1939), 579.

68. Washington to Knox, Mar. 30, 1788, to Lincoln, Apr. 2, 1788, to Langdon, Apr. 2, 1788, Fitzpatrick, ed., *Writings of Washington*, XXIX, 449, 451, 453.

69. Plumer, Jr., *Plumer*, 97; Orin Grant Libby, *The Geographical Distribution of the Vote of the Thirteen States on the Federal Constitution, 1787-8* (Madison, Wis., 1894), 72, 97-98; George Waldo Browne, ed., *Early Records of the Town of Derryfield now Manchester, N.H., 1782-1800*, Manchester Hist. Assn., *Collections*, 9 (1906), 145, 156-57; extracts from Hopkinton town records, Jan. 14, June 14, 1788 and from the Charleston town records, Jan. 29, Mar. 26, Apr. 15, 1788, N.H. Hist. Soc. Ebenezer Webster, a prominent delegate from Salisbury, was at first instructed to oppose ratification. He became convinced, it is reported, that the Constitution would make possible the payment of the national debt, and declared his confidence that Washington "will not mislead us." He was then authorized by the town to vote as he chose, but finally did not vote at all. John J. Dearborn, *The History of Salisbury New Hampshire* (Manchester, N.H., 1890), 115.

chusetts, and stands contrasted to all the wealth, abilities, and respectability of the State." [70]

Meanwhile the Constitution had received its second and more severe check in Rhode Island. This came as no surprise. The Assembly had voted not to send delegates to the Federal Convention, though by a very close vote, and now, in March, it refused to obey the injunction of that body to call a ratifying convention. Instead it ordered that the towns be polled so that the people could decide what to do. This democratic procedure was opposed by the Federalists, who insisted that the state was obligated to hold a convention whether the majority wanted one or not. The truth is that the Federalists recognized that the method adopted gave them no chance.

When the towns held their meetings, the Federalists refused in some cases even to vote.[71] In Providence only one man voted, and in Newport only eleven; it is obvious that both towns favored the convention although both were recorded in the negative. In some towns the Federalists did vote; they prevailed in Little Compton (63-57) and in Bristol (26-23). It is obvious, therefore, that the Antifederal margin of twenty-eight towns against a convention and only two in favor was deceptive.[72] Since slightly more than one-fourth of the adult white males usually voted in town elections, the maximum being over 40 per cent, it is likely that an abnormally small vote represents a Federalist boycott and perhaps a Federalist majority. We find a low proportion of potential voters recorded in Westerly, Warren, Jamestown, South Kingston, and Charleston. In the last two the Antifederal majority was too great to have been overcome,[73] but possibly the Federalists could have carried six or seven of the thirty towns. Such a division is con-

---

70. Sullivan to Belknap, Feb. 26, 1788 and to Gilman, Feb. 28, 1788, cited above, n. 66; Madison to Washington, New York, Mar. 3, 1788, Hunt, ed., *Writings of Madison*, V, 112.

71. *Conn. Courant* (Hartford), Apr. 7, 14, 1788. An attempt was made in Massachusetts to adopt this procedure; here also the Federalists opposed it for the same reason. Harding, *Ratification in Massachusetts*, 46-47.

72. Acts and Resolves, Mar. 1788, 11 (photostatic copy, Stanford Univ. Lib.). See the discussion in the *Conn. Courant* (Hartford), Apr. 7, 14, 1788.

73. Newport and Providence were the two major mercantile centers; Little Compton, Bristol, Warren, and Jamestown were all on the Bay, while Westerly was on the southern coast.

firmed by a vote taken the following fall, in which the legislature, by a three to one majority, again refused to call a convention, but instead agreed to distribute the message of the New York convention (calling for another general convention) and to poll the towns again.[74]

It is clear that in 1788 the Antifederalists controlled the entire rural part of the state and indeed everything except a few coastal, and probably commercial, towns. Fourteen of the Rhode Island towns were on the coast, most of them on Narragansett Bay; they were about evenly divided on the Constitution. The remaining sixteen were inland; every one was Antifederal. The division correlates very closely with that on paper money, all of the Federalist towns having opposed it and almost all of the Antifederal towns having supported it.[75] The same observation applies to the half-pay issue. A further correlation is that Federal towns had a larger number of slaves, on the average, than did the Antifederal, though there is less consistency in this regard. The significant division in Rhode Island was that of the coast versus the interior.

Thus it was that by mid-April there were still only six states which had ratified. With most of the returns in from the North, attention now shifted southward where four states had yet to vote. The first convention to meet was that of Maryland, and the result there would surely be of vital importance to the outcome elsewhere. The prospect was not pleasing to the Federalists. Many of the state's leading men were opposed. Samuel Chase, signer of the Declaration of Independence, and "radical" leader William Paca, also a signer and a former governor, and Thomas Johnson, also a former governor, all had refused to accept nominations to the Philadelphia Convention; John Francis Mercer and Luther Martin, who did attend, had refused to sign the Constitution, and the latter delivered a lengthy tirade against it before the House

74. Jeremiah Olney to Hamilton, Nov. 3, 1788, Shepley Lib., VIII, 108, R. I. Hist. Soc. For the New York circular letter as distributed in Rhode Island see Broadside A-1123, R. I. Hist. Soc. A three to one margin means that the division of towns was probably about 24-6, because Providence and Newport had ten votes between them whereas most of the towns had but two each.

75. Hillman Bishop writes, "There is no question but that the same towns and the same individuals who favored the paper money also opposed the Constitution." "Rhode Island," R. I. Hist., 8 (1949), 90.

of Delegates. James McHenry, who had signed, had been far from enthusiastic.[76] When the legislature considered the plan, the ratifying convention was postponed until April. This decision and an accompanying vote showed that there was potential Antifederal strength in the paper money stronghold of the northern and western (upper Potomac and Chesapeake) parts of the state. Chase's opposition became known; William Paca was expected to follow him; Governor Smallwood was Antifederal, and the opinion of other key leaders was doubtful.[77] Washington wrote urgently to two of them, warning that if Maryland failed to ratify—even if the convention merely adjourned—the Constitution would be defeated in Virginia, and thus forever.[78]

But then the tide turned. In most of the counties nobody came forward to challenge the Federalists (where they did, the Antifederalists won as often as they lost).[79] Newspapers printed very little on the subject, and most of what they did print was pro-Federalist. Two of the key figures, Johnson and Paca, limited their activity to an effort to obtain amendments, and the former did not try very hard even to do that much.[80] With the exception of Luther Martin, the Antifederalists wrote practically nothing and did not wage the kind of campaign which was necessary. As John Francis Mercer asserted, "All opposition being thus postponed & every necessary Step to inform the minds of our Citizens on one Side neglected— while unremitting Exertions by a Number of wealthy & respect-

76. *Md. Journal* (Baltimore), Apr. 27, 1787; *Md. Hist. Mag.*, 5 (1910), 139-50; Bernard C. Steiner, *The Life and Correspondence of James McHenry* (Cleveland, 1907), 100-7; Farrand, ed., *Records of the Federal Convention*, II, 649-50.

77. *Maryland Chronicle, or Universal Advertiser* (Fredericktown), Dec. 5, 1787; Madison to Jefferson, Oct. 24, 1787, Hunt, ed., *Writings of Madison*, V, 36; Samuel Chase to John Lamb, June 13, 1789, Leake, *Lamb*, 310.

78. To Thomas Johnson, Apr. 20, 1788, to James McHenry, Apr. 27, 1788, Fitzpatrick, ed., *Writings of Washington*, XXIX, 463, 471-72. Probably these letters were intended to be circulated.

79. There were contests in Harford, Baltimore, Anne Arundel, Washington, and Montgomery counties and in the towns of Baltimore and Annapolis. Crowl notes that there was no ticket in Frederick County and he was unable to find opposition elsewhere. *Maryland During the Revolution*, 136. Elections are not won without candidates.

80. Johnson to Washington, Oct. 10, 1788, quoted in Steiner, *McHenry*, 113n.

able characters were continued on the other—it cannot be surprizing that the Elections were generally favorable to the Constitution." Noting that few Antifederalists sought election and that few people voted, Mercer insisted that "four fifths of the people of Maryland are now in favor of considerable Alterations and Amendments." [81]

Several points stand out concerning the division in Maryland. First, the previously noted sectional division was maintained, except that the Antifederalist area had shrunk to include only three upper Chesapeake Bay counties (Anne Arundel, Baltimore, and Harford). Second, the paper money advocates were divided on the Constitution, although what Antifederal strength there was came from areas that had favored paper money during the previous two years: all three counties just named had subscribed to a currency emission in earlier votes. The Antifederalist leaders had supported paper money and similar measures; Crowl observes that "their personal fortunes would be jeopardized at least temporarily by the establishment of a stable currency and the regularized collection of debts." [82] The political history of the state and the attitude of the legislature showed that there was a large potential for Antifederalism; however the people waited to be led —as they were accustomed to wait [83]—and the active leadership was Federal. On April 26 the convention approved of the Constitution by the great majority of sixty-three to eleven.

The Antifederalists' failure in Maryland was followed a month later by defeat in South Carolina. By 1788 the distaste of the planters for a strong government, which had been partly based on a fear of Northern domination, had almost disappeared, and Charleston newspapers had been publishing articles calling for

81. "To the Members of the Conventions of New York and Virginia," Etting Coll., Autograph Letter, VI, Hist. Soc. Pa. For an account of the convention, in addition to published sources, see Daniel Carroll to Madison, May 28, 1788, Madison Papers, IX, Lib. Cong.
82. Crowl, "Anti-Federalism," *Wm. and Mary Qtly.*, 3rd Ser., 4 (1947), 446-69.
83. "Political dominance in each county fell easily into the grip of a few families whose wealth and social prestige made them the natural leaders of their particular localities." *Ibid.*, 452.

a stronger government.[84] The Constitution therefore met with general approval in the eastern part of the state. Not only were merchant-planters such as Henry Laurens enthusiastic, but so was Alexander Gillon, who had recently been supporting the state's debtor interest.[85] Yet opposition soon appeared and was expressed in the House of Representatives. The wealthy planter Rawlin Lowndes spoke for those who still feared oppression of the South by the North, and James Lincoln presented the backcountry view.[86] The impression made by these speakers was such that Arthur Bryan wrote to his father that he felt the Constitution would have been rejected, had a vote been taken in the House. (He was probably wrong.) He described the attitude of the interior counties where, he asserted, the Constitution was "universally reprobated," especially by the "second class of people." Other reports reached the North that "the Farmers" were Antifederal.[87]

The alignment on the Constitution was foreshadowed at this point by a vote taken in the House on a motion to hold the convention in Charleston on May 12. It was barely carried, seventy-six to seventy-five. The objections may have been to the place or to the date rather than to the meeting, but the division was prophetic: from the whole of the west all but two votes were cast in opposition to the resolution, whereas the east favored it with equal unanimity. In between, a group of parishes which had always fluctuated between the two poles, was divided.[88] The vote indicated that the alignment on the Constitution would resemble that on sectional and economic issues—a fact perceived by the Federal-

84. For example, Edward Rutledge to John Jay, June 29, 1776, in Johnston, *Jay*, I, 67-68, and the different emphasis a decade later in *ibid.*, III, 217. See *Charleston Morning Post*, July 7, 1786; *Charleston Evening Gazette*, Aug. 18, 23, 1786; *Columbian Herald* (Charleston), July 5, Aug. 23, 1787.

85. Laurens to Edward Bridgen, Oct. 8, 1787, Laurens Papers, Letter Book 13, S. C. Hist. Soc.; *Daily Advertiser* (Charleston), Jan. 26, 1788.

86. *Ibid.*, Jan. 21, Feb. 1, 1788.

87. Apr. 9, 1788, Bryan Papers, Box A24, Hist. Soc. Pa. David Ramsay thought that a great majority was for it. He added that in Charleston the opinion prevailed that if other Southern states refused to ratify, South Carolina would confederate with New England. To John Eliot, Jan. 19, 1788, Brunhouse, "Ramsay," *Journal of So. Hist.*, 9 (1943), 550.

88. *State Gazette of S.-C.* (Charleston), Jan. 28, 1788. This transitional tier of parishes has been previously described. On this issue they supported the west by a narrow margin.

ist historian, David Ramsay. Those who opposed ratification, he wrote, were apprehensive that "we can make no more instalment laws—no more paper money—& that we will be obliged to pay our debts & taxes. Some considerable opposition is expected from the favorers of instalment laws, valuation laws, pine barren laws & legal tender paper laws." [89]

There was thus considerable evidence of great Antifederal strength; nevertheless, when the convention met in May, the Federalists had a majority of between twenty-five and thirty. There were several reasons for this, most of which were discussed in an interesting letter from Aedanus Burke to John Lamb.[90] First was lack of organization. Burke admitted that there had been no previous meetings and no publications circulated; the Antifederalists had "no principle of concert or union." The planter Lowndes also lamented the absence of "a strong, systematic opposition." [91] Second, the newspapers had been strongly pro-Federalist. All of them were located in Charleston, and, Burke asserted, "The Printers are, in general, British journeymen, or poor Citizens, who are afraid to offend the great men, or Merchants who could work their ruin." Although the newspapers did publish the criticisms made in the legislature, and printed some Antifederal articles,[92] the weight of publicity was heavily on the Federal side. Third, and by far the most important, was the inadequate representation given to the western part of the state. Those eastern parishes which had for years united with Charleston against the back-country were almost unanimously Federal, and they had 122 out of the 236 votes. Finally, developments during the convention itself were unfavorable to the Antifederalists. Burke wrote: "The principle cause [for the ratification] was holding the Convention in the City where there are not fifty Inhabitants who are not friendly to it. The Merchants and leading men kept open house

89. To Rush, Apr. 21, 1788, Brunhouse, "Ramsay," *Journal of So. Hist.*, 9 (1943), 554.

90. June 23, 1788, Lamb Papers, Box 5, N.Y. Hist. Soc.

91. To Lamb, June 21, 1788, Leake, *Lamb*, 308.

92. The *Columbian Herald* published the objections of Mason, Lee, Yates, Lansing, and "Centinel" (Dec. 22, 1787, Jan. 7, Mar. 10, 17, 1788) while the *State Gazette* printed Martin's long address in 10 issues (Apr. 14 to May 22, 1788).

for the back and low country Members during the whole time the Convention sat." To the influence of prominent men was soon added another disadvantage: it was learned that Maryland had ratified. Prior to this time, Georgia had already agreed, and her decision may have been influential in the districts near the Savannah River.[93] But her action did not necessarily foreshadow what the other Southern states would do. Therefore Maryland's ratification "was a severe blow to us," wrote Burke, "for next day, one of our best speakers in the Opposition, Doctor Fayssoux, gave notice he would quit that ground, as Maryland had acceded to it." Actually the doctor continued to oppose ratification, but he no longer spoke, and admitted that Maryland's vote was decisive. His loss of hope seems to have been important, for it was fully reported in the newspapers not only in Charleston but as far away as Rhode Island.[94] Thereafter, Burke recalled, "we were every day afterwards losing ground & numbers going over to the Enemy, on an idea that further Opposition was useless." Meanwhile, letters from John Lamb were on the way bringing news of the Antifederal strength in New York, but they started too late (May 19) and took nearly a month to arrive, by which time it was all over. The first test of strength came on the twenty-second when a motion to adjourn until October was defeated (135-89). By this time some foes of the Constitution had given up, and it is likely that the original Antifederalist strength had been greater by eight or ten votes. The end came two days later when the Constitution was ratified (149-73).[95]

It is the first vote—that on adjournment—which furnishes the best guide to an analysis of Antifederalism, since it occurred before the defections revealed by the final roll call. The division was along geographical lines, and is strikingly similar to that already established on previous issues. The coastal parishes, which had traditionally sided with Charleston, cast 111 votes for and

93. The "Savannah and Edisto" district, which usually voted with the west, cast six votes unanimously for ratification.
94. *State Gazette of S.-C.* (Charleston), May 26, 1788; *Daily Advertiser* (N. Y.), June 11, 1788; *Providence Gazette*, June 7, 1788.
95. A. S. Salley, ed., *Journal of the Convention of South Carolina which Ratified the Constitution of the United States, May 23, 1788* (Atlanta, 1928), 13-23, 39-49.

only 9 votes against the Constitution.[96] Of the nine, four came from Prince Frederick, which lay on the border between east and west; however the Federalists received nine votes from this transition area which often in the past had determined the fate of a measure. The remaining fifteen Federal votes were cast by up-country delegates, some of whom had undoubtedly been chosen as Antifederalists, except, probably, the six representatives from the Savannah and Edisto district. The rest of the state—the whole interior—was Antifederal; excluding the last named district, up-country delegates voted seventy-two to nine for adjournment. Nearly 80 per cent of the white population lived in the parishes and counties which sent Antifederal delegates.[97] Burke's statement that four-fifths of the people detested the Constitution appears to have been accurate.

The nature of the division is also indicated by the fact that over three-fourths of the slaves were in the Federalist area. The Federalists included most of the wealthy men of the state, as well as lawyers, judges, merchants, planters, high-ranking army officers and state officials, and men of education and prestige. Few such existed among the Antifederal delegates, whose constituents were principally small farmers.[98] Burke's description seems accurate: "All the rich leading men, along the sea coast, and rice settlements with few exceptions, Lawyers, Physicians and Divines; the Merchants, mechanics, the Populace and mob of Charleston" were Federalist, and the opposition to the Constitution came "chiefly from the back country where the strength and numbers of our republick be."

It is also informative to note the nature of the shift which took place between the postponement vote and the final ratification. Those who changed sides were probably moderates who agreed with the Reverend Mr. Cummins of the backcountry that the Constitution, though faulty, was an improvement on the Articles,

96. Technically, on a motion to adjourn.
97. Greene and Harrington, *American Population*, 177-79.
98. In the Federalist parishes slaves were more than twice as numerous as whites; in the Antifederal counties whites were more than twice as numerous as slaves. McDonald has tabulated the property holdings of the delegates, and his figures demonstrate that the very great majority of large landholders and large slaveowners were Federalists. *We The People*, 217-34.

and that amendments were possible.[99] Most of these men were obscure, but it is interesting and significant that one was a lawyer, one a judge, one a merchant, and one a merchant who was also a large landowner. Of the fourteen who thus changed, just half came from the border region between east and west.

It can be concluded that Antifederalism in South Carolina was supported by the western part of the state—a region of small farms rather than plantations, with fewer slaves than the coastal section, where paper money and installment laws were popular among debtors, where the inhabitants had long struggled against the planters and merchants, had failed in their efforts to secure a more democratic state constitution, and now (as Burke tells us) saw themselves suffering still another defeat.

99. *Daily Advertiser* (Charleston), May 26, 1788.

Chapter X

RATIFICATION: THE FINAL DEFEAT

WHEN New Hampshire's adjourned convention met in June, the situation had changed in several respects, all of which favored the Federalists. Although New York's Antifederalist organization (the Federal Republican Committee) had sent some pamphlets to Joshua Atherton, and although the Antifederalists had been active in trying to maintain their early lead, yet the Federalists had been equally energetic and were even more successful in proselyting the public. Their control of the press was a great advantage; the Antifederalists claimed, and an examination of the newspapers makes it obvious, that Antifederal literature was virtually excluded.[1] In addition, the ratification by Massachusetts was important. When the New Hampshire convention met there was still, according to Atherton, a majority against the Constitution, but a number of towns had already reversed their positions, and during the convention others followed, the delegates either joining the Federalists or abstaining. The result was that the Constitution was approved on June 21 by a vote of fifty-seven to forty-seven.

Since all of the men who now changed sides came from the interior of the state, that section was in reality even more strongly Antifederal than appears from the final vote and must have been not far from unanimous earlier in the year. However, the towns along the Connecticut River were heavily Federal.[2] This has been

1. Tobias Lear to Washington, June 2, 1788, Sparks, ed., *Correspondence*, IV, 220-21; Joshua Atherton to John Lamb, June 11, 1788, Leake, *Lamb*, 321; Atherton to the Federal Republican Committee, June 23, 1788, Lamb Papers, N.Y. Hist. Soc.
2. Out of seventeen towns, thirteen were Federalist, casting eight votes; three towns cast three votes against ratification; and one did not vote.

attributed to a desire on the part of the people there to separate and join Vermont, but the wish seems to have nothing to do with this particular issue, nor did other such separatist movements have that effect.[3] It is a better guess that the river, which linked these towns with the commercial interest, played an important role. Perhaps too, the fact that many people in the upper valley came originally from Connecticut influenced them in following the Federalists of their old home. Moreover, the idea of ratifying with amendments, introduced in Massachusetts, had now become general, and laid fears to rest.

The Federalists also dominated the southeastern part of the state, which was influenced by the commercial centers of Dover and Portsmouth. A group of northern towns also voted for the Constitution, a fact which has been attributed to the local prestige of Judge Samuel Livermore.[4] Personal influence was doubtless of some importance, since the state's foremost politicians—John Sullivan, John Langdon, John Gilman, Josiah Bartlett, John Pickering, Pierse Long, Elisha Payne, and Livermore—were Federalists. Atherton wrote: "I believe it will be conceded by all, that they did not carry their Point by Force of argument and Discussion; but by other Means, which were it not for the Depravity of the humane Heart, would be viewed with the warmest Sentiments of Disapprobation."[5]

Both Joshua Atherton and Tobias Lear observed that the Federalists were wealthier. The latter informed Washington that "at least three fourths of the property, and a large proportion of the abilities in the State, are friendly to the proposed system. The opposition here, as has generally been the case, was composed of men who were involved in debt, and of consequence would be averse to any Government which was likely to abolish their tender laws, and cut off every hope of accomplishing their favorite plan

3. Several Massachusetts towns which wanted to join Rhode Island were Antifederal; the special desires of Maine and of the trans-Appalachian counties in Virginia and Tennessee had little or no influence on their position.

4. See the discussion in Libby, *Geographical Distribution*, 10-11. Colonel Elisha Payne is there stated to have influenced some Valley delegates.

5. To the Federal Republican Committee, June 23, 1788, Lamb Papers, N.Y. Hist. Soc.

of introducing a paper currency." [6] This is not literally true: some of the prominent Antifederal leaders were not paper money advocates, and a number of Antifederal towns were opposed to currency issues. However, the identification of Antifederalists with the cause of paper money tends to confirm the contemporary observation that they differed in wealth and status from the Federalists. That such was the case is also borne out by analysis of votes in the ratifying convention. Ten delegates were members of the upper house of the state legislature; of these, eight voted in favor of the Constitution, and of the remaining two, who did not vote, one was for ratification. All but one of the known college men were Federal, and virtually all of the wealthy delegates supported the Constitution. Differences in occupation are also significant: the business and professional men were usually Federal, while farmers were more often Antifederal.[7] Despite such differences in wealth and occupation, however, the division in New Hampshire is more evident on a sectional basis—the commercial areas near the coast and along the Connecticut River versus the interior.

Four days after the final vote in New Hampshire had been taken, the long struggle in Virginia also came to an end. In no other state was the situation so complicated; in no other state was there so striking a division among the political, social, and economic leaders. From the beginning, many of the most prominent men were either decidedly hostile to the Constitution or at best lukewarm and anxious for amendments. Patrick Henry's opposition was perhaps to be expected. To be sure, he had favored a stronger government, but this one went too far. Richard Henry Lee's opposition could have been confidently predicted, for Lee had opposed all efforts, thus far, to grant powers to Congress. His objections were given wide publicity and his influence was considerable.[8] The position of George Mason was also significant, and

6. June 22, 1788, Sparks, ed., *Correspondence of the Revolution*, IV, 224-25.
7. See Appendix E.
8. Sample newspapers which informed the public of Lee's stand were, the *Country Journal* (Poughkeepsie), the *Albany Gazette*, the *New Hampshire Recorder* (Keene), the *Columbian Herald* (Charleston), and the *Daily Advertiser* (Charleston).

his open, well-publicized refusal to sign the Constitution was welcome evidence to the Antifederalists that not all members of the Convention supported it. The same was true of Edmund Randolph's statement in criticism of the new plan.

Randolph, who fluctuated between Federalism and Antifederalism, was far from being the only Virginian who hesitated. Edmund Pendleton, while in favor of ratification, thought amendments should accompany the approval.[9] William Ronald of Powhatan at first opposed the Constitution "in terms that would be taken for absolute in all events," although he was reportedly determined "to do nothing which may . . . endanger the Union." [10] Others were also skeptical: General Thomas Nelson, St. George Tucker, George Lee Turberville, and Joseph Jones (of Fredericksburg) were either against ratification or had strong reservations; [11] moreover Benjamin Harrison, Theodorick Bland, William Grayson, the Cabells, John Tyler, Edmund Ruffin, and James Monroe were all to vote against ratification in Virginia's convention. Washington wrote plaintively, "It is a little strange that the men of large property in the South, should be more afraid that the Constitution will produce an Aristocracy or a Monarchy, than the genuine democratical people of the East." [12]

There were other ominous signs. Edward Carrington found opponents numerous even in the Northern Neck, and reports from the southern part of the state were alarming; adoption without amendments seemed improbable. Randolph declared: "the current sets violently against the new constitution." [13] A majority of the state legislature proved to be Antifederal, and though the margin against the Constitution was narrow, one discouraged

9. To [Unknown], June 14, 1788, Emmett Coll., No. 1133, N.Y. Pub. Lib.

10. Edward Carrington to Madison, Feb. 10, 1788, Madison Papers, VIII, Lib. Cong.

11. Archibald Stuart to Madison, Oct. 21, 1787, Hunt, ed., *Writings of Madison*, V, 40-41n.; Turberville to Arthur Lee, Oct. 28, 1787, Harv. Coll. Lib., photostatic copy in Lee Papers, Univ. Va. Lib.; Joseph Jones to Madison, Nov. 22, 1787, Mass. Hist. Soc., *Proceedings*, 2nd Ser., 17 (1903), 491.

12. To Lafayette, June 19, 1788, Fitzpatrick, ed., *Writings of Washington*, XXIX, 525.

13. Carrington to Knox, Jan. 12, Feb. 10, 1788, Knox Papers, XXI, 104, 139, Mass. Hist. Soc.; Randolph to Madison, Dec. 27, 1787, Madison Papers, VIII, Lib. Cong.

Federalist predicted that it would fail.[14] As early as November there were rumors that if Virginia did not ratify, the upper part of the state—presumably the Northern Neck—might secede from the lower.[15] Antifederalists took heart from rumors that the Baptists were opposed to ratification—in March the Virginia Baptist Association voted against the Constitution.[16]

Long before the elections it was clear that the Antifederalists would have a majority east of the Blue Ridge, and that the decision would be made by the west. From these western regions the early news was mixed: from Frederick County came reports of Federal success, but this was to be expected, since it was really part of the Northern Neck.[17] On the other hand, Kentucky proved to be inclined toward Antifederalism because of the fear that the navigation of the Mississippi would be surrendered by the Northern states under the commerce clause; moreover the Wilkinson group of land speculators felt that a stronger government would interfere with their Spanish intrigues.[18] A strongly worded memorial, signed by influential men in Fayette County, also indicated Kentucky's hostility.[19]

Prospects for a close race were borne out by the election returns. The Antifederalists made nearly a clean sweep of the Southside. The results from Amherst were indicative of public

14. Arthur Stuart to Madison, Dec. 2, 1787, *ibid.*; James Mercer to John Francis Mercer, Dec. 12, 1787, Mercer Papers, Va. Hist. Soc.; John Peirce to Knox, Nov. 12, 1787, Knox Papers, XXI, 49, Mass .Hist. Soc.

15. J. Hughes to Horatio Gates, Alexandria, Nov. 20, 1787, Emmett Coll., No. H, N.Y. Pub. Lib.

16. James Madison, Sr., to James Madison, Jan. 30, 1788, Hunt, ed., *Writings of Madison*, V, 105n.; Joseph Spencer to Madison, Feb. 28, 1788, *Doc. Hist. of the Constitution*, IV, 525; Robert B. Semple, *A History of the Rise and Progress of the Baptists in Virginia* (Richmond, 1810), 77.

17. *Pa. Packet* (Phila.), Nov. 5, 8, 1787; *Va. Journal* (Alexandria), Nov. 1, 1787; *Va. Independent Chronicle* (Richmond), Nov. 7, 1787.

18. George Muter to Madison, Mercer County, Feb. 20, 1787, and John Campbell to Madison, Pittsburgh, Feb. 21, 1787, Mass. Hist. Soc., *Proceedings*, 2nd Ser., 17 (1903), 451-55; George Nicholas to Madison, Apr. 5, 1788, *Doc. Hist. of the Constitution*, IV, 553-54; John Brown to Madison, May 12, 1788, Madison Papers, IX, Lib. Cong. Brown had heard from two important Kentuckians. For Wilkinson see Abernethy, *Western Lands*, 347, 347n.

19. Memorial to the Court of Fayette County on the Proposed Federal Constitution, Feb. 29, 1788, Draper MSS, 11J182, Wis. Hist. Soc.

sentiment in that area: the two Antifederal candidates had 327 and 313 votes against 23 and 5 for their opponents, who surrendered before the poll was completed.[20] East of the Blue Ridge, the Antifederalists led by at least a dozen delegates. This advantage, however, was overcome by the returns from the Shenandoah. The Federalists had swept the entire valley by large majorities. The results still farther west would tell the tale, but even when the convention met, the outcome was in doubt. The Antifederalists had carried Kentucky, but most of the West Virginia delegates inclined toward ratification. So far as could be determined, the Federalists had a slight lead in the convention, but there were a number of delegates in all sections whose position was uncertain, and the Antifederalists still had a chance. The issue would be determined by the waverers, especially those in the west.[21] Both sides were therefore busy in and out of convention. The Federalists may have been aided by the presence of Robert Morris, although his visit was connected with his business interests.[22] The Antifederalists, on the other hand, received encouragement from the Federal Republican Committee of New York, which sent letters in care of the Philadelphia printer Eleazer Oswald conveying news of strong opposition in New York.[23] As events proved, this Antifederalist support from outside was not enough: the Federalists secured the doubtful votes, and on June 25 the Constitution was ratified (89-79).

It is necessary, in explaining ratification in Virginia, not only to account for the interesting and significant sectional division but

20. *Va. Independent Chronicle* (Richmond), Mar. 12, 1788.

21. Various estimates were made of the situation. Grayson to Lamb, June 9, 1788, Leake, *Lamb*, 311; Henry to Lamb, *ibid.*, 307; Mason to Lamb, *ibid.*, Lamb Papers, N. Y. Hist. Soc.; Madison to Washington, June 13, 18, Hunt, ed., *Writings of Madison*, V, 179, 211; Henry Lee to Hamilton, June 16, Beveridge, *Marshall*, I, 434-35; Grayson to Dane, June 18, 1788, *ibid.*, 442-43; *Daily Advertiser* (N. Y.), June 27, 1788. Robert Morris wrote Horatio Gates from Richmond, "The knowing ones pronounce that the Event is doubtful," June 12, 1788, Emmett Coll., No. 9471, N. Y. Pub. Lib. See also Knox to Wadsworth, June 27, 1788, Wadsworth Papers, Box 138, Conn. Hist. Soc.

22. He was trying to collect from his debtors, one such being Carter Braxton. Morris to Alexander Montgomery, Richmond, June 18, 1788, Myers Papers, No. 507, N. Y. Pub. Lib.

23. Henry Lee to Hamilton, June 16, 1788, Beveridge, *Marshall*, I, 434-35; Lamb Papers, N. Y. Hist. Soc.

also the Federalist success in winning the support of the doubtful delegates from various parts of the state.[24] The Federalists had certain advantages in the contest. The Antifederal argument that necessary changes in the government could be made by another convention became less plausible as state after state ratified the Constitution. The Federalists insisted that no such convention was possible, and their argument gained strength after Maryland ratified without any qualification.[25] The Federalists also had a slight advantage in prestige. It is true that the influence of Patrick Henry, George Mason, Richard Henry Lee, Benjamin Harrison, Theodorick Bland, and William Grayson was great; yet Edmund Randolph was now working for ratification, as were Edmund Pendleton, George Wythe, George Nicholas, John Marshall, Ralph Wormeley, Francis Corbin, Henry Lee, James Madison, and, above all, George Washington.[26] Still another factor was the promise of amendments. Many among the Antifederalists felt that the Constitution could be rendered safe by some amendments, though of course they wanted these to be guaranteed before ratification took place. The Federalists insisted that amendments could be made after the government had been established, and they persuaded some delegates that this plan presented no danger.[27]

Such general factors operated equally in all parts of the state, but there were local factors of vital importance, especially in the counties lying west of the Blue Ridge, and it was here,

24. Just who the undecided delegates were is not known, but they are often referred to. Evidently some delegates from Kentucky and West Virginia were open to persuasion; arguments of local interest were important in influencing them. The rest probably came from among the following: William Ronald, David Patterson, George Parker, Paul Carrington, W. O. Callis, Cole Digges, Miles King, Burwell Bassett, Willis Riddick, and Solomon Shepherd. See Appendix B.

25. Joseph Jones to Madison, Feb. 14, 1788, Mass. Hist. Soc., *Proceedings*, 2nd Ser., 17 (1903), 495; Edmund Randolph to Madison, Feb. 29, 1788, in Conway, *Randolph*, 100; George Nicholas to David Stewart, Apr. 9, 1788, French Coll., Mass. Hist. Soc.; Madison to Washington, Apr. 10, 1788, Hunt, ed., *Writings of Madison*, V, 116-17; Washington to Benjamin Lincoln, May 2, 1788, Fitzpatrick, ed., *Writings of Washington*, XXIX, 488.

26. Monroe to Jefferson, July 12, 1788, in Stanislaus Murray Hamilton, ed., *The Writings of James Monroe*, 7 vols. (New York, 1893-1903), I, 186.

27. For example, R. H. Lee to Edmund Pendleton, May 22, 1788, Ballagh, ed., *Lee*, II, 472-74; George Mason to Lamb, June 9, 1788, Lamb Papers, N. Y. Hist. Soc.; *Daily Advertiser* (N.Y.), June 27, 1788.

of course, that the fate of the Constitution in Virginia was determined. In Kentucky circumstances favored the Antifederalists. During the previous years, the delegates from that region had usually supported the Northern Neck, but they had voted against the grant of the commercial power to Congress, fearing that the right to navigate the Mississippi would be relinquished by treaty with Spain. A Fayette County memorial had declared: "By the power to regulate Commerce, we loose the Navigation of the Mississippi; population will cease, and our lands become of little value." [28] During the debate over the Constitution, the Federalists tried to show that the fear was groundless, but the Antifederalists succeeded in proving it well founded, and there is no doubt that it was the decisive factor in Kentucky.[29]

The situation in the "Alleghany" counties, now West Virginia, was quite different. Although at first many of the delegates from these seven counties had wavered, they voted all but unanimously in favor of ratification. In the past this region had consistently supported the Southside: an analysis of eight key votes shows that West Virginia representatives had voted by a margin of four to one with the area which was now an Antifederal stronghold. Judging from personal property tax records, the social structure of the Alleghany counties resembled the Southside rather than the Northern Neck, for small, slaveless farmers predominated. Was there some individual of great prestige who controlled the vote in the convention? None such appears. Was it the superiority of the Federalists in debate? Assuming that this existed,[30] converts made in this way were usually few and scattered; there is no other instance of so large a bloc being won by persuasion. The technique of amendments, the prestige of Washington, the progress of the Constitution elsewhere—these were such as may have converted individuals, but not groups of thirteen from a single area. We must

28. Draper MSS, Univ. Wis. Lib.

29. Madison to Washington, June 13, 1788, Hunt, ed., *Writings of Madison*, V, 179; Elliot, ed., *Debates*, III, *passim;* John Brown to Jefferson, Aug. 10, 1788, Burnett, ed., *Letters*, VIII, 776; Hugh Williamson to James Madison, June 2, 1788, *N. C. Hist. Rev.*, 14 (1937), 160.

30. The debates as published may not be entirely accurate. George Mason twice observed that a Federalist had done the reporting and warned that they would be garbled. To John Mason, July 21, Dec. 18, 1788, Rowland, *Mason*, II, 298, 305.

look for some special reason which was powerful enough to override the tendency toward Antifederalism.

In the absence of definite statements about the subject, it is necessary to proceed inferentially, and one prime fact furnishes the required clue. In 1787 West Virginia had deserted its Piedmont allies and had supported the Northern Neck by the unanimous affirmative vote of seven delegates on a key issue: to repeal all laws in conflict with the Peace Treaty of 1783. These laws concerned the payment of British debts. There is no reason to believe that West Virginians were concerned about these debts—more than likely they were debtors and quite willing to see any debts remain unpaid. What did concern them was the British retention of the northwest posts—a violation of the treaty which was defended on the ground of American violations, and which (so it was believed) operated to encourage Indian attacks and generally to hinder the westward movement across the Ohio. A glance at the map will make it clear that although the West Virginians must have been concerned about the Mississippi question, they must have been even more immediately worried about foreign occupation of an area which lay directly to the west. It followed that a central government strong enough to repel Indian attacks and to seize the posts was essential to continued expansion. During the convention these Alleghany delegates were made fully aware that the adoption of the Constitution would strengthen the American position in the northwest.[31]

There remains, among the western regions, the valley of the Shenandoah, which was unanimously Federal in the convention. That Frederick and Berkeley counties favored ratification occasions no surprise and raises no questions, for they were part of the Northern Neck, and were therefore simply following the expected path. But the remaining five counties resembled the western Piedmont in social structure and on most issues supported the Southside. The explanation is indicated by the fact that on two questions during the 1780's Shenandoah delegates had deserted

31. Elliot, ed., *Debates*, III, 105, 238-39. It may be significant that the only county in Kentucky which favored ratification (Jefferson) bordered on the Ohio. Note also the two Federal votes from Washington County in southwestern Pennsylvania.

the Southside and voted with the Northern Neck. They had unanimously supported the law to enforce the collection of British debts, presumably because of its connection with the British posts. Hart is of the opinion that this was very important to the Valley.[32] Second, Valley delegates had voted overwhelmingly in favor of granting Congress power over commerce in 1785, a measure opposed by West Virginia, Kentucky, and the Southside. Hart believes that one reason for this stand was the extensive trade between the Valley and Maryland, which created a desire to put an end to the payment of interstate duties. Finally, the Valley depended for its prosperity upon goods exported through the Potomac River and other ports; a stronger federal government might provide funds for improving the river, and in any case would be in a better position to obtain favorable commercial treaties. Such economic interests are suggested by the fact that among the Valley delegates to the convention no less than eight were active in schemes to improve the navigation of the Potomac or the James.[33] Hart adds that the Valley expected to receive more effective representation in the new government than in the state government and a more equitable basis of taxation. Both of these considerations seem dubious. Hart points out too that the Valley had opposed paper money, and further suggests that Presbyterians and Baptists in the region endorsed the Constitution because it would secure religious liberty. This last Hart calls "an all-important factor." [34] If so, it is difficult to understand why these sects elsewhere were usually Antifederal. To be sure, residents of the Valley might have had opinions on the subject which were peculiar to themselves, but it sounds rather as though this were an argument used to persuade a strongly Presbyterian area by those who favored ratification on other grounds. It did not work in backcountry South Carolina, North Carolina, Pennsylvania, and New York, and one is inclined to believe that it was effective, if at all, only where there were more potent reasons for Federalism.

32. Hart, *Valley of Virginia*, 183-84.
33. Johnston and Stuart of Augusta, McKee and Moore of Rockbridge, Lewis and Jones of Rockingham, Woodcock and White of Frederick. *Ibid.*, 156, 158.
34. *Ibid.*, 187.

The interest of the Valley in the Ohio country and in commerce is quite sufficient to account for its attitude.

Virginia east of the Blue Ridge was separated into Federal and Antifederal territory by a line which was irregular but clearly defined. The major sections which had opposed each other during the Confederation period were the Southside and the Northern Neck, and the same alignment existed over the Constitution. The Northern Neck (including Frederick and Berkeley counties) was Federal by a great majority (19-5). The Southside was even more solidly Antifederal. The James-York River counties had supported the Northern Neck in the past and continued to do so, with some exception; indeed along the James, Federalist delegates were to be found even beyond the fall line.[35] The remaining "Tidewater" counties had never shown a really consistent pattern of behavior, but those nearest to the coast were now Federal, those inland (with the above-mentioned exceptions along the rivers) were Antifederal. It is perhaps this alignment which has given rise to the belief that the division in Virginia was between east and west, whereas the division was really between the Northern Neck plus the York-James counties versus the Southside, or southern Piedmont. The principal regions which had disagreed over the collection of taxes, the enforcement of the peace treaty, paper money and related issues, and the grant of power to Congress, once again were opposed. The difference between the alignments on former issues and the division over the Constitution lay in the Federalism of the coastal counties, some of which had in the past voted with the Southside. Yet even here there was a certain consistency: aside from the Northern Neck, the Federalists carried sixteen counties east of the fall line, of which ten usually supported the Northern Neck and only two did not;[36] the Antifederalists were successful in five, of which four had usually voted with the South-

35. Powhatan's vote was divided; its delegates had often voted with the Northern Neck. Albemarle, even farther west, had consistently supported the Northern Neck and did so now.

36. Middlesex, New Kent, James City, York, Elizabeth City, Northampton, Surrey, Southampton, Greensville, and Henrico were Northern Neck allies; Gloucester and Nansemond were not; Caroline, Norfolk, Princess Anne, and Isle of Wight counties had been divided

side, the fifth being neutral ground.[37] As for the Piedmont counties, here again old divisions were repeated; the only two counties which voted Federalist, Albemarle and Orange, had usually supported the Northern Neck. The striking fact about the alignment on the Constitution as on previous issues, was the influence on political behavior of the Potomac, Rappahannock, York, and James rivers, and of the type of society developed in the valleys of those streams.

Because of the Federalism of most of the wealthy eastern counties, one would expect to find that an analysis of the property held by delegates to the ratifying convention would reveal a considerable difference between Antifederalists and their opponents. This difference is, however, nearly eliminated by two major factors: first, Federal delegates west of the Blue Ridge, with a few exceptions, were, like their constituents, not particularly wealthy; second, Antifederalists frequently chose as their representatives the wealthiest residents professing their doctrine.[38] Although the Southside contained fewer men of great property than did the Northern Neck, some did exist, and those who were Antifederalists were then chosen. There were in the convention at least sixty-seven delegates who held 1,000 acres of land;[39] of these, thirty-six were Federalists, thirty-one Antifederalists. Of the large Antifederalist landholders, the majority came from the Piedmont where land values were lower. Of the very largest landowners (5,000 acres or more) eleven were Federalists, seven Antifederalists. There is a marked difference in the number of slaves owned, which reflects the sectional distribution of slaves in the state; forty-one delegates are known to have possessed individually at least fifty; of these delegates twenty-six (63½ per cent) were Federalists. Otherwise, there is not very much to distinguish

37. Essex, King William, Charles City, Sussex, Prince George. Of the remaining Tidewater counties, King and Queen, Accomac and Warwick were divided. These had usually supported the Southside, and it is possible that they were in reality Antifederal.

38. For example, the Cabells of Amherst were the richest residents of that county.

39. I say "at least" because property records are incomplete. Many of these held less than 1,000 acres in the county which they represented. John Tyler owned only 569 in Charles City but had 1,255 all told; Zachariah Johnston had 697 in Augusta and 536 in Botetourt.

between the Federalists and Antifederalists on the basis of personal property holdings. It is interesting, but may have no significance, that twice as many Federalists as Antifederalists held state or federal securities; the amounts held were usually small.[40] It is more suggestive if we examine the political convictions of the state's richest men, in or out of the convention. About two-thirds were Federalists.[41]

Nevertheless, when it is considered that the Shenandoah Valley and the frontier counties across the Alleghanies, with their numerous small farmers, were Federal, it is clear that a division along lines of wealth does not account for the alignment in Virginia. Far more decisive was the split between the counties near the coast or along the rivers and the counties of the interior; decisive too were the peculiar economic and political interests of the three regions west of the Blue Ridge. Sectional, not class, lines were of primary importance.

The news of Virginia's ratification arrived in Poughkeepsie just after New Hampshire's decision had become known, and the combination was fatal to the strong Antifederal party in New York. The history of the ratification of the Constitution in New York is of particular interest because, in addition to furnishing yet another opportunity to investigate the nature of Antifederalism, it offers a unique chance to study the campaign techniques employed. Only in New York was there an Antifederal "party" in the sense

40. Auditor's Items No. 44, 45, Va. State Lib.; Treasury Department, Public Debt Service, Office of the Commissioner of the Public Debt, Register of Loan Office Certificates, vols. 1078-1081, 1083, 1108B, 1109, 1110, 1110A, 1110B, 1111, 1118, Natl. Arch. Of those holding $1,000 worth or more in 1788 or before, eight were Federalists and two were Antifederalists in the convention. George Carrington, who came from the Southside yet voted Federalist, held £5,200 worth in 1785-86.

41. Of the wealthiest 100 there were 25 Federalists, 13 Antifederalists. I know something about the ideas of 14 others, of whom 13 were probably though not certainly Federalists. Thus the statement in the text is a guarded one. Among the next wealthiest 50 there were 11 or 12 Federalists and 6 Antifederalists. Whether the 2 : 1 ratio extends farther down I do not know. An examination of the property holdings of the delegates in the convention suggests the absence of a correlation between property holdings and attitudes toward the Constitution among wealthy men of lesser rank, but the convention delegates did not necessarily represent the economic status of the men who shared their views since, as we have observed, Antifederalists often chose their most well-to-do adherents.

connoted by that word—that is, an organization with a central committee of sorts which raised money, distributed propaganda, and corresponded with leaders within the state and in other states. This degree of organization owed its existence to the party machinery built by Governor Clinton and his assistants, which had dominated the state during the whole Revolutionary period. Long before the Constitution became an issue, candidates for office were running as Clintonians or anti-Clintonians on well-understood though informal, unwritten platforms and were voting in the legislature with remarkable consistency. The same was true also in Pennsylvania, but in that case the Federalists had pushed the adoption of the Constitution so rapidly that the Constitutionalists had lacked time to organize themselves as Antifederalists. In New York the Clintonians had a chance to organize with reference to the new issue, and were able to win an overwhelming victory in the elections to the ratifying convention.

As usual, the Federalists managed to launch the first publications, but during October the Antifederalists began to counterattack with articles by "Cato," "Brutus," "Sidney," and "A Republican."[42] New York newspapers also began to publish criticisms written in Pennsylvania; on November first alone, the *New York Journal* printed three Antifederal pieces, and then a spate of articles appeared in the *Journal* and the *New York Morning Post*, and outside the city in the *Hudson Gazette*, the *Albany Gazette*, and the *Country Journal* (Poughkeepsie). Not until February, however, did the Albany Antifederalists meet and appoint a committee to manage the elections, although publications had been sent out into the country somewhat earlier.[43] This committee consisted of seven persons, including John Lansing, Peter Yates, and Jeremiah Van Rensselaer; they began to correspond with New York City Antifederalists and to send articles to "impartial printers," by which they meant printers who would publish their criticisms without accompanying refutations.[44] Since the Albany

42. Peter Tappen to George Clinton, Sept. 29, 1787, Clinton Papers, Bancroft Transcripts, N.Y. Pub. Lib.; *Albany Gazette*, Oct. 4, 1787; *N.Y. Journal*, Oct. 18, 25, 1787.

43. Major North to Henry Knox, Albany, Feb. 13, 1788, Knox Papers, XXI, 143, Mass. Hist. Soc.

44. John Lansing, Jr., and others to Melancton Smith, Albany, Mar. 1, 1788, Yates, Jr., Papers, N.Y. Pub. Lib.

committee had not immediately adopted a name, the Federalists were able to assume the more popular one first; this being published, the committee was obliged to adopt the name "Anti-Federal." Meanwhile a town meeting of Kingston had also appointed a committee.[45]

The next step was to nominate delegates for the convention, the Senate, and the Assembly; a broadside was issued containing this information and some campaign propaganda.[46] Printers were engaged to reproduce literature. By April the Albany committee was getting pamphlets from New York and sending them out to Montgomery and Washington counties, where they were especially welcome because campaign funds were lacking.[47] In addition the committee took steps to counteract Federalist actions. It wrote to "Stephen Town" suggesting that attendants be placed at the polls and warned: "We are told that the Patroons Tenants are to fold up their Ballots in a particular Manner—if they do, you will direct the anti Voters to do the same." The Federalists themselves testified to the effectiveness of these measures.[48]

Meanwhile in New York City, the Federal Republican Committee had been established with General John Lamb, a one-time Son of Liberty, as chairman and his son-in-law, Charles Tillinghast, as secretary; Melancton Smith, Marinus Willett, Samuel Jones, and James M. Hughes were also members. By April they were distributing Mrs. Warren's "A Columbian Patriot" and sending out funds for printing; copies of "Centinel" and other Antifederal articles were distributed to consignees in the various counties.[49] In addition, an effort was made to co-ordinate activities with Antifederalists in those states which had not yet ratified the Constitu-

45. *N.Y. Journal*, Feb. 29, 1788.
46. Broadsides in the N. Y. Hist. Soc. and the N. Y. State Lib., No. 686; *Albany Gazette*, Mar. 27, 1788; *Hudson Gazette* (N.Y.), Mar. 20, 1788.
47. John Lansing, Jr., and Abraham Lansing to [Unknown], Mar. 23, 1788, Yates, Jr., Papers, N.Y. Pub. Lib.; the Committee of Albany to [Unknown], Apr. 12, 1788, Lamb Papers, N.Y. Hist. Soc.
48. Jeremiah Van Rensselaer to Benjamin Egbertson and others, Apr. 28, 1788, Accession No. 2135, N.Y. State Lib.; Abraham Oothout to James Duane, May 19, 1788, Duane Papers, N.Y. Hist. Soc.
49. Lamb Papers, N.Y. Hist. Soc. Someone sent copies of R. H. Lee's "Federal Farmer" to Connecticut in December. Jeremiah Wadsworth to Rufus King, Dec. 16, 1787, King, *King*, I, 264. Characteristically these arrived after the election.

tion—North and South Carolina, Virginia, and New Hampshire. Pamphlets were also sent to Maryland. Why these letters were not sent until late in May is a mystery—as it was, they arrived too late to be of any use. George Mason and others wrote to Lamb concerning proposed amendments, and indeed it was obvious that the Antifederalists needed to unite on specific recommendations; a merely negative attitude or a series of miscellaneous individual ideas could not substitute for or compete successfully with the concrete solution advanced and uniformly supported by the Federalists. But it was late June by the time Mason's letter had been forwarded to Poughkeepsie. A committee was appointed by the ratifying convention to continue the correspondence, but its reply to Mason was dated after the day of decision in Virginia.[50] It was all too late.

It does not seem that the Federalists in New York City had any formal organization such as the Clintonians established. The fact that most of them resided in more thickly settled areas made it easier for them to communicate personally; certainly they were busy writing to each other and sending out pamphlets and newspaper articles for distribution. The New York papers were filled with Federalist contributions; aside from the *New York Journal*, few newspapers in the city published any criticisms of the Constitution at all, and these few soon discontinued them. From the Federalist standpoint, all was well in the city, but it soon became clear that upstate New York was Antifederal, and counter measures were indicated. Federalists became active in Schenectady and Schoharie with little success; however, a Federal committee was established in Albany on March 12, candidates were nominated, and chairman Robert McCallen, an Albany merchant, urged vigorous action. The *Federalist Papers* and other pamphlets were sent up from the city for distribution, and from Albany emissaries were sent out with handbills by the thousands.[51] One Antifederal-

50. Yates to Mason, June 25, 1788, Emmett Coll., No. 9528, N.Y. Pub. Lib.

51. McCallen to James Duane, Mar. 12, 1788, John Myers to Duane, Duanesburgh, Apr. 5, June 23, 1788, Duane Papers, N.Y. Hist. Soc.; *Hudson Gazette* (N.Y.), Mar. 13, 1788; Broadside, Albany, Mar. 16, 1788, Mass. Hist. Soc.; Leonard Gansevoort to Stephen Van Rensselaer, Apr. 6, 1788, Accession No. 4069, N.Y. State Lib.

ist wrote: "On the first Day of this Month being the General Town Meeting Day the City was almost Destitute of the Better Kind of People they were at Several Polls in the Country Dispersing their General Letter Hand Bills Lists of Delegates and Assemblymen. Even the two Last order of Men have been on the Mission. The gentlemen are Indifaticable, they use many Measures in the Manor Renselear the Militia is Called by 2 and 3 Companies I may not Charge them with Design but have reason to believe they want the Opportunity to have the people Collected." [52] Clever broadsides were published refuting the Antifederal doctrine that the struggle concerned rich and poor by noting Clinton's wealth and the fact that many Antifederal candidates were lawyers.[53] These measures may have had some long-range effects, but they did not affect the immediate situation.

The result of the election was an overwhelming victory for the Antifederalists.[54] Carrying the entire state except for New York City, Kings, Richmond, and Westchester, they had a majority of forty-six to nineteen in the convention. Of this majority many were willing to vote for ratification if amendments were guaranteed, and were therefore susceptible to Federalist persuasion;[55] more important to the outcome, however, was the course of events elsewhere. As the convention deliberated, the news that New Hampshire and Virginia had ratified changed the situation entirely. The adoption of the Constitution ceased to be the issue; instead it was the question of whether New York should remain out of or join a union which would exist regardless of her decision. Aaron Burr, for example, felt that New York's adoption was a

52. Henry Oothoudt to John McKesson, Apr. 3, 1788, McKesson Papers, N.Y. Hist. Soc.

53. Broadsides, New York, Apr. 28, 30, 1788, Mass. Hist. Soc. The first of these stated that the Federalists wanted to adopt the Constitution but wished amendments, including one which would render the judiciary less oppressive and expensive, but such an amendment would not be proposed by the Antifederalists because the lawyers among them would oppose it!

54. *Daily Advertiser* (N.Y.), June 3, 4, 6, 7, 14; *N.Y. Journal*, June 5, 1788. Libby's estimate is wrong, and his analysis of the division is seriously erroneous. Mitchell in *Hamilton*, I, 429, 637, is misled by Libby's errors. See the discussions by Spaulding and Cochran.

55. William Duer to Madison, June 23, 1788, Madison Papers, IX, Lib. Cong.; Robert Yates to George Mason, June 25, 1788, Emmett Coll., No. 9528, N.Y. Pub. Lib.

"fortunate event and the only one which could have preserved peace; *after the adoption by ten States,* I think it became both politic and necessary that we should also adopt it."[56] Federalist arguments both in debate and outside of the convention may have had some effect, though Melancton Smith declared that "if my Sentiments are altered it is to think it worse." He was one of those who finally voted yea.[57] Hamilton has been given much credit for the outcome, but actually his views were so well known in New York that his activity was perhaps more of a liability than an asset to the Federalists. Charles Tillinghast reported, "You would be surprised did you not know the Man, what an *amazing Republican* Hamilton wishes to make himself be considered. But he is known."[58]

What had most weight with the Antifederalists was the thought of the possible consequences if New York failed to ratify. The Federalists made much of this point in debate, raising the ominous prediction that if the Constitution was defeated, the southern counties would secede and join the Union.[59] There is no doubt that this threat was made by persons of influence. John Jay wrote of it to Washington before the convention met,[60] and by that time the idea was familiar enough to Abraham Yates that he interpreted a remark by Hamilton to imply some sort of a division. His interpretation was probably correct, for a little later Hamilton was writing that this plan would become "the object of the Federalists."[61] Certainly the possibility was seriously considered during the convention. One Federalist wrote that "the Southern District are determined on a Separation," and another asserted that the

56. To Richard Oliver, July 29, 1788, Accession No. 10763, N.Y. State Lib.; see also King to John Langdon, June 10, 1788, King, *King,* I, 331; Abraham G. Lansing to Abraham Yates, June 22, 1788, Yates, Jr., Papers, N.Y. Pub. Lib.; Hugh Williamson to John G. Blount, June 3, 1788, Burnett, ed., *Letters,* VIII, 747.

57. Notes on the debates, McKesson Papers, N.Y. Hist. Soc.

58. To John Lamb, June 21, 1788, Lamb Papers, N.Y. Hist. Soc.

59. Gilbert Livingston, Notes on Debates in the New York Constitutional Convention, N.Y. Pub. Lib.

60. May 29, Johnston, *Jay,* III, 335.

61. Yates to Abraham G. Lansing, May 28, 1788, Yates, Jr., Papers, N.Y. Pub. Lib.; Hamilton to Madison, June 8, 1788, Henry Cabot Lodge, ed., *The Works of Alexander Hamilton,* 9 vols. (New York, 1885-1886), VIII, 187.

idea was spoken of "confidently." [62] The question is, of course, how much this possibility actually influenced the state's ratification. There is reason to believe it had considerable weight. Lord Dorchester in Canada was informed that it was a major factor. New York, he was told, did not dare remain out of the union, "knowing that their opponents had *determined* to separate the southern districts from the northern, . . . for which purpose they had actually concerted measures with such of the neighbouring States as had previously adopted the new constitution." [63] Finally George Mason, who was corresponding with the New York Antifederalists, wrote that they "thought themselves under the necessity of adopting also, for fear of being left out of the Union, and of civil commotions." [64]

Altogether, it appears that the threat of secession was made, that it was seriously intended, and that it was a factor in the outcome. The other horn of the Antifederalist dilemma was the conviction of many that New York could not remain out of the Union. This belief no doubt was also instrumental in changing their opinions. The ultimate result was that enough Antifederalists changed sides to carry the day (30-27). The shift in votes did not necessarily mean that these men now liked the Constitution. Even after ratification three of them—Nathaniel Lawrence, Melancton Smith, and Samuel Jones—joined a society which worked for another convention, and the next state legislature had a large Antifederal majority. [65]

The division in the state on the Constitution followed previous party alignments. It has earlier been observed that on internal financial matters and on the impost question New York City had been supported by other counties in the south, especially Kings, Suffolk, Richmond, Queens, and Westchester. The Federalist minority in the convention came exclusively from these counties—

62. General Samuel Blachley Webb to Miss Hogeboom, July 13, 1788, Ford, ed., *Correspondence of Webb*, III, 111; Francis Hopkinson to Jefferson, July 17, 1788, *Doc. Hist. of the Constitution*, IV, 796.

63. To Lord Sydney, Paterson Papers, N.Y. Hist. Soc.

64. To John Mason, Sept. 2, 1788, Rowland, *Mason*, II, 301. See also Spaulding, *New York in the Critical Period*, 255-56.

65. Lamb Papers, N.Y. Hist. Soc.; Journal of the New York Assembly, 1788-89, 102, 105, N.Y. State Lib.

Suffolk and Queens, at first Antifederal, ultimately shifted to their older allegiance on the final vote. Elsewhere the Clinton party remained in control. The town of Albany was once again on the side of New York, but it was now as so often before outvoted by the surrounding countryside. Antifederalist domination of the upstate counties persisted through the final vote, except that the delegates of Dutchess, which adjoined Federal Westchester, ultimately deserted the Antifederal ranks. The vote of individual delegates reflected the continuation of old alignments: Federalists had been pro-impost and anti-paper money; Antifederalists the reverse.

This long-continued sectional division represented a conflict between the commercial interest, including those landowners who were producing for export, opposed to the more isolated upstate farmers. The center of the Federalist party was New York City where, as one observer remarked, "the Mercantile Interest is strongly for [ratification]." [66] This interest was strong enough to carry the commercial towns and to attract the support also of the great landowners, as E. Wilder Spaulding has shown. Opposed to ratification, as Thomas Cochran puts it, were "men whose income was derived almost wholly from the cultivation of land, who had no direct interest in trade or commerce, and who had bought no government securities." To some extent the division also followed class lines, although within the commercial towns there seems to have been near unanimity. Spaulding is of the opinion that the Antifederalists were generally small farmers, tenants, and debtors,[67] an opinion in which the Antifederalists themselves seem to have concurred. In Albany, when the Federalists announced that their ticket had been nominated by a meeting of "very respectable citizens, and some of the first characters in the county," the Antifederalists gleefully presented their candidates as selected by "very respectable citizens ... though perhaps not the *first characters* in point of property" and published a broadside which declared: "In forming the list for Members of Convention,

66. Constable, Rucker & Co. to John Gray and Thomas Blount, New York, Nov. 30, 1787, Keith, ed., *Blount Papers*, I, 360.

67. Spaulding, *New York in the Critical Period*, 168; Cochran, *New York in the Confederation*, 83.

... particular attention was paid to exclude from nomination every person, whose very large possessions and intimate connections with a mass of the first property in the state, would afford him a hope that, if the government became vested in the hands of a few, his interest would be among the first particularly promoted by it." [68] This statement might be dismissed as no more than very effective propaganda, but the letters of the men involved show that it was sincere. Thus one writer refers to the Albany Federalists as "the better Kind of People" and "gentlemen," another contrasts the "Baneful Manor Interest" with the "Yeomanry," while others also refer to the rank and file of the Antifederalists as "Yeomanry" and "the common people." [69]

Something may also be judged from an analysis of the status and property of delegates to the convention. Five out of six merchants were Federalists, but only two out of five generals; more lawyers and large landholders were Antifederal. A simple numerical count is misleading, however, for there were at first more than twice as many Antifederalists elected. Proportionately there is a marked difference in occupation, wealth, and status. Fifteen out of nineteen Federalists (79 per cent) but only twenty-three of forty-six Antifederalists (50 per cent) were lawyers, judges, merchants, or large landowners. Proportionate to their numbers there were two and a half times as many men of wealth among the Federalists as among the Antifederalists. It is significant, moreover, that those Antifederalists who finally changed sides were among the more well-to-do, including one merchant, one large landowner, and three lawyers who were also large landowners, while four lawyers and a large landowner refrained fom voting. The alignment on the final vote therefore shows a more categorical difference between Federalists and Antifederalists. Although the number of lawyers and judges who voted on either side was equal,

68. The *Hudson Gazette* (N.Y.), Mar. 13, 20, 1788; Broadside, Mar. 15, 1788, N. Y. Hist. Soc.

69. Henry Oothoudt to John McKesson, Apr. 3, 1788, McKesson Papers, N.Y. Hist. Soc.; Abraham G. Lansing to Abraham Yates, Jr., July 20, 1788, Yates, Jr., Papers, N.Y. Pub. Lib.; Robert Yates to George Mason, June 25, 1788, Emmett Coll., No. 9528, N.Y. Pub. Lib.; Peter Tappen to George Clinton, Sept. 29, 1787, Clinton Papers, Bancroft Transcripts, N.Y. Pub. Lib. See also letter of Hugh Hughes, quoted in Spaulding, *New York in the Critical Period*, 113-14 and the discussion in *ibid.*, 213-24.

all of the merchants, most of the large landowners (9-4) and men of wealth (11-3) were Federal.[70] Among the college graduates, Federalists outnumbered Antifederalists at the beginning seven to three and at the end eight to one. All three directors of the New York Bank were Federalists from the first; the Antifederalists at first included three ex-loyalists, but all three shifted. The comparison in regard to public security holders is similar.[71] It seems clear that most of the wealthy landowners and merchants, in and out of convention, were Federalists and that the Antifederalists, while drawing some of their leaders from this class, were on the whole men of lesser means.

The decision of New York to accept the new government left only two states holding out: Rhode Island, where the towns had already refused to act, and North Carolina, where the convention did not meet until July.

It will be recalled that North Carolina was dominated politically by an exceptionally large group of small farmers. Only one section of the state consistently opposed their wishes and sided with the mercantile interest on most issues. This was the northeast region bordering Albemarle and Pamlico sounds, whose influence reached inland as far as Nash and Warren counties. These nineteen or so counties, and their commercial centers of Edenton, New Bern, and Halifax, were supported consistently by the town of Wilmington on the Cape Fear River and sporadically by some eight counties in the southeast. The latter, however, were to be found as often voting with the remainder, or western part of the state, which needed only a little support to control the legislature. When it is remembered that the state as a whole had the general

70. Of these categories combined, there were 20 Federalists and 12 Antifederalists. There was no difference in age except for the peculiar point that the Antifederalists who changed were markedly older than the average.

71. There were 13 Federalists and 21 Antifederalists who held federal securities, but on the final vote the count was 22-8. However not all of these had securities at the time and most of them held small amounts (only the Federalist Nicholas Low had a really large sum invested). Of those who had $100 worth or more when the convention sat, 7 were Federalists and 14 were Antifederalists of whom 8 changed sides or did not vote. The convention's second largest holder, Jesse Woodhull, was one of those who changed. Treasury Department, Office of the Commissioner of the Public Debt, vol. 545, Natl. Arch.

social structure and probably the economic interests of a Piedmont, it is not surprising that the Constitution had little chance of acceptance.

Too much stress should not be placed on the influence of individuals, but it was ominous for the Federalists that leading spokesmen for the western interest were critical of the new plan. Prominent among them were Willie Jones, the wealthy planter of Halifax County in the northeast,[72] Timothy Bloodworth of New Hanover County in the southeast, and in the west, Thomas Person of Granville, William Lenoir of Wilkes, and Samuel Spencer of Anson. All of these men were well-to-do, and most of them were wealthy; all had long been prominent and had usually voted with the west. They were aided by other men of means, experience, and influence, who had been less consistent in previous voting but had—significantly—supported the western demand for paper money.[73] It is therefore not surprising that the elections for the ratifying convention were swept by the Antifederalists.

There is no sure way of knowing how well-informed the voters were on the issues represented by the Constitution. The survival rate of North Carolina newspapers has been so low that it is impossible to tell what articles were published. However, the fact that elections were held six months after the Constitution had been submitted meant that it could be fully discussed even in the interior,[74] and the Antifederalists were active orally if not through the printed word.[75] The only clue concerning the extent to which the voters went to the polls in the election is supplied by an unusual case. In Dobbs County, out of 372 qualified voters, 281, or three-fourths cast ballots, and the Antifederalists were well

72. B. P. Robinson, "Willie Jones," *N. C. Hist. Rev.*, 18 (1941), 1-26, 133-70.

73. I have used here the property lists furnished by William C. Pool, in "An Economic Interpretation of the Ratification of the Federal Constitution in North Carolina," *N. C. Hist. Rev.*, 27 (1950), 119-41, 289-313, 437-61. Pool's work has made possible the identification of the more affluent Antifederalists, whose voting record was then examined.

74. It was being read in Surrey County on Oct. 18, 1787. Adelaide L. Fries, ed., *Records of the Moravians in North Carolina*, V, Publications of the N. C. Hist. Comm. (Raleigh, 1941), 2190.

75. Maclaine to Iredell, Dec. 25, 1787 and Jan. 15, 1788, McRee, *Iredell*, II, 183, 216-17.

ahead when some Federalists caused a riot and destroyed the votes. This incident suggests that a very high proportion of eligible voters were balloting, but the circumstances in this county were exceptional.[76]

In spite of the Antifederal victory, the Constitution was not rejected outright by the Halifax convention. While the convention was in session, Willie Jones, Thomas Person, and Timothy Bloodworth received encouragement and some pamphlets for distribution from the Federal Republican Committee of New York.[77] The news of Antifederal strength elsewhere was undoubtedly welcome and aided the determination to reject. Indeed, as Person wrote, a total rejection might have been effected by the delegates, but it was considered "more decent & moderate" merely to insist upon amendments and adjourn.[78] The decisive vote was taken when the Federalists tried to secure ratification with their own list of amendments but were defeated (184-84).

According to Antifederalists on the scene, there was a division along lines of class and interest. Person wrote to Lamb of the possible sacrifice of liberty to "Authority" and "Name"; Bloodworth reported that "The Attorneys, Merchants, and Aristocratic part of the community are in favor of the adoption with a few exceptions."[79] It has already been noted that the Antifederalists included a number of wealthy men; the adherence of the Tennessee region, most of the southeast, and some of the northeastern counties meant that well-to-do planters were found among their ranks. Their leaders, especially, tended to be men of substance, for the Antifederalists, like their opponents, were inclined to choose prominent persons to represent them. Nonetheless, there was some difference in wealth as between Antifederalist and Federalist delegates, and whether that difference was large or small, significant, or meaningless is a matter of interpretation. Pool

76. *Md. Gazette* (Annapolis), May 22, 1788; D. Witherspoon to Iredell, Apr. 3, 1788, McRee, *Iredell*, II, 222. All freemen who paid taxes could vote in this election. Clark, ed., *State Recs. of N.C.*, XX, 196-97, 370-72.

77. W. R. Davie to Iredell, July 9, 1788, McRee, *Iredell*, II, 231; Bloodworth to Lamb, June 23, 1788, Lamb Papers, N.Y. Hist. Soc.

78. To Lamb, Aug. 6, 1788, William K. Boyd, ed., "News, Letters and Documents Concerning North Carolina and the Federal Constitution," Trinity Coll. Hist. Soc., *Historical Papers*, 14 (1922), 80.

79. To Lamb, letters cited in *nn.* 77 and 78.

investigates the slave holdings of the delegates, and finds that among Federalists, seven delegates, or 8 per cent, held fifty or more slaves, whereas among Antifederalists, three delegates, or less than 2 per cent, owned that number. Thirty-one Federalists, or 37 per cent, had at least twenty slaves, as opposed to twenty-eight, or 15 per cent of the Antifederalists. Pool concludes that "those favoring and those opposed to ratification owned approximately the same number of slaves." [80] On the basis of his figures, it could equally well be maintained that proportionate to their numbers, more than twice as many Federalists had twenty slaves and five times as many had fifty. However, in another category of wealth, the ownership of land, the difference is very slight: 55 per cent of the Federalists and 47 per cent of the Antifederalists owned 1,000 acres; 15½ per cent of the Federalists and 6½ per cent of the Antifederalists held 5,000 acres or the equivalent. Nearly the same proportion held between 2,000 and 5,000 acres.[81]

It may be that a more meaningful approach is to examine the constituencies rather than the representatives. The striking fact is that the west and the northeast continued in opposition to each other, with the northeast now receding from its western limits, losing Northampton, Halifax, Warren, Nash, and Edgecomb.[82] The Tennessee representatives, previously divided in their allegiance, were almost unanimously Antifederal; this section, like Kentucky, was influenced by the fear that the navigation of the Mississippi might be endangered by ratification. Whereas in Kentucky important land speculators were opposed to the Constitution, in North Carolina the speculating interest represented by the Blount group was Federal, but its presence did not affect the outcome in the west.[83]

So far the sectional alignment followed precedents, but the Antifederalism of the southeast demands explanation. In this area,

80. Pool, "Economic Interpretation of Ratification in North Carolina," *N. C. Hist. Rev.*, 27 (1950), 125.

81. I am here estimating that one slave equalled about 40 acres.

82. Therefore the northeast, as previously defined, voted 60-24 in favor of ratification.

83. Hugh Williamson to Madison, June 2, 1788, *N. C. Hist. Rev.*, 14 (1937), 160; Trenholme, *Ratification in North Carolina*, 160, 194-95; Abernethy, *Western Lands*, 343.

which included about nine counties, the Federalists could gain only eleven votes, or one-fourth of the total; yet it was rich in slaves and contained a relatively large number of wealthy planters, many of whom swelled the Antifederalist majority in the convention. It must be remembered, however, that in previous years this section had often voted with the west: it had, for example, overwhelmingly favored an issue of paper money, and the evidence shows that this issue was important in the alignment on ratification. Moreover, this section appears to have been less commercially-minded than the counties of the northern coast.

The Federalism of the commercial elements is a striking fact. Not only New Bern, Halifax, and Edenton in the northeast, but Wilmington in the southeast and Salisbury in the west supported ratification, while an unrepresented town, in Edgecomb County, published a "testimony of reprobation of the unhappy issue" of the convention.[84] Pool dismisses in a few sentences the possibility that the division was along lines of commercial versus non-commercial issues on the ground that the state's trade was small. It is clear enough that most North Carolinians were not raising crops for export—a fact which accounts in part for the overwhelming Antifederal majority. Yet it is not correct to say that a commercial element did not exist. There was a considerable export, carried on not by the North Carolinians themselves but by Northern or British merchants, and sent abroad not so much from Edenton or New Bern as from ports out of the state. North Carolina's towns were small, but they were growing and exerting an influence,[85] and they served as collecting points for the agricultural and forest products which were ultimately to be exported. North Carolina newspapers published local export figures, and a lively and prosperous commerce flourished in the northeastern section.[86]

Another clue to the alignment is furnished by the critical series of votes concerning the disposition of western land. In these, speculator-commercial-business interests of the northeast were opposed by the west and also by the southeast. These votes cor-

84. *State Gazette of N.-C.* (Newbern), Sept. 8, 1788.
85. Hooper to Iredell, July 6, 1785, McRee, *Iredell*, II, 126.
86. *State Gazette of N.-C.* (Newbern), Jan. 15, May 14, 1789; Wright and Tinling, *Quebec to Caroline*, 270, 275; Charles Christopher Crittenden, *The Commerce of North Carolina, 1763-1789* (New Haven, 1936), chap. X.

relate in a remarkable fashion with the vote on the Constitution.[87]

The generalization which follows from these facts is that the Federalists included the commercial interest and those agricultural areas which were producing for export and which therefore were interested in financial stability, the payment of debts, and a government which could encourage commerce, whereas the Antifederalists represented those sections of the state which were not so immediately and directly concerned with mercantile or business affairs and which preferred inflation to a "sound," or deflationary financial system.[88]

During the year following the rejection of the Constitution, Antifederal strength slowly diminished. Ratification by eleven states ended all hope of a new convention, and attempts to act in concert with the New York opposition [89] subsided before the new Congress met. Federalists began to win elections even in the western districts of North Carolina and by autumn controlled the state Senate, though not the lower house.[90] There seem to have been threats that the Federal (northeastern) part of the state would secede if ratification were delayed.[91] The news that Madison was supporting amendments helped the Federal cause,[92] but of course the realities of the situation had most effect. When the

87. Clark, ed., *State Recs. of N. C.*, XIX, 613, 622, 643-44.

88. Crittenden, *Commerce of North Carolina*, 166-69, emphasizes the importance of commercial factors.

89. Bloodworth to Lamb, July 1, 1788 and Person to Lamb, Aug. 6, 1788, cited in *nn*. 77 and 78. At this time the North Carolina Antifederalists were still hoping to agree with those in New York on amendments and some way of forcing their adoption.

90. *State Gazette of N.-C.* (Newbern), Sept. 29, 1788; Hooper to Iredell, Sept. 22, 1788, McRee, *Iredell*, II, 238; Gen. H. W. Harrington to J. F. Grimke, Nov. 28, 1788, Gratz Coll., Case 4, Box 20, Hist. Soc. Pa.

91. Hugh Williamson wrote to John Gilman, "You are to note that the District of Edenton containing nine Counties, about the sixth Part of the State, is federal almost to a Man and I verily believe that if the State does not confederate, this District with the other two Districts on the Sea Coast will dissolve all connection with the interior Inhabitants and pray Congress to consider them as the State of North Carolina or as a separate State under some other Name. . . . I consider it as certain that unless we accede to the Union on the next Fall the State will be divided. I am inclined to believe that the Anticipation of such an Event will effect an Adoption of the new System." May 28, 1789, Bost. Pub. Lib.

92. W. R. Davie to Iredell, June 4, 1789, McRee, *Iredell*, II, 260.

new convention met in the fall of 1789, only a handful of Antifederalists, principally from the west, remained.

In Rhode Island, too, the Antifederalists slowly lost ground. The merchants, who had much to gain by joining the new government, agitated constantly for ratification, and the ruinous results of Rhode Island's remaining outside the Union were evident.[93] Nevertheless, when a new convention met in March 1790 a majority of the delegates were Antifederal. The Constitution was again rejected and a long list of amendments drawn up.[94] Not until fall were the Federalists able to secure a bare majority. Even at this late date, the final vote re-emphasized the persisting division between commercial and non-commercial areas.[95] Of the Narragansett Bay towns, every one was Federal except Warwick, which was divided. Four Federal votes came from the southwestern corner, near Connecticut. Otherwise the Antifederalists controlled the entire state, one town only excepted. Clearly the two years of dispute had seen the gradual conversion of the coastal towns until at last their combined strength was just enough to carry the decision. Once again the merchants had the support of the urban mechanics and eventually recruited enough votes from nearby farmers to assure victory.

93. The Browns, among others, owned valuable public securities. Hedges, *The Browns of Providence*, 321; Jabez Bowen and others to Christopher Champlin and George Gibbs, Jan. 12, 1790, Wetmore Coll., R. I. Hist. Soc.; Staples, *Rhode Island in Cont. Cong.*, 663-70.

94. Jeremiah Olney to Philip Schuyler, Feb. 15, 1790, Shepley Lib., IX, 115, R. I. Hist. Soc.; Cotner, ed., *Foster's Minutes*.

95. Staples, *Rhode Island in Cont. Cong.*, 672-73.

Chapter XI

CONCLUSION

I<small>T WILL</small> never be known whether a majority of the voters—to say nothing of all the people—opposed ratification. It seems likely that the Antifederalists outnumbered the Federalists by as much as four to one in Rhode Island and South Carolina and by perhaps three to one in New York and North Carolina, and that they were slightly more than a majority in Massachusetts and Virginia. Probably the two sides were nearly equal in New Hampshire in June 1788, although there had been an Antifederal majority earlier. On the other hand, almost all of the citizens in Georgia, New Jersey, and Delaware were Federalists. The situation in the remaining three states is uncertain; probably the Federalists had a clear majority in them, though perhaps not as large as the margin of victory in the ratifying conventions suggests. If we try to form an estimate of the entire white population, the two sides appear to have been nearly equal in numbers.[1] Of course in 1787-88 this was of no importance: what counted then was the ratification by nine states. Since the Federalists were a minority in at least six and probably seven states, they ought surely to have been defeated. Yet they came from behind to win.

A number of factors help to account for this. One of them, perhaps, was delay in the circulation of newspapers and letters. The Antifederalists complained that the residents of a state might not even know that opposition existed, and that this delay was an intentional effort on the part of the postal authorities to prevent the people from being informed. The Antifederalists also claimed

---

1. The Antifederalists probably had a very small majority—perhaps 52 per cent; but of course it is impossible to be exact.

that they were prevented from communicating promptly with one another in their efforts to organize and to combat misrepresentation. Most of the protest concerned the delivery of newspapers.[2] As far as private mail is concerned, George Clinton complained vigorously of poor service, with some reason if the dates he gave are correct, and continued, "I can only add, that while the new Constitution was in agitation, I have discovered that many letters written to me, have never been delivered, and that others especially those which came by private conveyances appeared to have been opened on their passage."[3] There were other complaints of slow mail too.[4] Whether these delays were intentional or accidental cannot be proven, but they handicapped the Antifederalists.

The pro-Constitution attitude of the newspapers was undoubtedly much more important. The number of papers which opposed ratification or even of those which presented both sides impartially was very few.[5] This was natural, for the city people were overwhelmingly Federal, and the printers were influenced by local opinion as well as by their own convictions; moreover, it was profitable to agree with the purchasers and the advertisers. In some cases pressure was used to enforce conformity: in Philadelphia the *Herald* was obliged to discontinue its coverage of the ratifying convention when almost one hundred readers stopped their subscriptions;[6] in New York City the *Morning Post* pub-

2. For example, the *Boston Gazette*, Jan. 28, 1788; the *Independent Chronicle* (Boston), Feb. 21, 1788; the *New Hampshire Spy* (Portsmouth), Mar. 18, 1788; the *N. Y. Journal*, Jan. 25, Mar. 10, Apr. 18, 1788; the *Independent Gazetteer* (Phila.), Feb. 8, 1788; "Centinel," in McMaster and Stone, *Pennsylvania and the Constitution*, 666; Harding, *Ratification in Massachusetts*, 18n.

3. To [Randolph], Oct. 4, 1788, Myers Papers, No. 1265, N.Y. Pub. Lib.; Rowland, *Mason*, II, 278-80.

4. Aedanus Burke to John Lamb, June 23, 1788, Lamb Papers, N.Y. Hist. Soc., and the discussion in Spaulding, *New York in the Critical Period*, 259-61.

5. Not more than a dozen; only half a dozen were Antifederal. Practically all of the Antifederal articles were printed in five newspapers: the *Independent Gazetteer* and *Freeman's Journal* (Phila.), the *N. Y. Journal*, the *American Herald* (Boston), and the *Va. Independent Chronicle* (Richmond).

6. *Independent Gazetteer* (Phila.), Jan. 29, 1788; Raymond Walters, Jr., *Alexander James Dallas* (Philadelphia, 1943), 19-20. The Federalists were then able to distort the account of the proceedings.

lished a number of Antifederal articles until January 9, after which they suddenly ceased to appear; in Boston the *American Herald* lost subscribers and ultimately moved out of the city.[7] The Federalist domination of news coverage permitted them not only to obtain more space for their own publications but to conceal or distort the facts. The objections of the Antifederalists were sometimes twisted so as to make them appear foolish;[8] at other times it was denied that there was any opposition at all to the Constitution. In Pennsylvania it was claimed that Patrick Henry was working for ratification;[9] in Charleston readers were informed that thirty-nine fortieths of the New Yorkers favored adoption;[10] in Rhode Island, readers were presented with an article which purported to originate in Richmond. "Out of all the members as yet returned to the Convention, *there are only three or four against the Constitution*; and it is the general opinion, that there will scarcely be found ten men in the whole state, who when they meet here in June, will set their opinions in competition with those of all the great and good patriots in America, and thus suffer themselves to be branded with the *odious and disgraceful* appelation of antifederalists."[11]

Issues of the *New-Hampshire Spy* are fairly typical. On October 9 a gentleman reputed to have made a tour of New England was quoted as having heard not a single dissenting voice in the four states; in New York no opposition was expected, and even Clinton favored the Constitution. On the 27th appeared an often-reprinted story concerning George Mason's reputed unpopularity in Alexandria;[12] three days later it was asserted that Mason was suffering "contempt and neglect" and that Patrick Henry favored ratification. On November 23, another frequently printed falsehood re-

7. Harding, *Ratification in Massachusetts*, 28. On the one-sidedness of newspapers see also Spaulding, *New York in the Critical Period*, 39.

8. *New York Morning Post*, Feb. 4, 1788.

9. *Pa. Gazette* (Phila.), Oct. 17, 1787.

10. *Daily Advertiser* (Charleston), Mar. 29, 1788.

11. *U. S. Chronicle* (Providence), Apr. 17, 1788.

12. Rarely was there published a denial of these lies, but in this case "A Lover of Truth" warned readers of the *N.Y. Packet* (Oct. 30, 1787) that "the fabricators of this falsehood are evidently among the number of those who are for *cramming down the new Constitution* by *force, fraud and falsehood.*"

lated that Washington had been on his feet for two hours at a time in the Federal Convention speaking in favor of every part of the Constitution. On December 7 the *Spy* informed its readers that "it is currently reported, that there are only two men in Virginia, who are not in *debt*, to be found among the enemies of the federal constitution." Subsequent issues gave false reports concerning Federal strength; on May 27, 1788, it was asserted that a majority of twenty was expected in Virginia and on the 31st the same margin was predicted in North Carolina. Evidently some Federalists believed their own propaganda; one of them wrote that even the Shaysites were for adoption![13] There is no way of determining how effective this misinformation was. When news arrived that opposition did exist, the public reaction to exposure of previous falsehoods may sometimes have undone what had been accomplished.[14] Yet it must have been discouraging for the Antifederalists to keep reading such gloomy reports in the newspapers, and it is even possible that some regions never knew that opposition existed—this was actually the case in Luzerne County, Pennsylvania.

The ability of the Federalists to outmaneuver their opponents was due in part to superior organization. The Antifederalists had not been able to unite, even within a particular state, in order to concert their efforts, until the creation of the Federal Republican Committee in New York. Everywhere they were too late. Thus a Pennsylvania Quaker sent Antifederal pamphlets to Maryland and Georgia in April, after the contest had ended in both states; his only hope was that another convention would be called.[15] On the

13. Lambert Cadwalader to George Mitchell, Oct. 8, 1787, Emmett Coll., No. 9414, N.Y. Pub. Lib. Another example of a wildly erroneous statement is in the *Pa. Gazette* (Phila.), Jan. 9, 1788.

14. The Federalists were infuriated when opposition appeared. James Winthrop wrote in some amusement, after North Carolina's rejection had become known in Massachusetts, "It is impossible to describe the anxiety of the victorious party in this state upon hearing the first report. They immediately began to vilify that State as being originally peopled by outlaws & convicts, who were driven from the more civilized parts of the world into the wilds of Carolina, where they had formed a settlement but little superior in morals to the infernal world." To Mercy Warren, Aug. 26, 1788, Warren Letters, IV, Mass. Hist. Soc.

15. R. Smith to George or Samuel Bryan, Apr. 26, 1788, Bryan Papers, Hist. Soc. Pa.

other hand the Federalists were consistently ahead of the game from the time when, in September, the "gentlemen" of Philadelphia rode out to harangue "the rabble."[16] Certainly their correspondence shows far better co-operation. Perhaps this evidence is deceptive and indicates only that more of their letters have survived; yet the results are to be seen in their better distribution of campaign propaganda and information.[17]

Still another advantage of the Federalists was the superior prestige of some of their leaders. In many of the states this advantage was very great. In New Hampshire all of the noted Revolutionary leaders were Federalists; in Massachusetts a majority of the prominent men favored ratification; in Connecticut almost all; and in New Jersey, Delaware, and Georgia all or nearly all backed the proposed Constitution. The weight of prestige was also on the Federalist side in South Carolina, Maryland, and Virginia. While it is true that some Federalists probably did more harm than good because their views and aspirations were known or suspected— among them Robert Morris, Hamilton, and Gouverneur Morris— yet there remained many whose opinions were trusted and whose intentions were known to be honorable. Pre-eminent among them were Franklin (though his age told against him) and Washington. The latter was assured by friends that his influence was decisive, and this was not just flattery, for observers on both sides agreed,[18]

---

16. David Redick to William Irvine, Sept. 24, 1787, Irvine Papers, IX, Hist. Soc. Pa. As a matter of fact the Federalists were organizing for the contest even before the Convention adjourned. See, for example, David Humphreys to Washington, Sept. 28, 1787, *Doc. Hist. of the Constitution*, IV, 302.

17. The Federalists in New York had an efficient line of communication established with New Hampshire at a time when the Antifederalists were still relying on the mails. Hugh Williamson to John G. Blount, June 3, 1788, Burnett, ed., *Letters*, VIII, 747; Spaulding, *New York in the Critical Period*, 262. An Antifederal emissary travelled from Philadelphia to Richmond and one rode out into New Hampshire from Newburyport, but these were just about the only such missionaries, whereas the Federalists were very active. On the Federalists, see Richard Sill to Jeremiah Wadsworth, Jan. 12, 1788, Wadsworth Papers, Box 138, Conn. Hist. Soc.; Alexander Contee Hanson to Thomas Bradford, Feb. 8, 1788, Misc. Colls., Hist. Soc. Pa.

18. G. Morris to Washington, Oct. 30, 1787, in Jared Sparks, *The Life of Gouverneur Morris*, 3 vols. (Boston, 1832), I, 289-90; Count Moustier to Count Montmorin, June 5, 1789, quoted in Bancroft, *History of the Constitution*, II, 495-96; Monroe to Jefferson, July 12, 1788, in Hamilton, ed.,

and the Antifederalists paid him the honor of newspaper attacks. The truth is that he was trusted, with reason, and his guarantee that the Constitution was a good one carried weight.[19]

The influence of these men of wealth and prestige was exerted in various ways, not, it seems, by bribery, for had efforts of that sort been made there would surely have been revelations of it, but rather by example and persuasion. Thus Nathaniel Barrell of York was informed from Boston that "you will meet the most pointed opposition from all your friends here."[20] Antifederalists who proved immune to arguments were occasionally treated with scorn or ridicule,[21] but more often, evidently, they were wined and dined, as in South Carolina where Aedanus Burke complained that the Charlestonians kept open house.[22] Everywhere there was talk. In some cases the men of small property and little prestige may have been impressed by the great ones, but more susceptible to conversion were Antifederal merchants, lawyers, planters, and well-to-do leaders in general, who were persuaded to coalesce with their Federal equivalents.

The course of events also favored the Federal cause. Ratification got off to a quick—albeit somewhat forced—start by the actions of Delaware, Pennsylvania, New Jersey, Georgia, and Connecticut. This momentum was never entirely lost. The fact that

---

Writings of Monroe, I, 186; Thomas B. Wait to George Thatcher, Jan. 8, 1788, *Hist. Mag.*, 16 (1869), 262. George Bryan observed that the women all admired him (Bryan Papers, Hist. Soc. Pa.).

19. The Federalists, especially in newspaper articles, constantly used the *ad hominem* argument. The fact that Washington would be the first President was also used tellingly. The *Conn. Courant* (Hartford), for example, published what purported to be an extract from a private letter: "Should the new Constitution be adopted, General Washington will unquestionably be President, and Governor Hancock Vice-President of the Union. With these great men at the head of government, all Europe will again acknowledge the importance of America." Feb. 4, 1788. Variations of the theme appeared frequently.

20. Joseph Barrell to Nathaniel Barrell, Dec. 20, 1787, Sandeman-Barrell Papers, Mass. Hist. Soc.

21. See, for example, Harding, *Ratification in Massachusetts*, 103-4; Ledlie to Lamb, Jan. 15, 1788, Lamb Papers, N.Y. Hist. Soc.; Smilie in McMaster and Stone, *Pennsylvania and the Constitution*, 784.

22. To Lamb, June 23, 1788, Lamb Papers, N.Y. Hist. Soc.; Harding, *Ratification in Massachusetts*, 106; Spaulding, *New York in the Critical Period*, 253.

every one of the five ratified by large margins was important in Massachusetts, and the outcome there was influential elsewhere. By the time the states controlled by the Antifederalists held their conventions eight states had already ratified. By pressing for a conclusion where victory was assured and staving off defeat in other cases (as in New Hampshire), the Federalists were able to extract the utmost benefit from circumstances. They took advantage of local forces and issues: the activities of the Boston artisans, the threat of secession in southern New York, the Indian menace in frontier Georgia, and the British posts in the northwest are examples.

Finally there was the promise of amendments without which the Constitution could never have been ratified. The Antifederalists included many persons who would under no circumstances accept ratification, but there were also many whose hostility was less intense, who in fact believed that the Constitution was fundamentally a good one, whose defects could be removed by amendment. The Federalists did not have to worry about those who wholly rejected the Constitution; they needed only enough votes for ratification—a dozen or so here, a handful there.[23] They themselves did not admit the need for any alterations. Publicly they preached that the Constitution was perfect, and wherever they had control (as in South Carolina) they proposed no amendments. But when the technique of conceding amendments to the opposition first proved its value in Massachusetts, winning over some waverers and enabling others who had already been convinced to violate their instructions with a clear conscience, it became the most valuable weapon in the Federal arsenal.

Fundamentally, the Antifederalists faced an insuperable difficulty in that they agreed upon the need for political changes. Although the Constitution was too radical a departure from the Confederation to meet their views, it was a substantial effort toward political reform. This fact persuaded large numbers of people to support the new plan despite its shortcomings. As

23. A shift of 24 votes would have meant defeat in 6 states instead of victory in 11. Rhode Island and North Carolina rejected the Constitution. The margin in New York was 3 votes (change of 2), in New Hampshire 10 (change of 6), in Virginia 10 (change of 6), and in Massachusetts 19 (change of 10).

George Bryan put it, "When the federal Constitution was proposed to the people, the Desire of increasing the powers of Congress was great and this Object had a mighty Influence in its Favor." Thus a few Antifederalists—just enough—felt that the Constitution was better than "anarchy and confusion," and the promise of amendments was enough to quiet their fears.

The final result was that the Federalists did surprisingly well in the elections and then succeeded in converting convention minorities into majorities. All told, at least sixty delegates, perhaps as many as seventy-five, who were chosen as Antifederalists, ended by voting for ratification. To study these men, who they were and where they came from, is to explain much about the nature of Antifederalism. Two facts emerge which are of especial significance: the converts came from the regions near the coast and from the upper socio-economic stratum of society.

Of some fifty-six delegates who are known to have changed sides, the majority represented areas in the east or in the transition zone between east and west. These geographical terms are to be understood in the ways previously explained; that is, by "east" is meant, in Massachusetts, the towns near the coast, in New York, those along the southern Hudson; by transition is meant, for example, the "border" parishes of South Carolina. Although converts to Federalism were made everywhere, for the most part these accessions represented a drawing together—a coalescing—of delegates from regions near the great commercial centers and along the paths of commerce, or the solidifying of strength in localities already Federal and the extension of Federal influence into adjacent areas. In Virginia, the first process is represented by the shift of Edmund Randolph of Henrico, the second, by that of William Ronald of Powhatan. Similar illustrations in Massachusetts are Charles Turner of Scituate and William Symmes of Andover, and in New York, Samuel Jones of Queens and Zephaniah Platt of Dutchess. So too the Federal tide in Rhode Island rose slowly from Providence and Newport to engulf the other bay towns, and in North Carolina swept inland from the sounds.

The second major fact about the converts is that they included many of the Antifederal leaders, men of superior wealth, position, and prestige. In some states the party was nearly decapitated. The apostasy of its leaders often influenced the event in other states. In Massachusetts, the prominent Revolutionary leaders Nathan Dane and Samuel Osgood, who were not chosen to the ratifying convention, were at first opposed to the Constitution, but changed their minds.[24] The shift of Hancock and Samuel Adams is well known. James Sullivan apparently also changed.[25] Charles Turner, William Symmes, Nathaniel Barrell, and John Sprague (of Lancaster) all voted in favor. Of this group, the first was a respected Congregational minister and one-time senator, the second was a lawyer, the third was a wealthy son of a tory, and the last was a well-to-do lawyer who had opposed Shays although he lived in the heart of the Shaysite country. In addition, there are indications that Charles Jarvis, a Boston doctor, and John Winthrop, a wealthy merchant, were at first uncertain, then voted for ratification; Samuel Holten of Danvers, a prominent and well-to-do doctor, failed to vote; while Capt. Isaac Snow of Harpswell, a shipowner, accepted the Constitution after amendments. In New York, the dozen who changed on the final vote included a merchant, a judge, and three wealthy landowners. Of similar significance were the stand taken by Edmund Randolph, when he emerged from his gyrations, the statement of the prominent Charleston doctor Fayssoux, the shifts of Humphrey Marshall and William Ronald in Virginia, of William Williams in Connecticut, of William Paca in Maryland, and of John Chesnut (merchant), Henry Pendleton (judge), the Reverend Mr. Cummins, and Alexander Tweed in South Carolina. Comparable, too, were the refusal of Abraham Clark to actively oppose the Constitution in New Jersey, the similar attitude of Thomas Johnson in Maryland, and the ultimate decision of Governor John Collins in Rhode Island that further resistance was useless.

About half of the delegates who changed sides were obscure men of only local repute, followers rather than leaders, whose conversion was not likely to influence many others. The other half, however, included a number of large property owners—indeed

24. Christopher Gore to Rufus King, Dec. 23, 1787, King, *King*, I, 265; Samuel Osgood to Samuel Adams, Jan. 5, 1788, Nathan Dane to Samuel Adams, May 10, 1788, Adams Papers, N.Y. Pub. Lib.; East, "Massachusetts Conservatives," Morris, ed., *Era of the American Revolution*, 376-77n.

25. Harding, *Ratification in Massachusetts*, 31-32n.

about a third of the total were well-to-do. There were three doctors, five merchants, a shipowner, at least four large landowners,
and no less than ten lawyers. The Federalists could appeal to such
men with particular success because of the nature of the Constitution. If the new government favored the well-to-do, as some
Antifederalists maintained, this was hardly an objection to those
who were of the "better sort" themselves. They might dislike an
aristocracy in theory, but in practice, rule by the educated, well-
bred, wellborn few was appealing. Insofar as the Constitution
helped to guard against popular uprisings, they were all for it—
the Warrens and their friends, for example, had not defended
Shays's Rebellion.[26] This is not to suggest that all men of property
were impressed by such arguments—some were repelled by
them;[27] yet the Constitution may have seemed less menacing to
those who would probably help to administer it, some of whom
were basically inclined to favor the few rather than the many.
Many, probably most, of the converts were hard-money advocates, who supported financial policies opposite to those which
the rank and file of Antifederalists preferred. Moreover, more
than most Antifederalists they were impressed with the need for
change,[28] perhaps because they lived nearer the commercial
centers and were influenced by the mercantile point of view. From
the first, therefore, they were less antagonistic to the Constitution,
its faults seemed fewer, its virtues more numerous. Their objections were more readily removed by arguments, or, when that
failed, by the promise of amendments. Thus Silas Lee, of Bidde-
ford, Maine, believed from the first that the Articles were
inadequate; his correspondents included staunch Federalists, and

26. See Oscar and Mary Handlin, "Radicals and Conservatives in Massachusetts after Independence," New Eng. Qtly., 17 (1944), 343-55.

27. Uriah Forrest wondered whether the makers had not been "too
strongly impressed" by Shays's Rebellion and continued, "I am obliged to
own myself one of those who do not wish to see the people more obedient to
their rulers in the next twelve, or any other twelve years, than they have
been in the last. A proper spirit of resistance is the best security for their
liberties, and they shou'd now and then warn their rulers of it." To Jefferson,
Dec. 11, 1787, Boyd, ed., Papers of Jefferson, XII, 416-17.

28. Antifederalists of every variety are recorded as wanting some alterations in the Articles, but the greatest number of those who sought the most
extensive changes were among the well-to-do.

he was ultimately persuaded that the Constitution, once amended, would serve to avoid the anarchy and confusion which the Federalists prophesied.[29]

An analysis of the Antifederalists who changed their vote suggests that Federalism attracted particularly the economic elite and also those who were connected with commerce. These key generalizations must now be tested against all that has been learned about the great controversy. Historians who have studied the division which took place in 1787-88 have arrived at very different conclusions: some have defended the sectional hypothesis as an explanation for political conflicts, others have suggested class antagonisms, or the presence or lack of vision, age, or religion. The first essential in reaching a conclusion is therefore to remove some of the errors.

The difference was not one of age. It is true that some of the "old patriots" were getting on, as Charles Warren says,[30] and that many were Antifederal—he lists ten who were over forty and contrasts them with nine Federalists who were younger. But a few selected examples do not prove a point. In Pennsylvania the Antifederalists were older by two years, but in New York there was no difference at all; in South Carolina the median age of eleven Antifederalists was 33, of thirty-two Federalists only 29; in Massachusetts the average Antifederalist was 52, the Federalist 51. All told, the Federalists were about two years younger than their antagonists. It is hard to see how this could have made any difference.

One explanation for the nature of the division stems from Charles Francis Adams's observation that "among the opponents of the Constitution are to be ranked a great majority of those who had most strenuously fought the battle of independence."[31] Unless the statement was meant to apply only to Massachusetts, it is not correct. Among the signers of the Declaration of Independence, Federalists outnumbered the Antifederalists nearly three to one, and of the latter, half finally voted for ratification; thus

29.   Silas Lee to George Thatcher, Mar. 24, 1788, *Hist. Mag.*, 16 (1869), 346. Lee was not a member of the convention.

30.   Charles Warren, *Making of the Constitution* (Boston, 1928), 759.

31.   Adams, ed., *Works of John Adams*, I, 442.

the margin becomes no less than six to one.[32] It is true that many of the signers were not enthusiastic about the Declaration and that all those who signed reluctantly became Federalists; but even when these are eliminated Adams's remark is inaccurate.[33]

Differences in religion also fail to provide a solution, whatever their importance in the earlier history of the country or their influence upon other issues. Some Antifederalists criticized the Constitution because it did not secure freedom of conscience; the omission would affect, presumably, the dissenting sects. But others objected to it because it tolerated all alike; this would affect those denominations which aspired to control the state. A majority of Congregationalists were perhaps in favor of ratification (certainly the ministers were);[34] yet there does not seem to have been any clear-cut alignment of Congregationalists behind the Constitution: thus while Connecticut favored adoption, central and western Massachusetts did not. The situation in regard to the Baptists is instructive. Those in Philadelphia were Federal, and in New York City a convention of Baptists of the middle states recommended ratification.[35] Baptists in eastern North Carolina

32. Out of 55 signers, 9 had died, the opinions of 7 are not known to me, 29 were Federal and two more probably Federal, 10 were Antifederal of whom 5 (Samuel Adams, Paca, Jefferson, Clark, and Williams) did not maintain their opposition.

33. Of the 48 signers of the Articles of Confederation, 23 were certainly and 2 more were probably Federal; only 6 were Antifederal of whom 4 (Samuel Adams, Hancock, Holten, and Collins) changed sides. Among those who were "radical" on the issue of Independence, the division was somewhat more equal, being Federal by about 4 to 3 and by 5 to 3 after the moderates had shifted. This is based on information concerning over 100 individuals, most of whom are listed in the D.A.B.

The future political allegiance of these men may be of interest. My data here are quite incomplete, being based on about 150 persons, but the pattern is very clear. Almost all of the Antifederalists became Jeffersonian Republicans. The exceptions have attracted notice because of their prominence but they are exceedingly few—only about one-sixth. That includes Henry who, after all, changed sides only at the very end of his life. Moreover the vast majority of Federalists remained Federal, only about one-seventh joining the Republicans. It should be added that I lack information on the rank and file.

34. See the New Haven Gazette, Oct. 25, 1787.

35. Ibid., Nov. 1, 1787, and other papers; American Museum, 2 (1787), 394-95.

and in eastern South Carolina were also Federal.[36] In New Jersey there were twenty-seven Baptist churches, but few Antifederalists.[37] On the other hand, the Virginia Baptist Association voted unanimously against ratification.[38] In Massachusetts most of the Baptists lived in the interior and were Antifederal, but the few who were in the east, including the prominent Isaac Backus, were Federal.[39] Elsewhere the Baptists were usually small farmers and were Antifederal. Obviously, the opinions of Baptists depended upon where they lived or what their other interests were, and the same was true of other religious or racial groups. Presbyterians of southern New York, eastern Pennsylvania, and the Shenandoah Valley were Federalists, but those of other sections were not. In North Carolina most of them were Antifederal, but W. R. Davie, a lawyer who represented the town of Halifax, was a Federalist. The Presbyterians were the strongest denomination in Federal New Jersey. Two other religious groups were fairly consistent in their Federalism: the Quakers in Pennsylvania and the Episcopalians; yet in the west they were often in the opposite camp. Antifederalist Charles Clay of Bedford County, Virginia, was an Episcopalian minister.[40] German sects divided irregularly. As Dorpalen discovered, they were for or against the Constitution for reasons other than their religion or national origin; he found that in Pennsylvania many Germans of whatever creed joined the Federalists but that in the South they were Antifederal because they resided in the backcountry.[41] In short the alignment on the Constitution was not affected significantly by religion.

On the other hand there is a good deal of evidence to show that the division followed class lines. There was no working class to any extent, but there did exist an antagonism between small and

36. *N. Y. Journal*, Nov. 30, 1787; Trenholme, *Ratification in North Carolina*, 155.

37. McCormick, *New Jersey in the Critical Period*, 53.

38. Semple, *Baptists*, 77; James Madison, Sr., to Madison, Jan. 30, 1788, in Hunt, ed., *Writings of Madison*, V, 105n.; Joseph Spencer to Madison, Feb. 28, 1788, *Doc. Hist. of the Constitution*, IV, 525.

39. See the account of Isaac Backus in the *D.A.B.* Silliman of Boston was Federal, Alden of Billerica was Antifederal.

40. Hugh Blair Grigsby, *The History of the Virginia Federal Convention of 1788*, 2 vols. (Richmond, 1890-91), I, 151, 255.

41. *Pa. Hist.*, 6 (1939), 233.

large property holders. It is true that such conflicts were tempered by exceptionally high vertical mobility, but there were nevertheless significant economic and social differences, well recognized at the time, that were continually reflected in political disputes. In the debate over the Constitution, several types of evidence are available to prove the existence of a division along class lines. First, there is the testimony of contemporaries. In Massachusetts the statements of King, Knox, Jackson, Thatcher, Sewall, Minot, Singletary, Lewis Morris, and Randal have been cited. Both East and Harding give other examples.[42] In New Hampshire, Sullivan, Madison, Atherton, and Tobias Lear testified that the Federalists were men of greater wealth. Hugh Ledlie referred to the Connecticut Federalists as men of "superior rank," while David Humphreys listed clergy, lawyers, physicians, merchants, and army officers. In Rhode Island, General Varnum observed that "the wealth and resources of this state are chiefly in the possession of the well-affected." [43] Similarly in New York, both sides noted a difference, the Federalists with pride, the Antifederalists with alarm.[44] The Pennsylvanian George Bryan discussed class differences, while Benjamin Rush contrasted the "people" and "their rulers." Observers in the South noted the same distinction, as Arthur Bryan did when he discovered that in South Carolina the "second class of people" were especially inclined to Antifederalism; Burke contrasted the "rich leading men" with "the Multitude." Timothy Bloodworth felt that the aristocracy favored adoption in North Carolina. Lord Dorchester was informed that "the partizans in favour of the new system hold the greater share of landed and personal property." John Quincy Adams also felt that there was a general class division over the Constitution. Even in Maryland, John Francis Mercer believed that the contest was between "wealthy men" or "the *few*" and "the People" or "the *many*," and another observer there believed that ratification was

42. See especially "Atticus," quoted in Harding, *Ratification in Massachusetts*, 11. East gives many commentaries on this fact. "Massachusetts Conservatives," Morris, ed., *Era of the American Revolution*.

43. Quoted in Bates, *Rhode Island and the Union*, 158.

44. In addition to previous citations see "A Citizen of America," in the *Daily Advertiser* (N.Y.), copied in the *Columbian Herald* (Charleston), Mar. 24, 1788.

secured by the aristocracy, not the "common class."[45] Some proof by implication may be drawn from the fact that Antifederalists generally criticized the Constitution for its undemocratic features,[46] while in contrast a considerable number of Federalists did not approve of the upsurge of the democracy and praised the Constitution as a check on popular majorities.

Another type of evidence is based on a study of individuals whose politics are known, especially members of the ratifying conventions. Such a study clearly reveals a class alignment. If it be conceded that there was some sort of a difference between "Esq." and "Mr." as used in New England, then it is evident that the Federalists outranked their opponents by a significant margin; they constituted nearly three and one-half times as many esquires. Second, it is probably true in New England and certainly true in the South that there was a correlation between socio-economic status and army rank. In every state for which information is available, except New York, the higher ranking officers were Federal by a margin of more than two to one.[47] On the other hand there were about the same number of lesser ranking officers on either side, lieutenants tending toward Antifederalism. Third, the holders of a college degree almost always came from the upper income groups and they were Federal by a margin of more than three to one. Fourth, certain professions carried with them superior prestige and usually higher income. Merchants were Federal by a five to one margin, lawyers and judges by well over two to one, shipowners, ship captains, and large manufacturers by over seven to one.

The highest political offices were at that time principally held by men of wealth and status (even aside from the property qualifications), and taking as representative of these offices the governors, state senators, and members of Congress, it appears

45. *Md. Journal* (Baltimore), May 16, 1788.
46. Especially "Agrarius," in the *Independent Gazetteer* (Phila.), Feb. 29, 1788; "Lycurgus," in *ibid.*, Oct. 17, 1787; "John Humble," in *ibid.*, Oct. 29, 1787; "Rusticus," in the *N. Y. Journal*, Sept. 13, 1787.
47. By available I mean available to me, but this means fairly complete information in states where Antifederalism existed, and exhaustive research would probably not change the generalization. Specific figures for members of the ratifying conventions are, generals, 30-12, colonels, 70-37, majors, 28-13.

that the Federalists held well over twice as many such posts in states where close contests occurred. Among the governors and former governors whose political opinions are known, twenty-seven were Federal and eleven were Antifederal, and of the latter, five changed sides. Men who had served in Congress were Federal by a four to one margin.

The political preference of the members of state senates is of particular interest. They were numerous (over eight hundred served at various times from 1775 to 1788) and influential because their approval was essential for the passage of all laws. The great majority of them were well-to-do merchants, lawyers, or large landholders. Among those whose opinions are known, nearly two-thirds voted for ratification. This may be attributed to their superior education and wider experience, or to the fact that as men of political knowledge they recognized the need for change. But economic status had something to do with it too. The wealthier senators supported the Constitution by a margin of over three to one; those who were merely well-to-do favored it two to one; but those of only moderate means opposed it by a small margin. The wealthier the senator, the more apt he was to be a Federalist.[48]

Indeed, men of wealth in general, in or out of the conventions, were usually Federalists. Almost all of them in New Jersey, Delaware, and Georgia apparently favored ratification, and nearly all in Connecticut and Maryland. In the remaining eight states, among almost three hundred men definitely known to have possessed considerable fortunes, nearly three-fourths were Federal.

48. Among 209 delegates to Congress living in 1788 whose attitude is known, 161 favored ratification from the start, and 9 more joined them eventually. The political ideas of about half of the senators are not known, but although further research may add a few, the generalizations will remain. The figures below include among the Federalists those who started as Antifederalists and then changed.

	Federal	Antifederal
wealthy	98	22
well-to-do	83	45
moderate means	28	39
unknown wealth	11	6
Total	220	112

Yet in these states the majority of the population was against the Constitution.[49]

Other evidence to the same effect may be stated briefly. In Pennsylvania, the Federalist delegates to the ratifying convention owned, on the average, half again as much land and other taxable property as the Antifederalists. In Massachusetts, Federal towns were wealthier. In Rhode Island, Federal towns contained far more slaves than did the Antifederal. Another type of property, public securities, was also unequally distributed, for much of the debt, worth millions of dollars, was concentrated in centers of Federalist strength.[50] Observers agreed that creditors, both public and private, tended to be Federal, while debtors were ordinarily Antifederal. Finally, the areas which supported Federalism, including the towns and the rich river valleys, contained most of the men who were well-to-do and a great proportion of the whole wealth of the country.

Still a third type of evidence in support of a class division is based upon a correlation between the alignment on ratification and that on earlier issues which involved conflicts between rich and poor, large and small property owners. Allowing for the inevitable exceptions, the Antifederalists had in the past supported the more democratic state constitutions which increased the political power of the majority, whereas the Federalists had preferred to restrain or "manage" the democracy; the Antifed-

49. Since my research was directed primarily toward discovering Antifederalists, the error here, if it exists, probably lies in understating the proportion of wealthy Federalists. The exact figures are: Federalists, 209, Antifederalists, 79, of whom 6 changed sides. Where exact figures concerning property were available the standard for admission into this class was 50 slaves and 5,000 acres, or the equivalent, or an estate valued at £10,000. "Well-to-do" indicates an estate of £2,000. Usually it was necessary to rely on general statements in biographies, genealogies, or local histories; their tendency to exaggerate was allowed for.

The union of rich men in support of the Constitution was more striking in the North (nearly 80 per cent) than in the South (barely 70 per cent). The only state in which the division was nearly equal was North Carolina. If *all* the states were included, then it would surely be safe to say that well over three-fourths of the economic elite were Federalists.

50. Again I am indebted to the work of E. James Ferguson. Detailed research into the question of private debts and into the distribution of other types of property is essential. Until this is done, all generalizations must remain tentative.

eralists had supported paper money, lower interest rates, legal tender clauses, valuation and instalment and stay laws, and other measures favorable to debtors; they had attempted also to reduce the state debts so as to render taxes less burdensome to the majority, while the Federalists upheld the creditor interest and favored the taxes necessary to pay the debts at par. Similarly the Antifederalists, in combating the loyalists, opposing the Bank of North America, obstructing enforcement of the British treaty, striving for lower court fees, and checking the increase of power in government, had defended the interest of the many against the few. The struggle over the Constitution was in part a continuation of a long history of social conflicts which extended far back into colonial times.

All of this evidence proves that there was a division along lines of class. It does not, however, prove that the struggle over ratification can be explained exclusively in terms of class conflict. There are several states in which the concept obviously does not hold. In Georgia both wealthy planters and yeomen farmers agreed on ratification. In North Carolina and Virginia a large number of planters were Antifederal, and in the interior of the latter state, two large sections inhabited by small farmers favored ratification. Maryland does not fit the theory, nor do Delaware and New Jersey. Delegates from small farmer strongholds in Connecticut, New Hampshire, Pennsylvania, and even Massachusetts (parts of Hampshire County) were Federal.

But the most serious of all objections to an interpretation based exclusively on an alignment along class lines is the complete absence of a division of opinion in the towns. Where there should have been the most feeling, the least existed. This is a fact of such significance that it deserves fuller discussion.

In Charleston a solidly Federal delegation was elected without any sign of opposition. Alexander Gillon, who had been anti-Morris, skeptical of the impost, pro-debtor, and spokesman for the common man, was Federal. His ally Dr. John Budd voted for ratification. Aedanus Burke noted that everyone in the city, rich and poor alike, was "boisterous to drive it down." [51] In neighbor-

51. See also Phillips, "South Carolina Federalists," *Am. Hist. Rev.,* 14 (1908-1909), 542.

ing North Carolina, the towns of Wilmington, Halifax, and Salisbury, all situated in Antifederal areas, were themselves Federal, as was an unrepresented town (Tarborough) in Antifederal Edgecomb County. Edenton and New Bern likewise supported ratification. Only Hillsborough, farther west, did not. Both Williamsburg and Norfolk in Virginia elected Federal delegates; Fredericksburg was Federal in an Antifederal county (Spotsylvania); the freeholders of Alexandria voted for ratification, as did the inhabitants of Winchester (unanimously) and Petersburgh.[52] The town of Baltimore in Maryland was not unanimous, but the Federalists polled over 70 per cent of the vote,[53] whereas in the county they were defeated. In Annapolis, too, Federal candidates won in an Antifederal county.

Pennsylvania towns united in support of the Constitution. The Antifederalists could gain only an average of 150 votes per candidate in Philadelphia, scarcely one-eighth as many as the Federalists; George Bryan declared that "most townsmen were for it," and far to the west the residents of Pittsburgh favored ratification.[54] A hopeful letter written the next spring reviewed Antifederal gains in Pennsylvania, but admitted that the town of Carlisle had many Federalists and that Lancaster was Federal; Northampton and Easton also approved of their delegates' vote for ratification.[55] In New York City a few former leaders of the Sons of Liberty days, headed by General John Lamb, tried to organize the artisans as of old; but even Governor Clinton could get only 134 votes; Federalists polled well over 90 per cent of the votes cast in the city. Moreover they carried the city of Albany, at a time when all of the upstate counties were lost, and were victorious in Lansingburgh and Hudson too.[56] In Rhode Island there were only two towns with more than a thousand inhabitants, and in these the Antifederalists managed to poll exactly twelve votes. The mass

52. Monroe to Madison, Fredericksburgh, Feb. 7, 1788, Hamilton, ed., *Writings of Monroe*, I, 181; *Pa. Packet* (Phila.), Oct. 18, Nov. 6, 1787; Hart, *Valley of Virginia*, 172-73.
53. Crowl, *Maryland During the Revolution*, 165.
54. Konkle, *Bryan*, 305; *Pa. Packet* (Phila.), Dec. 13, 1787; *Pittsburgh Gazette, passim.*
55. *N. Y. Journal*, Apr. 18, 1788; *Pa. Packet* (Phila.), Jan. 3, 31, 1788.
56. Spaulding, *New York in the Critical Period*, 9, 220, 228-29.

meeting of the Boston mechanics to hail the Constitution has been previously noted, and other Massachusetts towns with populations of over nine hundred favored ratification, twenty-four to four. Portsmouth, Dover, and other large New Hampshire towns were centers of Federalist strength. Indeed in the entire United States there was scarcely a town that was not Federal.[57] Was this perhaps due to the absence of any class conflict during this period? Far from it: throughout the 1780's there were numerous clashes within the cities along class lines. The history of Charleston, for example, reveals important internal disputes. But there was no such contest between urban classes over the ratification of the Constitution.

If urban classes were not divided, was there not a class division implicit in a sectional alignment over the Constitution? This thesis, which was most fully developed by Libby, set east versus west, or, to be more accurate, seacoast versus backcountry. Libby's protagonists were the debtor areas of the interior and the creditor, mercantile centers near the coast. Emphasizing the issues which separated the two general regions, he stressed the correlation between Antifederalism and paper money as a proof of his hypothesis.

This interpretation has much truth. There had most certainly been just such a division all during the colonial period, and it continued to be of great importance for many decades. There is an abundance of evidence to support this explanation; as a matter of fact, the contrast between seacoast and interior was in some cases even more marked than Libby believed. The strength of Antifederalism was greater in upstate New York and backcountry South Carolina than he appreciated, and he did not fully exploit the possibilities of Rhode Island or of Maine. It is also true, as he contended, that paper money was a factor in the contest. In Massachusetts, towns opposing paper were Federal by about four to one, while pro-paper money towns were Antifederal by an even wider margin.[58] The hard (or less soft) money towns in New

57. Excluding, of course, the rural New England towns.
58. Based on scattered sources. Pro-paper money towns cast only 3 votes for and 22 votes against ratification; anti-paper money towns favored ratification 29 to 7.

Hampshire were Federal; most of the Antifederal strength in Connecticut was found in paper money districts; and the case of Rhode Island is sufficiently familiar. In New York it was the Clinton party which favored bills of credit in 1784, 1785, and 1786. Delegates from the Federal counties of New York, Kings, and Richmond, had voted against such issues; and when Suffolk and Queens counties finally changed sides and voted for ratification, they joined long-time allies on the paper money question. The same was true of the individuals involved: New York's Federalists had opposed paper money, whereas Antifederal members of the convention had voted for it, twenty-one to eleven; of the eleven Antifederalists who had opposed paper money, no less than seven were among those who ultimately changed sides on the Constitution or refrained from voting. Thus the advocates of hard money drew together in support of the Constitution. In Maryland and in Virginia the paper money forces opposed ratification. This was also the case in North Carolina, while in South Carolina, Antifederal strength lay in the backcountry, which had favored inflation.

All of the foregoing, however, does not prove an exact correlation between Antifederalism and the advocacy of paper money. There are a large number of exceptions, and of course there is a limit to the number which may be admitted without invalidating a rule. Leaving aside the fact that many Antifederalists, especially the leaders, specifically denounced state currency emissions, we have to consider the following exceptions: (1) in South Carolina, a large number of planters, most of whom became Federalists, supported the state's paper emission; (2) most Antifederalists in Virginia (including the planters) were opposed to paper money; (3) in Maryland, according to Crowl, attitudes toward paper money are not the key to the situation, and indeed the correlation with opinions on the Constitution is certainly not high; (4) New Jersey endorsed both paper money and the Constitution; (5) in Pennsylvania, although it is probable that a majority of the people were Federal, a majority favored paper money; (6) in Connecticut, paper money sentiment was far stronger than Antifederalism. Other exceptions could be cited.

That paper money sentiment was in some degree a factor in the existence of Antifederalism is scarcely to be doubted—the Antifederalists drew more heavily by far than their opponents from the ranks of paper money advocates; however the correlation is by no means complete. A different approach is necessary if all, or even most, of the facts are to be explained, and the real causes for the alignment understood. It will be necessary first to examine the positions taken by the different social or economic groups.

Among the groups into which the population might conceivably be divided, there were some whose members did not take a consistent stand on the Constitution. It has already been observed that religious and racial groups insofar as they voted together seldom did so for reasons connected with religion or race. Speculators in western lands varied in their attitude toward the Constitution; their votes were determined by local factors or personal interest.[59] Members of the "intelligentsia," if such a thing existed then—the writers, teachers, artists, and the like—were divided almost equally; doctors showed a slight but indecisive tendency toward Federalism.

Merchants, on the other hand, were virtually unanimous in endorsing the Constitution. It would not be quite accurate to say that every one of them supported ratification, but at least 80 per cent of them were Federal. It did not matter where they were located—in Boston or in Savannah, Pittsburgh, or Alexandria—nor what their economic status was, they were Federal almost to a man. In addition all, or very nearly all, of those who were immediately dependent upon commercial activities held similar views. This was the "Mercantile Interest" which, as John Adams once defined it, included "Merchants, Mechanicks, Labourers." [60] Understood in this way, the word takes in important segments of the population, including shipowners, seamen and other persons in maritime industries, the "mechanics and artisans," the apprentices and other hired employees in almost every town, and all those

59. Hugh Williamson wrote to Madison, "For myself I conceive that my opinions are not biased by private Interest, but having claims to a considerable Quantity of Land in the Western Country I am fully persuaded that the Value of those Lands must be increased by an efficient federal Govt." June 2, 1788, *N. C. Hist. Rev.*, 14 (1937), 161. But most leading citizens of Kentucky and Tennessee were of a different opinion. Most land speculators in the North were Federalists.

60. To James Warren, Oct. 20, 1775, Burnett, ed., *Letters*, I, 240.

who depended upon any of the above.[61] But the commercial interest was not just urban. The commercial centers were supported by nearby rural areas which depended upon the towns as markets and as agencies through which their produce was exported overseas. That is to say, the commercial interest also embraced large numbers of farmers, and the influence of each town radiated, perhaps in a degree relative to its size or commercial significance. The same influence permeated the rich river valleys and bound the great planters and other large landowners in the commercial nexus. Just as in physics each point along a beam of light itself acts as a point source of light, so also the major channels of commerce, rivers or roads, influenced the country through which they passed. The mercantile interest, understood in this broad sense, is the key to the political history of the period. Its counterpart is the non-commercial interest of the subsistence farmer. This is a socioeconomic division based on a geographical location and sustains a class as well as a sectional interpretation of the struggle over the Constitution.[62]

A brief review of the evidence will make clear the importance of this generalization. In Maine, the seacoast towns, dependent on the export of fish or lumber, favored ratification by a margin of over two to one, while the largely self-sufficient towns of the interior were Antifederal. The towns along the Connecticut River favored ratification. This was true in Connecticut, Massachusetts (with a few exceptions in the northern part of the state), New Hampshire, and possibly Vermont, where the southeastern counties became Federalist strongholds. The situation in Rhode Island is also striking. At first Federal strength was probably limited to four towns, all on the coast, including the only important commercial centers. Three other towns which may have been Federal in 1788 were also coastal. In 1790 all of the towns which supported

61. It is beyond the scope of this work to examine in any detail why individuals or groups became Federalist but it is evident that the mechanics and artisans, among other things, hoped for protection against British competition.

62. The division was to continue, at least into the next decade. Manning Dauer, in his study, *The Adams Federalists* (Baltimore, 1953), 7, contrasts the political behavior of "the more self-sufficient farming sections" with that of "the exporting agricultural sections." The resemblance between his conclusions and my interpretation is very striking.

the Constitution were with two exceptions on the coast. From Narragansett Bay, the center of commercial activity, Federalist strength gradually reached out into the adjacent hinterland. In New England, then, the major division was between the areas, or people, who depended on commerce, and those who were largely self-sufficient. That the distinction was recognized at the time is shown by the observations of the residents of Spencer (Worcester County) who referred to their town as one of those whose "Distent Situation, from the metropolis . . . Renders the profits, of . . . farmes, Very Inconsiderable, to Those, of an equal Bigness, and Quality, near, the Maritime And, market Towns." [63]

In New York and in the remaining states the data cannot be quite so precise because the political unit was the county rather than the town, and it is therefore more difficult to distinguish the commercial from the non-commercial interest. The Federalism of the towns, however, is obvious and has been sufficiently discussed. The Federalism of the countryside surrounding New York City is also to be noted; so too is the remark of Thomas Tredwell that the contest was "between navigating and non-navigating individuals." [64] Spaulding notes the opposition of merchants and non-merchants and observes that "the Clintonians were scarcely interested in commerce," [65] while Cochran defines the Antifederalists as farmers "who had no direct interest in trade or commerce." [66]

The vote in Pennsylvania is also significant. Counties which had immediate access to the Delaware (Philadelphia, Bucks, Northampton) or which were but a score of miles distant (Montgomery and Chester) together with the counties adjoining the lower Susquehanna (Lancaster and York) cast thirty-seven votes for

63. Quoted in Oscar and Mary Flug Handlin, *Commonwealth; A Study of the Role of Government in the American Economy: Massachusetts, 1774-1861* (New York, 1947), 32. Spencer opposed the supplementary fund, opposed the impost, favored paper money, was active in Shays's Rebellion, opposed sending troops into the Shaysite country, and favored Hancock over Bowdoin, in the election of 1787, by 87 to 7. James Draper, *History of Spencer, Massachusetts, from its Earliest Settlement to the Year 1860: including a Brief Sketch of Leicester, to the Year 1753* (Worcester, n. d.), 61-67. It was of course Antifederal.

64. Elliot, ed., *Debates*, II, 396.

65. Spaulding, *New York in the Critical Period*, 7, 28.

66. Cochran, *New York in the Confederation*, 168.

and only one against the Constitution, whereas the remainder of
the state cast twenty-two votes against and nine for ratification.
George Bryan believed that an important feature of the division
was the fact that men of trade and their supporters were Federal;
he contrasted the counties near to and remote from "the navigation" and observed of the mechanics, "such as depend on commerce and navigation, in favor." John Armstrong found that Antifederalism was dominant among the "country people." [67] New
Jersey and Delaware do not quite fit this, or any other pattern,
although it might be noted that both were favorably situated for
supplying domestic and foreign markets. In Maryland the only
Antifederal support came from the country; the location of the
state between the Chesapeake and the Potomac may be compared
with that of the Northern Neck between the Potomac and the
Rappahannock.

In assessing the situation in Virginia, it is illuminating to consider the vote in 1785 granting commercial powers to Congress.
Although it is not quite a straightforward test of the commercial
and non-commercial interests, yet the correlation between the
alignment on this issue and that on the Constitution is striking.
The Federalist counties (including the "Alleghany" region)
favored the measure by a margin of over two to one, while Antifederal counties rejected it by nearly three to one.[68] It is true that
there were few merchants or commercial towns in the state, but
the great planters were essentially commercial farmers who recognized that their future depended on trade, and it is no accident
that Virginians took the lead in the effort to bestow the commerce
power on Congress. On the other hand large parts of the state
were further from the trade routes, so that many people either
had nothing directly to do with commerce or did not recognize
any identity of interest with the mercantile community. It has
already been noted that the division within the state was fundamentally that of the river valleys versus the non-valley areas. The
vast majority of counties which bordered the major streams were

67. To General William Irvine, Carlisle, Jan. 9, 1788, Irvine Papers, IX,
Hist. Soc. Pa.
68. That is, when adjustments are made to allow for the votes of several
men who were for a grant of commercial powers but opposed the particular
measure in question.

Federal, whereas Antifederal strength lay principally in the regions more distant from such waterways, notably in the Southside.

The fact that North Carolina contained a large proportion of subsistence farmers certainly was instrumental in shaping its Antifederalism. Evidence has already been adduced which indicates that the planters in the southeastern portion of the state, in spite of their greater wealth, had on several issues been opposed to the merchants, whereas the northeastern planters had voted on the other side. It is significant that the Constitution's sole support came from the Albemarle Sound counties and from the towns.

Still farther south, the foreign trade of South Carolina had always been of fundamental importance, symbolized by the interrelationship of planter and merchant in Charleston; all along the coast the producers of rice, indigo, and forest products voted with the city. On the southern border, the Savannah River drew inhabitants of both banks into the Federal camp, for not only did South Carolinians dwell under its influence but nearly the entire state of Georgia was at this time contained within the single river valley.

In all parts of the country, therefore, the commercial interest with its ramifications, including those who depended primarily and directly upon commerce, were Federal, and the "non-navigating" folk were Antifederal.

The mercantile interest drew many groups into its orbit. Manufacturers were with few exceptions comprehended within the term "artisans and mechanics." They were skilled workers with a small shop or master craftsmen with a few apprentices. Such men either depended directly upon overseas trade, producing goods for export (coopers, sailmakers, and dozens of others) or sold their products to those who were merchants or closely associated with merchants. In addition it is well known that they hoped for protection against British competition. They are therefore to be included as part of the commercial interest, and their very livelihood seemed to them to depend upon the adoption of the Constitution. Few of these men were chosen to the ratifying conventions, but many voted, or expressed their opinion in less formal ways (as in Boston), and their attitude is clear. In addition there were some, though not yet many, who owned fairly large establishments. A number of these men—upwards of a dozen—did attend the conventions and were Federalists with but one or two exceptions. Other businessmen were also dependent upon commerce. The majority—indeed nearly 70 per cent—of the lawyers and judges favored ratification. When they lived in non-commercial areas, such as in parts of Virginia, they were Antifederal, or where peculiar circumstances existed the usual condition might be changed: in North Carolina the lawyers (Federal) and judges (Antifederal) had been previously opposed,[69] while in New York the Clintonian party contained its share of both. Judgeship or a law practice in itself did not determine political belief, but it did predispose the individual to act in concert with those of equal status or similar economic interest.

With regard to the creditors of the federal government the situation is somewhat different. The whole question of the debt is a very complex one, but some tentative observations may be made. It is almost certainly true that most of the debt was held by Federalists, for the certificates were concentrated in the more wealthy and the urban areas. It does not require more than a superficial examination of the records to secure the evidence of this.[70] Three different groups may be distinguished. First, there were those holding public securities who lived in states which were paying the interest in a fairly satisfactory manner. These men, in their capacity as security holders, would not be vitally affected by the Constitution unless they feared a local change of policy. Second, there were those owning certificates who lived in states which were not paying the interest in a satisfactory manner. These men

69. The judges had been chosen by the legislature and had taken the popular side throughout the decade. For example the lawyers were defending the property rights of loyalists whereas the judges upheld state laws unfavorable to the tories. A. Maclaine to Iredell, Mar. 6, 1786, McRee, *Iredell*, II, 137-38, 183; *Daily Advertiser* (Charleston), Jan. 1, 1788; Trenholme, *Ratification in North Carolina*, 153.

70. I have studied the records for New York, Massachusetts, Pennsylvania, and Virginia, but again rely heavily on the work of E. James Ferguson. See his "State Assumption of the Federal Debt during the Confederation," *Miss. Valley Hist. Rev.*, 38 (1951-1952), 403-24. His book, *The Power of the Purse*, read in manuscript, makes it clear that the importance of the debt was greater than indicated in the text. Until a detailed study is made of the political views of the larger holders it is impossible to be certain.

would gain heavily by the ratification. Third, there were those who held no securities. The last two need further discussion.

The mere fact that a person held securities did not mean that he favored ratification. Most of the creditors owned too small amounts to constitute a vital interest. In Virginia, although about a third of the members of the ratifying convention subscribed to the loan of 1790, only a handful had $1,000 in securities. Fully 85 per cent of the delegates either had no securities or their holdings were too small to have constituted a motivating factor. Six of the large holders, moreover, were Antifederal. Presumably these men can be exempted from the imputation of economic motive, and in the case of certain other known creditors it is evident that other considerations governed their decision: Isaac Vanmeter, a West Virginian; Archibald Stuart of the Shenandoah Valley; John Marshall; and Edmund Randolph. When all the facts are considered, it becomes evident that the personal holdings of the delegates were not an important factor in shaping their political convictions. Similarly, in Pennsylvania only nine members of the convention held large amounts; four of them were Antifederal. In New York security holders were at first more numerous among Antifederal than Federal delegates to the convention, but it is instructive to note that about half of the Antifederal security holders were among those who changed sides on the final vote. Only seven of those who had securities held large amounts; four of these were chosen as Antifederalists, and three of the four changed sides.

It seems clear that of the approximately three hundred members of the conventions in these three important states, not over 10 per cent could have been persuaded to favor ratification because of the public securities they held. It is true that outside of the conventions there were large security holders, and that a great deal of money was at stake, but it is evident that the public creditors comprised only one of many interests.

In regard to those who did not own public securities the situation is quite complex. It would be to their interest to keep the tax burden as low as possible, but in some cases the Constitution might actually be advantageous. McCormick argues convincingly that New Jersey favored ratification because the taxes for payment of the debt would be lowered. In other cases ratification would make little difference if taxes were already being levied for the purpose. In still other states the non-holders did stand to lose, and there were objections to the Constitution on that ground. The division certainly was not simply one of holder versus non-holder. A majority of the former favored ratification and a majority of the latter opposed it, but in neither case was the distribution of the debt at all decisive; probably, with some exceptions, it was not even very important compared with the influence of commercial factors.

The influence of private debts was undoubtedly very great. In the absence of extensive data concerning who owed whom, it is necessary to proceed by inference; this, however, may be done with some confidence. There were two major types of debtors: those who had fallen into debt because they were poor (typified by the small farmer), and those who had borrowed although they had considerable property (typified by Southern planters). Just as there is no strict dividing line between farmer and planter, so also one variety of debtor merges into the other; nevertheless a broad distinction exists. The different classes of debtors behaved differently. George Bryan remarked that in Pennsylvania debtors as a group did not agree on ratification, for, as he pointed out, "debtors are often creditors in their turn." Those who were engaged in business had to pay their debts promptly if they were to receive the further credits which were essential to them, and such men therefore held creditor views about "sound money" and "honesty in business." This category included most characteristically the merchants, but many, if not most, of the large landowners as well. In general, it seems that the class of what might be termed well-to-do debtors were divided in their attitude toward the Constitution, but that a majority of them were Federal. In South Carolina, measures benefiting debtors had found much support in the Federal eastern parishes; many Virginia planters who were in debt to British or American merchants were Federal; in Pennsylvania some prominent Republicans supported a paper money bill. In New York the Federalist Henry Remsen and other merchants petitioned for relief from debts due to British merchants.[71] The Shenandoah Valley delegates were Federal, though at least

71. Spaulding, *New York in the Critical Period*, 26; see also pp. 8, 71n.

six of them were well-to-do debtors.[72] Another student has found that those owing money to British merchants were divided politically.[73] It may be concluded that although some large property holders opposed the Constitution because of their debts, the majority were Federalists regardless.[74]

The other type of debtor, typified by the small farmer, was numerically more important. The testimony of contemporaries, the number of court suits, and the passage of various laws demonstrate the prevalence of debtors in every state. The decided majority were in the Antifederal column. We have seen that advocates of paper money were apt to be Antifederalists; so also were those who favored other measures aiding debtors. In South Carolina, for example, a valuation law, an instalment law, and a "Pine Barrens" law were supported by the western counties; the votes on such matters previously discussed reveal an alignment very similar to that on the Constitution, even including the uncertain stand of those parishes which changed sides.[75] Benjamin Rush and Charles Pinckney both emphasized the importance of these issues.[76] In Virginia the votes on bills concerning the British treaty are especially significant, as are those postponing taxes in 1783 and 1784.[77] Similar correlations existed elsewhere: in North Carolina, New York, and all of the New England states. In general, then, creditors were usually to be found on the Federalist side; debtors, with many exceptions especially among the more well-to-do, were Antifederal. This fact confirms the generalizations that have been previously made concerning the alignment on ratification.

72. Hart, *Valley of Virginia*, 123, 132.

73. Ben R. Baldwin, The Debts Owed by Americans to British Creditors, 1763-1902 (unpubl. Ph. D. diss., Indiana Univ., 1932).

74. See for instance the list of those owing debts to British firms as given in Isaac Samuel Harrell, *Loyalism in Virginia* (Philadelphia, 1926), 27-28, 171; most of them were Federalists.

75. For example, on a vote to change the depreciation table, Federal parishes voted 56-10 in the negative (of the ten, four came from the west), while Antifederal parishes and counties voted affirmatively, 40-8, and those divided or shifting on ratification voted 11-10 in the negative. *State Gazette of S.-C.* (Charleston), Mar. 12, 1787.

76. Rush to Ramsay, in Brunhouse, "Ramsay," *Journal of So. Hist.*, 9 (1943), 554; Pinckney in Elliot, ed., *Debates*, IV, 334.

77. In the last year cited, Federal counties east of the Blue Ridge opposed postponement 27-7, Antifederal counties favored it 24-13.

When a question so complex as the ratification of the Constitution is examined, it is to be expected that any generalization will be surrounded by exceptions. If too much attention is devoted to these exceptions, the generalization may become obscured or disguised, if not entirely hidden, so that one may even be mistaken for the other. On the other hand, if the over-all view is to be successfully maintained, and the generalization proved valid, the exceptions must be accounted for. In the case we are considering, it would be too much to contend that the division between commercial and non-commercial elements entirely accounts for the alignment over the Constitution, and even when it is added that a division along class lines is also evident, much remains unexplained.

Along the great arc of the frontier, for example, were two areas which were Federal because of their peculiar circumstances. These are, first, backcountry Georgia, which wanted protection from the Indians, and second, a region including West Virginia, the Shenandoah Valley, and western Pennsylvania, which hoped that a strong central government could drive out the British and Indians. In these areas, military and diplomatic considerations, rather than socio-economic factors, determined a preference for the Constitution. There were also several instances in which the influence of prominent local leaders brought Federalism to unlikely spots. Such was probably the case in northern New Hampshire, Huntingdon and Luzerne counties in Pennsylvania, and parts of Berkshire County in Massachusetts. Another exceptional instance is the strength of Federalism in the interior of Connecticut, which is especially surprising when contrasted with the Antifederalism of Rhode Island; the reasons are to be found in the quite different economic, political, and perhaps even cultural backgrounds of the two areas.[78]

78. Connecticut and Rhode Island did not share quite the same cultural background: orthodox Congregationalism and Episcopalianism in Connecticut exerted a different influence than the more heterodox faiths of Rhode Island. Economically, the farmers of Connecticut seem to have been more prosperous than those of Rhode Island. In Rhode Island, the great anti-impost feeling stimulated by the merchants had predisposed opinion against the Constitution. The merchants, who were changing their minds about centralization, secured political power in 1786, but passed some unpopular

The magnitude of the Antifederalists' victory in New York and their quick defeat in Pennsylvania are equally puzzling; the Hudson was a great commercial highway which should have recruited strength for Federalism in the interior, whereas much of the Quaker state was backcountry and should have adhered to Antifederalism. Here the major explanation lies in contrasting political trends in the two states. In Pennsylvania, the conservative Republicans were increasing in strength, whereas in New York the Clintonian party had governed so successfully that it had never lost control. Special circumstances, like those we have already noted, governed the situation in other states, such as New Jersey, Delaware, and Maryland.

But after all of these facts have been taken into account, we can return to the major generalization: that the struggle over the ratification of the Constitution was primarily a contest between the commercial and the non-commercial elements in the population. This is the most significant fact, to which all else is elaboration, amplification, or exception. The Federalists included the merchants and the other town dwellers, farmers depending on the major cities, and those who produced a surplus for export. The Antifederalists were primarily those who were not so concerned with, or who did not recognize a dependence upon, the mercantile community and foreign markets. Such people were often isolated from the major paths of commerce and usually were less well-to-do because they produced only enough for their own purposes. Because of this basic situation, a majority of the large property holders were Federal, but this division along class lines did not exist in the towns and not everywhere in the country. It was real enough however to find reflections in the political ideas of both sides. Because the Federalists dominated the towns and the rich valleys, they included most of the public and private creditors, great landowners, lawyers and judges, manufacturers and shipowners, higher ranking civil and military officials, and college

---

measures and were promptly repudiated with resultant loss of prestige. In Connecticut, on the other hand, the future Federalists managed to retain the respect of the majority. In Rhode Island the commercial towns were therefore left isolated, whereas they had much backcountry support in Connecticut.

graduates. Although the Antifederalists derived their leadership from such men, the rank and file were men of moderate means, with little social prestige, farmers often in debt, obscure men for the most part.

Antifederal thought was shaped by the composition and objectives of the party, but was modified by the social and political attitudes of the articulate leaders through whom it was expressed. Only a few of these leaders came from the small farmers or truly represented them. They frequently defended views somewhat less democratic than those of their constituents, and they were often out of sympathy with the economic demands of the rank and file, especially in the case of paper money and debtor relief legislation. As a result, Antifederalism as formulated by its most prominent spokesmen sometimes lacks the democratic overtones we have attributed to it.

But the democratic implication existed. As a body of political thought, Antifederalism had a background in English and American political theory long before the Constitution was drafted. Its principles were embodied in the Articles of Confederation; later they were elaborated in the controversy over the impost. Always the emphasis was on local rule and the retention of power by the people, which were democratic tenets in that age. Such a body of thought could of course be used by special interest groups; its bare political doctrine was put forth in opposition to the impost by the merchants of Rhode Island and Massachusetts. But it was always more congenial to the many than the few. Throughout the 1780's, whenever the question of sovereignty arose, the same men representing the same interests rehearsed the arguments they were to employ in debating the Constitution. Although the Antifederalist position was employed to mask special interests, it was fundamentally anti-aristocratic; whoever used its arguments had to speak in terms which implied, if they did not clearly define, a democratic content. It was therefore peculiarly congenial to those who were tending toward democracy, most of whom were soon to rally around Jefferson. The Antifederalists, who lost their only major battle, are forgotten while the victors are remembered, but it is not so certain which is the more memorable.

Appendix A

SEPARATE CONFEDERACIES

The statement is frequently made by historians that the Antifederalists wanted separate confederacies as an alternative to the Constitution. This is probably based on their opposition to the new plan of government, on their belief in state sovereignty, and on the doubts they raised as to the feasibility of centralized government in so extensive a country as the United States. Cited as evidence is the fact that Patrick Henry was believed to have favored such an arrangement. Henry's words do not quite deny it.[1] In addition Luther Martin asserted during the Federal Convention that "he had rather see partial Confederacies take place, than the plan on the table."[2]

The possibility of two, three, or four such confederacies was much talked of, and advocated by several newspaper articles which were widely reprinted in 1787.[3] Possibly some of the Antifederalists favored the idea; however the evidence is very strong that most of the talk about separate confederacies was generated by the other side. Whereas Monroe considered the idea and positively denounced it,[4] Madison discussed it in his letters and did not reject it entirely,[5] and among those who were definitely friendly to the idea were such ardent Nation-

1. Madison to Randolph, Jan. 10, 1788, Hunt, ed., *Writings of Madison,* V, 80-81; John B. Smith to Madison, June 12, 1788, *Doc. Hist. of the Constitution,* IV, 703; Elliot, ed., *Debates,* III, 161.
2. Farrand, ed., *Records of the Federal Convention,* I, 445.
3. "Reason" and "Lycurgus" were published by newspapers in New York, Philadelphia, Hartford, Charleston, Boston, and Baltimore. See also the *Independent Chronicle* (Boston), Feb. 15, 1787; the *New Haven Gazette,* Apr. 26, Nov. 8, 1787; the *Gazette of State of Georgia* (Savannah), quoted in Phillips, "Georgia," Am. Hist. Assn., *Ann. Report,* 1901, II, 18; the *Mass. Centinel* (Boston), Dec. 8, 1787.
4. To Jefferson, Aug. 19, 1786, Burnett, ed., *Letters,* VIII, 445, and to Patrick Henry, Aug. 12, 1786; *ibid.,* 424.
5. Madison to Pendleton, Feb. 24, 1787, Hunt, ed., *Writings of Madison,* II, 319-20.

alists as David Ramsay, Benjamin Lincoln, Theodore Sedgwick, William Bingham, David Humphreys, Rufus King, and Benjamin Rush.[6] The evidence certainly does not warrant the conclusion that the Nationalists as a whole favored such a plan; on the contrary it is clear that only a minority did so, and these principally in the North. But it is equally clear that what little support the idea did receive came more from them than from the Antifederalists.

6.   Ramsay to Jefferson, Apr. 7, 1787, Boyd, ed., *Papers of Jefferson*, XI, 279; King to John Adams, Nov. 2, 1785, Lincoln to King, Feb. 11, 1786, King, *King*, I, 113, 160; Sedgwick to Caleb Strong, Aug. 6, 1786, Burnett, ed., *Letters*, VIII, 415; Bingham in Madison Papers, notes, Feb. 21, 1787, *Doc. Hist. of the Constitution*, IV, 81; Humphreys to Washington, Apr. 9, 1787, Humphreys, *Humphreys*, I, 408; Rush to Richard Price, Oct. 27, 1786, "The Price Letters," Mass. Hist. Soc., *Proceedings*, 2nd Ser., 17 (1903), 353. See also James McClurg to Madison, Aug. 5, 1787, *ibid.*, 471.

Appendix B

THE ANTIFEDERAL MAJORITY
IN VIRGINIA

Most historians have agreed that a majority of Virginians opposed the Constitution.[1] Patrick Henry certainly believed that this was the case.[2] There is also the fact that the legislature was Antifederal in the fall of 1788, as is indicated by the choice of senators and the desire for a new convention.[3] Secondly, the ratifying convention was more Federal than the people, and several delegates voted against the wishes of their constituents.[4] Finally, the total population of the Antifederal counties exceeded that of the Federal. These last two points require further examination.

It has been supposed that as many as fifteen delegates voted for ratification in spite of the Antifederalism of their counties. Actually the number was probably far less. John Marshall's word may be taken that he and Governor Randolph were chosen by an Antifederal county, though it is unusual to find Henrico on that side.[5] Caroline County also opposed ratification but elected Federalists.[6] Humphrey Marshall of Fayette County, Kentucky, admitted that he was instructed to oppose the Constitution.[7] William Ronald of Powhatan was elected as an

1. John Scott, *The Lost Principle* (Richmond, 1860), 102-3, 234-38 (but Scott is unreliable); Grigsby, *Virginia Convention*, I, 41; David John Mays, *Edmund Pendleton*, 2 vols. (Cambridge, 1952), II, 391n.; Beveridge, *Marshall*, I, 381-82.
2. To Lamb, June 9, 1788, Leake, *Lamb*, 307.
3. George Lee Turberville to Madison, Nov. 10, 1788, Madison Papers, N.Y. Pub. Lib.; *Journal of Va. House of Delegates*, 44.
4. Scott, *Lost Principle*, 234-38; Grigsby, *Virginia Convention*, I, 41n.; William Wirt Henry, *Patrick Henry, Life, Correspondence and Speeches*, 3 vols. (New York, 1891), II, 377.
5. Beveridge, *Marshall*, I, 365.
6. Mays, *Pendleton*, II, 202-3.
7. Humphrey Marshall, *The History of Kentucky*, 2 vols. (Frankfort, 1824), I, 287.

Antifederalist but changed his views.[8] As to the remaining supposed examples, proof is lacking. Hart has refuted the claim that the Rockbridge delegates violated their instructions.[9] The prior voting record and the economic interests and personal connections of Levin Powell (Loudon) and Paul Carrington (Charlotte) make it probable, though not of course certain, that they were known to be Federalists at the time of their election. Cole Digges of Warwick, W. O. Callis of Louisa and George Parker of Accomac may have changed their ideas, but there is no proof. We may accept it as proven that in addition to the counties which the final vote showed to have been Antifederal, Henrico, Fayette, Caroline, and Powhatan opposed ratification, but nothing further can be said with certainty.

As it has usually been presented, the proof of an Antifederal majority rests upon dubious methodology. In order to be certain of the result, the actual vote in each county would have to be known. If, for example, the Federalists were narrowly defeated where they lost, but won by large majorities in the counties they carried, then Virginia was Federal. The only votes which have been preserved, however, suggest that Federal as well as Antifederal majorities varied greatly in different counties. In the Piedmont, the Federalists carried Orange by a four to one margin, but the Antifederalists led in Amherst by over twenty to one.[10] Elsewhere, in Powhatan (divided), Henrico (Federal), and Princess Anne (Federal) the results were very close, but the Antifederalists swept Essex by a two and one-half to one margin.[11] Probably the testimony of Henry and others that the Southside was overwhelmingly Antifederal may be accepted, and probably elsewhere east of the Blue Ridge the Federalists may be assumed to have carried their counties by the same margins that the Antifederalists obtained in theirs. In the Shenandoah, the Federalists won by majorities varying from "safe" to "unanimous"; [12] of Kentucky and West Virginia nothing is certainly known. But taking into consideration all of these facts, and estimating the number of eligible voters from a study of the tax records for the various counties, the guess may be hazarded that the Antifederalists included at least 60 per cent and possibly more of the eligible voters.

8. Madison to Jefferson, Apr. 22, 1788, Hunt, ed., *Writings of Madison,* V, 121.
9. Hart, *Valley of Virginia,* 176.
10. Brant, *Madison,* III, 118; *Va. Independent Chronicle* (Richmond), Mar. 12, 1788.
11. Edward Carrington to Madison, Apr. 8, 1788, *Doc. Hist. of the Constitution,* IV, 565-66; *Norfolk Journal,* Mar. 12, 1788; Princess Anne County Deed Book No. 21, 346-54 and Essex County Deed Book No. 33, 108-10, Va. State Lib.
12. Hart, *Valley of Virginia,* 176.

Appendix C

AUTHORSHIP OF ANONYMOUS ARTICLES

A Republican Federalist	James Warren	See Warren, "Gerry"
Helvidius Priscus	James Warren	See Warren, "Gerry"
A Columbian Patriot	Mercy Warren	See Warren, "Gerry"
Agrippa	James Winthrop	See Warren, "Gerry"
Candidus	Benjamin Austin	See Warren, "Gerry"
Sydney	Robert Yates	See Ford, ed., *Essays*
Brutus	Robert Yates	See Ford, ed., *Essays*
Centinel	Samuel or	See Ford, ed., *Essays*
	George Bryan	See Ford, ed., *Essays*
The Plain Dealer	Spencer Roane	See Ford, ed., *Essays*
An Officer of the Late Continental Army	William Findley	See Ford, ed., *Essays*
Cato	George Clinton	See Spaulding, *Clinton*
A Countryman	DeWitt Clinton	See Spaulding, *Clinton*

Appendix D

CHRONOLOGY OF RATIFICATION

	Convention Met	*Division* *	*Final Vote*	*Division*
Delaware	December 3	30-0	December 7	30-0
Pennsylvania	November 21	46-23	December 12	46-23
New Jersey	December 11	39-0	December 18	39-0
Georgia	December 25	—— **	January 2	26-0
Connecticut	January 1	128-40 (?)	January 9	128-40
Massachusetts	January 9	170-190	February 16	187-168
New Hampshire	February 13	30-77	June 21	57-47
Rhode Island	(in March towns voted not to call a convention 16-48) (?)			
Maryland	April 21	62-12	April 26	63-11
South Carolina	May 12	126-98 (?)	May 23	149-73
Virginia	June 2	equal	June 25	89-79
New York	June 17	19-46	July 26	30-27
North Carolina	July 21	75-193	August 4	75-193

* Federal strength is given in the first figure here and on the final division. The first vote is approximate. When the figures on the vote are dubious, it has been indicated with a question mark.

** A large Federal majority was reported.

Appendix E

OCCUPATIONAL TABLES

The following tables showing the occupations of delegates to ratifying conventions are drawn principally from town histories and genealogies.

PENNSYLVANIA

	Federalists		Antifederalists	
Merchants	6		2	
Large manufacturers	3		1	
Lawyers	9		1	
Large landowners	3		0	
Doctors	2		0	
Ministers	2		1	
Total	25	54%	5	22%
Innkeepers	2		1	
Millers	8		4	
Artisans	1		0	
Miscellaneous	4		2	
Total	15	33%	7	30%
Farmers	6	13%	11	48%
Grand Total	46	100%	23	100%

CONNECTICUT

	Federalists		Antifederalists	
Merchants	15		2	
Lawyers	36		3	
Large landowners	5		0	
Doctors	7		1	
Ministers	2		2	
Total	65	51%	8	20%

	Federalists		Antifederalists	
Shopkeepers	1		0	
Innkeepers	4		1	
Surveyors	1		2	
Millers	1		0	
Manufacturers	1		0	
Total	8	6%	3	7½%
Farmers	11		8	
Unknowns	43		21	
Total	54	43%	29	72½%
Grand Total	127	100%	40	100%

NEW HAMPSHIRE

	Federalists		Antifederalists	
Merchants	8		0	
Lawyers	4		3	
Large landowners	5		2	
Doctors	5		2	
Ministers	5		2	
Total	27	47½%	9	19%
Traders	3		1	
Innkeepers	1		1	
Millers	3		6	
Surveyors	1		0	
Ferry owners	1		0	
Total	9	16%	8	17%
Farmers	15		19	
Unknowns	6		11	
Total	21	36½%	30	64%
Grand Total	57	100%	47	100%

Appendix F

Socio-Economic Divisions in Maryland:
Slave Ownership, Geographical Location, and Vote on Paper Money

County	Percentage of families with twenty slaves	Location of county	Position on paper money 1785	Position on paper money 1787
Prince George	16	lower Potomac	for	for
Anne Arundel	10	middle Chesapeake	against	for
Charles	9	lower Potomac	against	against
St. Mary's	8½	lower Potomac	against	against
Queen Anne's	8½	middle Chesapeake	for	for
Dorchester	8	lower Chesapeake	against	against
Talbot	6½	lower Chesapeake	against	against
Calvert	?	lower Chesapeake	for	against
Somerset	?	lower Chesapeake	divided	against
Cecil	6	upper Chesapeake	for	for
Kent	5	middle Chesapeake	for	for
Baltimore	4	upper Chesapeake	for	for
Harford	4	upper Chesapeake	against	for
Worcester	4	eastern	for	for
Frederick	4	western	for	against
Montgomery	4	western	for	for
Caroline	3	eastern	for	against
Washington	2	western	for	for

HISTORIOGRAPHICAL AND BIBLIOGRAPHICAL ESSAY

Modern interpretation of the struggle between Federalists and Anti-federalists began with the publication in 1894 of Orin Grant Libby's *The Geographical Distribution of the vote of the Thirteen States on the Federal Constitution, 1787-1788*, which applied Turner's hypothesis of sectional conflicts to the controversy over ratification. This brief monograph, which still has value, was largely displaced two decades later by Charles A. Beard's *An Economic Interpretation of the Constitution of the United States* (New York, 1913). Beard argued that the Constitution was written by men who held large "personal" as opposed to "real" property (for example, public securities rather than land), who did not believe in democracy, and who wished to protect their economic interests by a government especially designed for the purpose. This position eventually became standard among historians and was supported by a large number of monographs.

Very recently Beard's conclusions have been seriously questioned. Robert E. Brown argues indeed that they were totally invalid. In *Charles Beard and the Constitution: A Critical Analysis of "An Economic Interpretation of the Constitution"* (Princeton, 1956) he points out that although Beard assumed the existence of classes in the new nation he did not prove that they existed; the truth is, Brown insists, that they did not exist. Rather, the country was middle class and democratic. Moreover, Brown declares, the Constitution was written for just such a society. He demonstrates that Beard's methodology was faulty and his research inadequate. Brown did not succeed in proving Beard wrong, for to do so would have required much work in the primary sources, but he did shift the burden of proof and suggested new hypotheses for future research.

An even more substantial criticism was made by Forrest McDonald in *We The People: The Economic Origins of the Constitution* (Chicago, 1958). Whereas Brown refuted Beard on the basis of his own evidence, McDonald introduced much new data. Like Brown, he concluded that the framers of the Constitution represented the country

as a whole, and were not motivated by economic interests characteristic of any particular class or section. Moreover, there was no such
difference as Beard had maintained between Federalists and Antifederalists; instead, both represented the same groups in society.
McDonald has not set forth an alternative theory, contenting himself
(for the moment) with the destruction of previous assumptions.

The result of all this is that everything is reduced to anarchy and
confusion (to borrow Washington's favorite phrase). On the one
hand, Beard can no longer be accepted without serious reservations. On
the other, Brown and McDonald have not entirely destroyed the older
work, nor have they succeeded in replacing it with a fresh view.
McDonald's book in particular has been severely criticized in Jackson
T. Main, "Charles Beard and the Constitution: A Critical Review of
Forrest McDonald's *We The People*," *William and Mary Quarterly*,
3rd Series, 17 (1960), 86-110. Obviously the points in dispute must be
resolved by some hard work. The present volume is a beginning. Although it follows neither Libby nor Beard, it does accept the view that
great property distinctions existed, thus differing from Brown's assertion, and in contrast to McDonald's argument it does find significant
differences between Federalists and Antifederalists. In these respects
it stands closer to Beard than to his detractors. Unfortunately, Lee
Benson's *Turner and Beard: American Historical Writing Reconsidered*
(Chicago, 1960), which is an effort to resolve these contradictions,
became available too late for me to consider here.

The lack of agreement among historians, and the fact that on a
great number of subjects little or nothing has been written, require the
student to depend heavily on primary materials. Manuscripts relevant
to a study of Revolutionary politics and ideas are scattered in scores
of libraries. Especially valuable for this book were the Knox Papers
in the Massachusetts Historical Society, the Bryan Papers and the
Etting, Gratz, and Greer collections in the Historical Society of Pennsylvania, the Samuel Adams Papers and the Emmett Collection in the
New York Public Library, the Lamb Papers in the New York Historical
Society, the Washington and Madison Papers in the Library of Congress, the Wadsworth Papers in the Connecticut State Library and in
the Connecticut Historical Society, and the many unpublished records
contained in the state archives of Massachusetts, New York, and
Virginia.

Newspapers are of fundamental importance, especially because so
many of the Antifederalist writings have not been published. Unfortunately the most valuable ones for a study of Antifederalism are not
yet on microfilm, although the *Providence Gazette* is available. A
special effort should be made to read the *American Herald* and the

Independent Chronicle, both of Boston, the *Massachusetts Gazette* (Springfield), the *New York Journal*, the *New York Gazetteer* (first published in Albany, then in New York), the *Freeman's Journal* and the *Independent Gazetteer* in Philadelphia, and the *Virginia Independent Chronicle* (Richmond).

Many of the state records have been published, and all of the legislative proceedings are now available on microfilm. See William S. Jenkins and Lillian A. Hamrick, eds., *Guide to the Microfilm Collection of Early State Records* (Washington, 1950). Important documentary collections include Edmund Cody Burnett, ed., *Letters of Members of the Continental Congress*, 8 vols. (Washington, 1921-1936); Jonathan Elliot, ed., *The Debates in the Several State Conventions, on the Adoption of the Federal Constitution, . . .*, 5 vols. (Washington, 1854); and Max Farrand, ed., *The Records of the Federal Convention of 1787*, 3 vols. (New Haven, 1911, 1937). Essential to a study of political ideas are the materials in Peter Force, ed., *American Archives*, 4th Series, 6 vols., 5th Series, 3 vols. (Washington, 1837-1856). The writings of very few Antifederal leaders have been published; exceptions are James Curtis Ballagh, ed., *The Letters of Richard Henry Lee*, 2 vols. (New York, 1911-1914), and Harry Alonzo Cushing, ed., *The Writings of Samuel Adams*, 4 vols. (New York, 1904-1908). Many letters are contained in Kate Mason Rowland, *The Life of George Mason*, 2 vols. (New York, 1892). Some criticisms of the Constitution appear in two collections edited by Paul Leicester Ford: *Pamphlets on the Constitution of the United States* and *Essays on the Constitution of the United States* (Brooklyn, 1888, 1892).

Helpful for politics during the Confederation are Julian P. Boyd, ed., *The Papers of Thomas Jefferson*, 13 vols. (in progress, Princeton, 1950 to date); John C. Fitzpatrick, ed., *The Writings of George Washington*, 37 vols. (Washington, 1931-1940); Worthington Chauncey Ford, ed., *Letters of Joseph Jones of Virginia, 1777-1787* (Washington, 1889); Gaillard Hunt, ed., *The Writings of James Madison*, 9 vols. (New York, 1900-1910); J. Franklin Jameson, ed., "Letters of Stephen Higginson, 1783-1804," American Historical Association, *Annual Report*, 1896, vol. I; Charles T. King, ed., *The Life and Correspondence of Rufus King*, 4 vols. (New York, 1894-1897); "Letters of William Plumer, 1786-1787," Colonial Society of Massachusetts, *Transactions*, 11 (1906-1907), 383-403; Griffith J. McRee, *Life and Correspondence of James Iredell, . . .*, 2 vols. (New York, 1858); and "Warren-Adams Letters," Massachusetts Historical Society, *Collections*, 73 (1925). The student of the struggle over ratification should also read William K. Boyd, ed., "News, Letters and Documents Concerning North Carolina and the Federal Constitution," Trinity College Historical Society, *Historical Papers*, 14

(Durham, 1922), 75-95; Worthington C. Ford, ed., "The Federal Constitution in Virginia, 1787-1788," *Massachusetts Historical Society, Proceedings*, 2nd Series, 17 (1903), 450-510; "The Thatcher Papers," *Historical Magazine*, 16 (1869), 257-71, 337-53; and Charles Warren, "Elbridge Gerry, James Warren, Mercy Warren and the Ratification of the Federal Constitution in Massachusetts," *Massachusetts Historical Society, Proceedings*, 64 (1930-1932), 143-64.

Reliable secondary accounts of the period are surprisingly few. For New Hampshire there is nothing at all after 1783, and a more thorough study is needed to replace Richard Francis Upton's *Revolutionary New Hampshire* (Hanover, 1936). A history of Massachusetts is badly needed too. The best account is the article by Robert A. East, "The Massachusetts Conservatives in the Critical Period," Richard B. Morris, ed., *The Era of the American Revolution* (New York, 1939), 349-91. Reliable and helpful are Robert J. Taylor, *Western Massachusetts in the Revolution* (Providence, 1954), and Lee N. Newcomer, *The Embattled Farmers; a Massachusetts Countryside in the American Revolution* (New York, 1953). Also good is Samuel Bannister Harding, *The Contest over the Ratification of the Federal Constitution in the State of Massachusetts* (New York, 1896). For Shays's Rebellion, see Richard B. Morris, "Insurrection in Massachusetts," in Daniel Aaron, ed., *America in Crisis* (New York, 1952), 21-49. None of the books on Rhode Island do the job properly and it is best to start with Hillman Metcalf Bishop, "Why Rhode Island Opposed the Federal Constitution," *Rhode Island History*, 8 (1949), 1-10, 33-44, 85-95, 115-26. There is not even a good article to help one study Connecticut. Altogether it is amazing to find that so little has been done on the New England states, especially when the published primary sources are so good and the libraries so full.

The situation is better in the middle states. Excellent are Richard P. McCormick, *Experiment in Independence: New Jersey in the Critical Period, 1783-1789* (New Brunswick, 1950), and John A. Munroe, *Federalist Delaware, 1775-1815* (New Brunswick, 1954). Neither E. Wilder Spaulding, *New York in the Critical Period, 1783-1789* (New York, 1932), nor Thomas Childs Cochran, *New York in the Confederation; An Economic Study* (Philadelphia, 1932), are complete accounts of the period but together they cover New York's politics quite well. Robert L. Brunhouse, *The Counter-Revolution in Pennsylvania, 1776-1790* (Harrisburg, 1942), is good on politics but weak on the economic and social background. Much primary material is published in John B. McMaster and Frederick D. Stone, *Pennsylvania and the Federal Constitution, 1787-1788* (Lancaster, 1888). Philip A. Crowl furnishes a thorough and reliable account of Maryland's politics in *Maryland During and After the Revolution: A Political and Economic Study* (Baltimore, 1943), and "Anti-Federalism in Maryland, 1787-1788," *William and Mary Quarterly*, 3rd Series, 4 (1947), 446-69.

Farther south, there is great need for a book on Virginia in the Confederation. Meanwhile see W. A. Low, "Merchant and Planter Relations in Post-Revolutionary Virginia, 1783-1789," *Virginia Magazine of History and Biography*, 61 (1953), 308-18; Jackson T. Main, "Sections and Politics in Virginia, 1781-1787," *William and Mary Quarterly*, 3rd Series, 12 (1955), 96-112; Irving Brant, *James Madison the Nationalist, 1780-1787* (New York, 1948); Freeman H. Hart, *The Valley of Virginia in the American Revolution, 1763-1789* (Chapel Hill, 1942); and David John Mays, *Edmund Pendleton*, 2 vols. (Cambridge, 1952). The ratification in North Carolina has been discussed by Louise Irby Trenholme, *The Ratification of the Federal Constitution in North Carolina* (New York, 1932), and William C. Pool, "An Economic Interpretation of the Ratification of the Federal Constitution in North Carolina," *North Carolina Historical Review*, 27 (1950), 119-41, 289-313, 437-61, but neither are entirely satisfactory and a detailed account of the period is sorely needed. Charles Gregg Singer, *South Carolina in the Confederation* (Philadelphia, 1941), should be replaced by a work more detailed and broader in scope. For Georgia, see Kenneth Coleman, *The American Revolution in Georgia, 1763-1789* (Athens, 1958). William W. Abbot, "The Structure of Politics in Georgia: 1782-1789," *William and Mary Quarterly*, 3rd Series, 14 (1957), 47-65, is excellent.

For general background, the basic account is Merrill Jensen, *The New Nation* (New York, 1950). Indispensable guides to the economic history of the era are Robert A. East, *Business Enterprise in the American Revolutionary Era* (New York, 1938), and E. James Ferguson, *The Power of the Purse* (Chapel Hill, 1961). Allan Nevins, *The American States During and After the Revolution, 1775-1789* (New York, 1924), though now superseded at many points, contains much detail. The political ideas of the "Federalists" have yet to be fully examined. See Merrill Jensen, "The Idea of a National Government During the American Revolution," *Political Science Quarterly*, 58 (1943), 356-79. Cecelia M. Kenyon reaches conclusions different from those presented here in "Men of Little Faith: The Anti-Federalists on the Nature of Representative Government," *William and Mary Quarterly*, 3rd Series, 12 (1955), 3-43. The basic political doctrine out of which Antifederalism developed is best studied in two first-rate works: Merrill Jensen, "Democracy and the American Revolution," *Huntington Library Quarterly*, 20 (1957), 321-41, and Elisha P. Douglass, *Rebels and Democrats* (Chapel Hill, 1955).

Index

"A. B.," 115
Adams, Charles Francis, 259
Adams, John, 3, 62, 87, 104
Adams, John Quincy, 133, 174-75
Adams, Samuel, 9, 14, 109, 152, 169; political ideas of, 115, 122, 201, 205, 257
"Agrarius," 174
"Agricola," 75, 110
Agricultural interest, 35, 50, 65, 86, 87, 88-89, 91
Agriculture, commercial, 5
"Agrippa" (James Winthrop), 182, 287
Albany, N.Y., 48, 98-99, 234-35, 240-41, 267
Albany Antifederal Committee, 139, 173, 181
Albany County, N.Y., 48, 50, 240
Albany Gazette, 234
Albany Plan, 15
Albemarle County, Va., 12, 29, 232
Albemarle Sound, 33, 242, 274
Alexandria, Va., 30, 70, 267
"Alleghany" region, Va., 1, 30, 32, 273. *See also* West Virginia
Amendments, to Constitution, 161-62, 175, 222, 227, 255; on presidency, 141-42; on tax power, 145-46; on army, 148; on elections, 151; on ten-mile area, 152; on judiciary, 157. *See also* under individual states, ratification in
American Herald, 251
Amherst County, Va., 225-26
"Amicus Patriae," 114
Annapolis, Md., 267
Annapolis Convention, 114
Anne Arundel County, Md., 38, 39, 215
Appalachian Mountains, 14
Appointments, power over, 139, 141-42
Aristocracy, 44, 77; feared, 66, 78, 81, 103-4, 129-34, 150; favored, 104; in Senate, 137, 138
Armstrong, John, 273

Army, power over, 14, 16, 72, 122, 141-42, 144, 146-48, 151; fear of, 15, 74, 81, 106; and politics, 44
Arnold, Jonathan, 88
Articles of Confederation, 15, 16-17; effort to strengthen, 72, 103; terms of, 73, 79, 105, 106, 128, 136, 142, 161; defended, 77, 83, 138, 185; inadequacy of, 113, 114, 117, 180; in Antifederalist thought, 281
Artisans, 41, 70; and mechanics, 48, 99, 190, 191, 193, 219, 248, 270, 274-75. *See also* Mechanics
Ashfield, Mass., 13
Ashmead, Samuel, 192
Atherton, Joshua, 152, 157, 221-22
Athol, Mass., 57
Atkinson, N.H., 68
Augusta, Ga., 37
Austin, Benjamin, 201; as "Candidus," 287

Backcountry, of S.C., 22-28
Backus, Isaac, 261
Bacon, John, 202
Baltimore, Md., 30, 38, 267
Baltimore County, Md., 215
Bank of New York, 48-49, 242
Bank of North America, 42, 44-46
Baptists, 225, 230, 260-61
Barnstable County, Mass., 55
Barrell, Nathaniel, 177, 203-4, 254, 257
Barrington, N. H., 67
Bartlett, Josiah, 222
Bayard family, 48
Beccaria, Marquis di, 80
Belknap, Jeremy, 163
Bellingham, Mass., 87
Benson, Egbert, 48
Berkeley County, Va., 229
Berks County, Pa., 190
Berkshire County, Mass., 60, 202-3
Berthoff, Baron de Beelen, 76-77
Bethlehem, Pa., 192

Bill of Rights, in state constitutions, 19. *See also* Constitution, U.S.

Bingham, William, 47, 284

Bishop, Phanuel, 116

Bland, Theodorick, 224, 227

Bloodworth, Timothy, 35, 36, 37; political ideas of, 113, 135, 172, 181, 243-44; on aristocracy, 132-33

Blount, William, 34

Blount Papers, 34

Blue Ridge, 29, 32

Bodman, William, 144

Boston, Mass., 44, 61, 70, 87, 268; and impost, 85, 86, 87

Bowdoin, James, 60, 61, 136

Bristol, R.I., 212

Bristol County, Mass., 55

British trading posts, 31, 33

British treaty, 32, 35, 229-31

Brown, John, 88

Brown, Nicholas, 88, 89

Brown family, 248

Brown University, 88

"Brutus" (Robert Yates), 61, 129, 154, 234, 287

Bryan, Arthur, 216

Bryan, George, 114, 190, 191, 193, 197, 273; on amendments, 161; admits need for reform, 256; on Pennsylvania ratification, 267, 277; as "Centinel," 287

Bryan, Samuel, 110; as "Centinel," 173, 287

Bucks County, Pa., 41

Budd, Dr. John, 266

Burke, Aedanus, 107, 133-34, 217-20, 254, 266-67

Burgh, James, 8-14, 19, 77

Burr, Aaron, 237-38

Cabarrus, Stephen, 34

Cabells, the, 224

Calhoun, Patrick, 171

Callis, W. O., 286

Calvert County, Md., 38

Camden County, S.C., 28

"Candidus" (Benjamin Austin), 287

Cape Cod, Mass., 55

Cape Fear River, 242

Carlisle, Pa., 189, 267

Carlisle Gazette, 188-89

Caroline County, Va., 285

Carrington, Edward, 224

Carrington, Paul, 286

"Cato" (George Clinton), 10, 12, 13, 14, 19, 234, 287

"Centinel" (George or Samuel Bryan), 170, 188, 235, 287

Centralization, fear of, 15, 103

Charles County, Md., 38, 39

Charleston, N.H., 211

Charleston, R.I., 212

Charleston, S.C., 21-22, 28, 37, 70, 96, 251; opposition to Morris, 44; and ratification, 217-20; Federalists in, 266-67; class conflicts in, 268

Chase, Samuel, 132, 175, 213

Checks and balances, 13, 16

Chesapeake Bay, 38, 39, 41

Cheshire County, N.H., 65

Chesnut, John, 257

Chester County, Pa., 41

Cincinnati, Society of, 63, 107, 109, 191, 208

"Cincinnatus," 124, 137, 160, 165, 174, 179

Clark, Abraham, 195, 257

Class, structure, 2-5; upper, 3-4, 132; middle, 4-6; lower, 4, 105; urban, 70; and ratification, 261-68. *See also* under individual states

Clay, Charles, 261

Clergy, 198. *See also* Ministers

Clinton, DeWitt, as "A Countryman," 287

Clinton, George, 48, 173, 234, 250, 251, 267, 287; and impost, 97-98; political ideas of, 113, 118, 138, 148; as "Cato," 287

Clintonians, 48-50, 272, 280

Cochran, Thomas, 240, 272

Collectors, of impost, 74, 81, 90 93, 98

College men, 223, 242, 263

Collins, John, 257

"A Columbian Patriot" (Mercy Warren), 235, 287

Commerce, 47, 106, 110-11, 149, 181-82; in Va., 29, 30; in Md., 38; in R.I., 52, 76; in Ga., 196; in Shenandoah Valley, 230; in N.C., 246

Commercial interest, 69-70, 100, 270-74, 280; in N.C., 35, 242, 246-47; in N.Y., 50, 240; in Mass., 86, 87; in R.I., 88-90, 213, 248; in Pa., 193; in N.H., 222-23

Commercial powers, 273

Commutation, 86-92 *passim*

Confederacies, separate, 169, 283-84

Confederation, preferred by Antifederalists, 80, 121, 137

Confederation, Articles of. *See* Articles of Confederation

Conflicts, social, and the Constitution, 266. *See also* Class
Congregationalists, 260
Congress, powers of, 15, 16, 47, 79, 84, 106, 110-11, 184, 231; requests funds, 26, 44, 45 58, 73; and Shays's Rebellion, 63; members favor ratification, 263-64
Connecticut, 6, 11, 17, 51-52, 107-9, 276; paper money in, 52, 91, 198, 200; and impost, 90-92, 200; and ratification, 198-200, 269, 289-90. *See also* Commercial interest; Debtors
Connecticut Courant, 198
Connecticut Gazette, 198
Connecticut River, 55, 58, 60, 69, 70, 86, 87, 199; and ratification, 206, 221, 271
Conscience, rights of, 154
Consolidation, fear of, 75
Constitution, U.S., 9, 72, 109, 121, 149, 279; objections to, 77, 120-29, 133-34, 136-58, 161; attitudes toward ratification, 119-20, 264-65, 277-78, 288; ambiguity, 126, 153-55; and democracy, 129-34, 169-76; and Bill of Rights, 158-61; economic aspects, 162-67; Antifederalists vote for, 177. *See also* Securities, public; Debt, public; under individual states
Constitutionalists, in Pennsylvania, 42-47, 97, 170, 188, 190
Constitutions, state. *See* under individual states
Convention, recommended in 1785, 103; second proposed, 178, 189, 213, 227, 239, 285. *See also* under individual states; Federal Convention
Convention, Philadelphia. *See* Federal Convention
Corbin, Francis, 227
"A Countryman" (DeWitt Clinton), 287
County Journal (Poughkeepsie), 234
Courts, federal, 164
Creditors, 32, 84, 162-67, 191, 195, 275-77
Crowl, Philip, 215, 269
Cumberland County, Me., 65
Cummins, Rev., 219-20, 257
Currency. *See* Money, Paper Money
Cuyler family, 48

Daily Advertiser, 61, 104
Dane, Nathan, 112, 172, 176, 201, 257
Davie, William R., 34

Debt, 7, 19; federal, 7, 46-47, 73, 75, 82, 83, 84, 89, 91, 145, 275-77; state, 7, 26, 46-47, 52-59 *passim*, 66, 91, 163, 194, 195
Debtor laws, 164, 278
Debtors, 70, 262-67, 277-78; in S.C., 25, 26-27, 217, 220; in Va., 32, 33; in N.C., 36; in Md., 39; in Conn., 52; in R.I., 53; in N.H., 66, 211, 222; in N.Y., 240
Debts, 6; private, 7, 164-67, 277-78; in S.C., 24-25; in N.C., 35; in R.I., 53; in Mass., 55, 56, 59; in N.H., 65; in Md., 215; pre-war, in Va., 31, 33; British, 32, 36, 165-66, 229-30; public, 162-64, 275-77; in N.C., 35
Declaration of Independence, 259
Delaware, 18, 50, 193-94, 249, 273; and impost, 97
Delaware River, 194, 272
Democracy, 11, 13, 49, 108, 263; and government, 129, 135, 156; and Whig tradition, 8; and suffrage, 14, 17; in state constitutions, 19; in S.C., 24; in Pa., 42; in Mass., 63; opposed, 104, 105, 116-17; defended, 80, 118; and Antifederalists, 129-34, 169-76, 184, 281
"Democritus," 10, 79
Depression, 31-32, 35, 49, 51, 53, 56; minimized, 178-80
Derryfield, N.H., 211
Despotism, 142
Dickinson, John, 47
Digges, Cole, 286
Dobbs County, N.C., 243-44
Doctors, 208, 258, 270
Dollard, Patrick, 181
Dorchester County, Md., 38, 39
Dorchester, Guy Carleton, Lord, 163, 238
Dorpalen, Andreas, 261
Dover, N.H., 222, 268
Drowne, Solomon, 88
Duane, James, 48
Dukes County, Mass., 55
Dutch loan, 179
Dutchess County, N.Y., 47, 240
Dwight, Timothy, 202

East, Robert A., 203
Easton, Pa., 41, 192, 267
Edenton, N.C., 33, 70, 242, 246, 267
Edgecomb County, N.C., 245, 246
Elections, 12, 140, 149-51; annual, 16, 18, 42, 43, 135, 136
Electoral college, 140

Ellsworth, Oliver, 163
Enfield, Conn., 115
Entail, 19
Episcopalians, 41, 47, 192, 261
Epping, N.H., 211
Essex County, Mass., 55, 60
Essex County, Va., 286
Executive, 13, 16, 18
Exeter, N.H., 66

Fairfield, Conn., 91
Fairfield County, Conn., 51, 199
Fall line, 29
"A Farmer" (David Howell), 122, 164,
    180
Farmers, 4-8, 45, 61, 109, 112, 266;
    small, 39, 40; subsistence, 2, 271-74;
    in Va., 29, 30, 233; in S.C., 26-28,
    216, 219-20; in N.C., 33, 34-35, 36,
    242; commercial, 40, 271; in Pa., 41,
    46, 191; in N.Y., 48, 49, 240; in
    Conn., 52, 200; in R.I., 53; in Mass.,
    64, 86, 87; non-commercial, 70; and
    impost, 75, 100; in N.H., 223
Farmington, Conn., 107, 108-9
Fayette County, Va., 225, 228, 285
Fayssoux, Peter, 218, 257
Federal Convention, 114-18, 119, 121,
    126, 140, 163, 212, 252
Federal Republican Committee, 221,
    226, 235-36, 244, 252
Federalism, nature of, 127, 280; in
    Pa., 191-92; in Del., 194; in N.J.,
    195; in Conn., 198-200; in N.H.,
    211, 222-23; in Md., 215; in S.C.,
    216-19; in R.I., 256
Federalist Papers, 153-54, 236
Federalists, ideas of, 119-20, 121; and
    support, 4, 252-59 passim; and Whig
    tradition, 8; in Va., 92, 226-33; de-
    fend Constitution, 126-27, 151, 153;
    and bill of rights, 158; promise
    amendments, 161, 255; and creditors,
    164; and democracy, 171, 172-73;
    objectives of, 177-78; take initiative,
    185; in Pa., 187-88, 189, 192; in
    Mass., 201-9; in R.I., 212; in N.H.,
    221-22; in N.Y., 234-37; in N.C., 245
Fees, 7, 59
Finances, state, 37
Findley, William, 12, 43, 47; political
    ideas of, 136, 138, 154, 161, 180; on
    aristocracy, 132; denies emergency,
    178; as "An Officer of the Late Con-
    tinental Army," 287
Forrest, Uriah, 258
Foster, Theodore, 88

Franklin, Benjamin, 190, 253
Franklin, Mass., 87
Franklin County, Pa., 189, 190
Frederick County, Va., 225, 229
Fredericksburg, Va., 267
Freeman's Journal, 188
Frontier, 1, 30, 33, 37, 279
Fryeburg, Me., 122

Galloway, James, 181
Gardner, William, 166
"General welfare" clause, 122, 124-25,
    154-55
Georgia, 1, 17-18, 37, 110, 218, 252;
    and impost, 74, 96-97, 196; and rati-
    fication, 195-97; Federal majority in,
    249; economic interest of, 274. See
    also Commerce, Indians
"A Georgian," 156
Germans, 42, 192, 261
Gerry, Elbridge, 103, 116-17, 121, 198,
    201; political ideas of, 111, 113, 122;
    and democracy, 171; moderate Anti-
    federalist, 177
Gillon, Alexander, 22, 216, 266
Gilman, John, 222
Gilman, Nicholas, 210
Gloucester, Mass., 61
Goforth, shoemaker, 50
Gordon, Thomas, 8-14
Gordon, William, 20
Gorham, Nathaniel, 203
Goudy, William, 127, 150-51
Governors, favor ratification, 263-64
Grayson, William, 113, 224, 226
Great Barrington, Mass., 202
Greene, Nathanael, 95

Habersham, Joseph, 196
Hagerstown, Md., 41
Half-pay, 106
Halifax, N.C., 242, 246, 267
Halifax County, N.C., 245
Hamilton, Alexander, 48, 112, 116, 238,
    253
"Hampden," 94
Hampshire County, Mass., 55, 59
Hancock, John, 60, 61, 85, 86; and
    Constitution, 201, 205-6, 209, 257
Hancock, N.H., 211
Harford County, Md., 215
Harrington, James, 10
"Harrington," 105
Harrisburg, Pa., 41
Harrison, Benjamin, 75-76, 113, 147-
    48, 149, 224; influence of, 227
Hart, Freeman H., 230, 286

Harvard, Mass., 61, 121, 180-81
Hatfield, Mass., 55
Hawkins, Benjamin, 34
"Helvidius Priscus" (James Warren), 201n, 287
Henrico County, Va., 285, 286
Henry, Patrick, 2-3, 166, 184, 251, 283, 285; and impost, 75, 93, 94, 100; admits need for reform, 113, 181; on democracy, 131; opposes ratification, 223; influence of, 227
Herald (Philadelphia), 250
Higginson, Stephen, 63, 104
Hillsboro County, N.H., 65
Hillsborough, N.C., 36, 267
Holten, Samuel, 103, 257
Hopper, William, 171
Hopkins, Joseph, 199
Hopkinton, N.H., 211
House of Representatives, U.S., 134-36
Howell, David, 81, 88, 110. *See also* "A Farmer"
Hudson, N.Y., 267
Hudson Gazette, 234
Hudson River, 70
Hughes, Hugh, 9-10
Humphreys, David, 62, 284
Huntingdon County, Pa., 189, 190, 279

Impeachment, 139
Impost, 81, 82, 107, 183; 5 per cent, 71, 72-102, 106, 127; significance in Antifederalist thought, 281. *See also* under individual states
"Independens," 92
Independent Gazette, 188
Indians, 31, 229; in Ga., 37, 197
Iredell, James, 34, 35
Izard, Ralph, 95-96, 169, 171-72

Jackson, Henry, 204
Jackson, Jonathan, 171, 207
James River, 28, 29, 30, 32, 92, 230, 232; valley, 111
Jamestown, R.I., 212
Jarvis, Charles, 205, 257
Jay, John, 3, 48, 61, 238
Jefferson, Thomas, 281
"John DeWitt," 179-80
"John Humble," 156
Johnson, Thomas, 213-14, 257
"Jonathan of the Valley," 110, 115
Jones, Joseph, 93, 113, 177, 224
Jones, Samuel, 235, 239, 256
Jones, Willie, 35, 243, 244

Judges, in Pa., 18-19, 191; in Conn., 200; in Mass., 208; in S.C., 219; favor ratification, 263; in N.C., 275
Judiciary, 13, 19, 42, 43; under Articles of Confederation, 16; under Constitution, 122, 124, 125, 155-58, 184
Jury, trial by, 159-60
Justices of the peace, 19

Kent County, Md., 38
Kentucky, 1, 31, 225, 226, 228, 286
Killingworth, Conn., 107
King, Rufus, 58, 62, 104, 198, 202, 207, 284; and democracy, 171
Kings County, N.Y., 48, 99, 237, 239, 260
Kingston, N.Y., 235
Kinlock, Francis, 142
Knox, Henry, 62, 63, 163, 176, 207

Lafayette, Marquis de, 63
Lamb, John, 132, 133, 175, 217, 235; admits need for reform, 181; correspondence, 218, 236, 244
Lancaster, Pa., 192, 267
Lancaster County, Pa., 41
Land, cost of, 6; prices in Georgia, 37; western, 246-47, 270
Landholders, large, 258; in N.Y., 48, 241-42; in Pa., 191; in Conn., 200
Langdon, John, 222
Lansing, John, 116-17, 121, 128-29, 234
Lansingburgh, N.Y., 267
Laurens, Henry, 25, 216
Lawyers, 21, 254, 258, 263. *See also* under individual states, politics and ratification of
Lawrence, Nathaniel, 239
Lear, Tobias, 222
Ledlie, Hugh, 109, 199
Lee, Henry, 62, 227
Lee, Richard Henry, 15, 173, 175, 187, 198; and freedom of press, 160; and democracy, 169, 172; moderate Antifederalist, 177; opposes ratification, 223; influence of, 227
Lee, Silas, 154, 160, 258-59
"Legion," 115
Lenoir, William, 127, 243
Libbey, Jeremiah, 163
Libby, Orin Grant, 268
Liberty, 8, 14-15, 19, 147, 158; loss of feared, 78, 80, 82; endangered by Constitution, 129, 133-34, 142
Lincoln, Benjamin, 61, 284
Lincoln, James, 133, 160, 216

Lincoln County, Me., 65
Litchfield County, Conn., 52
Little Compton, R.I., 212
Livermore, Samuel, 222
Livingston, Gilbert, 151, 177
Livingston family, 48
Lloyd, John, 25, 105
Locke, John, 13
Locke, Matthew, 166
Long, Pierse, 222
Long Island, 48
Low Country, S.C., 22-28
Lowndes, Rawlins, 149, 166, 216-17
Loyalists. *See* Tories
Luzerne County, Pa., 188, 190, 252, 279
"Lycurgus," 156, 173-74

McCallen, Robert, 236
Maclaine, Archibald, 34, 35, 75
McCormick, Richard N., 194-95, 276
M'Dowall, Joseph, 130
McHenry, James, 214
Madison, James, 69, 96, 153-54, 211, 247, 283; influence of, 227
Maine, 1, 58, 60, 64-65, 206-7, 271
Manufacturing, 41, 56, 191, 208, 263
Marlborough, N.H., 68
Marshall, Humphrey, 257, 285
Marshall, John, 131, 227, 276, 285
Martha's Vineyard, 55
Martin, Gov. Alexander, 36
Martin, Luther, 117, 121, 166, 181, 213-14, 283
Maryland, 7, 236, 252, 291; senate of, 18; politics in, 37-39, 273; constitution of, 38; slaves in, 38, 291; planters in, 38-39; paper money in, 39, 215, 291; classes in, 39; sections in, 39, 215, 291; and impost, 73, 74, 96; and ratification, 142, 145, 149, 185, 213-15, 218, 227, 269. *See also* Commerce, Debtors, Debts
Mason, George, 116-17, 172, 236, 239, 251; political ideas of, 94, 113, 121, 123, 125, 135, 149, 151-52, 154, 160, 177, 223-24, 227; and democracy, 131, 171, 175
Mason, Thomson, 11
Massachusetts, 6, 18, 55-65, 103, 107, 249; sections, 55, 59; taxes in, 55, 56, 58, 59; merchants of, 56, 207, 208; lawyers of, 57; paper money in, 59, 87, 268; constitution of, 59, 60, 63; and impost, 73, 74, 85-88; and ratification, 131, 136, 145, 200-9, 210, 221, 255, 268; classes in, 207-9.

See also Commercial interest, Debts, Shays's Rebellion
Massachusetts Centinel, 56
"A Mechanic," 46
Mechanics, 56, 219, 248. *See also* Artisans
Medway, Mass., 87
Mercantile interest, 5, 48, 65, 194, 270-74. *See also* Commercial interest
Merchants, 61, 70, 100, 258, 270; British, 31; Antifederal, 254. *See also* under individual states
Mercer, John Francis, 113, 116-17, 121, 158, 166, 262-63; and democracy, 175; opposes ratification, 213-15
Meredith, N. H., 211
Middlesex County, Mass., 55, 59, 60
Middlesex Gazette, 198
Middletown, Conn., 109
Ministers, 208
Minot, George Richards, 121, 136, 202-4
Mississippi River, 31, 139, 225, 228, 229, 245
Monarchy, favored, 104, 142, 168
Money, 5, 139; shortage of, 35, 52, 53, 56, 59. *See also* Paper money
Monopolies, 153
Monroe, James, 15, 113, 131, 140, 224, 283
Montesquieu, Baron de, 80
Montgomery County, N.Y., 48, 235
Montgomery County, Pa., 41, 272
Morning Post (New York), 234, 250
Morris, Gouverneur, 118, 253
Morris, Robert, 44-46, 74, 87, 94-95, 100, 226, 253
Morris family, 48
Munroe, John A., 194

Nantucket County, Mass., 55
Narragansett Bay, 52, 54; politics of, 88-90, 213, 248, 272
Nash County, N.C., 242, 245
Nationalists, 84, 107, 117. *See also* Federalists
"Necessary and proper" clause, 122, 124, 125, 154-55
Nelson, Gen. Thomas, 224
"Nestor," 113
Netherlands, the, 80
New Bern, N.C., 33, 70, 242, 246, 267
New Braintree, Mass., 61
Newburyport, Mass., 202
New Hampshire, 6, 65-69, 236, 249, 279; and impost, 92, 101; and secession, 65, 222; sections of, 65, 221-23; and ratification, 145, 210-12, 221-23,

233, 237, 268-69, 290. *See also* Commercial interest, Debtors, Debts
New-Hampshire Spy, 251-52
New Hanover County, N.C., 36
New Haven, Conn., 70
New Haven Gazette, 198
New Jersey, 7, 18, 50, 182, 249, 273; and impost, 97, 101, 195; and ratification, 194-95, 276; taxes in, 195
New Jersey Plan, 117. *See also* Paterson Plan
New London, Conn., 70, 91
Newport, R.I., 52, 88-89, 212
Newspapers, pro-Federalist, 201, 204, 210, 214, 215, 217, 221; delay in circulation, 234, 249, 250
New York, 47-50, 116, 249, 272, 280; classes in, 48-50, 240; merchants of, 48, 98-99, 241-42; sections of, 48-50, 99; paper money in, 49-50, 74, 98, 99; and the impost, 76, 97-99, 239; and ratification, 141-42, 146, 152, 157, 185, 213, 226, 233-42, 269; and secession, 238-39. *See also* Commercial interest, Debtors
New York City, 48-50, 70, 98-99, 234-40 *passim*, 269
New York Journal, 234, 236
Nicholas, George, 227
Non-commercial interest, 69-70, 271-74, 280. *See also* Agricultural interest
Norfolk, Va., 70, 267
Northampton, Pa., 267
Northampton County, N.C., 245
Northampton County, Pa., 41, 272
North Carolina, 2, 17, 33-36, 94, 116, 236; taxes in, 5, 35; Piedmont of, 34, 35, 243; land speculators in, 34, 245; sections of, 35-36, 242-48; planters in, 36, 244-45; and impost, 96; and ratification, 130, 142, 145, 149, 152, 185, 242-48, 269; political alignment of, 249, 252, 274, 275. *See also* Commerce, Commercial interest, Debtors, Debts
Northern Neck, Va., 29, 30, 32, 33, 38, 92, 111; and ratification, 225, 231-32
Northumberland County, Pa., 189, 190
Northwest Territory, 31
Norwich, Conn., 91, 108

Office-holding, qualifications for, 13, 18, 38
"An Officer of the Late Continental Army" (William Findley), 287
Officers' pay, 74, 86, 90-91, 198, 208, 219, 263-64

"An Old Whig," 188
Orange County, N.Y., 47
Orange County, N.C., 14
Orange County, Va., 29, 232, 286
Osgood, Samuel, 104, 152, 201, 203, 257
Oswald, Eleazar, 226
Otto, Louis, 63, 76, 112, 178

Paca, William, 213-14, 257
Pamico Sound, 33, 242
Pamunkey River, 28
Paper money, 7, 100, 165-67, 268-70. *See also* under states
Pardon, power of, 141-42
Parker, George, 286
Paterson Plan, 185. *See also* New Jersey Plan
Payne, Elisha, 222
Pendleton, Edmund, 224, 227
Pendleton, Henry, 257
Pennsylvania, 41-47, 170, 272-73; constitution of, 12, 17-18, 19-20, 42-43; merchants of, 41, 191; west, 42, 46; and impost, 47, 97, 101; test oath, 48; and ratification, 131, 132, 187-94, 276, 277, 289; and Antifederalists, 136, 189-93, 280. *See also* Commercial interest, Constitutionalists, Republicans
Person, Thomas, 96, 243, 244
Peterborough, N.H., 211
Petersburgh, Va., 267
Petersham, Mass., 13-14
Pettit, Charles, 61
Phelps, Oliver, 203
Philadelphia, 41-47, 70, 190-92, 253, 267
Philadelphia convention. *See* Federal Convention
Philadelphia County, Pa., 41, 272
"Philadelphiensis" (Benjamin Workman?), 180
"Philanthropos," 174
Pickering, John, 222
Pickering, Timothy, 188
Piedmont, 100. *See also* North Carolina, Virginia
Pinckney, Charles, 278
Pittsburgh, Pa., 41, 192, 193, 267
Pittsburgh Gazette, 189
"The Plain Dealer" (Spencer Roane), 287
Planters, 2, 254, 266. *See also* under individual states
"Plato," 162
Platt, Zephaniah, 256

Plymouth County, Mass., 55, 60
Pool, William C., 244-46
Portsmouth, N.H., 69, 70, 222, 268
Posts, western, 229-30
Potomac River, 28, 29, 30, 70, 230, 232
Poughkeepsie, N.Y., 233
Powell, Levin, 286
Power, fear of, 9-10, 11, 76, 93, 115, 127-29, 150; reservation of, 10, 14, 16, 19, 124, 125
Powhatan County, Va., 29, 286
Presbyterians, 230, 261
President, U.S., 119, 140-42, 146, 184
Press, freedom of, 125, 154, 160-61
Price, Richard, 170-71
Prince Edward County, Va., 94
Prince Frederick Parish, S.C., 219
Prince George's County, Md., 38
Princess Anne County, Va., 286
Providence, R.I., 52, 88-89, 212
Providence Gazette, 88
Public securities. *See* Securities, public

Quakers, 41, 42, 43, 48, 192, 261
Queen Anne's County, Md., 38
Queens County, N.Y., 48, 99, 239-40, 269

Ramsay, David, 95, 217, 284
Randal, Benjamin, 144
Randolph, Edmund, 76, 93, 105, 116-17, 131, 285; and democracy, 171; criticizes Constitution, 224; influence of, 227; converted to Federalism, 256-57; as public creditor, 276
Rappahannock River, 28, 29, 32, 232
"A *real* Federalist," 185
Recall, 16, 138, 184
Redick, David, 118, 176, 187-88
Reed, Joseph, 11
Religion, freedom of, 159, 230; and ratification, 260
Remsen, Henry, 277
"A Republican," 234
"A Republican Federalist" (James Warren), 287
Republicans, of Pennsylvania, 42-47, 188, 190, 280
Requisitions, 17, 73, 82, 144, 182-84
Responsibility, of U.S. Senate, 138, 139; of officials, 184
Revolution, American, 11, 15, 41
Richmond, Va., 70
Rhode Island, 6, 7, 17, 53-54, 116, 146, 251; politics in, 52-54; and impost, 53, 73, 74, 88-90; and paper money in, 89, 90; and democracy,

169; rejects Constitution, 212-13; and ratification, 248; Antifederalists in, 249, 279; Federalism in, 267; alignment in, 271-72. *See also* Commerce, Commercial interest, Debtors, Debts
Richmond County, N.Y., 48, 99, 237, 239, 260
Riots, during 1780's, 6-7
Rittenhouse, David, 190
Roane, Spencer, 150; as "The Plain Dealer," 287
Rochester, Mass., 87
Rockbridge County, Va., 286
Ronald, William, 224, 256-57, 285-86
Rotation in office, 12-13, 16, 18, 140-41; opposed, 113; defended, 136, 184; in Senate, 137-38
"Rough Hewer" (Abraham Yates, Jr.), 78*n*, 98
Ruffin, Edmund, 224
Rush, Benjamin, 190, 278, 284
"Rusticus," 174

St. John's (Colleton) Parish, S.C., 27
St. Mary's County, Md., 38, 39
Salaries, and farmers, 7; of S.C. governor, 24; of U.S. Congress, 153
Salem, Mass., 61
Salisbury, N.H., 211
Salisbury, N.C., 36, 246, 267
Savannah, Ga., 37, 70
Savannah and Edisto District, S.C., 219
Savannah River, 196, 274
Schenectady, N.Y., 236
Schuyler family, 48
Schoharie, N.Y., 236
Scotch-Irish, 192
Secession. *See* New Hampshire, New York
Sectionalism, 291. *See also* under individual states
Sections, in South, 40. *See also* under individual states
Securities, public, in R.I., 53; and Constitution, 162-64; and Federalists, 208; in N.Y., 242; and ratification, 275-77; federal, in Va., 233
Sedgwick, Theodore, 171, 202, 284
Senate, U.S., 13, 138-39, 174; criticized, 136-39; and Antifederalists, 137, 184
Senates, state, 18, 43, 91, 200, 223. *See also* under individual states
Senators, state, favor ratification, 263-64
"Senex," 25
Shays's Rebellion, 13, 59-63, 66; effects of, 51-52, 105, 198, 199, 201, 207

Shaysites, 252
Shenandoah Valley, Va., 30, 32, 33, 226, 229-31, 278, 286. *See also* Commerce
Sheffield, Mass., 202
Shipowners, 34, 208, 263
Ship captains, 263
"Sidney" (Abraham Yates, Jr.), 79n, 234
Singer, Charles Gregg, 95
Singletary, Amos, 131, 144
Sitgreaves, John, 34
Slaves. *See* Maryland, Virginia
Smallwod, William, 214
Smilie, John, 43, 45, 47, 131, 147, 158, 160
Smith, Melancton, 131, 135, 138, 144, 156, 203; and ratification, 235, 238-39
Snow, Capt. Isaac, 128, 257
Society of Cincinnati. *See* Cincinnati, Society of
Somerset County, Md., 39
South, fear of North, 110-11
South Carolina, 7, 18, 24-25, 236; politics of, 21-28, 249, 274; and impost, 73, 74, 76, 94-96; and ratification, 215-20, 269, 277, 278. *See also* Debtors
South Kingston, R.I., 212
Southside of Va., 30, 32, 33, 111, 228; opposes ratification, 225, 286; favors ratification, 231
Sovereignty, 16, 72, 111, 120-25, 128
Spaight, Richard D., 34
Spanish, and expansion, 31
"A Spartan," 49-50
Spaulding, E. Wilder, 240, 272
Speculators, land. *See* North Carolina
Speech, freedom of, 160
Spencer, Samuel, 150, 181, 243
Spencer, Mass., 272
Sprague, John, 257
Staten Island, 48
Staunton, Va., 93
Stuart, Alexander, 163
Stuart, Archibald, 276
Suffolk County, Mass., 55, 60, 87
Suffolk County, N.Y., 48, 99, 239-40, 260
Suffrage, 14, 17, 21
Sullivan, James, 257
Sullivan, John, 222
Supplementary fund, 58, 107
Supreme Court, U.S., 125, 126, 155-60
"Supreme law of the land" clause, 122, 124, 144, 184-85
Susquehanna River, 272

Sutton, Mass., 61
Switzerland, 80
"Sydney" (Robert Yates), 287
Symmes, William, 127-28, 166, 256-57

Talbot County, Md., 38
Tarborough, N.C., 267
Tarleton, Gen. Banastre, 93
Tax, poll, 7, 22, 145
Taxation, power over, 15, 47, 71, 72, 77-79, 122, 123-24, 143-46; in Va., 31; and Antifederalists, 182-84
Taxes, 7, 207; land, 7; direct, 183. *See also* under states
Tenants, 29
Ten Broeck, Abraham, 48
Ten-mile area, 125, 151-52
Tennessee, 244-45
Term of office, of U.S. Senate, 137-38; of U.S. President, 140, 142; of state senates, 18; of local officials, 18; shorter, 184
Test oath, 42, 43-44, 48
Thatcher, George, 207; as "Scribble-Scrabble," 65n
Thompson, Gen. Samuel, 128, 180
Tidewater. *See* under individual states
Tillinghast, Charles, 235, 238
"Timoleon," 154-55, 160
Tories, 57
Towns, Federalism in, 266-68
"A Tradesman," 66
Treaties, power over, 139, 141
Treaty, British. *See* British Treaty
Tredwell, Thomas, 181
Trenchard, John, 8-14
Tucker, St. George, 166, 224
Turberville, George Lee, 224
Turner, Charles, 177
Tweed, Alexander, 257
Tyler, John, 224

Ulster County, N.Y., 47
Unicameral legislature, in Ga., 37; in Pa., 42, 43; defended by Antifederalists, 136-37, 184
Upcountry, S.C., 19

Van Cortlandt family, 48
Vanmeter, Isaac, 276
Van Rensselaer, Jeremiah, 234
Van Rensselaer family, 48
Varnum, Joseph Bradley, 262
Vermont, 1, 17-18, 62, 222
Veto, power of, 141
Virginia, 7, 80, 111, 139, 211, 236, 252; politics in, 28-33; Tidewater,

28, 29, 231; slaves in, 29, 232; constitution of 31; Piedmont, 28, 29, 30, 231-32; taxes in, 32, 93, 231; and impost, 74, 76, 92-94; and ratification, 131, 142, 145, 149, 152, 185, 223-33, 237, 269, 276, 277, 278; sections of, 223-33; and Antifederalists, 249, 273-74, 285-86. *See also* Commerce, Commercial interest, Debtors, Debt, Northern Neck, Southside

Voting, 17

Wadsworth, Jeremiah, 198
Wait, Thomas, 129, 153
Wales, Ebenezer, 64
Warren, Charles, 259
Warren, James, 78, 113, 173, 201; as "Helvidius Priscus," 201n; as "A Republican Federalist," 287
Warren, Joseph, 11
Warren, Mercy, 114, 140, 169, 186, 235; as "A Columbian Patriot," 287
Warren family, 258
Warren, R.I., 212
Warren County, N.C., 242, 245
Warwick, R.I., 248
Wateree River, 1
Washington, George, 62, 141, 197, 228, 238, 252; on Federal defeat in N.H., 211; and impost, 74, 94, 95; on ratification in Md., 214; in Va., 224; influence of, 227, 253-54
Washington County, N.Y., 47, 235
Washington County, Pa., 189, 190
Welton, Capt., 11
Westchester County, N.Y., 48, 50, 99, 237, 239
Westerly, R.I., 212
Western land. *See* Land
Westminster, Mass., 14
West Springfield, Mass., 15

West Virginia, 30, 33, 226, 228-29, 286. *See also* "Alleghany" region
Whig tradition, 8
White, Abraham, 144
Whitehill, John, 190
Whitehill, Robert, 43, 124, 142, 156
Whitehill family, 47
Wilbraham, Mass., 128
Wilkinson, James, 225
Willard, Samuel, 144
Willett, Marinus, 235
Williams, William, 199, 257
Williamsburg, Va., 267
Williamson, Hugh, 34
Wilmington, N.C., 242, 246, 267
Wilson, James, 47, 118, 180, 190, 192
Winchester, Va., 267
Winthrop, James, 150, 169, 172, 178, 201; as "Agrippa," 287
Winthrop, John, 205, 257
Worcester County, Mass., 6, 59, 86, 87
Workman, Benjamin, 190; as "Philadelphiensis," 180
Wormeley, Ralph, 227
Wrentham, Mass., 87
Wyoming Valley, 1
Wythe, George, 227

Yates, Abraham, Jr., 79, 80, 110, 112, 156, 238; as "Rough Hewer," 78n, 98; "Sidney," 79n
Yates, Peter, 234
Yates, Robert, 116-17, 121, 125-26; as "Sydney," 287; as "Brutus," 287
York County, Maine, 65, 208
York County, Pa., 41, 272
York River, 28, 32, 111, 232
Yorktown, battle of, 74, 99

Zenger case, 160